FROM SAVAGE TO SHAMAN

A FIGHTER PILOT'S JOURNEY TO HIS HEART

JOHNNY MEDICINEBEAR

For Karsen
"You are never alone"
Blessings
Johnny Medicine Bear
24 Aug 2024

FROM SAVAGE TO SHAMAN
A Fighter Pilot's Journey to His Heart

Copyright © 2024 by John Doerr (Johnny MedicineBear)

All rights reserved.

No part of this book may be reproduced in any form or by any electronic or mechanical means, including information storage and retrieval systems, without written permission from the author, except for the use of brief quotations in a book review.

I have tried to recreate events, locales and conversations from my memories of them. I may have changed some identifying characteristics and details such as names, physical properties, occupations and places of residence. Mentions of names of people in my past are to acknowledge their importance in my life. They are true to the best of my memory, and are in no way meant to misconstrue any part of an individual's life. The views expressed are solely those of the author. They are part of "my" story and are entirely my memory.

There are also fictional stories in this book. Names, characters, businesses, places, events, locales, and incidents are either the products of the author's imagination or used in a fictitious manner. Any resemblance to actual persons, living or dead, or actual events is purely coincidental.

ISBN: 979-8-9906628-0-3 (Print Version)

LCCN: 2024900307

DEDICATION

From Savage to Shaman is dedicated to the many that never found their way out of their darkness and paid the ultimate price. And From Savage to Shaman is also dedicated to you, Dear Reader, to guide and assist you out of your darkness, through your shadow, and into your light.

DEDICATION

FOREWORD

    This book is a gift. A gift for all those who, for whatever reason, have been in darkness. Whether from childhood emotional trauma, addiction, low self-esteem, guilt, regret, or the many other possible destructive influences in life, those struggling will embrace this book as a gift of understanding, compassion, and empowerment to move beyond the darkness. But actually, John Doerr (later Johnny Medicine-Bear) has given us all a remarkable gift of his authenticity and genuine hope to rise above the struggles, and even the ashes, of our lives. His own story of redemption is all the more remarkable because of his most unusual background.

    I have had the privilege of knowing, working, and flying with many military pilots. Fighter pilots, however, are a breed apart. Descendants of the first cadre of WWI fighter pilots whose life expectancies in combat were forty-five days, these aviators lived life with gusto, humor, and a "spit in your eye" bravado. Still today, they are exceptional specimens overflowing with situational awareness, independent spirit, self-assuredness, competitive nature, and overall ability. John Doerr was no exception. He was a perfect savage and warrior combination…capable and jovial despite the harshness around him, and consistently successful at completing his mission. He exhibited all the fighter pilot traits when we served together, yet fortunately for all of us, he also had hidden and not-yet-discovered character traits not often seen in this breed...traits such as introspection, vulnerability, and a willingness to take the road less traveled. His discovery of his deeper self is truly, "situational awareness" in afterburner. Once a savage embracing destruction, he is now the spiritual-warrior with a mission of service to empower others to rise above the misery of addiction, guilt, and defeat.

I've known Johnny for nearly fifty years, since our death-defying flight above the Arctic Circle and the frozen fiords of Norway. He exploded into my life with all the color and grandeur of a Hollywood actor and gave me the gift of knowing what it's like to live on the edge. He admits now that he was in darkness, but he was a brilliant light for me. In his Shadow period, I was given the opportunity to help him regain his former grandeur after a long battle with addiction and guilt. I see this was not a wasted effort, as he has, by telling his story, found his light and he is now using it to benefit others.

Yes, *From Savage to Shaman* is a story of redemption, the stuff of ancient myths, where from the depths of darkness, a battered human fights his way, not only to regain his self-esteem but also to guide others to their own light.

Roger Landry, Col USAFMC (retired)
Cape Cod, Massachusetts
2 September 2023

PREFACE

About twenty-five US military veterans commit suicide every day. I am grateful to no longer be concerned about the "horrors-of-war" pit, and the demons that attack when the mind slides into that space of emptiness, depression, and worse. Some suggested that I write a book sharing my journey from darkness and despair, to freedom and joy. Having never written a book, I was stuck and did not know where or how to begin.

Then a spiritual teacher arrived and through her, divine inspiration and guidance were received. *From Savage to Shaman* was born.

I committed myself to share, through this book, the path I've traveled and the tools I've acquired along the way. Those that suffer from depression and worse will find themselves in this book and may use these tools to assist and guide them out of their darkness, through their shadow, and into their light.

I have poured my heart and soul into this project and have been lovingly supported by friends and Spirit along the way. This book is a gift from my heart to yours.

From Savage to Shaman is atonement for my participation in the Vietnam war. And if just one person finds what they need to heal from suicidal thoughts and actions, then this four-and-a-half-year book project will be double worth it.

There is nothing more important in your life than you. Do your inner work and join me on the peaceful path of love, compassion, and service to all beings.

From my heart,
Johnny MedicineBear
2 September 2023

INTRODUCTION

Neither healing inner trauma nor reading this book is for the faint-of-heart. But if you have an interest in healing yourself and moving forward with your life, then this book is for you.

We all suffer as children. To feel better, we run toward addictions and the military where we may fly jet airplanes, drive tanks, or crew on an aircraft carrier. But somewhere along my path, I stopped running from life and began walking toward life. YOU CAN TOO. That is what this book is all about.

I am Johnny MedicineBear and this is my story from a childhood of direct and indirect abuse, through a Vietnam combat tour flying fighter-jets, to my present-day space of freedom and joy. But this is also your story on a slightly different angle for it transcends gender, cultural, and religious boundaries.

From Savage to Shaman applies to civilian, military, male, and female alike. It is inclusive, not exclusive.

Whatever traumas you suffer from, you will find yourself in this book. You will also find the tools to illuminate your path from hopelessness, depression, and suicidal thoughts toward your light.

Into the Darkness (Section 1) is the story of my abusive and lacking childhood, and most of my twenty years in the Air Force. You will easily relate to this section.

Into the Shadow (Section 2) is my story of exploring many spiritual paths of recovery and healing. As I matured and assumed ownership and responsibility for myself, life began unfolding in more meaningful and compassionate ways.

Into the Light (Section 3) is my journey with a spiritual teacher. I share the various paths, tools, and concepts that I now embrace.

I am confident that you can improve your current state of mind and body with commitment and dedication to doing your inner work. This book is your guide for doing that.

You are number one in your life. Now commit to doing your work. And remember that Johnny MedicineBear walks with you every step along your earthwalk. You are never alone.

From my heart,
Johnny MedicineBear
2 September, 2023

AUTHOR'S MESSAGE

At our spiritual core, you and I are the same. It is only through our personalities that physical, emotional, intellectual, cultural, and other aspects of individuality arise. To benefit the most from this book, it is essential that you relate to our sameness and find yourself in these pages. See yourself in my story, for it IS your story as well albeit on a slightly different angle. This book is intended as a healing tool, not simply a Johnny MedicineBear adventure novel.

From *Savage to Shaman* is your pointer for you to find your way to a meaningful, pleasant life. The road I've traveled to arrive at a peaceful space is available to everyone. Your road may be different, however, the encouragement to start or continue your journey of self-discovery is found in these pages. Please use *From Savage to Shaman* as your tool to unlock the chains that restrain you and move forward toward freedom and joy.

Some ideas, or concepts I've incorporated in these pages may be foreign to you. I encourage you to use the enclosed glossary to assist you in your understanding. And Johnny MedicineBear walks with you as you journey into YOUR darkness, through YOUR shadow, and into YOUR light.

jmb

CONTENTS

Foreword   5
Preface   7
Introduction   9

Author's Message   11
Glossary - Definition of Terms Used   18

PART I
INTO THE DARKNESS

Section Introduction   25
The Name Game   27
Sheriff Roy Rogers - Cowboys and Indians   29
Parents - Sister - Grandparents   32
Model Airplanes-Toy Guns-Grade School   38
Uncle Russell and the Christmas Socks   42
Third-Grade Art Class   44
Eighth-Grade Book Report   46
Little League Baseball   49
The Wall And The Dishes   51
Boy Scouts   53
The Safety Patrol   55
Paperboy And Jobs Through High School   57
Middle Of The River   61
The Large Box Of Tide   64
Johnny's Birdhouse   67
Shooting The Little Bird   69
Mr. Joseph's Market   72
Terrified To Tell Dad The Truth   79
Cigarettes   82
Cutting The Coconut   85
I Can Do It Myself   87
Rutgers University   90
The Day My Love Died   93
Am I Valuable Or Suicidal   97
Free, White And Twenty-One   99
Work After College - Bradley Field   103
Us Air Force Pilot Training   106

Assignment to Fighters - The F-4 Phantom	111
Learning To Fly The F-4 Phantom	114
Vietnam – Arrival	117
Mr. Song's Mission	120
The Air-War In Cambodia	125
Vietnam - More	127
Light Humor - In The Darkness	131
Germany – Bitburg Air Base	134
The Doc	138
Delivering Supplies To The British Royal Navy	143
Stopped by Police - The Gunnery Team	148
Dee - I Married My Father	150
Stealing? - Beer Doesn't Count	154
Daughters - Sarah And Jennifer	156
Sobriety - 8 March 1985	158

PART II
INTO THE SHADOW

Section Introduction	163
The Human Shadow	165
Alcohol Rehab	168
Home After Rehab - Initial Sobriety	172
Sarah And Jennifer - After Sobriety	175
Do the Right Thing - Even When No One is Looking	177
Instant Karma - There is No Free Lunch	180
Sammy - The Ground Squirrel	182
Ronnie	184
Best Friend Or Worst Enemy	189
A Broader Perspective	191
The I Know Game - Listening in Presence	193
Phantom Backseater Rick	195
American Airlines	199
Honesty - Jennifer And The Lemonade	203
Monster Boy	205
Mom And The Airplane Strobe Lights	209
Playing With The Clouds	212
Controlling The Stock Market	214
Can We Change The Past?	216
The Drainboard	219
Rusty Vision	221
The Men's Room	225
The Shadow Weekend	228
Mr. Song's Letter	233

The Inca Medicine Wheel	238
Dutch & Harley	247
Fear Of The Dark, The Coal Mine	251
The Haunt	255
Beyond Fear	257
Karishma	260
Gifting	262
The Money Box - What's Money For?	265
Beyond Courage - Gail Laughing Water	267
Synchronicity	271
I Killed My Daughters	274
Gift Exchange With Dad	277
Dad's Passing	278
Driving Tips	280
Mom and Ginny Jaguar	287
Respecting The Goddess	290
The Warrior's Creed - The Wimp's Creed	291
The Middle Path – Non-Duality Reality - And More	295
Dreams - Visions - Personal Journal	302

PART III
INTO THE LIGHT

Section Introduction	331
The Beginning	333
Round and Around I Go - Where I Stop, I Don't Know	337
Earthlings	339
Baby And Sweetheart	341
Leah	343
Try This, Try That, Not This, Not That	345
The Work Of Byron Katie	347
The Building-Of-Life	349
Relationships - Partnerships	352
Addictions	354
Lying And Denial	357
Control - Guidance	361
Judgement	364
Traveling On - Goddesses & Mantras	365
Having Fun - Experiencing Joy - Balance	367
Glacier Park	369
Growing Up	373
The Black Hills Motorcycle Rally - Sturgis, SD	376
Safety - Safe to Live, Safe to Love, Safe to Shine	381
If I Spot It, I Got	384

Physical And Non-Physical Reality	386
Knowledge And Knowing	390
What Do I Do with the S.O.B.s	392
Food	395
A Chipped Bottle May Hold Pure Water	397
The Journey Continues	398
Medicinebear's Terrorist Group	400
The Personality Loves Noise - The Soul Loves Silence	402
Revisiting The F-4 Phantom	404
Religion And Spirituality	407
Belief and Knowing	412
Perspective	415
Trust	418
Truth	421
Tap-Dancing	423
My Suicide - Killing Parts of My Ego	426
Asking a Reasonable Question	429
Johnny's Lily Pad - Dark Johnny	432
Afraid to Go and Afraid Not to Go	437
There Is No Such Thing As Failure	440
Success Has Its Genesis In Failure	444
Deep Work	446
Unraveling Judgement	452
Mom and Dad - Who They Truly Were	453
Dream - The Funeral Pyre	455
The Greatest Psychology Book Of All Time	457
Spiritual Work Is Your Life's Work	459
Us Or Them - Pink Floyd	461
Living Life Closer To The Bone	464
Hi-Ho, Hi-Ho, It's Off to Europe We Go	469
Sitting In A Chair	471
Casual Bantering Humor	473
It's Only A Mushroom	475
Mary And The Web Of Life	478
Alignment	480
A Mountain Is, A Mountain Is Not, A Mountain Is	482
It Could Not Possibly Happen - But It Did	484
The Personality/Ego And The Soul	486
Who Am I	489
Suffering on the Pilgrimage	491
The Cloakroom	496
Resisting	500
The Master - Teacher's Role	504

The Wounded Masculine	507
Why We Fight Wars and The Way Out	511
Pushing My Button	514
The Man In The Mirror	516
Quick To Defend	519
Soller, Mallorca, Spain	520
The Water-Fast	522
The Spiritual Pilgrimage – Mallorca, Spain	528
Killing My Parents - Over the Cliff They Go	534
Deep Work Is Hard Work	537
How to Find Authentic Spiritual Teachers (and Know That They are Authentic)	545
India - Arrival	547
India - The Swan	549
India - The Pundit Master Astrologer	552
India - Dee - Wife Revisited	554
India - The Ayurvedic Doctor	556
India - Releasing Karma	558
India - Return Home	560
Other Thoughts	561
Ending	563
Epilogue	565
Acknowledgments	567
About the Author	569

GLOSSARY - DEFINITION OF TERMS USED

3-D: The 3-D refers to physical reality. It is defined by the three physical dimensions of length, width, and height. However, it also includes the fourth dimension of non-reversible physical time.
Animistic: A perspective of reality where everything is alive.
Ashram: A spiritual retreat center.
Aura: The luminous energy field emanating from a living being. In this book, it is the same as one's auric fields, energy fields, or luminous body.
Auric Fields: See Aura.
Ayurveda: A system of health and wellness incorporating herbal medicines, special diet, meditation, yoga, massage, and other alternative practices in conjunction with modern medical practices. It is a vast body of knowledge practiced widely in India and Nepal.
Belief: An intellectual acceptance of something as truth without tangible evidence that it is true. Believing something is true does not make it true. With belief, one lacks direct knowledge. The more fundamental and deeper space beyond belief is knowing.
Chakras: Vortices of spinning energy associated with the physical body that allow for life-force energy flow into and through the physical body. They are also known as energy centers. Properly functioning chakras are essential for optimal health.

Delusion: A persistent false psychotic belief regarding the self, other persons, or objects outside the self that is maintained despite irrefutable evidence to the contrary.
Denial: A defense mechanism whereby one fails to acknowledge an unacceptable truth or emotion and admit it to consciousness. This is different than lying where one knows that they are untruthful. With denial, one believes that they are truthful.
Denial Systems: Psychological systems developed to support denial.
Dharma: The inherent nature of reality, regarded as a cosmic law underlying proper behavior and social order. When one lives in accordance with their Dharma, they are aligned with the cosmic laws and universal truths of reality.
Divine-Time: Spiritual time or God's time. Events occur when they are of the greatest value for soul expansion. Divine-Time is outside of clock time and schedules.
Divinity: The higher spiritual realms of reality. Also, the highest spiritual energies or spiritual beings.
Dutch or Motorcoach-Dutch: Johnny's 2005 40' Newmar Dutch Star motorhome that has been his full-time home since November 2004.
Earthwalk: In this book earthwalk means a physical incarnation on the planet Earth. If you are reading this text, you are experiencing an earthwalk.
Ego: The 3-D personality (physical being), or physical self. Also, it is one's sense of self, self-worth, and the image of oneself. In this book, it mostly references the 3-D, or physical personality.
The Energetic: Another name for the spiritual world. Those dimensions of reality beyond the physical that exist only in energy form.
Energy Fields: See Aura.
Faith: Complete trust or confidence in someone or something. Complete belief in religious doctrines without tangible evidence, validation, or proof.
God: See Life-force.
Guilt: The unpleasant or negative feelings arising from doing something wrong. Guilt arises from one's actions and is about what I've done, not who I am.
Harley or Motorcycle-Harley: Johnny's 2006 Harley-Davidson Softail Deluxe chromed to the hilt, world class motorcycle.

Hooch: A small rustic hut, shed, or home usually constructed from basic materials and topped with a thatched roof.
Hope: A feeling of expectation and desire for a certain outcome.
Identity: In this book, it means the nameless core essence or the soul of a being. It is nameless, everlasting, has no form, and is the most fundamental expression of a being.
Knowing: Knowledge acquired through direct personal experience. Knowing is the more fundamental space beyond belief.
Karma: Universal Cosmic Law of cause and effect. The energy of every action (cause) will eventually return to us (effect). How you treat others is how you will eventually be treated. Compassionate deeds engender compassionate returns. Destructive deeds engender destructive returns. This karmic cycle may take only a short while or it may take many lifetimes to complete. But, by cosmic law, it must complete.
Life-Force: The highest, creative, vital, animating energy or force present in everything and is ubiquitous. It is the impartial, non-judgemental energy of creation in all physical and non-physical reality. Known also as Source, Source-Energy, Divinity, The Creator, Great Spirit, The One, and God.
Luminous Body: See Aura.
Medicine: In this book it refers to one's spiritual strength, personal power, and healing abilities. It embraces much more than our western concept of medicine as tonics and pills.
Medicine Person: A shaman and healer using physical and non-physical tools and techniques to heal both body and spirit. A Medicine Person is of impeccable character and pure intent.
Mind: A non-physical component of our aura. One may relate to the mind as a go-between of our physical and non-physical bodies. The brain is the on-board bio-computer that controls and operates the physical body. The mind is not the brain. One may relate to the mind as "mission control" that directs and influences one's thoughts, actions, and activities.
Morality - Morals: Principles and standards concerning the distinction between right and wrong, good and bad. Morals define what is, and what is not, acceptable behavior.
Neurosis: A relatively mild mental disorder that is not caused by organic disease, involving symptoms of stress (depression, anxiety, or

obsessive-compulsive behaviors). There is no radical loss of touch with reality as in psychosis.
Non-Physical Reality: All that exists beyond and outside of physical reality beyond length, width, height, and non-reversible time.
Ossified: To harden into bone. To become rigid or fixed in attitude or position.
Personality: The physical being and the qualities and characteristics of that being. This includes desires and emotions and the mind.
Physical Reality: All that exists on the physical planes of reality with the dimensions of length, width, height, and non-reversible time.
Pranayama: Yoga breathing techniques.
Presence: The state of being present. In this book, it means that one's awareness is not regretting the past nor fearing the future but is focused on the here and now.
Psychosis: A severe mental disorder where thought and emotions are so impaired that contact with reality is lost.
Pundit: A learned person or expert on a subject or field of knowledge who is frequently asked to offer opinions or advice about it. An authoritative teacher.
Religion: A particular set or system of attitudes, beliefs, and practices, usually supporting a superhuman controlling power, or God.
Savage: A person who embraces brutal behaviors and kills, injures, and destroys without conscience. A savage is the antithesis of a warrior.
Session or Group: A dedicated sharing time rooted in respect, and truth. One person shares without interruption till completion, then another may respond or share. Use of a "talking stick" is encouraged.
Shadow (Human): The parts of the human psyche that are hidden and repressed where violence, anger, and hate generally reside.
Shaman: A Medicine Person of compassionate heart and pure intent, dedicated to selfless service for all beings.
Shame: Painful feelings arising from the belief that I am dishonorable, improper, or defective. It is not about what I have done, but about who I am.
Soul: The spiritual non-physical component of a being that is immortal. It is who we were before our earthwalk began, who we truly are today, and who we will become when this earthwalk is complete.

Spirit: A general term referencing non-physical reality, the spiritual world or the world of spirit. In this book, a message or vision received from Spirit means that the message was received from the spiritual realms and that the identity of the originator is either irrelevant or unknown.

Spirit Guide: A non-physical being of the spirit world that is of supportive service to physical beings. It is similar to or the same as an angel.

Spiritual: Of, relating to, or affecting the spirit, usually relating to sacred matters or practice.

Spiritual Pilgrim: A seeker of truth, a Spiritual Warrior.

Spiritual Warrior: A seeker of truth, a Spiritual Pilgrim.

Synchronicity: The simultaneous occurrence of events which appear significantly related but have no discernible obvious connection.

Talking Stick: A small stick, feather, or similar object that is used in session or group to designate the person sharing. The holder of the talking stick may speak without interruption till complete. The stick is then passed to another.

Warrior: One who embodies the energies of protection, compassion, and service with strength and endurance. The warrior is conscious and trustworthy. The discriminating guard at the castle gate is the archetype of the warrior that protects and never harms. Warriors are conscious beings of compassionate heart and service. A warrior is the antithesis of a savage.

Yoga: An ancient practice designed to bring mind and body in alignment with life force energies. It incorporates breathing exercises, meditation, and postures designed to still the mind and relieve suffering.

PART I
INTO THE DARKNESS

SECTION INTRODUCTION

"Where did you grow up, Johnny?"

"I haven't," I replied. And I'm pleased that today I have a lighthearted, active little boy running around somewhere inside this slightly more mature body. That little boy was born a trusting, loving child, eager to explore life from his radiant heart. But through cultural, religious, family, and inter-personal experiences, he matured into an ego-centered savage. He lost his way.

This type of conditioning happens to many of us. And some adults believe that their physical bodies and mind are all that they are. They are unaware of their true-self and identify solely with their personality. They have forgotten who they were when they were born, and where they came from before they were born.

The ego forms during early childhood. And I began sliding *Into the Darkness* as a child at home, continuing the down-slide through high school, university, and sixteen of my twenty years in the United States Air Force. The fun-loving, radiant little boy disappeared somewhere, and for survival, I grew into an ego-centered, self-righteous, savage. Even when surrounded by friends or in a crowd, I was alone. By high school graduation, I was lost and out of control.

This was all subconscious, of course, and I thought that my life was normal. I believed that most everyone drank alcohol and partied, that humans were untrustworthy, and that wars were inevitable.

The story of Johnny MedicineBear IS the story of most every one of us. Divine inspiration and guidance encouraged me to bare my soul, share my life experiences, and write this book. I hope you relate to my adventures and use *From Savage to Shaman* as a tool to embrace your darkness, journey through your shadow, and emerge into your light.

Journey with me now *Into the Darkness*.

THE NAME GAME

I am Johnny MedicineBear. But before I assumed that name, I went by several others and wish to share why I am Johnny MedicineBear rather than the name on my driver's license.

John Charles Doerr was given to me at birth. Charles was my father's name and John was his father's name. As a young boy, I was Johnny, and I liked it. Somewhere, perhaps entering high school, I felt too grown-up to be Johnny anymore. So, I became John. That lasted through high school, college, and about sixteen years of my twenty-year Air Force tour.

When I transitioned to sobriety in 1985, I assumed the name JC, using the initials of my first and middle names. It was a rite-of-passage name change. JC was a reminder for me that I was a new person traveling a sober path, not the old me at the bar.

JC stuck with me for my last Air Force tour and my time as pilot with American Airlines. JC had an individuality to it as there were few JCs flying American Airlines jets. I liked it and it also had rite-of-passage significance to it. I earned that name.

Elsewhere in this book, I share my experience of working with teachers of the Inca Medicine-Wheel. In 1995, in a guided meditation during one of those workshops, I was shown a lifetime where I was of great service. MedicineBear came to me in that experience. He was the village medicine-man, or shaman. Shortly thereafter, MedicineBear began appearing in dreams and visions. Over time, our connection strengthened, and he is now an integral part of me. We have established a line of communication, and he has been one of my spirit-friends since 1995.

As my connection to MedicineBear matured, I identified more with him than with the persona of John Doerr. I related to his cultural and spiritual practices more than I do to the cultural and spiritual practices of my current environment. As I embraced his truths, his philosophies, and his way of life, I assumed the name Johnny MedicineBear. It was another rite-of-passage.

SHERIFF ROY ROGERS - COWBOYS AND INDIANS

I'm up early this "Funday" morning, and excited to play cowboys and Indians with my neighborhood friends. Jumping out of bed, I slip on my dungarees with holes in the knees and don my special Roy Rogers shirt with glitzy little fringe strings hanging down from the breast pockets. Wriggling into my real leather brown cowboy boots, all scuffed from "riding the range," I smile while pinning on my sheriff's badge. It's big, shiny, heavy, and bulletproof too, with SHERIFF written in bold, black letters. Undoubtably, I strike terror into the hearts of everyone who sees me.

Opening my closet, I retrieve my gun belt holstering two pearl-handled super-fast-action cap-pistols with extra bullets sheathed along the back of the leather belt. I check the trigger, hammer, and barrel on each gun for smooth and proper action and install a full roll of caps in each pistol. With surgical precision, I trim the red tape centering the first cap directly beneath the hammer. "My irons will not fail me when needed," I whisper, twirling my pistols around my finger and sliding them smoothly into their holsters.

All grown up now with my loaded pistols hanging around my waist, I'm eager to rid the world of outlaws. Big bad Little Johnny is all set for a play day pretending to be a man.

Sneaking downstairs, I peek into the kitchen and see Mom by the sink and Dad reading the paper. Jumping around the corner with both guns drawn, I holler, "Stick 'em up, I'm the sheriff and don't anybody move or else I'll give it to ya." They smile and play along with me. Mom puts her hands up over her head and says, "Good morning, Johnny, uh, Mr. Sheriff, can I please put my hands down now and finish the dishes?" "OK, Mom," I say, then Dad smiles, nods his head, and continues reading his paper.

Nice job, Sheriff Johnny, I got 'em just where I want 'em. No problems anymore here in the kitchen as the great Sheriff Little Johnny once again restores law and order in the grub-house.

Twirling my guns a few times for effect, I slide them smoothly into their holsters and slowly saunter bow-legged toward the grub table. I'm hungry and ready for breakfast. A man holstering two real pistols, not a little boy with cap guns, prepares his bowl of Wheaties "Breakfast of Champions."

That was me, Sheriff Roy Rogers, with my two pearl-handled cap-pistols and big shiny sheriff's badge pinned to my fringe-shirted chest. I was in another world and loved feeling grown-up and unafraid. While I was Sheriff Roy Rogers, I was a powerful man. I dismissed all thoughts that these grown-up feelings would end when I hung up my gun-belt and closed the closet door. Finishing breakfast, I thanked Mom and Dad for playing along and left to hunt down my friends to play Cowboys and Indians.

I was prejudiced toward Indians by ten-years-old. And Indians, (we never referred to these people as Native, Original, or Indigenous) were not civilized human beings like me, my family, and my friends. They were lesser people that lived in strangely painted tents called teepees, exhibited strange behaviors, dressed unconventionally, spoke strange languages, and performed weird rituals with dancing and drumming, while whooping and hollering like savages. They didn't lead normal lives like I did, go to school like I did, live in a heated home like I did, shop in stores like I did, and ride in cars like I did. I did not understand them or their culture, nor wanted to, and assumed we were right and they were wrong about everything.

In the 1950s, inequality was evident on TV shows and in movies. Cowboys like Roy Rogers, Gene Autry, Hopalong Cassidy, and The Lone Ranger were privileged white male heroes, while others on these shows, both male and female, were inferior, subservient, and dumber. As a young boy, I gave this little thought and ignored these obvious prejudices. I related solely to the white male heroes, worshiped them, and placed them on pedestals.

"Funday" was a great day playing cowboys and Indians, riding bicycles, and even building a crane with my erector set. Life was good. But all good things eventually come to an end.

"Oh Johnny, it's almost bedtime, so brush your teeth and set out your clothes for school tomorrow." Wow, it's almost 9 o'clock already Sunday evening and I still haven't reviewed for my history quiz tomorrow. Playing is so much more fun than doing homework.

"OK, Mom," I replied. I quickly dismiss school thoughts and lovingly put away my erector set with its shiny metal girders, gears, and electric motor. I moved the crane to a special space on my desk where at night it reflected the outdoor street lamp shining in my window. In Johnny's dreamland, I designed and constructed several of the world's tallest buildings all by myself, assisted by my erector set crane.

"I'm all set for tomorrow, Mom. Please come scratch my back so I may have pleasant dreams." And Mom always did.

Lying in bed, I did not fall asleep easily as my fifth-grade teacher's voice whispered about the little history quiz scheduled for tomorrow. I ought to know enough to pass that little quiz, I mused. Why do I need to know about the stupid Louisiana Purchase that happened a few hundred years ago, anyway? I fell asleep reminding myself that I'm fairly smart, very cute, and can butter up the teacher a bit when necessary.

That was the childhood of Little Johnny playing with his toys and hiding behind his Roy Rogers Sheriff's Badge and pearl-handled cap-pistols to feel worthy and grown-up. I learned that boys and men suppress feelings and emotions and don't talk about them like girls and woman do. I learned that men don't cry. I learned to lie and manipulate, relying on my cuteness and cleverness to get my way. I became skilled at "buttering-up" when necessary to achieve my objectives. So, I super-glued a smile on my face, and hid my heavy heart and tear-filled eyes.

That was the genesis of Johnny MedicineBear.

PARENTS - SISTER - GRANDPARENTS

My father was both my hero and my tormentor. He was Mr. God to me and whatever he said I believed, and whatever he did, I imitated. But he was inflexible, angry, and emotionally distant. I was frequently in trouble for trivial things and became the outlet for his unresolved anger and rage.

There were also creative and humorous aspects of Dad that occasionally emerged. He was very capable and was always busy building or fixing something. He also helped many people, but his humorous, light-hearted side rarely surfaced.

Dad never showed his feelings, and I was convinced that men were born as either sharers or stuffers. Frequently, Mom would say, "Your dad (it was always your dad when she was serious) is a stuffer and that's how he processes his feelings and emotions." I was forty-years-old before I learned that stuffing emotions was not a healthy way to process feelings. It did not help that Dad was in the Army and fought the last year of WWII somewhere in the Pacific Theatre. He saw everything as polarized; either right/wrong, good/bad, white/black, friendly/enemy, etc. I imitated my father and embraced his limited contracted views.

When I tried to talk to Mom about Dad's abusive behavior toward me, she would say, "He's hard on you for your own good, Johnny. Someday you'll understand why he's so tough on you." But I did not understand, and neither did Mom nor Dad. Our family dynamic never changed. We were trapped in a dysfunctional triangle of the tyrant, the victim, and the rescuer. Like stone statues, we were frozen in our roles.

Mom and Dad were not aware of their dysfunctional behaviors. So, they passed their childhood traumas on to sister Pat and me. It did not matter that it was or was not the best Mom or Dad could do. It only mattered that I was not truly loved and nurtured at home by my parents. When Dad would call me from his workshop, "Hey Johnny, come on down, I want to show you something," my reaction was fear, not elation. *What did I do wrong?* I would think. I remember being excited about what Dad and I did, but not excited about doing it with Dad. He no doubt had a rough childhood. But having never looked inward, he projected his fears, anger, rage, and prejudices mostly on me. And Mom, terrified of Dad, stood by, watched, and defended his behavior. I minimized and tried to forget these traumatic incidents, love my father, smile, pretend everything was fine, and hope that someday Dad would show me his love.

Dad only went to eighth-grade, then left school to help work his small family farm. He was very smart with a ton of common sense, but always saw himself as uneducated and lacking. He knew more than most and had tremendous creative gifts. He could build anything and fix it too, usually better than when it was new. In his spare time, he designed and built our home. This included not only the brick-and-mortar structure, but the plumbing, heating, and electrical as well.

Tearing down a car engine and rebuilding it in a week was child's play for Dad, and he did that with an airplane engine once. But his limited formal education undermined his sense of self-worth and haunted him his entire life. Dad only did what he did well. Many times, I asked him to toss a baseball with me, but he never would.

Sometimes, Dad would physically hurt me, and I remember him strapping me across my butt with his leather belt till I was raw and screaming. He did this to "teach me a lesson" and the emotional scars of fearing my father lasted a lifetime. Screaming from the burning pain and the trauma of being strapped by the man who supposedly loved me created more turmoil, confusion, and chaos within. I vowed that if I became a father, I would never do to my children what my father did to me...and I never did. Dad's anger and rage engendered distance between us. Projecting my fear of Dad on others, I avoided confrontation and conflict. I remained fearful of big men and authorities for the rest of my life and rarely, if ever, got into a knockdown, drag-out fight.

Dad's anger was always just below the surface. In my mid-forties one afternoon, I searched for Dad's portable drill in his shop. Not finding it, I asked him where he last saw it. He said, "Chuck borrowed my drill a bit ago and hasn't returned it."

"When did he borrow it, Dad?"

"Let's see, about six months ago, Johnny."

"Well, for sure Chuck's finished with it, Dad, and he forgot to return it, don't you think? I'll go over and get it."

"No, you won't, Johnny, it's Chuck's job to remember what he's borrowed. It's not my job to remind him."

So, Chuck kept the drill, and Dad kept his anger. I was glad that I could hold my parents in loving light and not be caught-up in their self-created negative dramas.

My mother was a great mom. During childhood she tucked me in at night, fixed great breakfasts, scratched my back, and made the best lemon meringue pie in the world. Mom was a gentle soul, had a pleasant disposition, and was easy to be with. I felt safe near Mom. However, her not protecting me from Dad's rage was a huge betrayal. She witnessed his brutality, yet remained passive during these events. Sometimes she would make a verbal gesture and ask him to stop, but never, not even once, did she physically put herself between us, or get in Dad's face about his behavior toward me. She never, in any meaningful way, put herself on the line.

Mom's betrayal impacted me and affected my relationships with women. I repressed the anger I held toward my mother and projected it on the women in my life. I did not trust women or engage in any deep, loving relationships. I disrespected women, and in a broader sense, disrespected all Goddess/feminine energies, including the Earth Mother. I felt uncomfortable and trapped in intimate relationships. Subconsciously carrying my mother's betrayal, I believed that any intimate loving relationship with a woman would end in betrayal. My denial systems, however, kept this betrayal of my mother hidden until I was seventy-five years old. It took the guidance of a teacher to bring that suppressed betrayal into awareness.

When Dad finished punishing me, I'd run off and hide in a closet. Mom would find me, soothe my wounds, minimize Dad's brutality, and offer me a treat if I'd come to the kitchen and forgive him. Dad never apologized for his behavior. I carried the fear of my father and the repressed anger of betrayal toward my mother with me most of my life.

Mom and Dad were also visionaries and had a lighter-brighter side. They set the expectation for sister Pat and me to go to college from early childhood forward. It was never "if you go to college," it was always "when you go to college." They were both born poor, lived through the 1930s depression as teenagers, worked hard all their lives, survived WWII, and were in many ways extraordinary. They took us with them on vacations, and Santa Claus always visited at Christmas.

Sister Pat (just Pat from here forward) and I both graduated from university debt free because of Mom and Dad's vision and efforts. They wanted us to have opportunities that they never had. No others in our immediate family, except Pat and I, went to university. The opportunity to fly airplanes in the U.S. Air Force and with American Airlines would not have happened without their vision.

Dad's sense of humor and quick wit made him likable to most, including me. But my underlying fear of Dad was always there and contaminated every aspect of our relationship.

Pat was two grades ahead of me throughout school. We each had our own circle of friends and did not interact socially much because of our age difference. But as a young boy, I found comfort in knowing that I had a sister who was intelligent, strong, and a foot taller than me. I felt protected by Pat.

We had different interests and never really played much together as kids. Pat remembered one morning when I was about ten, that I slipped on the rug at the top of our steep staircase and slid all the way down on my butt. Dad came after me for "fooling around and sliding down the stairs." Pat saw it all and when Dad was going to hit me, she went into action. She told me to step away from Dad and stood between us. She said, "Johnny did nothing wrong, he just slipped, and if you want to hit someone, hit me, I'm more your size, anyway." Dad backed down.

Once Dad strapped Pat across her bare legs with his belt for something. After she stopped screaming, she showed him the red welts on her legs and said, "Don't you ever hit me again." The fire in her eyes and the strength behind her words were apparent; he never hit her again.

My warrior energy of protection was killed off early by Dad, and I never found the courage to stand up to him as Pat did and hold him accountable for his actions. Pat is a fine woman and we are very close.

My grandfathers both passed before I was born. But I had two available loving grandmothers who were my saving grace. Both unconditionally loved me, but they weren't always there.

My mother's mother, who lived with us the last several years of her life, arrived as a teenager alone at Ellis Island, New York, in 1900. She spoke Ukrainian, but was illiterate in English. Over time, she learned to speak English but never learned to read or write it. Our relationship lacked depth and, in my ignorance, I thought she was dumb and attributed her broken English and heavy accent to stupidity.

My father's mother was a gentle woman who lived locally in the house where Dad was born and raised. As a young boy, I frequently rode my bike to Grandmom's and was always loved and nurtured by her. Although poor, she always had a nickel so that I could buy an ice-cream bar on my way home. I loved spending time with my grandmothers. Both grandmothers were gone by the time I joined the Air Force at age twenty-four.

Until I was forty-two-years-old, I saw my family and early home life as normal. I believed my childhood was nurturing and loving until I got sober and began looking at my early life with clearer vision. Then, for several years, I cursed my parents for the childhood they provided and blamed them for my alcoholic behaviors. Eventually, I realized that they, like me, also had traumatized childhoods and unresolved issues. They did the absolute best they could. This does not excuse their behaviors, but helps me to understand their behaviors and move past them.

In their generation, few went to therapy, and recovery from alcohol was not nearly as common as it is today. Taking responsibility for my life after sobriety, I eventually came to love them. By doing my inner work, I became my own parent.

Today, even though they have both crossed over, I have a loving relationship with Mom and Dad.

MODEL AIRPLANES-TOY GUNS-
GRADE SCHOOL

"Thank you, Santa Claus," I said in a loud, excited voice as I opened my gift and held the box containing the plastic model of an F-86 Sabre Jet. Wow, this was the fighter that knocked the Mig-15s out of the sky in Korea a few years back, and now I was going to build one. As a young boy, I spent countless hours building plastic models of my favorite fighter-jets and occasionally I'd hear one fly over and would run outside to glimpse this marvelous machine. In a million years, I could not have imagined myself flying a real fighter-jet. Fighter-jet pilots were gods reincarnated on the planet Earth and birthed with skills beyond human comprehension. I lovingly built my plastic model F-86 Sabre-Jet and frequently fantasized about flying it. The aircraft carrier came next with an entire squadron of fighter-jets that I shuffled all over the flight deck simulating launch and recovery operations. I lived in a fantasy land with my models and dreamed of flying these powerful planes. However, I was only a little boy and fighter-jet pilots were god-like men.

The Shaman says, "First we dream it, then we manifest the dream." My dream of flying jets came true 15 years later when I joined the United States Air Force and began jet-pilot flight training.

Today, I see that what was normal play planted seeds of violence and desensitized me to the horrors of war. At an early age, I played with cap pistols pointing these simulated weapons at others, shooting them, and watching them drop dead. Sometimes, I got shot and went through the *I'm dying* drama as well. I sometimes wondered how it would feel to take a bullet in the chest for real, fall to the ground gasping, experience the burning pain, and finally die. I did not know, of course, but I imagined it was very painful and frightening. I brushed these thoughts aside rather quickly, told myself it was only a game, and played on. I was reinforcing my denial system about the purpose and dangers of pistols, rifles, and guns.

We routinely played with cap pistols and shot each other repeatedly. I dismissed this as normal behavior because that's what boys do. Discussion about how simulated violence plants seeds for actual violence never happened. None of our parents, as I recall, ever discouraged us from playing with toy guns.

Fighter planes were magical, and I glued on bombs and missiles never connecting them with death and destruction. The planes, bombs, and missiles were just toys. It was only play and nobody ever gets hurt during play. But never did I, nor any of my friends, talk about the real bombs, real crashes, and real people dying; nope, just play.

I accepted war as a common and inevitable occurrence and viewed my F-86 Sabre Jet as a fun-to-fly toy, not as a weapon of war. Thoughts of dying, killing others, dropping bombs, and the other horrors of war never arose. My denial system was in full force by ten-years-old.

I went to the same elementary school that my father, his siblings, their children, and my sister attended before me. The old solid brick building schoolhouse had steam heat radiators that clanked loudly and spit occasionally, cloakrooms instead of lockers, real blackboards with white chalk, wooden desks, and no intercoms or security systems. We left our bikes outside in the playground bike rack unlocked, and boys and girls entered through separate entrances with BOYS and GIRLS chiseled into the granite stone above the entry doors. There was no cafeteria, but we had a huge auditorium with a big raised stage. The janitor brought milk in small containers to our classroom at noon and we ate our made-by-mom lunches from Hopalong Cassidy and Superman lunch boxes at our desks. The old building had lots of character.

Directly behind the school building was a small fenced-in area that was home of "the Liberty Bell." The school custodian pulled the rope and rang this huge bell every morning at 9:00 am, signaling the start of school, 12:00 noon, signaling the start of lunchtime, and 1:00 pm, signaling the beginning of afternoon classes. It could be heard quite a distance away. We all respected the Liberty Bell, and I do not recall ever hearing it ring other than at its normal times and always by the man assigned to ring it. Respect for others' property and authority was the norm for young people in the 1950s.

We also had practice nuclear attack drills during school. We were told that this is only a drill, it is not for real, and that a ballistic missile coming from Russia with a nuclear bomb warhead was on its way and would explode nearby shortly. Kneeling on the floor under our little desks, we would put our heads down, cover our eyes with our hands, and stay there in terror and fear until the teacher said it was OK to get up. This exercise occurred several times each school year during my entire grade school experience.

Rather than question, I assumed that war was an inevitable occurrence every twenty or thirty years and eventually it would happen. The thought of nuclear war as ultimate insanity never crossed my mind. I simply learned to hate the Russians and saw them as enemies for launching nuclear missiles at us. It was their fault we had these drills and might die in a nuclear holocaust. I could not grasp that these people that were apparently our enemies were from the same general area that my mother's mother was from. Were they nuts? Grandmom would never do this. I could not wrap my brain around any of the insanity of nuclear war, so I just pretended that it was a bad dream and did not think about it.

All our smaller school desks were constructed for right-handed children with the armrests on the right side. There were no left-handed school desks in our school. Pat is left-handed and I recall her complaining about this obviously biased and unfair situation. Left-handed people in the 1950s were treated unequally, as inferior, and even by some as akin to witches and freaks. Something was wrong with left-handed people, and Pat's complaints about the lack of small left-handed desks fell on deaf ears. Even today, you will probably never find a vintage left-handed small wooden school desk in any antique shop or yard sale. *(If perchance you do, please forward me the contact information so that I may purchase it and have it sent to Pat, even though she's now well beyond eighth grade. Thanks.)*

I acquired the savage energy of unconscious killing and destruction during childhood. On the surface, I was gentle, kind, and non-violent. But below the surface, these destructive seeds took root, and I became a stereotypical, patriarchal, privileged, white male without conscience and a blindness toward violence.

God is on our side; the USA is always right; the Russians are our enemies and might attack with nuclear warheads at any minute; it is a man's job to defend our country; do not question or think for yourself; and trust our government for they would not lie. Over time, these ideas became deep-rooted beliefs. Reciting the Pledge of Allegiance every day in school and a few other nuggets of indoctrination daily reinforced my patriotic conditioning.

One grade-school teacher taught us that George Washington never told a lie. This translated to our government never told a lie. Even though I knew that this was not true because every child lies sometimes about something, I never questioned its validity. I tried to be a good little boy, not make too many waves, and go along with the program.

UNCLE RUSSELL AND THE CHRISTMAS SOCKS

"Mom, can I please ask Uncle Russell for a new baseball this Christmas rather than another pair of those stupid argyle socks?"

"No, Johnny, you can't. What would he think if you asked him for something other than what HE wants to give you? And you WILL like his gift and be grateful no matter what! You simply cannot ask him for something, otherwise it would not be a gift from him. And you must make him believe that you really like whatever he gives you, Johnny. You sure don't want to hurt his feelings, do you? And that's all there is to it!"

A week later, as Christmas approached, I was at Uncle Russell's home and he asked me what I wanted for Christmas. I hesitated, replaying Mom's stern words over and over and finally said, "Whatever you wish to give me, Uncle Russell."

"Well, I guess you must like those argyle socks, Johnny. I'll bet they are your favorites to wear to school." "Oh yes, they are, Uncle Russell, they are my favorite socks for sure," I lied. And so, another Christmas rolled around and this little eight-year-old boy received another pair of Uncle Russell's argyle socks.

I did not like it one bit. It was confusing to me to not talk openly with my wonderful uncle and share what I REALLY wanted from him, especially since he asked what I wanted for Christmas. I imagined that a new baseball cost about the same as a pair of argyle socks. But open and honest communication was not the norm in our family. Smiling, pretending everything was just fine, and not making waves took precedence. As an eight-year-old, I did not understand the trauma that suppressing feelings, lying, and not appropriately speaking one's truth had on the entire family. I learned to pretend that everything was just fine.

We practiced looking good, pretending gratitude, and stuffing feelings. It was very confusing. Uncle Russell was rather poor, was blind in one eye, and had limited sight in the other. He did not drive or get out much and probably had others Christmas shop for him. He most likely gifted me what someone else bought, wrapped, and labeled from Uncle Russell. Although he asked what I wanted for Christmas, I could not speak openly with him. I was too afraid and the issue was closed.

Uncle Russell and the argyle socks is an example of communication within my family. Appearances were everything and I remember a lot of, "You can't say that to them!" and "What will they think if you told them that?" And so, I learned to assume responsibility for others' feelings, and that if I spoke the truth or from my heart it might offend someone. So, I didn't do that. I just stuffed and sat on my feelings. So, there we all sat at Christmas dinner, everyone pretending that everything was super-peachy-fine.

It takes a lifetime to unravel behaviors learned in childhood.

THIRD-GRADE ART CLASS

"Today, we will draw trees," said our third-grade teacher, Miss Oliver. I visualized Mr. Oak, the giant oak tree that lived in our backyard with my swing tied to one of his strong arms. Mr. Oak always held me safe as I swung for hours, forth and back. I loved that swing, and I loved Mr. Oak Tree. We were friends, and I relied on him to always hold me safely on my swing, and he always did. Even in strong winds, Mr. Oak was there for me with his big sturdy arms with leaf clusters like open hands, welcoming me to come join him in play. He let me climb on him all the way to the top sometimes.

I selected colors from my box of Crayola Crayons and drew the biggest, strongest tree I could imagine. I ran off the edge of the paper as my tree was so big and strong that he just would not quite fit my paper. Coloring the huge brown trunk, I ripped a hole in the paper, taped it up, and completed my drawing. "OK children, let's all show our pictures" and one by one, we went to the front of the class and presented our trees. Wow, Peggy drew a Christmas tree, and it looked so real with lights and a big star on top, and Mary had a little cherry tree with beautiful leaves and little red cherries that looked very real. I wanted to pick and eat one. I glanced at my oak tree and felt a little knot of fear. I cannot show them my tree, for it doesn't even look much like a tree compared to the others.

"Johnny, your turn." Up I went to show my tree that barely looked like a tree and had a rip in the trunk with tape over it. I held up my drawing and there was silence and a few little snickers. "What is it?" hollered the class bully, Willard. I hated that kid because he was fat, stupid, and should have been in fifth grade, having already failed two grades so far. "It's Mr. Oak Tree that lives in my backyard and holds my swing and we're best friends," I said. More snickers and giggles, and I felt about two-foot tall. "Ok, Johnny, thank you and Billy, please show the class your tree." I walked back to my seat, sat down, and tried to hide my embarrassment. I would let no one know how I felt, but I wanted to run away, never come back, and smash that big fat Willard right in his ugly face. I gently placed my tree picture into my desk, never to be admired again.

Later Miss Oliver came and asked to see my tree drawing. She looked at it with a critical eye, told me that the perspective was not accurate, the colors were wrong, especially for an oak tree and that it wasn't centered on the paper correctly. I listened patiently, then tried to explain to her that Mr. Oak and I were special friends and he was so big that he couldn't fit on the paper, but she didn't hear one word of it. "Johnny, your picture also doesn't have a border and it, blah blah blah," and I closed my ears to her critical comments. When she left, I crumpled Mr. Oak, and along with my creative, intuitive, artistic talents and skills and tossed them all into the trash can. I never drew again.

EIGHTH-GRADE BOOK REPORT

All through grade school I was a pretty good student. I did my assignments, got As and Bs and was headed for a university someplace. But I didn't enjoy learning about things I had little interest in and pushed those assignments off till the last minute. I disliked reading, never learned how to read rapidly, was not skilled at content retention, and when it was necessary to read, did so slowly. With book reports, there were questions to answer, and it was challenging for me to complete an assignment. I found little enjoyment in reading and had no interest in English Literature or writing. To me it was all a waste of time.

We read Hamlet in school and I could not get into it. I saw it as stupid. I'd rather be outdoors playing baseball than inside reading this book. What good is this going to do me? How is this going to help me? Why do I need to know this stuff, anyway? My questions went unanswered, and I was not really interested in answers, anyway. I already had Dad's "I can do it myself" attitude. Dad never asked for help, so neither would I.

I hated English and that was all there was to it. I never talked much to Mom or Dad about my feelings concerning school, for they lacked understanding and compassion. The few times I tried to discuss my deep feelings with Mom, her repeated response was, "There are some things that you just have to do and that's it, Johnny." This is true, but I felt that there was something inherently wrong with me. Somehow it was my fault, and there was no one for me to discuss and process those feelings with, nor do I recall being given any helpful suggestions. I would drive myself half-crazy asking *why do I have to do this if it makes no sense.*

The teacher told me, "Johnny, you need to know this subject to be a well-educated boy and grow into a well-educated man, so people will respect you and admire you. You don't want people to think you don't know Shakespeare, do you?"

"Well, I guess not, Miss Yates." I did not relate very well to Miss Yates sometimes.

Mom said, "Johnny, what's wrong with you? You only do well in subjects you like. Why can't you also do well in the subjects you do not particularly enjoy, like reading and writing?"

"I don't know, Mom," and I would leave our discussion now more confused and dejected. There was something wrong, and I did not know what. I was obviously not with the program and did not have a clue how to get with the program. I assumed I should just try harder.

So, I slowly read and reread Hamlet by Shakespeare, then struggled to write, edit, and rewrite the book report over a weekend while my friends were outside playing and having fun. It took a long time to complete, and I hated every minute.

I turned in my book report during Monday's English class. On Tuesday, Mrs. Yates returned my book report with a red F on the front page. I felt a knife entering my heart. How could this happen? I'm not that stupid, am I? I placed my paper in my desk and closed the cover. What am I going to tell Mom and Dad, for an F was a big deal in our family.

Dejected and forlorn, I sat down at dinner and Mom asked, "How did your book report go, Johnny? Did you get it back yet?"

"Yes, Mom." Silence.

"Well, did you receive your grade, Johnny?" More silence.

"Well?" Dad chimed in.

I looked up and replied, "Yes." More silence.

"Stop fooling around! What did you get?"

More silence and I whispered, "An F."

"What? An F! What's the matter with you? You stupid or something?"

And I got up and went to my room and closed the door.

At thirteen-years-old, I hear Dad in the hall saying, "And no son of mine cries either? You know what's the matter with you, Johnny?" Dad hollers from the hallway, "Your tear-bags hang too low."

Crying, frightened, and heartbroken, I remained in my room till bedtime. The next day, I threw my book report into the trash along with my creative writing gifts and skills.

LITTLE LEAGUE BASEBALL

Baseball was my favorite boyhood sport. I played shortstop on our local little league, and listened to major league games on my small seven-transistor Admiral AM band portable radio that was the leading-edge technology in the mid-1950s. I was "one of the boys" playing on the team and I liked the feelings of community, team spirit, and acceptance among my peers. Outwardly, I showed great team spirit and enthusiasm, but inwardly I felt inferior and afraid of failure.

Riding my bike to evening practice, I tried to convince myself that I was an excellent short stop, and I always gave 100% for our team. But my fear of failure clouded my enjoyment, and I found little true pleasure playing on our team.

Our coach was sometimes a drill sergeant kind of man. When one of us muffed a play, sometimes he would holler, "GET IT RIGHT! THE REST OF THE TEAM IS COUNTING ON YOU! IF THAT'S THE BEST YOU CAN DO, I'LL GET SOMEONE ELSE TO PLAY YOUR POSITION!" His loud demeanor kept me on edge and reminded me of Dad. While fielding, I would pray that the batter would not hit the ball to me, fearing I would muff the play. Sometimes, however, I would make a marvelous catch or ground stop and an accurate bullet-fast toss to first base making the out. Several times our coach remarked, "Johnny, you're a very good short stop." I just did not know it, and was focused on failure rather than success. Pretending that all was well, smiling, and daring the batters to hit to me was all bravado.

At bat, I dreaded striking out. Fear of failure kept me from letting loose and hitting the long balls. But I would trudge up to the plate and try. And occasionally I'd hit solidly and get on base. But batting like fielding was in failure mode and the cloud of doom and gloom seemed to hover over me.

I began having headaches on baseball evenings and started missing practices and games. Mom and Dad could not figure out "what was wrong with me" and why I was getting headaches only on baseball evenings, yet neither ever asked about my feelings, struggles, or fears. I eventually quit the team, and that ended my baseball career.

THE WALL AND THE DISHES

"Hey Pat, Johnny, come on down here to the living room. I've got a treat for you two." In record time, we were standing in our living room with Dad holding two big hammers.

"Hey, what's going on?" I chimed, all excited and clueless.

"Well, Mom and I are going to construct a built-in bookcase right over there in the center of that wall. So that entire section of sheetrock that I've marked with tape has got to come down. But rather than just cut it out, I thought you two might enjoy beating down the wall with these hammers. Take out all your frustrations on the wall and pound the heck out of it with all your might."

"Wow! What a treat!" And it was. For the next half hour, we beat up on the wall, smashing it to smithereens.

"Thanks Dad, that was a lot of fun." It takes a special father to do something like that for his children. There was a very special side of Dad that sometimes jumped out. I loved that piece of Dad.

Also, around that time, Dad found a pile of dishes in a box while working. As a cable splicer for the local telephone company, he installed phone systems in hotels and occasionally brought things home the establishments were going to trash. That is my recollection of how Dad acquired the dishes that he brought home for Pat and me to smash. HOW MUCH FUN IS THAT!

So, we stood next to our two-car parking apron and, one-by-one, tossed these dishes up as high as we could and watched them return to earth and smash to pieces on ground impact. IT WAS TONS OF FUN! "Get all of it out of your system, you guys." Perhaps Dad and Mom also smashed a few dishes and might have even taken a swing or two at the wall. Those details faded long ago.

But Dad did these fun things for Pat and me, and so did Mom. And I include them here to honor my parents for the fun things that they brought forward to make our life enjoyable. Thank you, Mom and Dad.

BOY SCOUTS

I loved Boy Scouts and the encouraging, helpful family of boys and leaders that I encountered. Scouting was not competitive like little league baseball and I trusted and respected my scout brothers and our scout leaders. I was a part of our Boy Scout team.

Our scoutmaster was an amiable man. Being honest and approachable, he treated us with respect and dignity. He never talked down to anyone, and I did not fear him. He nurtured us, respected us, appropriately assigned responsibilities, and related to us with a sense of maturity. I never heard him, even once, raise his voice, threaten, or punish anyone. He sat patiently, listening to us with a smile and understanding. Everyone in our troop loved and respected our scoutmaster.

I worked through our Boy Scout handbooks, adhered to the scout codes and laws, and respected the scout honor system. I earned a shoulder sash with merit badges, recognition patches, and event pins. Ending each meeting, I proudly played taps on my official Boy Scout bugle.

On special weekends, we camped about 40 miles away at a little lake. I totally got into scout signaling using a wigwag flag. I would dip the flag left and right signaling morse code dots and dashes while we pretended we were in enemy territory maintaining radio silence. I would signal a crucial message over a long distance of perhaps a few hundred yards. It was my responsibility to pass vital information to headquarters, and I'd flap my wigwag flag signaling another scout.

Several hours later, over our campfire dinner, we'd compare messages, laugh, and playfully blame each other when the message sent didn't quite match the message received. It was great sport.

Boy Scouts was laughter, fun, learning, and I was part of a team. I belonged here. Scouting was a safe-haven for me. But at fourteen, I entered High School and left scouting forever.

THE SAFETY PATROL

I joined the grade-school safety patrol at the beginning of seventh-grade in early September, 1956. We did not have adult crossing guards as there are today, but rather a volunteer force of senior students who helped the younger ones cross the streets safely. In our kindergarten through eighth-grade school, being a seventh-grader was hot stuff.

Wearing my safety patrol belt with the metal badge across the chest strap, I felt as powerful and important as the town chief of police. My corner was busy with five streets like spokes converging and several traffic lights.

In 1956, parents rarely drove their kids to school and most children either walked or rode their bikes. Abductions and random shootings were nonexistent, and the older ones helped the younger ones get to school safely.

My job was to make sure that kids remained on the sidewalk and crossed the intersection when the lights were favorable and traffic was clear. I took my job seriously and was always out on my post regardless of weather for approximately a half-hour prior to school and a half-hour after school. In eighth grade, I was the captain of the safety patrol and still remember my badge saying Captain-Safety Patrol. I enjoyed feeling important and responsible.

Safety patrol crossing guards were not permitted to step into the street and direct traffic, of course. But being playful, I engaged in a little game with a long-distance bus driver that passed through my intersection most every afternoon.

He drove a big inter-city bus, and initially I just waved at the driver as he turned the corner in front of me every day. We became waving friends. Then one day I did something a little different. The big bus waited at the red light, and when it switched to green, I stepped out into the street, and facing the bus, held my hand up in a stop signal. After he drifted toward me a few feet and stopped, I motioned a few children across the street. Complete, I stepped back onto the sidewalk and with a big grin waved the inter-city bus through the intersection. My bus driver friend smiled, saluted, and blew his air-horn as he accelerated away. He knew I was in heaven stopping his big bus, and I felt like the chief of police directing traffic. Every day that the inter-city bus caught the red light, we played this game and always waved and smiled at each other.

I felt important, alive, and valuable. Perhaps this made up for feelings that were lacking in my home. I thank you, Mr. Inter-City Bus Driver, for playing the "stop the bus and let a few kids cross the street" game with me.

PAPERBOY AND JOBS THROUGH HIGH SCHOOL

"Oh boy, it's time to go deliver my newspapers," I said, and raced out of my seventh-grade classroom at 3 pm. Completing my safety patrol obligation, I rode my bike home and retrieved my newspapers. It was a pleasant ritual for me which I performed diligently, without fail, in all kinds of weather seven days a week for two years except for a few vacation or sick days. I was excited and carefully, even lovingly, folded each paper then slipped on a rubber band to hold the fold. Packing my papers into the oversized paperboy basket on my twenty-eight-inch Schwinn bicycle, off I'd go for my daily round of deliveries. I felt important and valued. "The mail must get through" was the mantra of the mailman, and my paperboy mantra was "I must deliver my papers dry and on-time no matter what." I meant it and I did it.

I experienced a dream/vision of a customer waiting at his door as I approached on my bicycle in torrential rain with my papers covered with a tarp. I pulled one out and handed it to him, and he returned a smile. The man went inside, began reading his dry, delivered on-time newspaper and made an in-his-favor, life-changing decision from the information he gleaned from THE DRY ON-TIME newspaper delivered by that unsung hero, the best paperboy in the world, Little Johnny. In my vision, I saw the man with a smile on his face, knowing that all was well now and he said, "I owe a lot of gratitude to that fine young paperboy, Johnny, for getting this newspaper here on time every day. If it were not for him, I never could have made such a fine decision. Thank you, Johnny." It felt good to know that I was doing a fine job and that I cared about my customers. My mother and father instilled that work ethic in me as a young boy. To this day, I have a strong sense of commitment and purpose for any job I do. Thank you, Mom, and Dad.

This job also paid me well. I recall weekday (Monday through Saturday) papers sold for five-cents apiece, Sunday papers were fifteen-cents apiece, and my cut of the forty-five cents collected for one week's papers was fifteen cents (ten-cents for the six dailies, and five-cents for the Sunday paper). I earned about $7 per week, and with tips, perhaps closer to $10. That was big money and lots of responsibility for a twelve-year-old boy in 1956. I did it well and loved it.

When there was a blizzard or deep snow that prevented me from riding my bicycle, dad would drive his 1950 Mercury four-door sedan around my route with me in and out of the back seat running the papers to the customer's front porch. Dad helped me out on those occasions, and my customers were always served. I was very grateful to Dad for helping me. Many days I would come home after delivering my papers on my bike in heavy rain and cold, shivering and drenched to the bone, but warm in my heart for having done an important job well.

Mom was the village postal clerk, and many of my customers remarked how much they appreciated me and how thoughtful, pleasant, and polite I was. I genuinely felt good about these compliments passed to me through Mom. As a paperboy, I was on my own. No one was hanging over me telling me what to do, how to do it, or when it needed to be done. I had no boss. I was sad to release that job when I began high school, but circumstances prevented me from continuing and so ended my wonderful paperboy career. Perhaps some other piece of me ended as well.

I've had a job ever since early childhood and recall Dad saying, "If you have a job, Johnny, you'll always have a dollar in your pocket and you'll never be poor." I observed Dad to be the most responsible man in the world and he transferred his work ethics to me. I sold vegetable and flower seeds to the neighbors in third, fourth, and fifth grades, cut the neighbors' lawns with my dad's ancient rotary lawnmower, occasionally babysat our neighbor's little ones, and worked in my cousin's lawn business as a gardener all before my eighth-grade graduation.

In high school during summer break, I was the dock-boy at Dick's Marina a mile from home. I loved working at the marina and was there at six every morning setting up fishing boats for hire and ran the fuel service dock. I worked twelve-hour days during my early teens and loved it. Being responsible and trustworthy, I ran the cash drawer at the marina without question or supervision.

Dad taught me a valuable lesson somewhere during my childhood. He said, "Johnny, do not intentionally take anything that is not yours home from your workplace, not even a paperclip or a pencil. Steal nothing, no matter how insignificant it may appear. For once you compromise your work integrity by intentionally taking something, it becomes easier to further compromise your values. Shortly after taking a paperclip or pencil that your employer will never miss, you might next take home a pad of paper, or a box of paperclips. Your credibility and integrity are now gone. There is no such thing as a minor theft." Underneath Dad's anger and rage was a wise and intelligent man.

It was many years before I recognized these special pieces of my father. During college summers, Sealtest Dairies hired me as a retail delivery milkman, ice-cream freezer man, and truck loading man. It was fun and paid well. This was the mid-1960s with no product expiration dates on bottles, cartons, or containers, and milk was home delivered in reusable glass bottles. Most of the time, this job was hard work and total fun.

I had one customer who I called The Old Crone. She was not pleasant, was very demanding, abrupt, rude, never tipped and looked kind of like a witch. I did not like her. One day, I called in to the office before leaving my area to check for messages. "Hey, Johnny, one of your customers wants an additional quart of fat-free milk."

"Thanks, Tom," I replied. It was the Old Crone.

Swearing under my breath, I checked for fat-free milk in my truck and found none. Now what? Using a bit of engineering ingenuity, I took a quart of non-homogenized milk, drank off the cream, filled the space that used to be cream with water from a garden hose, retrieved a green fat-free bottle cap from my spare stash, and delivered the quart of fat-free to Ms. Crone. Mission accomplished.

In retrospect, I see how immature and arrogant I was at nineteen-years-old. It was all about me. I never tried to truly relate to her or understand her in any meaningful way. I just made fun of her and ridiculed her. It was all I knew how to do. I didn't have the awareness, or maturity to see her simply as a being on her earthwalk, nor the inner compassion to accept her just as she was. It was far beyond me to understand and appreciate her as a divine being. She was a teacher for me, for Ms. Crone is the only customer I remember some fifty-plus years later. She was a mirror reflecting to me an image of some aspect of me hidden underneath my outer shell of shallow pleasantries and baked-on smiles.

During college, I held a part-time assistant engineer job at the Modess Manufacturing Plant producing woman's sanitary napkins. My job was to assist in any way I could to keep the machines running and the napkins rolling. I enjoyed my part-time employment and saw it as on-the-job-training for life after graduation.

My parents and I both assumed that upon university graduation, I would get a job and become one of the zillion robot engineers that make American industry function. I did not believe that there were other options available to me.

Thoughts of alternative life paths outside the box were too big a stretch for me to consider, and that was all there was to it. I never checked in or asked, "What is important to me? What do I REALLY want to do? Is this truly in MY best interest? What is my passion?" No dialog like that ever occurred, and I went through life like a zombie on autopilot, in constant fear and anger, smiling at the world, and praying no one would ever discover how frightened and alone I was.

MIDDLE OF THE RIVER

"Hi Matt, let's go play," I hollered as I hopped off my bike in his backyard. I loved my friend Matt and his older brother Mark, who lived close to me in our neighborhood. They were one and three years older than I and were very smart, wore thick glasses, had big noses, were very Jewish, had an operational pinball machine, and were nerds. They were the only non-Christian boys in our neighborhood gang of six or seven and I was the only one that played with them. They were wonderful friends, and we rode our bikes endlessly around our neighborhood. I wore their yarmulkes and ate matzah during Passover even though it tasted a bit like dried cardboard to me.

I was about ten when I experienced this profound vision. I saw myself standing in the center of a small river. On one bank was our Methodist Minister surrounded by countless followers, all holding up crosses and chanting, "We are right, this is the way, the one and only way." On the opposite bank was a Rabbi surrounded by Matt, Mark, and countless followers all wearing yarmulkes chanting "we are right, this is the way, the one and only way." I stood in the middle of the river and asked the Methodist Minister how he could be sure his way was the one and only way when there were countless people on the opposite bank with a different view chanting the same thing? He did not reply and kept up his chant. I then asked the Rabbi the same question and received a similar response. I awoke confused and unsure who to believe. Truth had to be somewhere in the middle of the river.

As a boy, I often wondered why people individually or in groups could not get along, regardless of their beliefs. Why weren't people tolerant of others from different cultures with a different mythology?

Exclusion and separation made no sense to me and I was uncomfortable accepting without question what our Methodist Minister put forward as truth. I wondered why the Reverend and the Rabbi did not go to the center of the river, honor each other, and become friends and brothers. The river vision cracked open a door for me to become more tolerant of other religions, cultures, and ethnic groups. Rather than separate from others different from me, I opened the door to learn from others different from me. I knew that no religion was the absolute answer and did not comprehend why others could not see this simple logic. I suspected religions condition most people to believe what they are taught and told without question early in childhood. I never shared this vision or these thoughts with my parents being too afraid to rock the boat. Spiritual expansion and expression of feelings were not encouraged in our home.

"Why can't you be a good little boy? Why can't you act nice like the other boys?" and the most terrifying question from Mom or Dad was, "What are you going to tell God when he finds out that you've been a bad boy?"

I tried to answer when Mom or Dad asked these questions, but never could find the words. I was terrified, especially about how I would answer God about my "bad behavior." I thought somehow that I ought to know these answers and was scared to death standing there in front of Mom and/or Dad mumbling under my breath, "Gee, I don't know."

"Well, you better think about it Johnny, because you never know when you will meet your maker."

Terrified, I would go hide, again.

I had no answers to these questions, no one to talk to, and they did not even make sense to me. What kind of God would ask a little boy or girl questions like that? I would hide in my bedroom and hope that I wouldn't die before I found out the answers so I could meet and talk sensibly to God. I would then try to forget how frightened I was. It is a painful way to end a beautiful day of carefree fun for a little boy.

THE LARGE BOX OF TIDE

Even though Dad was very tough on me, he was the best and most available father in our neighborhood gang of about 7 boys. In many ways Dad was a good father. Sometimes he took me fishing with a few of my friends, but we fished his way. He taught me how to drive a car at an early age, his way of course. He tried to teach me how to build things, use tools, and do repairs around the house his way. I remember Mom saying, "There is everybody else's way to do things, Johnny, and then there's your Dad's way and his way is always the best way." She meant it and she was right. I believed Mom and tried to feel grateful that he was my dad.

Whenever I completed a job, Dad would come and inspect it. He would line up a screw head just a smidge straighter, trim around a fence post just a smidge neater, or notice that I missed some insignificant paint spot. "Do it right or not at all, Johnny," was the mantra I heard repeatedly, which translated into do it Dad's way.

That was impossible, of course, as he always found some flaw or fault. Dad discarded anything unusual or creative, and he showed criticism toward me when I tried to do things my way. He was trying to teach me his way so I could eliminate mistakes. I see that now, but at ten or eleven I didn't.

"Johnny, please ride your bike to the grocery store and buy a LARGE box of Tide laundry soap for Mom."

"I'm on my way, Dad," I remarked and set off with money in my pocket and clear instructions to buy a LARGE box of Tide laundry soap. I felt at ease and enjoyed the bike ride to the neighborhood grocery store.

Mom and Dad will be proud of me when I arrive home with exactly what they want, I thought. I will successfully complete this mission and perhaps get a dime reward for doing it well.

Let's see, I am looking for a LARGE box of Tide laundry soap, and they are right down this aisle. There was a small box, a medium box, and a large box. But the small box was labeled LARGE, the medium box was labeled JUMBO and the large box was labeled GIANT ECONOMY. What do I do now? If I return with the box marked LARGE, and Dad wanted the largest box, I failed. I can hear him now. "I don't care what it says on the box, I sent you to get the large box of laundry soap." And of course, if I bring home the GIANT ECONOMY box, and he wanted the box marked LARGE on it, he will say, "Look, Johnny, the box you brought home says GIANT ECONOMY and our empty box says LARGE and I told you to get the LARGE box of Tide!" I don't recall the outcome, but my memories of fear and confusion remain. I was terrified of making mistakes.

This was a typical experience from my childhood, and I rarely found the courage and confidence to decide on my own without fear. Constantly I repeated to myself, "What if I'm wrong?" or "What will Dad say when I get home, if it's not what he wanted?" I could not confidently bring home a box of Tide and if it was not what he wanted, say, "I did my best, Dad, I'll just take it back and return it for the other." Dad always pointed the finger of blame at me, never at himself. He seemed incapable of ownership and I rarely heard, "I understand the confusion, Johnny, we'll just use this box. Thank you for going." Rather than relating respectfully, it was always bruised egos, finger pointing, and blame and shame. That was my typical childhood experience.

Dad's authoritarian attitudes and rigid inflexible ways were the result of his unresolved childhood trauma. He projected that trauma on me. I am not suggesting right or wrong here. I am merely attempting to understand and explain the reality of our relationship and Dad's behaviors toward me.

He refused to talk about his punitive treatment of me, or look at other ways to parent. Doing emotional work was out of the question for Dad. Whenever someone suggested that he was wrong, or too hard on me, or that he ought to look at his anger, he'd respond, saying, "I'm fine, nobody's going to psychoanalyze me!"

Since he was the unchallenged King of the Castle, he bullied his way around and got away with it. He was not challenged, as no one wished to face the tyrant. The result was very destructive to all of us. I filled my basement trauma center with his unresolved anger, rage, and fears, and he carried his unresolved trauma to his grave. It did not help that he was drafted into WWII and spent the last year of that war as a grunt, dodging bullets and fighting from foxholes somewhere across the Pacific Ocean.

When Dad physically hurt me by strapping me across my bare butt. I'd run screaming to my room as soon as it was over and feared him even more.

I was a good boy, and never ran away from home, had no problems with the police, never got suspended or expelled from school, was a Boy Scout, played shortstop on a little league team, held small jobs around our neighborhood, and was responsible and pleasant. But I pretended that all was well while living in constant fear, with no place to take my heavy heart.

If you, dear reader, truly love yourself and love your family, you will do your inner work, no matter what. If you find yourself in this story, especially as the tyrant, you have a choice to either resolve your trauma or not. Parents make the choice to either heal themselves or pass on their darkness to those close to them, especially the children.

JOHNNY'S BIRDHOUSE

"Hey Dad, come check out my new birdhouse!" I shouted. Excited, I set my little birdhouse on his workbench and proudly waited for Dad to come downstairs to his basement workshop and admire my beautiful creation that I designed and built all by myself.

"Well, let's see, Johnny, what kind of bird is this house for?" asked Dad.

"Gee, I don't know, Dad. I guess any kind of bird, for they all gotta live somewhere, right?"

"Well, I suppose so, but the hole looks kind of small, and the perch peg isn't very long, and it's set too far below the door hole."

"Well gee, Dad, I just thought..."

"See that's the trouble, you don't think things out before you do them, Johnny, and you wind up with a mediocre birdhouse. Also, the roof isn't caulked and will leak, and the walls aren't very straight either."

"I didn't think birds cared about how straight the walls are, Dad," I said, turning my face away from my father so he wouldn't see the disappointment in my eyes.

"It's not what the birds want, Johnny, it's what YOU want. Now if the walls are not straight and the roof properly aligned and caulked,

YOU'LL know you built a half-assed birdhouse, and that is not the way to do this or any job. If you're going to build a birdhouse, build it right!"

I turned away, unable to hold back a flood of disappointment. I left my dad alone in his shop as he scratched his head, staring at my little birdhouse. He did not even notice I was gone. At eleven-years-old, I desperately wanted my father's love and approval, but I didn't get much of it.

Several days later, I sulked back down into the workshop and found my little birdhouse perched on Dad's workbench. Looking carefully at my creation, I now saw only ugliness and flaws. My little birdhouse was no longer beautiful. Gently, I lowered my birdhouse along with my creative energies into the trash can. Dad hadn't a clue how destructive his derisive comments were to me.

A month later, Dad called me to his workshop and showed me his new two-story, eight-room, wren birdhouse, with a three-tone paint scheme, mitered walls, roof overhangs, and little shutters near the perfectly sized holes. "Now that's a birdhouse, Johnny, that you can be proud of, and I'll show you how to make one just like it."

"Thanks Dad, it's beautiful, but I'm going to go ride my bike."

"And by the way, Johnny, where's your birdhouse?"

"I don't know, Dad, must have got misplaced somewhere."

"Well, if you find it, Johnny, we can hang it outside and maybe some bird will use it."

"Thanks, Dad, your birdhouse is beautiful."

"And Johnny, if you build it as I tell you, you'll have yourself a perfect birdhouse that you can be proud of too."

I turned and walked away, went to my room, closed the door, and felt my heart sink into despair and sadness. I did not even know why I was crying because my father to this little boy was Mr. God and therefore always right. I would tell myself that he's just trying to teach me how to do it right. But the constant criticisms and pain of him not recognizing my creative gifts and allowing me to be an eleven-year-old was too much for me to bear. I assumed that I just was not good enough. It had to be something like that. It sure couldn't be Dad, for he was everything to me and I listened and believed every word he said. It just had to be me. Maybe if I just try harder.

SHOOTING THE LITTLE BIRD

"Hey Johnny, come out here. I want to show you something," Dad called from the back porch.

"OK Dad, I'm coming," I replied. It was a warm summer afternoon as I slipped outside to our small back porch where Dad was sitting with his .22-caliber rifle resting across his lap.

"Johnny, I want to show you how to safely use this rifle."

I had little interest in real guns and rifles, but I sat down next to Dad, anyway. I was about eleven. "First, always check that the rifle is unloaded, Johnny." Dad opened the breech and showed me where to look to ensure that the chamber was empty. "Trust no one when they tell you a gun or rifle is empty or unloaded. Always verify it for yourself, no matter what." That seemed like a good idea to me.

Dad was harsh, but he always stressed safety and I have been safety conscious all my life thanks to him. We checked that the rifle safety was engaged, checked for an empty breech, inspected the barrel, and verified that the magazine was empty. We both knew that this rifle was safe to handle. It felt awkward and heavy and I noticed some feelings of uneasiness arising. I knew that guns and rifles were not my thing, and my mind and body began resisting.

"Let's load her up with a few rounds and see what we can pick off," said Dad. So, he slipped in several rounds and loaded the chamber.

Dad looked around and saw several small birds on the telephone wires by our back fence and said, "I bet I can pick off one of those birds, Johnny. Watch this!"

"But Dad, they're just little birds that haven't done anything wrong. How about I go set up a few cans on the fence for you to shoot? I can easily get them from the trash."

I was up and started for the trash when his hand grabbed me and he said, "Sit down, Johnny, it's only a bird!" I sat down, and Dad pulled the rifle to his shoulder. BLAM, the first round fired, but all the birds were still there. "Damn! I missed."

I moved a little away from Dad and thought about my little parakeet safe inside his cage in the house. In my mind, there was negligible difference between my pet parakeet and these little birds on the wire. I could not relate to killing for sport. BLAM and a little bird fell from the wire, and we heard the thunk as its body hit the trash can lid directly below. Is killing little birds for sport what it means to be a man? That's what Dad was doing, and he was my hero, my model of manhood, and I wanted to be just like him.

"OK, Johnny, your turn!" I wanted to run away but sat there conflicted. *What do I do?* I reluctantly took the rifle, held it as Dad instructed me to, and aimed at one of the remaining little birds on the wire. "Now, Johnny, when you got the bird in your sights, aim for his head, for there will be a little drop in your bullet and then gently squeeze the trigger, don't jerk it."

"OK, Dad." I held the rifle, looked through the sight, saw the little bird's head, then adjusted my aim off to one side. Holding my breath, with the rifle pulled tightly to my shoulder, I squeezed the trigger. BLAM! The report startled me, but I missed the bird and felt relief.

"Try it again." I did, and each time I moved the sight away from the little bird and missed and missed and missed.

"You'll never make a hunter, Johnny," laughed dad, and he took back his rifle. I was glad to give it back. "Let's go see where the one I shot fell." We walked to the fence and there on the trash can lid lay the body of the small bird. Dad picked up the lid, tilted it sideways, and we watched the little bird slide off into the trash. "How skilled is that!" boasted Dad. "Didn't even have to pick him up."

I went inside and visited my little parakeet, Chirp. I told him how sorry I was that Dad shot one of his friends. I let Chirp sit on my finger and stroked his head. How can Dad let Chirp fly around our house as a pet and then shoot his feathered brother or sister outside? Birds were birds and senseless killing for sport made no sense to this young boy. I hoped I would never experience this situation again. At eleven years old, I thought being a man meant killing little birds and not feeling any sadness or remorse. Stuffing feelings and not showing emotions or remorse was also a sign of manhood, I thought.

I witnessed some of this same senseless brutality from Dad with our fishing experiences. We lived near saltwater tidal bays along the New Jersey shore and had a small boat. I loved going out in our boat and, at thirteen, became a skilled boat operator. Dad taught me about safety, and I applied this knowledge to all boating activities. Safety consciousness was a gift from Dad.

Flounder were plentiful in our area and these flat fish were exciting to catch and made delicious dinners. Sometimes Dad did not seem to care how he treated these fish after we caught them. Some fishermen had little boxes that floated in the water that kept fish alive and in minimal pain till they reached the dock and were cleaned. It was somewhat respectful. Sometimes Dad would use a wooden fish box to keep our fish alive in water, but sometimes he just tossed them into the bottom of the boat to flop around in a few inches of water. I watched as they gasped for water to breathe and slowly died. I asked Dad about this, and he commented that, "They're only fish, Johnny. They don't feel pain like we do." I knew he was wrong just watching them jerk, squirm, and gasp, and it was disturbing to me. But I didn't push it too much, for Dad was my hero and I wanted to grow up to be a man's man, just like him. I did not want him to think I wasn't strong, couldn't take it, or had a weak stomach. My father was the archetypical "man's man." He was set in his ways, inflexible and showed little or no emotion.

MR. JOSEPH'S MARKET

I was about nine or ten, and, along with my friends, a member of the Little Men's Club in our neighborhood. The half dozen of us boys would meet at our tree fort and plan out our next adventure. What would grown men do? We would ask questions like this to ourselves and spend countless hours pretending we were grown men. Usually, we'd talk about adventures of questionable character if you get my drift. But we were all good kids, rarely got into any real trouble, and talked a lot louder than we acted. It was a lot of fun imagining pulling off some of those shenanigans.

We worked out a plan to wreck the local freight train as it crept down the branch-line tracks through town, hauling maybe three cars and racing along the rails at a blistering ten miles per hour. The cars always swayed excessively on the horribly maintained track.

We decided that our best bet to derail the locomotive was to put a crowbar on one rail. It was early 1950s and steam locomotives still worked this branch line. "What would we do if the crowbar worked, and the engine jumped the track?" someone muttered. "We'd have the police after us and be in REAL trouble then! And suppose the locomotive tipped over and the engineer or fireman died or something like that?"

None of us ever did anything that destructive or dangerous, but it was fun to pretend and brag about what we could do, just like grown-up men. We backed off the crowbar idea and settled on leaving a few pennies on the rail. No harm came to the locomotive, of course, and we got a few squashed pennies in the deal. We talked loudly, but were just boys pretending.

Mr. Joseph Wisehart and his wife Marie, owned and operated the Wisehart Market neighborhood grocery store a few blocks away. We all went there occasionally for small grocery items, ice-cream bars, soda pops, and penny candies. The Wiseharts were gentle caring people with "wise hearts" and everyone, including us youngsters, called him Mr. Joseph and her Mrs. Marie and generally referred to the market as Mr. Joseph's Market.

The building was an old two-story wooden structure with the grocery store on the first floor, and their living quarters upstairs. Unlike modern markets with aisles and shelves throughout the store, Wisehart's market had shelves along the outer walls, and tables, barrels, and bins in the center area. The long counter on the right side held the cash register and the penny candies. I remember the tall ladder that Mr. Joseph would roll along the outer wall shelves and climb to retrieve items beyond his reach. It was a true mom and pop market with a rather small selection of items but lots of character.

The bins of penny candies like Mary Janes, Tootsie Rolls, and a few others were on the counter right out in the open near his cash register. Mr. Joseph and Mrs. Marie were trusting people.

"Hey," said Frank, "I got an idea to prove how grown up we are. Let's each go separately to Mr. Joseph's store, steal a piece of his penny candy and not get caught."

"But that's really stealing, not just play stealing," one kid said.

"What's the matter, you chicken or sometin?"

"Of course not, but it's still stealing."

"We're supposed to be big men, and it's only a little piece of candy!" chimed in Donny.

So, we all decided to do it and each boy was to do it alone. We allowed ourselves three days to complete the robberies, then meet back at the fort to show each other what we had stolen and share how we did it. We felt that stealing was the stuff that men do and we were big strapping men of nine or ten. I felt uncomfortable, for I was an honest kid and stealing wasn't something I did. However, the need to belong to the club and to prove I was a man had the greater influence and overrode any thoughts I had about honesty and integrity. I could not have faced the gang in three days without a penny candy and a true story of how I bravely pulled the robbery of the century off without a hitch.

"Hello Mr. Joseph," I chimed, all smiles.

"Well, hello, Johnny, what can I get for you today?" *He is being awfully nice to me today*, I thought. He must know I'm up to no good. Maybe it's written on my face. These thoughts raced through my mind as I meandered through Mr. Joseph's store toward the cash register and the penny candies.

"I've got a nickel for a fudge bar, Mr. Joseph. May I have one, please?"

"Of course, Johnny, I'll go get it for you from the freezer." As he turned and started toward the back of the store, I turned away from him, put my hand in the Mary Jane candy bin, and pulled out one little Mary Jane. Quickly, I slipped the stolen goods into a pants pocket.

"Here's your nickel fudge bar, Johnny." I felt my Mary Jane candy with my fingers as I rummaged through my pocket, retrieving the nickel. "Thank you, Mr. Joseph, I'll be on my way now."

"OK Johnny, thank you for coming by."

I was home free and started toward the door and safety.

"Uh Johnny."

"Yes, Mr. Joseph?" My heart stopped.

"Would you come back for a minute, please?"

"Sure Mr. Joseph," I said and returned. Mr. Joseph was now sitting in a chair in the center of his store. He beckoned me to sit on a chair facing him. "Yes, Mr. Joseph?" I blurted out, feeling my forehead growing moist with sweat.

"Johnny, I want to tell you a brief story that happened to me when I was a young boy about your age. My parents owned a little farm, and, of course I helped Dad with the chores and also helped Farmer Sid Parker our neighbor as well. Farmer Parker grew excellent vegetables and prided himself on the quality of his root vegetables especially his beets. He didn't have a tractor back then and used a team of draft horses to pull his plow and hung his old horseshoes on a wall in his barn. There must have been fifty horseshoes hanging on his wall and I wanted four of them to use with a horseshoe pit I was planning to build near Dad's barn.

"Dad had a steam tractor and didn't have extra horseshoes hanging around. But rather than ask Farmer Parker for four old horseshoes, I decided to steal them. I thought if I asked him and he said no, then I would be out of luck. So, I snuck over to Farmer Parker's barn one evening just after dark. I remember how frightened I was and how heavy the four horseshoes were as I took them down from the wall and placed them in my canvas bag. Opening the barn door to leave, I bumped into Farmer Sid Parker standing right there in front of me. He appeared ten-feet tall and he caught me red-handed.

"But Farmer Parker was a compassionate man, and he knew I was an honest boy. He said, 'Well young Joseph, out for an early evening stroll in my barn? What do you have in your bag Joseph?' I could have died right there. 'Well, sir?' I stammered. 'Joseph,' interrupted Farmer Parker, 'I'll bet you have a few horseshoes in that bag.' 'Well, uh.' 'It's ok if you do, son, I understand.' I put my bag down and pulled out the four horseshoes. 'Young Joseph,' said Farmer Parker, 'I know you're a good boy and an honest boy, too. But somehow maybe you've a bit of pride or faulty reasoning that is preventing you from simply asking for a few old horseshoes. I have many on that wall. And rather than trying to teach you a lesson by punishing you and telling your dad what you did, I'll make you a little offer.' 'OK, Farmer Parker,' I replied.

"He continued, 'Stealing a few horseshoes really doesn't hurt me much Joseph since I've a ton of them, anyway. But it hurts you, for it compromises your integrity. So, if you put the horseshoes back, then come and help me for a few hours doing odd jobs around my farm, we'll call it even. When you're done, you can have four horseshoes as a gift and this issue will be closed. This will remain our little secret, and I will not tell your mom or dad. We will deal with this ourselves, man to man. Do we have a deal?'

"Johnny, I gladly accepted Farmer Parker's deal and realized how afraid I was of people that I didn't have to be afraid of, and how reluctant I was to tell the truth. I felt instant relief. I was also very grateful that Farmer Parker did not tell my parents and we would deal with this ourselves. I felt ashamed, but I also felt like I grew up a bit because of Farmer Parker's understanding and compassion. He was more interested in helping me than getting even and punishing me.

"I put the horseshoes back on his wall, helped him with home projects a few days later, built my horseshoe pit and, for many years, tossed ringers with Farmer Parker's horseshoes. When Dad asked me where I got the horseshoes, I told him that they were a gift from Farmer Parker for helping with a few odd jobs around his farm.

"Johnny, I've known you for years and I know you are an honest young boy. And I have had just about every trick pulled on me here in this little store. I noticed you were nervous when you came in, and so I just watched you because I felt you might be up to something that you might regret doing.

"There's a mirror on the wall near the ice-cream freezer and when I turned away, I immediately saw you in the mirror turn and put your hand in the penny candy bin. So, I turned and watched you finger a Mary Jane and I'll bet it is still in your right pants pocket. You needn't be afraid, Johnny. I shared my horseshoe story so that you know I did similar things as a boy and understand how you feel. You may have been dared by one of your friends, or something else may have encouraged you to pocket the Mary Jane. But on your own, I don't think you would steal a candy. You are just too honest for that."

My eyes grew moist as I felt the loving understanding of Mr. Joseph. I reached into my pocket and pulled out the little Mary Jane candy.

"Johnny, here's the deal. Since what you did was dishonest, I believe there ought to be a consequence for your action. This is to atone for the wrong and make it right. How about next Saturday morning, you come here and help me stock a few shelves or sweep up for a few hours? That's your atonement. You may keep the Mary Jane as a gift and a reminder of this talk we've had. I will not say one word to your mom or dad or anyone else about this, for it's our business and we are dealing with it ourselves, man to man. If you agree, then this issue is closed."

I agreed.

Mr. Joseph then added that, "This talk with you today, Johnny, happened because I was shown understanding and compassion from Farmer Sid Parker many years ago. And someday, Johnny, perhaps you'll have the opportunity to show understanding and compassion to a young girl or boy when the circumstances offer you the opportunity sometime in the distant future."

I thanked Mr. Joseph for his wisdom and kindness and left.

The entire gang was at our tree fort as I entered and sat with my friends. I shared with them what happened at Mr. Joseph's market and how kind and understanding he was. I told my buddies how anxious I felt on my way over to Mr. Joseph's market, how anxious I felt in the store, and how scared I was when I pocketed the Mary Jane. I expressed how awful I felt when he asked me to return and sit with him. I shared that I did not want to ever experience these feelings again.

I pulled out the Mary Jane, cut it into six tiny pieces, and passed them around. I felt relief and knew now that being a real man was not about seeing what I could get away with, but like Mr. Joseph, it was about being kind, honest, and understanding. We gave up our plans of stealing Mr. Joseph's penny candy.

On Saturday morning, I went to Mr. Joseph's store accompanied by my five buddies to help sweep his floor and stock his shelves. When we finished, Mrs. Marie gifted us each a fudge bar and our choice of five penny candies apiece. We all felt good about helping Mr. Joseph and Mrs. Marie and talked non-stop about these great feelings of helping all the way home. We understood by demonstration that the feelings generated by helping far exceed the feelings generated by getting away with something. We were sure glad to have Mr. Joseph and Mrs. Marie in our lives as role models to look up to and hoped that someday we could be as kind and understanding as these two adults were to us.

Love, compassion, and understanding are attributes of the spiritually mature. They create a compassionate community rooted in honesty. Atonement for one's misguided actions is the path of healing.

Atonement is not punishment. It is a necessary reciprocal gift to restore balance. Threats, punishments, and physical responses to events create more disorder and chaos. They encourage separation between the parties involved and push one away from resolution. These are actions of the spiritually immature. Imagine if Mr. Joseph had told my father what I did and when I got home, Dad was waiting with a leather strap to "teach me a lesson I'd never forget." It is obvious which outcome encourages a boy to walk a path of compassion and service and which outcome encourages a boy to resist, rebel, and fight back to get even.

I had to reach deep to recall the hazy memories of the Wisehart Market and Little Johnny the penny candy thief. It occurred about seventy years ago and it's way too deep in my fuzzy past to accurately recall all the details. But it did occur, and it occurred something like I've shared. The story of little Johnny, the penny candy thief, and the Wisehart Market caper is retold right here in all its beauty.

TERRIFIED TO TELL DAD THE TRUTH

I loved our small sixteen-foot boat with its twenty-five horsepower Evinrude outboard motor. We kept her docked at the local marina, where I worked during high school summers only a mile from our home. At thirteen or fourteen, after much instruction mostly centered on safety, Dad allowed me to take our boat out by myself. I would ride my bike to the marina, fuel up, hand crank our trusty Evinrude and off I'd go. Salt spray in my face. I was very grown-up and loved running around and fishing the inner back-bays near Atlantic City, New Jersey.

A few other boys also had similar boats, and we'd meet up, fish, and sometimes water-ski behind a boat. Of course, we raced each other to see whose boat was the fastest. I imagine I could coax about twenty-five mph out of her. To me, she was the fastest thing on water. It was great fun. Dad, of course, told me to "be careful, don't take chances, and don't fool around."

One day, Dave and I were racing each other down a small creek toward a little bridge. We were neck and neck and we both chose the same span to pass under. It wasn't quite wide enough and as we went shooting under the bridge neck and neck, we gently bumped sides. It wasn't a big deal, but our collision put a small 1" x 3" hole in the plywood side of my boat near the stern just under the gunwale.

I panicked, for I was TERRIFIED to tell my father that I had disobeyed him, was fooling around, racing, and put a hole in the boat's side. I had some explaining to do and felt that I just could not tell Dad the truth.

So, I lied when I told him about the hole in the boat and I do not remember what his reaction was or what punishment I received. I just remember how TERRIFIED I was about disobeying my father and how unwilling I was to speak the truth. It was not safe for me to be truthful in my home.

A few days later in a few hours, dad patched the hole, painted it, and that was the end of it. I remember, however, the traumatizing, paralyzing fear I held toward my father.

Perhaps in a safer environment, this incident may have unfolded differently. I imagine my father now as my hero, my friend, and one that nurtures and loves me from his heart. Let us listen in on the conversation that might have been:

"Dad, I've something to share that is hard for me to tell you."

"What's going on Johnny?"

"Well, I took our boat out today and met up with Dave in his boat out in the bay. We fished for a while and then called it quits and came back to the Marina. Running back with Dave on one side of the creek and me on the other, we approached the low bridge next to the Marina. Both of us headed for the same bridge span to pass under. I guess we each thought the other guy would let up, but neither of us did. I suppose neither of us wanted to chicken-out so we shot under the same span, neck, and neck. His boat tapped the side of ours just below the gunwale, near the stern, and there is now a small hole in the plywood a few inches long. It is way up high so the boat is in no danger of sinking. I'm really sorry, Dad for fooling around and with a little help, perhaps I can repair it."

"Well, Johnny, the important thing is that you, Dave, and the boats are OK, and it sounds like the damage is minimal. I know boys will be boys and even though I set the guidance, I know you'll push it a little. All boys do. When I was a kid, I did the same sort of stuff and did things I wasn't supposed to do as well. How about after dinner we go look at her and you and I will get us a little plan to repair our boat, so she's as good as new. I am glad you told me, Johnny. Now let's put it behind us and go enjoy one of Mom's fine dinners."

CIGARETTES

"Hey Johnny, what brand of cigarettes did you bring?" asked Dave. I reached into my duffle bag and produced my pack of Winstons. Then we went off into the woods away from the camp to experiment with our forbidden activity.

Dad smoked cigarettes in the car and around the house. In the 1950s, smokers smoked on busses, in restaurants, on airplanes, and just about everywhere else. Smoking was a sign of maturity and manhood.

Since Dad smoked, I decided I would too, and it began in Boy Scouts at about thirteen years old. Dave and I lit up, took a few shallow puffs, choked, and coughed a lot, tried each other's brand, and came back to camp hoping no one saw us. That scenario repeated itself every Boy Scout camping trip during my last few years of scouting.

My early experiments with cigarettes and smoking were forced and unpleasant. I could not imagine how anyone could enjoy smoking cigarettes. But, if I tried hard enough, perhaps I'd learn. It seemed like almost every man I knew smoked cigarettes. It was the cool thing to do, and I was going to do it even if it killed me.

High School was the big league to this just turned fourteen-year-old freshman and the city bus, which doubled as our school bus, was exciting to ride. We would laugh and play during the three-mile ride to school and it provided an opportunity to be with the grown-up juniors and seniors. The protocol was that upperclassmen rode in the back of the bus and the lower classmen rode up front. Smokers, however, all rode toward the back of the bus.

During my sophomore year, I acquired a flip-top Zippo lighter and polished the chrome till it shone like a mirror. I loaded the soft cotton fuel cell with lighter fluid and practiced sliding my fingers off the top to pop it open, then snapping a finger on the striker wheel which created the spark that ignited the fuel and the wick burst into a perfect flame. I practiced for months till I was very skilled at the "flip-snap-burst into flame" zippo lighter act. This was like my Sheriff Roy Rogers gun-twirling quick-draw maneuver that I frequently used to maintain law and order around our home a few years prior. I practiced for hours until I could pull this Zippo flip-snap-burst-into-flame act off with style and grace.

I also practiced smoking until I could inhale without choking or coughing and became an expert at blowing picture perfect smoke rings. I was ready to let the world see this young boy do his Zippo act and smoke on the school bus.

About mid-sophomore year, I boarded the school bus one morning, sauntered down the aisle to a seat near the back, slid out a Winston and, with flair and finesse, pulled off my little Zippo lighter routine. The big boys were impressed, and I felt like a man, at least a bit. Smoking, I believed, was on the path to manhood. I also noticed that the girls near the back of the bus seemed more mature even though they did not give me a second glance. I was in!

I never thought about health risks, costs, addiction, or anything like that. Growing up was the only thing on my mind.

I smoked for about 10 years on and off, mostly on. I never really liked it, but I identified maturity, adulthood, and being a man with cigarettes, and it just felt cool to smoke. Sometimes, after a party, I could barely breathe the following morning, but that didn't deter me from continuing.

In Air Force pilot training, I quit smoking almost every Monday, would abstain all week, then go back full force on Friday evening at the Officer's Club stag bar. I would pull out all the stops for drinking and smoking almost every weekend. This cycle repeated itself over and over.

One Sunday morning in January 1970, I awoke coughing and wheezing from the pack of cigarettes I smoked at Saturday night's party. Hacking away, I looked in the mirror and hardly recognized the bloodshot eyes staring back at me. I did not know what was worse, my hangover, or the shortness of breath and constriction I felt in my chest. I was not ready to quit drinking, but I was ready to ditch the cigarettes. "Dear Lord"! I muttered, "I've tried a hundred times to quit smoking. God, please help me." "JOHNNY, EITHER YOU TAKE CARE OF THESE CIGARETTES, OR THESE CIGARETTES WILL TAKE CARE OF YOU!" I had no clue where the voice came from but I heard it loud and clear. I showered, shaved, and tossed my cigarettes into the trash.

The following Friday, I had no urge to smoke at the bar and held the line with minimal effort. The second week was easier than the first, and as I went to bed at the conclusion of the second week, I realized I hadn't thought about smoking for several days. I abstained from cigarettes over the second weekend, and the desire and urge to smoke was history. I was twenty-five and free of the cigarette addiction.

CUTTING THE COCONUT

"Johnny, we're rehearsing our senior play, South Pacific, and Randy is the hula dancer. This coconut will be his you-know-whats. Can you cut this coconut in half and tie them across his chest please?"

"Sure Pat," I replied. I was fifteen. Grabbing a big kitchen knife, I carefully examined the coconut. I checked and rechecked it out thoroughly. Then, holding the knife over the coconut, I prepared to cut. *Nope, that's not quite right*, I thought, *let's see, how about like this*? *Nope, that's not quite right either.* I examined the coconut several times from several angles and just could not settle on how to make the cut.

"What are you doing, Johnny?" asked Dad, strolling into the kitchen.

"I'm about to cut this coconut to make a pair of you-know-whats for hula dancer Randy to wear."

"Well, go ahead! What are you waiting for?"

"Well, I never cut a coconut before, Dad."

Feeling unsure and self-conscious because of Dad's presence, I examined and re-examined the coconut several more times.

Finally, Dad said, "Would you like me to cut the coconut Johnny?"

"Sure, Dad."

He confidently took the coconut in one hand, placed it on the cutting board, picked up the knife and wham, he cut the coconut.

"Nice job, Dad. Where did you learn to cut a coconut?"

"That was the first coconut I ever cut. And if you've never cut a coconut before, Johnny, and you're asked to cut a coconut, just look it over, select the knife, and cut the coconut."

That was helpful, instructive support. But I took it as criticism. I was unable to accept support from Dad and confidence in my abilities slipped deeper into the basement.

I CAN DO IT MYSELF

College was tough, and I failed first semester freshman English Comp. I hated writing and needed tutoring. Yet I refused extra help and blamed my failure on the professor. My "I can do it myself" attitude, ingrained from my "I can do it myself father," plagued me my entire life (at least the part I've lived so far). Dad never asked for help, and he could do anything all by himself. So, by golly, if Dad never asked for help, then I won't ask for help either. I would not want to be a wimp, for only wimps ask for help, or so I thought. I was reluctant to ask for help with anything.

I'm blessed with a musical ear and taught myself to play guitar during college. I watched a guy strum a few chords and simply copied what he was doing. Within a few weeks I could chord and play a few simple folk songs. Shortly thereafter, I could chord and strum practically any song on the guitar after hearing it a few times.

But I never practiced to become proficient with bar-chords or finger-picking. I had the talent, but my "I can do it myself, I don't need your help" attitude prevented me from becoming an accomplished guitar player. I simply needed a teacher and a bit of practice. But I never engaged a teacher, never took a lesson, never had a dedicated practice, and never progressed beyond being a good campfire guitar player. My attitude and thick skin blocked my talent.

Rather than encourage and authentically support each other, put-downs and cheap shots were more the norm in our family. Mom and Dad were proud and supportive of Pat's and my accomplishments. But it takes only a few put-downs and cheap shots to erase the genuine support and compliments. The focus, as I remember it, was more on failures than accomplishments. Failures were met with sarcasm and put-downs rather than concern and helpful suggestions. It hurt!

Needy people extract energy from others by taking cheap shots. Needy people are not aware of this, of course, but that's what they do. The victim gives a little energy away when absorbing any cheap-shot. It happened a lot in my family, especially to me from my father, "What are you, stupid or something? Just kidding! Har har har."

I heard that a lot and was always devastated.

Dad would say, "Here's Johnny, the flower of the family, a blooming idiot! Har har har, just kidding, Johnny!"

I told Dad how his remarks hurt me, and he said, "Don't be so thin-skinned. You got to learn to take a joke." Of course, nobody ever took a cheap shot at Dad.

During Christmas dinner when I was in my early fifties, thirty years after my college graduation, my University English Composition failures became the dinner topic of discussion. I felt like I was shot in the heart at close range. Retired as a veteran combat fighter pilot from the Air Force, and currently flying as a pilot with American Airlines, my family focused on a painful experience and I was the brunt of their laughter and amusement.

It may have been just Dad doing this as my memory after all these years is hazy. But I recall how lousy I felt about having these thirty-year-old unpleasant memories brought up again and put next to the turkey and stuffing on the Christmas dinner table. I heard, again, probably from Dad, "You got a pretty thin skin, Johnny, can't you take a little ribbing? What's the matter with you?" Is it any wonder that I left home at eighteen, returning only for college summers to work and brief visits after university graduation? I was not comfortable nor was it ever safe for me to be around my father.

As a boy, when Dad made these demeaning remarks to me, it was God speaking to me and it took a ton of work and many years to undo the damage.

Family today is more expansive than my biological tribe. My "family" are my supportive loving brothers and sisters that accept me as I am, love me as I am, and support me without judgement, as I am.

RUTGERS UNIVERSITY

I left home for Rutgers University in early September 1962, with little confidence and a lot of fear. My classmates at Rutgers College of Engineering were mostly young men, just like me. But I perceived them as smarter, wiser, and more capable than myself. I felt like I did not belong. I saw myself as a four-foot boy in a college full of six-foot men. I believed that I was in way over my head. Confused and alone, I began my university experience.

"Gentleman," said the College of Engineering Dean, "please introduce yourself to your classmates sitting on both sides of you. Next semester, one of them won't be here." Washout of fifty percent first-semester freshman engineering students at Rutgers University in the early 1960s was normal. What if I fail? My family is counting on me and sacrificing much so I can go to college. The pressure was on and that added to the already heavy burden on my overloaded shoulders. I did well in high school, but this was the big league, and failure was not an option.

The legal drinking age in New Jersey in the 1960s was twenty-one. However, Rutgers University allowed students to consume beer (no wine or hard liquor) in dorms and fraternity houses on campus. The first weekend, my roomie, also an eighteen-year-old, asked if I wanted to kick in for some beer. I never drank in high school but I am on my own and this is college, so here's my dollar.

He was gone in a flash and returned shortly with a six-pack. My first beer, my first real drink in that dorm room a few weeks after my eighteenth birthday, turned me into a six-foot, handsome, debonair, charming MAN. I could not believe how wonderful, capable, and alive I felt. My self-confidence was restored.

What? What is this subtle feeling? What am I seeing here? Something from my past was coming into focus and I visualized myself as a boy dressed as Sheriff Roy Rogers with my gun belt holstering two pearl-handled pistols strapped to my waist. Just as I became a man many years ago by donning a Roy Rogers silver SHERIFF's badge, I became a man by drinking a can of beer. Drinking for me was never normal.

The next morning, I was not quite the man I was when I went to bed. Johnny was again a four-foot-tall frightened freshman college student in over his head with a hangover. Now began the management program of only drinking on weekends, only a few if there was a test on Monday, blah, blah, blah. A terrorist group soon became permanent residents of my mind. They argued endlessly whether I ought to have a beer, or two, or abstain this weekend, etc. Doom and gloom slowly spread over me, but I kept smiling and telling the world that everything was fine.

Second semester freshman year, I pledged one of several dozen Greek social fraternities on Rutgers University campus. I loved the camaraderie of our brotherhood and especially the social functions. I found beer, music, and girls Saturday nights downstairs in our party room. One party evening, brother Bruce entered our bar, strapped on his guitar, and sang a few verses of "Tom Dooley." Shortly, a few girls sat down in front of him and glued their eyes to him and his guitar.

The next day, I asked Bruce to teach me how to play his guitar. Having music in my blood, I learned quickly and shortly I was on the barstool playing "Tom Dooley" and other simple folk songs with my brand new ten-year-old yard-sale guitar. I didn't need much encouragement and loved being center stage. I felt valuable.

I was not on the dean's list, but was succeeding socially, and partying became a top priority. The guitar attracted girls, and I milked it for all it was worth. Perhaps I was getting the approval that I longed for and did not get from my father as a little boy. It just felt good.

Senior year, I assumed the responsible position of "Social Director of Kappa Sigma Fraternity" responsible for the beer, the bands, and the parties. Fumbling my way through academics, I graduated with a major in Industrial Engineering, and a minor in fraternity parties. But I was lost, overwhelmed, unprepared, immature, and frightened of the future. Meanwhile, I kept smiling at everyone and pretending that all was well. It wasn't.

THE DAY MY LOVE DIED

September 1961 was memorable. I got my driver's license one week after my seventeenth birthday and began senior year in our brand-new high school. Three local communities merged into a new regional school, and I knew only one-third of my classmates, as the other two-thirds had gone to a different school. We were the first graduating class. As always, with change, I felt unsettled in this unfamiliar environment.

I played trumpet in our marching band and did not take part in any sports. I felt inferior to the jocks and athletes. Julie, a marching Majorette from my neighboring town, liked me and we became great friends through band and academics. She lived only a mile away and soon I had special feelings for this special young woman. She was attractive, intelligent, playful, and we just hit it off. Her family loved me as much as my family loved her. We had similar interests and meshed well together in all activities.

We did not go to many student parties and were among the "straight ones" that did not experiment with alcohol. We simply preferred to be with each other doing simple things. We fell deeply in love and shared first intimacy.

Studying was enjoyable with Julie, and she was better at the creative subjects like English and history, while I was the engineer, good at science and math. We complemented each other. During senior year, we spent Christmas, Easter, and proms together. I had dreams of us in a little house with a picket fence, our baby in the swing, and a little dog running around the yard barking at butterflies.

A year later, in September 1962, I entered Rutgers University, while Julie began studies at a school some distance from me. It was not possible to be with each other very often. We settled for a long-distance relationship, seeing each other only on major social weekends.

I pledged a social fraternity second semester freshman year and Julie came to Rutgers several times that semester for party weekends. Our love grew and although we were not going steady and agreed to see and date others, she remained the love of my life. Sophomore year began as a repeat of freshman year, with us managing our long-distance relationship. Julie stayed mostly at her school while I remained at Rutgers.

Early second semester sophomore year, letters from Julie became less frequent, and I became a bit anxious. Communication in the early 1960s was mostly by written letters through the U.S. mail, not by phone. In our fraternity house, as example, we had only one pay phone for use by all the brothers.

In February 1963, Julie shared in a letter that she had gone to a party a few months prior, got drunk, slept with her date and now was several months into her unplanned and unwanted pregnancy. She told me she loved me, that I was not the father, and that she felt obligated to have her child and marry this man. "I'm so sorry, Johnny, but this is what I must do. I love you and wish you well."

I was devastated. My Julie, my Goddess, my beautiful love, the love of my life, my dreams, her dreams, our dreams, gone, shattered. I died that day. Her parents, dominated primarily by her stiff, stoic, and rigid father, basically disowned her.

That was the last I saw or heard from Julie for twenty-five years. My despair knew no bounds. Mom and Dad were sympathetic and watched as I sank deeper into depression, relieved only by shallow sensory pleasures. I felt betrayed. Why her? Why me? What did we do wrong? It went on and on and my life of parties, drinking, casual dating and not caring about myself or others continued. All the while I smiled, feigned sincerity, and pretended that I was unaffected by this event. I stuffed, as my father taught me, the whole affair into my dark basement and leaned heavily against the basement door to hold it shut.

Senior year, I became the social chairman of my fraternity and organized the parties, bought the beer, found the bands, and invited the girls. I did that well. I tried to erase Julie from my consciousness and escape the pain of the hole in my heart. But her face showed up on many of the women that I casually dated. I didn't know whether to run from them or embrace them.

Life went on, of course, and I continued drowning my pain in beer and whiskey. I drank way too much, partied way too much, and had a devil-may-care attitude.

Today I see I laid all my pain and suffering on her. SHE became pregnant; SHE betrayed ME; SHE destroyed OUR dreams; SHE ruined MY life. My maturity level was low during college and I simply could not be there for her. I could not even be there for myself to process this event. I never discussed this meaningfully with anyone, or asked for, or was open to, genuine help.

Certainly, since we were intimate and took risks, it could have been us getting pregnant rather than them. Occasionally, Julie and I were sexual after a wild fraternity party, and yet I simply blocked all that out.

Twenty-five years later, at age forty-four, I retired from the U.S. Air Force, was hired by American Airlines, and after completing my initial training, went to visit my parents in New Jersey.

"Hi Mom, hi Dad." I felt great, looked great in my American Airlines Uniform, and was on top of the world. Mom and Dad were very proud of me.

"Guess who I chatted with a few weeks ago, Johnny?" said Mom.

"Who?" I asked.

"Julie," Mom replied. My heart stopped. "She looks great, Johnny. Her mom was having a yard sale, so I stopped and there was Julie." My heart had not restarted. Memories were flooding back, as I had not thought of Julie in years.

"Really Mom, that's nice," I finally managed.

"She said that her son has finished school and has left home. She's also recently divorced." My heart stopped again. "I told her you would be home soon, and she gave me her number. She asked me to pass it on to you. I believe she'd love to chat with you, Johnny." My heart fluttered.

Timing is everything. I was divorced and my daughters were with their mom. I took Julie's number and phoned her.

A few days later, I drove to her home and stayed for several days. She looked like she was still in college, but our experience together was totally different. The magic and spontaneity were gone. Julie was gone. And she probably felt the same about me. We were two different people now. But it was great to catch up and put closure on our "love" from so many years prior. It was pleasant, but distant.

She shared about her life and how unavailable her father was to her after she got pregnant and needed him the most. She said that her mom was powerless to help her and that her dad disowned her. That is what many fathers did to their daughters in 1964. The pill was just coming in, and I recall several surprises with my fraternity brothers and their girlfriends.

She asked about my life and I shared about my marriage with Dee, our two daughters, flying in the Air Force, my time in Vietnam, my new employment with American Airlines, and being sober for about four years now. Our time together was pleasant, and I finally got the closure I needed with my love, Julie.

We saw each other one more time shortly after that and then communication dwindled as we each moved on with our lives.

AM I VALUABLE OR SUICIDAL

During the time I spent with Julie just after my retirement from the U.S. Air Force, she asked me if I was ever suicidal. My response was instantaneous and I blurted out, "Nope, never thought about taking my life." And this is true in the sense that I never consciously thought about putting a gun to my head, slitting my wrists, or taking a handful of poison pills. She pressed the question further.

"Johnny, just give a short answer to these few questions, please."
"OK Julie," I responded.
"Were you obligated to join the military, or did you volunteer?"
"I volunteered."
"Did you volunteer for pilot training?"
"Yes."
"Did you volunteer to fly fighter-jets?"
"Yes."
"Did you volunteer for combat duty in Vietnam?"
"Yes."
"So, you didn't have to go into the military during the Vietnam war. But you gave up your safe engineering job, joined the military (dangerous), went to pilot training (more dangerous), trained in fighter-jets (even more dangerous), and volunteered for combat in Vietnam (much

more dangerous). So, you volunteered to fly combat missions in the middle of the night over North Vietnam in all kinds of weather being shot at by surface-to-air missiles, anti-aircraft-artillery, and perhaps a few of their fighter-jets, correct?"

"Well, yes, I guess I did."

"And you say you've not entertained suicidal thoughts."

"I never thought about it that way, Julie."

Perhaps I just did not care enough about myself to make choices that would keep me out of harm's way. There are several ways to look at this, I suppose, but I voluntarily placed myself in harm's way. I remember the devil-may-care attitude I had toward life and saying, "What the hell, if I die, I die." That was my attitude about the precious gift of my life. I was disconnected from my soul. My view of life was a blur out of a fighter-jet canopy flying at the speed of sound.

It is impossible to change by simply saying, "I'm more valuable than how I'm treating myself, and I am right now going to change." One may say this, but change does not come until the deeper self is ready and chooses to change. It is necessary to experience the darkness to loosen the ego before one elevates into the light.

Please use caution if you are slogging around in your basement. Find a trusted teacher or friend who will stand ready with a life-preserver as you move through your darkness.

FREE, WHITE AND TWENTY-ONE

"Congratulations, son, you're finally a man!" said Dad on my twenty-first birthday. "And you ought to be grateful, Johnny, for you are not only a man, but you are free, white, and twenty-one." Those were my father's exact words (free, white, and twenty-one). I held the world in the palm of my hand. I was fast becoming the stereotypical, patriarchal, privileged white male with birthrights in this special class. I was convinced that on my twenty-first birthday, I received a rite-of-passage entitlement. As a member of this elite social group, I could travel anywhere, visit any store, take any table in any restaurant, and sit anywhere I wished on the bus. I played social second fiddle to no one.

I referred to women as broads, cracked blonde jokes, and laughed at racial slurs about Blacks, Poles, Italians, Jews, Orientals, and others. I did it all with my privileged white male friends. I would laugh and was glad that I was free, white, and twenty-one and not one of the others. God obviously favored me, for he birthed me into this elite class of people.

I also felt conflicted because some piece of me did not believe this lie. The slurs, jokes, etc., made me a little uncomfortable, but I was not emotionally or spiritually mature enough to walk a path of truth. I caved in and went along with the crowd. I was one of the privileged, so I suppressed the inner voice that whispered, "This isn't right, Johnny. This is not who you really are. You are living a lie."

Dad said that with an engineering degree, I would not have to work "menial labor" jobs because, "You're above that, Johnny." I loved hearing that. It was September 1965, and race and gender discrimination were all over the United States. But being a white male put me at an advantage for job selection, job promotions, and other social privileges.

In the 1960s, women held mostly teaching, secretarial, and nursing jobs, while minorities performed the labor jobs. And I, the entitled white-male, held the management, supervisor, and professional positions. There were exceptions, of course, but this was the norm.

Being in the privileged group, I reaped all the advantages and gave little or no thought to the obvious discriminations. I did not rock the boat.

It takes courage to listen to the quiet voice of truth within, but I was enjoying the benefits of my white male entitlement way too much to pay attention to that voice. I ignored the obvious and shoved this voice of truth into a dark corner of my basement.

After graduation from University, I took employment as an engineer for a large corporation. In my group of about fifty engineers, all were white males just like me.

There were few women and few non-white men in the officer ranks when I joined the Air Force in January, 1969. And of the roughly 500 student pilots at my Air Force flight training base, all were white males. During my military time from 1969 to 1989, I knew only a few non-whites or women pilots. I accepted this as normal, gave it little or no thought, and did not rock the boat because I was one of the privileged. I was free, white, and twenty-one.

Indigenous societies send their young men and woman on vision quests. This is an initiation experience into adulthood where the youth remains alone in the wilderness for several days, fasting. They stay until receiving a spiritual vision providing direction and guidance for their adult life. During their time alone, they suffer from hunger, thirst, and fear. Suffering is necessary, for it loosens the ego sufficiently to allow a spiritual experience to occur. If it is easy, it is probably of little value. We must suffer to grow.

Dad condensed my vision quest initiation and rite-of-passage into just a few minutes of time and the words-you're free, white, and twenty-one, Johnny. I was now a man, simple as that, having experienced no pain and no suffering. I believed every word my father said to me and that was the end of it.

During the city riots in the 1960s, I judged blacks as lazy, inferior, not quite up to snuff, and looking for a handout. I believed this, for I needed to believe it to remain distant from reality and enjoy my entitlement. I liked attending Rutgers University, liked being a pilot in the Air Force, and liked the other perks of the privileged class. My denial system grew stronger and my skin thicker. I did not care about the blacks in Los Angeles or Detroit and went about my business of living a privileged life.

During my early teens, Dad mentioned, "You can't trust a black person, Johnny," and although I felt differently, I did not question him about his comment. He was prejudiced, bigoted, biased, and found ways to stay angry. Dad could not drive a mile without making derogatory comments about other drivers, especially women. His anger was always just below the surface looking for ways to percolate out and release.

Forty years ago, I avoided people of different skin tones, and those that wore different clothing or spoke foreign languages. I just labeled them as weirdos and hung around with those who looked and acted like me. I looked for the differences between people and found many reasons to keep people distant.

It took years for my father's voice to soften sufficiently for me to allow people different from me to be close to me. But with work, it happened.

Seeing oneself as privileged is dangerous for one tends to treat others with less respect than they treat their privileged brothers and sisters. They see themselves as better than others.

In the eyes of divinity, all beings are equal and no one is any more or any less special than anyone else. The personality wants to feel superior, hold power over, and exercise its authority over others to create, support, and sustain an illusion of superiority. The spiritual warrior on a spiritual pilgrimage recognizes truth and sees through this illusion. They treat every being with love and compassion-no exceptions.

As you begin to see through this illusion, some in your community may challenge you. Some may push you away and some will try to convince you that you have strayed from the fold. Some may treat you as an outsider for your rebellious attitudes.

When one gets sober, one's interests and friends are no longer found in the tavern and the bar gang gets discarded. Others, more evolved and more aligned with your new interests, will appear and fill the space.

I encourage you to sit peacefully, ponder your deepest beliefs, and question their authenticity. Because you disagree with a concept does not mean you oppose it. Be the seeker of truth. Ask yourself, "Where are my beliefs coming from? Are my beliefs truly valid? Who am I and why am I here?" These questions take a lifetime to answer.

WORK AFTER COLLEGE - BRADLEY FIELD

Graduating with an engineering degree from Rutgers University in May 1967 was a big deal for my parents and me. Mom and Dad shared in my excitement and sense of accomplishment of becoming a college graduate engineer.

As children, Pat and I heard, *when* you go to college, not *if* you go to college. Neither Mom nor Dad had the opportunity to pursue higher education, but they held that vision for Pat and me. I have been eternally grateful for my parents' selfless gift they gave us. Thanks to Mom and Dad, both Pat and I graduated from university debt-free.

I started my new job just a few days after graduation in Windsor Locks, Connecticut. Being away from my parents allowed me to lead a life as I wished, which included lots of drinking and partying. My job was draft-deferred freeing me from the dreaded military draft lottery then in effect. The job description said that "this position is vital to the security, safety, and defense of our country." I could not imagine that, but wasn't about to argue or reject my stay-home-free card. Let someone else go fight the war raging in Vietnam, I thought. I felt special.

Within weeks, I grew uncomfortable with my job and soon intensely disliked it. I did not enjoy wearing a jacket and tie, was uneasy around my colleagues, and again felt four-foot-tall in an environment full of six-foot people (mostly men). I was in over my head, and my childhood fears of decision making and relating to fellow workers, kept me feeling worthless and low. I was trapped and frightened. But I had a car, a place to live, girls to date, a few dollars in my wallet, and lots of booze to dull the pain. I convinced myself that I was doing just fine.

Driving my 1966 VW "bug" home one snowy evening from a local pub, I snapped to attention as a telephone pole flashed by my windshield in slow-motion. Instantly, I became a passenger in a double rollover maneuver, to a full stop landing right side up off the side of the road. My heart pounded as I sat, eyes closed, in my old VW bug. Terrified to open my eyes or move, I did not know if I was dead or alive. After several agonizing minutes, I realized I might not be dead, and mustered the courage to check things out. So, I pried open my eyes, took stock, and checked body parts for damage.

The door resisted but finally, with force, squeaked open as I killed the engine and climbed out. Not a scratch! The popped out rear window fit nicely into the back seat, and I saw that I had rolled over twice between a telephone pole and its support guidewire, coming to rest on all fours facing the road, engine running, and lights on. Now I not only had booze helping me through life, but God was obviously on my side too. I could have died, or at least have been seriously injured in my acrobatic maneuver.

In place of driver and passenger airbags to cushion a head-on collision as in a modern car, the sixty-six VW bug had a ten-gallon fuel tank forward of the driver, in the trunk up front. That was all that separated the driver and passengers from whatever they collided with. I climbed back in, started the engine, and drove home. Upon awakening the next morning, I dressed as usual and went to work as if nothing had happened. Insanity was now the norm.

I stumbled and faked my way through about a year of engineering employment, not enjoying the work, and feeling inadequate. Then, in the summer of 1968, I had a magical experience with an F-102 fighter-jet flying at Bradley Field, just across the street from my employment.

I loved jet fighter planes and frequently stopped along the perimeter fence of Bradley Field (Hartford - Springfield) Airport to watch the Air National Guard F-102 Delta Dagger fighter-jets taxi by and take off. This day, I stepped out of my car and waved at the pilot only a hundred feet away as he taxied past. Great looking aircraft; delta wings, shiny silver fuselage, sleek and racy from nose to tail, loud, and a god-like pilot in the cockpit waving back. Helmet, gloves, oxygen mask hanging down loosely with the dark visor pulled down protecting his eyes, I envisioned myself in that cockpit flying that jet fighter. The pilot went through his pre-take-off checks, closed his canopy, and taxied onto the runway. I watched as he ran up his engine, then BOOM! The hard-light afterburner rattled my bones as the pilot released brakes and began his one-and-a-half-mile take-off roll. Slowly the fighter-jet accelerated down the runway and in less than a minute, was airborne.

"THAT'S IT!" I knew in a heartbeat that I, too, could be a U.S. Air Force pilot flying a fighter-jet. A plan rapidly formed in my mind and within minutes I saw flying as my future and somehow it would happen. How cool would it be to fly a fighter-jet and see the world from a tiny cockpit way up there in the sky? In that one-minute take-off roll of the F-102 fighter-jet, I decided to quit my safe, boring, and stressful, draft-deferred job, join the United States Air Force, and become a jet pilot.

I was closing the door on my boring, unexciting life and choosing a road of dreams, adventure, and the unknown. In the next few months, I transitioned from civilian to military life. My agenda at twenty-four-years-old was to fly fighter-jets, drink all the booze I could afford, and chase all the girls that came into view and would slow down a bit. I now had a life vision that offered excitement beyond my wildest dreams. And my childhood vision of flying my plastic model F-86 fighter-jet was unfolding.

US AIR FORCE PILOT TRAINING

I was in heaven arriving at Reese Air Force Base, Lubbock, Texas, in early April 1969 for basic flight training. The Air Force provided me a place to live, flight suits to wear, jet planes to fly, paid for the instructors and fuel, sold whiskey cheaply, and put a few dollars in my bank account every month. What a great deal!

As a new second lieutenant in 1969, I was one of about 500 student pilots at Reese Air Force Base. The pilot's stag bar at the Officer's Club on Friday night was right out of Top Gun and Star Wars. Imagine about 500 wanna-be pilots and instructors, all thirsty as hell, all trying to out-drink each other, and all trying to look cool, and you have an idea of the noise and chaos at the Officer's Club pilot stag bar. Booze was cheap and plentiful, and flowed till the last guy dropped. I loved flying airplanes and discovered that I was a natural pilot. I did well in flight school.

Flying U.S. Air Force jets through the Texas skies was easy and lots of fun. I thought little about the Vietnam War or how I might shortly become involved in hostilities. For me, the Air Force was all about having a good time.

The Commanding General of Air Training Command visited Reese AFB and said, "Every student pilot better want to go to combat, for that's what the Air Force is all about and that's why you're training to fly." I did not want to hear anything about war or combat or danger, so I just blocked him out. I was an out of control six-year-old in a slightly more mature body enjoying flying jets over Texas. The Vietnam War was a million miles away.

Wing Vice-Commander Colonel Howard J. Pierson and I were scheduled to fly my T-38 weekend cross-country training flights together. He was frequently at the O' Club Bar and was always available to chat with new lieutenants. He was the epitome of a fighter-pilot's fighter pilot. Top Gun's Maverick had nothing over this man. I felt a little apprehensive about flying with Colonel Pierson, as he was one of the highest-ranking officers on our base. But with cleanly cut hair and spit-shined boots, I presented myself to Colonel Pierson at base operations on the morning of our departure to flight plan and organize our trip.

He was an exceptional man-tall, confident, bald, easy-going, respectful to everyone regardless of age or rank, and a patient teacher for me. He showed up later in my life several times in very positive ways. We pre-flighted, took-off, and flew our first leg uneventfully to England AFB, Louisiana. After a brief stop for fuel and flight planning, we strapped in for launch, and found that the starter motor on our left engine in our two-engine T-38 aircraft had failed. I assumed the mission was scrubbed since there was no way to start our left engine without maintenance. Colonel Pierson, however, had different thoughts. "Johnny, start the right engine and let's taxi," and I did. Pierson planned to make a single-engine take-off in our two-engine airplane and I was the 200 pounds of baggage along for the ride in the front seat.

His voice crackled reassuringly through my headset, "Johnny, just remember that there are many airplanes flying around that only have one engine, like the F-100, F-102, F-104, and F-105, to name a few. They fly just fine with only one engine and so will we. I'll fly the take-off and give you control after we're airborne once you air-start our left engine."

"Yes, Sir," I replied.

My mind whispers that Colonel Howard J. Pierson is flying our airplane and he's the most capable fighter pilot in the entire USAF. If he says we can do it, then we can. I check my parachute risers, re-familiarize myself with the seat ejection handles, and hope that I will still be alive in 10 minutes. He's a colonel with a ton of flying experience and I'm a second lieutenant student pilot. So, I gritted my teeth and did not say one word. I would never live it down if I called him on this obvious and blatant major violation of safety and rules. "Sir, isn't this dangerous performing this insane, stupid, unnecessary, single-engine take-off?" I thought. I would rather die in the fireball than say that to Colonel Pierson. My lips remained sealed.

Pierson ran our operable engine to full power, plugged in the afterburner and released the brakes. Off we went, sluggishly at first, but gaining speed. Acceleration was nowhere like the normal rapid take-off of a T-38. But our speed increased, and I watched the airspeed needle creep through 130, then 140, as the end of the runway grew closer. With my unobstructed front-seat panoramic view, and approaching 155 knots with only a few hundred feet of runway remaining, I felt the nose rise slightly, and we lifted off about midway through the 1,000-foot overrun.

"That wasn't very close now was it, Johnny?" Pierson's calm voice whispered through my headset.

"No sir, plenty of room to spare." Lying and denial are part of being a fighter pilot.

After air-starting our left engine, we accelerated to climb speed and flew on like nothing unusual had happened. Oh well, I mused, just another day at the office. I wondered what my pre-Air-Force engineer friends in Windsor Locks, Connecticut, were doing today. A big smile spread across my face.

I sat through two more single-engine take-offs during our cross-country weekend adventure with Colonel Howard J. Pierson at the controls. He was a fine pilot.

On Sunday, our final day, we refueled at an east coast training base where T-38 maintenance fixed our left engine starter. With both engines operable, I flight planned for our return leg to Reese AFB, Lubbock, Texas.

It is a very long flight against headwinds from Georgia to Texas, but Colonel Pierson, always the optimist, said, "Johnny, plan it all the way, and we'll keep a sharp eye on the fuel and perhaps stop somewhere if necessary. But I'd sure like to get home without a refuel stop as I don't wish to keep Suzi waiting."

"Yes, sir," I replied. "Colonel, my flight plan shows we will land at Reese with zero fuel."

But Pierson optimistically remarked, "Headwinds are probably not as strong as predicted and might shift direction in our favor, Johnny."

"Yes, sir."

So, we took off and climbed to 49,000 feet for maximum range and minimum fuel burn. Half-way to Texas, I keyed the interphone and said, "Colonel, the headwinds haven't shifted or lessened, and I still show zero fuel at touchdown."

Pierson calmly replied, "Let's press on a little further, Johnny, for there's one more opportunity to land and refuel if we need it."

"Yes, sir." I figured that Suzi waiting for him back in Lubbock must be awfully pretty to bias his decision-making to this extent.

We flew on past all refueling opportunities with my calculations continually showing zero fuel at touchdown. Pierson reassuringly said, "We'll make some fuel during the descent, Johnny." I did not remember reading anything about "making fuel" in any of the training manuals, but, hey! I am flying with Colonel Howard J. Pierson, the greatest aviator in the United States Air Force and kin to God.

Approaching Reese AFB, I rechecked my parachute risers and re-familiarized myself again with the seat ejection handles as we flew a minimum fuel descent profile and glided to a touchdown and safe landing at Reese. I shut down one engine during our landing rollout to save fuel and increase our odds of making it to the parking ramp without flaming out.

Parked and chocked, I shut down the remaining engine and noted 0.0 on the fuel gauge. Climbing out, I overheard Pierson telling the crew chief, "She's a bit low on fuel, Sergeant, but enter a normal amount on your fuel form, please."

"Yes, sir," replied the crew chief." Pierson sealed the deal with a $20 handshake. What a guy. Colonel Howard J. Pierson is the man, and I cannot wait to brag about this adventure at the bar.

"Johnny, best we keep this just between us, OK?"

"Yes, sir," I replied and told no one of this adventure except my roommate who I swore to secrecy under oath and threat of death.

Disregard the rules, lie when convenient, and take unnecessary risks is what we did, and that is what men do. And that is how I learned to fly in the United States Air Force. My excitement bar had risen from this adventure, and I looked forward to my life in the Air Force filled with more stories, excitement, and adventures. I stuffed my feelings deeper and looked forward to my next adrenaline rush.

In April 1970, Mom and Dad attended my USAF Pilot Training graduation ceremony at Reese AFB, Lubbock, Texas. It was important for all of us and I was recognized and honored as a Distinguished Graduate, (the top ten percent) of my pilot training class. Reflecting on the "cut the coconut incident" in high school nine years prior, Dad leans over and says, "I knew you could cut the coconut, Johnny."

At the completion of Air Force Pilot Training, I was a capable, creative, intelligent, talented, young man of twenty-five, but could not see or access these qualities. I perceived myself as mediocre. To feel better than mediocre, I continued to drink alcoholically and use other sensory pleasures to feel good about myself.

Denial and addiction are incredibly strong, and it takes a lifetime of work to clear the trauma of childhood conditioning. I held an Industrial Engineering degree from Rutgers University and was now a Distinguished Graduate of the USAF Undergraduate Pilot Training Program, but I still felt four-foot tall in a world full of six-foot men.

ASSIGNMENT TO FIGHTERS - THE F-4 PHANTOM

"Check it out, Dave," I hollered to my roomy, "not one fighter plane on the class assignment sheet! What a bummer!" So, this young second lieutenant elected to fly the C-141 transport based at Travis AFB in Vacaville, California. Since fighters were not available, this would be a pretty good runner-up.

The C-141 was an airliner sized, four-engine, jet transport plane and I'd fly it all around the world. What a great deal! Although flying fighter-jets was my passion, this assignment would also be filled with adventure and challenges. Perhaps fighter-jets will come into my field-of-view further down the road, I thought.

It was great fun flying this huge jet plane and almost every month I flew to Vietnam, delivering troops and supplies to the never-ending war raging in Southeast Asia. During my first return trip from Vietnam, somewhere over the Pacific Ocean, I walked back into the cargo hold for a look around. An unfamiliar, unpleasant, pungent smell greeted me. "Hey Sarge," I asked the loadmaster, "What's that smell?"

"Well, Lieutenant, this must be your first trip. Look over there on the far side of that pallet, and you will see several coffins. One bag must be leaking a little and you're smelling death."

I never forgot that smell as I stood in silence, thinking about the soldier riding home in a leaky plastic bag inside a gray metal coffin. It frightened me, for if life had unfolded a bit differently, I might have been that guy in the leaky bag riding home in a gray metal coffin. It's war, Johnny.

While flying the C-141 transport, I visited the assignments office and filled out my dream-sheet. Pilots like me, about a year out of flight school, were being rotated for a tour in Vietnam flying small transports, spotter aircraft, ranch-hand sprayer planes, and others. It was all dangerous flying, and that's what was on my horizon.

"Lieutenant, your next aircraft will not be a fighter because according to the regs, you don't currently qualify," mused pilot assignment officer Major Randy Ellestad. "You might as well put down something reasonable on your dream-sheet rather than this list of fighters you've written here."

"Thank you, Major. I realize that currently I don't qualify for fighters but those are my assignment preferences so please accept my dream-sheet. If I cannot get a fighter for the next assignment, I don't really have a preference." I thanked the Major for his explanation and genuine concern. However, I stuck to my plan and signed my dream-sheet, listing every fighter I could think of. I placed it on the Major's desk, saluted, and left.

A month later, while enjoying leave at my parent's home in New Jersey, Dad hollered, "Hey, Johnny, long-distance phone call from some major, at your base in California," and Dad handed me the phone.

"Yes sir, yes sir, yes sir, yes sir, thank you, sir! Good day, sir." I hung up the phone, stunned, and a warm glow ignited in my gut.

"Lieutenant, this is Major Ellestad, pilot assignments at Travis."

"Yes, sir."

"Lieutenant, they've changed the regs for fighter pilot assignments and you now qualify."

"Yes, sir."

"And although there are fifteen pilots in front of you for reassignment for a Vietnam tour, none of them requested fighters and I don't want to give this first and perhaps only one to a pilot that does not want to fly fighters."

"Yes, sir."

"Since you are the front pilot in the queue that has fighters listed on his dream-sheet, I am offering you this slot to go fly the F-4 Phantom in a few months followed, of course, by assignment to Vietnam. Do you accept?"

"Yes, sir."

"The assignment is now yours, Lieutenant. Come to my office when you return from leave to fill out the papers and officially accept. Good day, Lieutenant."

"Good day, sir."

I could not believe that I was going to fly the Phantom, the finest front-line fighter in the entire world and flown by both the U.S. Air Force and the U.S. Navy.

I went to my bedroom and there was my plastic model F-86 Sabrejet resting patiently on my desk. I lovingly held her and soared all around the room, doing loops and rolls and thanking the spirits for making my dream come true. I was approaching my twenty-seventh birthday and extreme excitement and fear were colliding in my gut. Regaining composure, I blocked out the fear and Vietnam visions, seeing now only the joy and freedom of flying this top-of-the-line fighter-jet aircraft.

LEARNING TO FLY THE F-4 PHANTOM

The F-4 Phantom is a two crew member aircraft with the pilot in the front seat, and the radar operator/navigator/extra set of eyeballs, in the rear seat. When the major assigned me to the F-4 in August 1971, both Phantom crew members were assigned from the pilot pool, and I would be trained as a GIB (Guy-In-Back) and be flown around by the old head GUF (Guy-Up-Front). I would not be the pilot flying the Phantom because the GIB, even though trained as a pilot, operated the airborne intercept radar, inertial navigation system, and assisted the GUF every way he could. The only way to become a GUF was to first have a one-year tour as a GIB and then upgrade to GUF if one survived. Oh well, I was not very excited about this situation, but I was all in and there was nothing I could do about it, anyway.

Returning to Travis AFB after my leave, I visited assignments and completed the paperwork.

"Lieutenant, I cannot believe how much luck you have," said assignments officer Major Ellestad. "Not only do you get the one and only, so far, fighter assignment at Travis AFB, but the Air Force made another significant change in your favor as well. The rear cockpit crew member is now being filled by navigators. That means that you'll go straight to the front seat of the F-4 when you begin your training soon and your GIB will come from the navigator pool."

"Thank you, sir." I was one of the first Air Force pilots to be assigned to fighters from transport aircraft, and one of the first to go directly to the front seat of the Phantom. Overjoyed falls far short.

Thirty-two young F-4 crew member trainees, sixteen pilots and sixteen navs, sat with smiles making small talk, waiting for the Squadron Commander. "Gentlemen, ten-hut," barked the admin sergeant, and we all snapped to attention. "At ease, gentlemen, and welcome to Luke Air Force Base. Sergeant, please roll the movie clip of the first flight of a brand-new F-4." We all watched as the shiny jet rolled down a runway, rotated its nose and lifted off. It continued, however, to increase its nose-high-pitch-up, stalled, rolled over on its back, and fell back to the runway in a huge fireball. Both crew members ejected safely.

The movie next focused on the crew members walking toward the camera, lugging their parachutes, and scratching their heads in bewilderment. "Welcome to the Phantom, gentlemen. Anyone care to leave?" said the commander with a smile. We all stayed, of course, as he explained that this Phantom on its first flight, had a malfunctioning stabilator which froze in full nose-up pitch position. It was a record for the shortest flight of an F-4. Brake release to impact lasted just fifty-four seconds and covered only about two-thirds the length of the runway. He emphasized the ever-present dangers of flying fighter planes and the reliability of our Martin-Baker ejection seats. I reflected about how close I was to ejecting with Colonel Pierson in our T-38 during several single-engine takeoffs and near fuel starvation experience a few years ago. The Air Force was exciting, and I loved the electric atmosphere and champed at the bit to go fly the Phantom.

"Hello, Johnny and Jim, I'm Rusty and I'm your flight instructor while you're in training at Luke." We lucked out. Rusty Waller was a gentle, congenial major with a laid-back attitude that blended well with both my paired-student GIB, Captain Jim Clooney, and me. Completing his tour in Vietnam, Rusty, also a Korean War veteran, knew everything about flying fighter planes and was very willing to show us the ropes of how to fly our Phantom.

During our six months at Luke, Jim and I learned to fly the

Phantom to its limits and use it as a weapons platform. We learned about bombs, missiles, our twenty-mm cannon, and many munitions. I was becoming a trained killer, and did not even seem to realize it. Bombing missions, shooting down other aircraft, low-level ingress, and egress into and out of target areas, all became normal activities for me. I was very engaged in the fighter pilot mission and image. We were Maverick and Goose in Top Gun. But Jim and I were preparing for war, not a movie.

The danger of flying fighters was brought home when one of our student crews crashed on a training mission at the air-to-ground gunnery range. The GIB ejected safely, but the pilot died in the ejection attempt. I felt no remorse, just a little sorrow. I shrugged my shoulders and mused, "It's just part of the job."

Somehow, I always felt safe and secure in my Phantom jet and knew that my Phantom would bring me home and she did. I imagine that many who did not return also thought their Phantoms would bring them home as well.

VIETNAM – ARRIVAL

Stepping from the transport onto the tarmac at midnight, beads of sweat formed on my forehead. Ubon Air Base, Thailand, was a hot muggy sauna, even at midnight. It was mid-August 1972, and I was here to help win the Southeast Asia war. Even at this late hour, my survival knife could cut the calm, heavy, moisture-filled air. Sweat flowed down my body as I walked across the ramp toward the small terminal.

"Hmm!" I muttered and mused, "I wonder why the rescue chopper is launching?" Looking northeast, I saw a dull orange glow forming on the horizon as the rescue chopper cleared the perimeter fence and flew into the darkness toward the glow and Vietnam. Thick black smoke eerily rose skyward now in the dull ghastly light and I knew a plane had just crashed and exploded. Chills shivered down my spine, cooling my sweaty body as I watched, bathed in the oppressive jungle heat. "God, please help that crew come back and live another day."

The next morning, I checked in with the 497th Nite Owls, Tactical Fighter Squadron. "Hello, Captain," said the admin sergeant, "welcome to the Nite Owls. The fireball off the end of Runway 05 last night was one of our Phantoms. Preliminary rumors say that the pilot apparently mistook a fire or light on the ground as flight lead's afterburners and tried to join up on it. He drove his Phantom into the ground just a few miles off the end of runway 05 in full afterburner, with no distress call or attempt to eject. We will clear the pilot's hooch and, as soon as we get his belongings out of there, the room is yours. Glad to have you with us, Captain."

Moving into the dead pilot's vacant hooch that afternoon, I thought very little about my deceased brother and that he had slept in my bed only a few nights prior. Instead, I went exploring and found the base bottle shop and whiskey. I am amazed sometimes at what my memory retains and recalls. As I write about my arrival at Ubon, I had to dig deep to retrieve the faded details about the fireball-crash, and the move into the dead pilot's hooch. However, I vividly remember that at the base bottle shop, I switched my main drink from scotch to bourbon because Johnny Walker Red scotch whiskey was $4.50 a half-gallon, and Jim Beam bourbon whiskey was $2.50 a half-gallon. That was an easy decision. Welcome to the war.

Ubon Royal Thai Air Force Base was very busy with six squadrons of Phantom fighters flying combat missions round the clock, plus Thai Air Force aircraft and the U.S. Air Force C-130 "Specter" Gunships. It was late August 1972.

A typical day began about noon with a bit of exercise, a three-mile run, a meal, and a walk to squadron operations about four pm. Our missions launched in the evening and with planning, briefings, pre-flight, flying, and de-briefing took an entire day to complete. I was busy and reveled in the excitement and adventure. Every day was an adrenaline rush. At completion of duty at 1 or 2 am, I would mosey to the "Owl's Nest," our party hooch, toss down a few, and swap stories about how great it was to fly the Phantom in the middle of the night over North Vietnam. Then bed, sleep, and awake about noon to repeat the cycle again the next day. That was my life for one year.

The Nite Owls flew at night, so I saw little of the landscape, and little of the destruction and devastation that I was contributing to. It was usually very dark to pitch black outside my cockpit. It was safer flying and bombing with moonlight than on a pitch-black moonless night or below an overcast. With a little moonlight, I could see the ground and easily determine which way was up. In total blackness, with no visual cues, determining which way was up came only from our on-board flight instruments. If what I saw (or thought I saw) outside disagreed with what my instruments were telling me, spatial disorientation and confusion rapidly set in. I was trained to trust my instruments, not my eyeballs, and if they did not agree, then I had only a second to sort out the confusion and act. Several pilots during my tour became spatially disoriented and collided with the ground.

There were few lights on the ground in Thailand, Cambodia, and Laos, and no lights on the ground in South and North Vietnam. When I say no lights, I mean no lights, period. I do not recall ever seeing a house light, headlight, streetlight, or any light anywhere in North Vietnam or the northern area of South Vietnam. The joke was that nobody even smoked in North Vietnam and there were no lightning bugs either. It was so dark most nights that cigarettes and lightning bugs could be seen from our Phantoms a mile in the sky.

Flying as a wingman, my world was flight lead's small red or green wingtip light and little else. To add to the excitement, during monsoon season, we worked our way to and from the target areas over, under, around, and sometimes through 45,000-foot thunderstorms. Fighter-jets do not have the fuel to travel hundreds of miles avoiding storms as do airliners. So, we tightened our seat belts and picked our way through walls of huge active thunderstorms in the middle of the night, experiencing a very rough ride and blinding flashes of lightning. It was a super realistic video game to me before video games and I loved it.

When a crew was killed, we would go to our party hooch, raise a toast and sing "Throw a nickel on the grass, kiss a fighter pilot's ass." That's how I processed the death and destruction of war. I never gave a moment's thought of the Vietnamese people and what I was doing to them and their land.

The dream of flying my plastic model F-86 Sabre Jet was now reality.

MR. SONG'S MISSION

Looking away slightly to avoid the blinding glare of flight lead's afterburners, my cockpit illuminates brightly then fades as flight lead's Phantom slowly begins its take-off roll down his half of the two-mile runway. Deafening noise, muffled by the thick glass canopy and custom fitted helmet, slowly diminishes.

After 20 seconds, I release brakes, push the throttles forward, then outboard into the afterburner quadrant. I smoothly advance the throttles forward to full afterburner/max power. The engine nozzles swing open and I feel my body pushed deeper into the seat-back. It's 9 pm, and the familiar sensations reassure me that our Phantom is operating at maximum power, and Willie and I begin our two-mile-long take-off roll. Acceleration feels normal as our speed increases. At 185 knots, I gently ease the control stick aft and feel the heavy nose of the Phantom slowly rise to take-off attitude and stabilize on the main gear for a few seconds. We lift off into the blackness at 205 knots (235 mph) with less than 1,000 feet of runway remaining. An adrenalin shiver surges through my body. I smile as my left hand reaches for the gear handle.

Gear up, flaps up, and I see the twin flames of flight lead's afterburners a few miles ahead and aim my jet toward them. Easing back on power at 400 knots, I rapidly close on flight lead and join to close formation. This is what flying is all about, and I grin and giggle a little to myself.

Dim light signals pass between our jets indicating all is well, and I slide out a few feet off leads right wing and relax slightly to reflect on our mission tonight into North Vietnam. Checking in with the airborne command post, we get assigned target area Route Pack One, the most southern area of North Vietnam. It's a simple routine mission so far and all is well, yet I know conditions can change from comfort to disaster in a heartbeat or less.

Willie, my close friend in the aft cockpit just six feet behind me, is my favorite mate to fly with. He's jovial, responsive, and can find targets on his radar like he was born with a joystick controller in his hand. We make small talk to kill time, yet both know that danger lies ahead. I quickly brush off these thoughts and focus on flying our Phantom.

Directed to Hickory Tanker, we join up and refuel in radio silence. It's eerie and a bit spooky up here in the middle of the dark night, heading toward North Vietnam. I reflect a bit as I fly precisely twenty feet off the refueling tanker's wing.

Let's see, flight suit, G-suit, survival vest, gun belt with my 38-caliber revolver, parachute harness, helmet, mask, gloves, my big long survival knife strapped to my right calf, and two frozen water bottles in my lower G-suit pockets. They'll be thawed yet still cold when I want them in a while.

Then, there is the Phantom: 58,000 pounds of mean fighting machine with bombs, radar and heat-seeking air-to-air missiles, a 20-mm cannon, power to spare, and built solid as a tank. I am invincible in my Phantom jet and remember as a boy how powerful I felt when I wore my Roy Rogers cowboy shirt with my big shiny sheriff's badge and two pearl-handled six-shooters strapped to my waist. I experienced the same invincible feelings while flying my Phantom jet. The story today is different, but the feelings are the same.

Eerie sensations creep up and down my spine crossing the invisible border into North Vietnam en route to our assigned target area in coal-mine blackness. Lead's red beacon flashes once, signaling he's descending to have a look around. Reducing power, I slowly glide down to 10,000 feet, and set up an orbit in the dark North Vietnamese sky. Clouds above are clearing and the moon breaks through, while below, it's total blackness, with no lights visible anywhere. "Target area is close to the sea," Willie reminds me, "but I'll keep watch on the mountains to the west with the radar, Johnny."

"Thanks, Willie," I whisper. I can now concentrate totally on bombing targets, for Willie will keep us a safe distance from the dangerous hills. In the darkness of night flying, sky and ground blend into a total-surround blackness with zero discernible references or horizon. The mountains to the west are the final resting place of many young men, including several of my flying brothers.

Lead's flares illuminate an area near Dong Hoi along the North Vietnamese coast and he fires a white phosphorous (Willie Pete) marking smoke rocket at an indiscernible target for me to bomb. With eyes glued on the smoke, and without looking inside, I select and arm cluster bombs. "Hit my smoke" crackles through my headset and I call "Phantoms in from the east." I check wings level then roll left, drop the nose, roll out in a 30-degree dive and quick check inside to verify that what my eyes see matches what the instruments say. At 4,000', I "pickle" and feel the cluster bomb canister release, pull aggressively on the stick, and simultaneously jink hard right to throw off the ground gunners that are always there.

Over my shoulder, I see my bombs explode all around the marker smoke and a sense of joy and accomplishment fills my heart. I whisper, "What a great night, Willie."

"A few tracers came at you from ground gunners, well behind you now. Nice job," lead says.

After an additional bomb pass without significant damage, flight lead's voice crackles in my ears, "I'm going further inland, and maybe I'll find better targets there."

After a few minutes, I whisper to Willie, "Flares ahead about 10 miles" and I fly toward the lights.

"Trucks along a tree line," crackles through my headset. "Smoke's away," says lead, and I see the white plume rising on the ground from his marking rocket. "Trucks 50 meters east of my smoke. Make your pass north-to-south."

"Roger," I reply, and line up with cluster bombs armed for a north-to-south pass. I'm hyper-aware with adrenaline pumping through every cell and concentrating totally on bombing those trucks. I'm in a war in North Vietnam in a fighter-jet with real dangers from anti-aircraft guns and surface-to-air missiles. It's all here, and the world is counting on me to save them from the bad guys. And only I can do it for I'm six-foot-tall and have no fear while strapped into my indestructible Phantom jet suit-of-armor.

Fully alert, I roll left, drop the nose, roll out on parameters, and pickle off my bombs as the gun sight covers the target. A hard jink, g-forces, the familiar pull-out experience, and I see my bombs explode around the marking smoke. Several trucks blow-up and Willie and I know that we've done well and will have a story to brag about at the bar later tonight.

"Nice bombs," lead says, "and at the end of the tree line, there's a small hooch, get it."

"Roger," I grunt.

I spot the hooch and circle south for alignment. "Five-hundred-pound bombs ought to do it, Willie," I say, and he agrees. Selecting a stick of three bombs set to release with a slight delay between each so they won't drop into the same hole, I roll in, drop the nose, accelerate, check parameters, and pickle. Aggressively, I pull up into a climbing turn, glance over my shoulder, and whoop it up as the bombs explode and the little hooch disappears. I did not see in the dark of night the small man standing near the little hooch watching me on my bomb pass. Twenty years later, this small man would reappear in my life and become a mentor, teacher, and soul-brother of Johnny MedicineBear.

"Switches safe, we're heading home," comes flight lead's voice through my headset. Low on fuel and out of ordinance, we fly toward a tanker somewhere in the blackness for a quick drink, then head home.

Flying and bombing was a game to me. Vietnam wasn't real. The people were Gooks, not humans. The communists were coming closer to us. They had to be stopped somewhere and better here than the California coast. I bought it all.

As a young boy playing Sheriff Roy Rogers, I learned to use guns like a man. As a high schooler, experimenting with cigarettes, I learned to smoke like a man. As a college student with alcohol, I learned to drink like a man. And as a fighter pilot in Vietnam, I learned to kill like a man.

I never asked or thought about the tough questions like, "What does it REALLY mean to be a man? Why am I killing people in the name of peace? What is the purpose of my life? Why am I here on this planet?" Descending deeper into the darkness, loneliness, and terror of depression and despair, I continued to block these thoughts from my mind and drown myself in the free-flowing relief found in every whiskey bottle.

The cycle of flying, drinking, sleeping, flying, drinking, sleeping continued for about one year. I once went on R&R (Rest & Relaxation) to Bangkok, Thailand for a week with a few flying buddies and don't remember a thing about it. Opportunity lost.

THE AIR-WAR IN CAMBODIA

Late in the war, Willie and I were flight leader supporting friendly troops in southern Cambodia. Arriving in the target area, we found the U.S. Air Force Forward Air Controller (FAC) flying his OV-10 Bronco aircraft and checked in with him on the radio. The FAC was trying to help a Cambodian Army unit that was engaged with the enemy somewhere in our vicinity. There was a skirmish going on and a small group of about six or eight enemy were on the run.

The FAC passed us some info and requested that I go down and take a closer look at the target area. "Roger," I said into my face mask, "I'll fly a look-see pass over the target area and check it out." I swooped down low, jinking right and left. "I see a small hooch and six or eight men just ran inside."

"You're cleared to bomb that hooch, and beware Phantom, as anti-aircraft fire is intense in this area. I've been shot at several times today," the FAC said.

Pulling up over my target, I set the weapons panel to drop three bombs with a slight delay between releases. "Phantom's in from the north," I grunted into my sweaty oxygen mask. The G-forces increased as I pulled tightly into a rolling nose-down dive and rolled-out for my bomb pass.

"Five thou, four thou, ready pickle," Willie's voice whispered in my helmet. I felt the slight weight shift as the bombs released. "BREAK LEFT, JOHNNY!" Willie yelled and without thought I slammed the stick left and pulled into a 6-g level turn as our Phantom's nose came tightly around. The red tracers went above, and I rolled out and pulled up into the clear, bright sky.

"Christ, Willie, that was a little close, but we're out of range now."

"Can't wait to get back to our night routine, Johnny. It's safer when they can't see us," chided Willie.

I laughed. The dangers at night were different, but just as deadly.

"Nice bombs, Phantom. The hooch is gone. Your second bomb went right through the roof." The FAC was ecstatic that we destroyed the little hooch and the people in it.

I whispered, "Phantom's low on fuel, out of ordinance, and we're heading home."

"Nice job, Phantom. The Cambodian Army Commander thanks you for taking out that little pocket of resistance. You're cleared off."

"Switches safe, Willie, we're heading home." I pointed our Phantom north to get a drink from a tanker, then home to debrief and go to the bar.

I had not thought till now as I am writing this book that there may have also been civilians in that hooch as well.

Flying home, Willie and I felt we had single-handedly won the war. The hero returns once again. After our flight debrief, I enjoyed a meal, and drank sufficiently to keep the inner demons at bay. I felt no remorse, guilt, or shame. If I had allowed myself to see the reality of my actions, I would either have hung myself with a rope or blown my brains out with a gun. Hence, my denial system thickened, and I thirsted for more action to satisfy my thrill-seeking addictions. I pushed my soul a little further away and laid another layer of denial over the door to my dark shadow basement.

Today, I am committed to a life of service for all beings. My soul, the soul of the young dashing pilot, was fractured, splintered, and lost in Vietnam. This book is a big part of my atonement.

VIETNAM - MORE

"Looks like a great night to fly, Willie," I quipped as we step off the crew van into pouring rain on a dark, overcast, hot, muggy night facing our F-4E Phantom. Sloshing through the puddles on the tarmac, we quickly became soaked and make no effort to stay dry. The steady downpour continued.

"Maybe it'll let up a bit before we come home, Johnny, or we can just strip and take our after-mission shower outdoors tonight."

I smiled as we began our preflight of airplane and ordnance, paying particular attention to details as I had never flown an E model Phantom before. Normally we flew F-4Ds from our squadron pool of aircraft (497th Nite Owls), but tonight would be a special adventure for both of us flying a slightly unfamiliar aircraft into combat in the black of night in torrential rain. Oh well, I thought, if I survive, perhaps I'll have something to write about in a book someday.

There are several differences in the airframe, engines, radar, nav systems, and weapons release panels, and I assumed I'd fly a local familiarization ride before piloting an "E" into combat. But that didn't happen. "Willie, are you familiar with this beast?" I asked.

"Johnny, I've flown in an E-model several times and know the rear cockpit, so I'm willing to go if you're OK with driving this machine." I loved Willy's attitude.

"OK, Willie, let's take her for a ride and I'll learn how to fly her on the take-off roll." We laughed at our light-hearted humor and, in the pouring rain, climbed the ladder and strapped in.

The cockpit instruments and switches were familiar, of course, but I could not get the six main primary flight instrument lights on the dashboard directly in front of me to illuminate. In the pouring rain, I wave the crew chief back up the ladder. "Chief, seems like these primary instrument lights are inop. Any suggestions?"

He looked at me wide-eyed, with a look on his face saying, *are you sure you're a pilot?* "Captain, have you flown an E-model before?"

"Nope, this is my first flight."

"OK, Captain, down by your right elbow at the rear of the right-side panel you'll find seven small rotary knobs, a master and six minors. Turn up the master, then adjust the minors individually for your six primary flight instruments lights."

I bent my arm around, reached behind me on the right, twisted a few knobs as instructed, and the primary flight instruments illuminated. "Well, everything else looks fairly familiar, Chief," I quipped with a smile. "I appreciate your help and don't worry; I imagine she flies similar to the D-model and I'll bring her back home tonight."

"Have a safe flight, Captain."

"Thank you, Chief." I watched the water whip off his baseball cap as he disappeared down the ladder, scratching and shaking his head. I saw his lips move and could almost hear him telling his helper, "We better go look for a replacement jet because that guy doesn't even know how to turn on the instrument lights, let alone fly our airplane."

We started, taxied, and approached take-off position as I chatted with Willie about how heavy this Phantom felt and bet him that we were a few thousand pounds over gross weight. We decided to check when we returned, and found we were about 2,000 pounds over our 58,000-pound max gross weight. She flew just fine. Our E model Phantom had a 20-mm internal cannon with 600 rounds of ammunition, two external fuel tanks hanging on the wings with 4,800 pounds of fuel, electronic jamming pods in the forward missile wells, two sparrow radar-guided air-to-air missiles in the aft missile wells, two sidewinder infra-red heat-seeking missiles on shoulder stations, and munitions hanging on every available underwing and underbelly attachment point.

The philosophy was if there's a place to hang it on the jet, hang it. With both J-79 turbojet engines in full afterburner, the Phantom had sufficient power to push itself airborne no matter how heavy the load. We just used a bit more runway, and came unstuck a little faster, that's all.

I remember flight instructor Rusty's words when I asked him about computing take-off data for the Phantom. "There's no need for take-off data, Johnny. Just plug in the afterburners, check for two good burner lights, come back full aft with the stick around 170 knots, and she'll fly off when she's ready. If you run out of runway first, then eject to avoid becoming part of the fireball. That's all there is to it. It's pretty simple." And that's just what we did in the pouring rain at UBON Thailand on that dark stormy night. Twenty seconds after flight lead rolled, I released brakes, checked for two good burner lights, and flew off into the pouring blackness at 205 knots (235 mph), with less than a thousand feet of runway remaining. I loved it.

As a fighter pilot in Vietnam, I developed and sustained a huge denial system supporting combat flying in my F-4 Phantom. Had I related to the Vietnamese people as humans, I would have been horrified that I was killing them and destroying their homeland. Instead, returning from a mission, I would join my friends at our bar, drink, and sing songs about killing the enemy, the beauty of war, and how right and brave fighter pilots are.

This was commonplace, accepted behavior. Drinking alcohol was encouraged, and in my case necessary, to keep me from waking up to my participation in this war. I was not protecting the United States flying patrol missions along the California coast, but bombing Vietnam 10,000 miles away. My denial systems allowed me to justify behaviors that would otherwise have destroyed me. I had no ill feelings against the Vietnamese people until I was conditioned into believing that they were enemies, and if we don't stop them over there, they will soon be over here attacking us at home.

I became suspicious of people that dressed differently, were from foreign cultures, and practiced other religions. I learned to look for terrorists behind every tree, sleep with one eye open, and suppress emotions. This was the only way I could take part in this war and survive. I loved flying my F-4 Phantom fighter-jet, and that, plus several medals and ribbons, were my rewards for participating in this insane war.

Few on the planet will ever have the thrill of flying a supersonic, top-of-the-line fighter-jet in the heat of battle. I paid a huge price for this experience. All the while I was engaged in war, I thought that my behavior was normal. Those who chose to run away from their obligation by moving to another country, or claiming conscientious objector were, in my mind, cowards and they obviously didn't have the big picture like I did. I believed major wars were going to occur about every thirty years and that war was an inevitable life event. My awareness did not allow for the possibility that humans could get along with each other and live in peace and harmony with all creation, including animals, plants, and our precious Earth. There was no room in my mind for that level of awareness or consciousness. The lower levels of consciousness are necessary for the soldier to be a savage and carry out brutalities without question.

The savage IS unconscious killing, destruction, and violence, rationalized and justified away. There was no room for anything else in my mind-no light, no love, no deeper self, just robotic, unconscious, destructive behaviors. It is no surprise that many returning veterans waking up to a glimpse of reality, entertain and/or act on suicidal thoughts.

LIGHT HUMOR - IN THE DARKNESS

"Hey, Johnny, the bomber crew asked if the Pave Poet was with us tonight. You're getting famous up there with the B-52 (known as the BUFF: Big-Ugly-Flying-Feller) crews."

I swiveled on my bar stool, greeted my friend, laughed, and poured another swig of whiskey down my throat. It was my night off. I love the playful six-year-old that jumps out occasionally, and sometimes, even in war, finds opportunities to have a little fun. "Thanks Joe," I chimed, "I'm fragged for a midnight pathfinder mission tomorrow. I'll give 'em a little poem to brighten the black night sky."

During June and July 1973, several of our Phantoms were modified with a LORAN (Long Range Aid to Navigation) nav system that allowed for precision navigation and bombing from high altitudes. This LORAN was also known by the unclassified code name PAVE. Hence, I acquired the name Pave Poet. Apparently, our LORAN system in our Phantoms was more accurate than anything the BUFFs had on board. So, we flew pathfinder missions and lead them on bombing runs.

We would locate and rendezvous with our assigned flight of three BUFFs in the high skies over Vietnam. They flew a trail formation with the second BUFF following the leader one mile behind and 500' higher. The third BUFF flew one mile behind and 500' higher than the second.

The lead Buff followed us using the on-board radar one mile behind and 500' above. Number 2 and number 3 BUFF kept station behind the leader using their on-board radars.

It was a challenge to locate and join with our BUFFs sometimes but with back-seater Willie using our on-board radar, it usually worked out well. He was a master at locating the BUFFs and directing the intercept. This was done at 30,000 feet, in the black of night, in clear or cloudy skies, and sometimes with massive thunderstorms along our route. We had a war to fight and so we did what we could to have a successful mission.

It was both challenging and exciting. Several times we flew too close for comfort to thunderstorms for the BUFFs, and our big brothers simply broke off the formation and headed toward home. Oh well, I thought, we tried.

It was also a little ego game, as the flight of three B-52s consisted of one and a half million pounds of airplanes and bombs, twenty-four engines, and fifteen crew members. We were one little Phantom jet with two crew members and two engines. Yet we were leading our big buddies around the sky. I loved that part. However, we didn't have some of their conveniences like a crew bunk, coffee maker, or lav.

On my second PAVE BUFF mission, I penned out a simple, "Roses are red, violets are blue," poem, finishing the verse with something like, " I'm glad I fly a Phantom, not a B-fifty-two." I enjoyed making up little funny simple poems. I'd read them to our big friends when our mission was complete before we broke off and flew home. It was fun.

"Mission's complete, heading home from afar. By the time you get back, we'll be drinking at the bar." It was always a little silly poem like that, and I'd sign off with, "You just heard an original from the Pave Poet." Perhaps it brought a little humor to an otherwise dangerous and not so humorous experience.

I played another fun game a few times with our air-refueling tanker crews. Joining up on the KC-135 tanker one late afternoon before sunset with Willie in the rear cockpit holding the stick for a bit, I extracted my rubber gorilla mask from my crew bag, took off my helmet, slipped the mask over my head, replaced my helmet, and came back up on the intercom.

"What the hell are you doing, Johnny?" asked Willie. "You'll see in a minute, Willie. Watch the boomer on the tanker after we rendezvous and plug in."

I had enlarged the eye holes sufficiently to have unrestricted vision, and I looked like a gorilla with a crash helmet on flying a Phantom jet. We plugged in and saw the boomer laughing and hollering to his buds to come and have a look at the gorilla flying the Phantom. Quickly, the cameras were out and snapping away. "You are sure one ugly dude," quipped the tanker boomer.

"You think I'm ugly, you ought to see my buddy in the back seat! And toss us a couple bananas, too, while you're filling us up, will ya?" I replied. Willie and I laughed and giggled as we flew refueling formation till our Phantom was full. It was such great fun. And although I never received a photo as promised by several tanker boomers, I imagined what I looked like. If, while surfing the net, you ever stumble across a photo of a Gorilla driving a Phantom, it just might be yours truly under that mask.

GERMANY – BITBURG AIR BASE

Nothing could replace the thrill of war. However, flying Phantoms over the rolling hills of Germany was a close second. Returning from Vietnam, I was excited about flying Phantoms at Bitburg Air Base, in the beautiful Eifel region of Germany. All appeared well on the surface, but a deep sense of remorse and regret, like a cloud of doom and gloom, was evident. I had a casual attitude toward my flying, and my off-duty behaviors were out-of-control.

I tried to dull the ache in my heart and minimize my recent participation in war with excess consumption of German beers and wines. There were Flying Rules of Engagement (ROE) in Vietnam, but it was relatively easy to comply with those directives. In Germany, however, there were also many ROEs and they were taken seriously by commanders at all levels. I followed some when it was convenient, but not all, and lived on that edge of out-of-control to relieve my inner dull ache. I was the first at the bar Friday evening, and the last to leave. My smile hid my heavy heart. Abnormal, over the top, out-of-control behaviors were my norm.

I was proficient in the fine art of driving my car home from the Bitburg Air Base officer's club at midnight with one eye closed to keep from seeing double centerlines on the rural two-lane German highway.

I'd swear off booze almost every morning and sustain till mid or late afternoon. This went on and on, over and over. I was in the repetitive, never-ending loop of the alcoholic. I suppressed all emotions, feelings, and my Vietnam experience.

A few months after I arrived in Germany one Friday afternoon, the pilots gathered in our squadron main briefing room for commander's call. "Squadron, TEN HUT," barked the admin sergeant. We snapped to attention and our Commander entered. "Gentlemen, please remain standing."

"Captain John Doerr, please come forward."

What's going on I wondered? I walked to the front of the room and the admin sergeant began reading. "Captain John Doerr distinguished himself by heroism while participating in aerial flight as an F-4D Aircraft Commander over North Vietnam on 18 December 1972. On that date, Captain Doerr displayed outstanding airmanship and courage while on a night strike against strategic military targets located deep within the Red River Delta. Despite heavy concentrations of extremely accurate high-caliber anti-aircraft artillery, multiple launches of radar-guided surface-to-air missiles, and attacks by hostile interceptor aircraft, he delivered his ordnance on target with extreme precision and accuracy to achieve success in this complex air operation. The outstanding heroism and selfless devotion to duty displayed by Captain Doerr reflect great credit upon himself and the United States Air Force."

The Commander took the Distinguished Flying Cross medal from its case and pinned it to my flight suit. I recalled watching several B-52 bombers being shot down by Surface to Air Missiles (SAMs) during that mission and knew that some that night did not return home. I felt like a hero. We partied on at the officer's club till midnight with my Distinguished Flying Cross medal hanging like a Roy Rogers Sheriff's badge on my chest for all the world to see.

Thirty miles north of Bitburg Air Base was the small German Helicopter base, Mendig, with a short, 2,000-foot runway designed for helicopter and low-speed aircraft operations. Frequently, we'd fly near this little base returning to Bitburg from training missions.

Returning home one day, I had a little extra fuel and decided to have a little fun. "Hello, Mendig tower, Snake Flight here."

"Guten Tag, Snake Flight, how may I help you?" came the deep, guttural German voice of Mendig tower through my helmet ear pads.

"Roger, Mendig, Snake is one Phantom jet, request overhead traffic pattern for a low approach."

"Roger, Snake, Mendig landing runway two-six, please call two-mile initial."

Great! Games on. "Mendig, Snake is two-mile initial for the overhead runway two-six."

"Roger, Snake, you are cleared for the overhead and low approach. Make left break."

Left hand lightly on the throttles, right hand caressing the stick, thumb on the trim button, and toes gently touching the rudder pedals, I enter the traffic pattern 1500 feet above the airport at 400 knots. Over the runway numbers, I slam the stick full left, retard the throttles, snap into a 90-degree bank, pull 3 g's in the break, and roll out on inside downwind, 250 knots and close to the runway. Gear down, flaps full, I roll off the perch at 190 knots and hold the tight turn till short final. "This runway sure is short," I whisper to Jack in the rear cockpit. Coming close to the runway, but not touching down, I stabbed the mic switch, "Snake's on the go, Mendig, request closed pattern for gear-up low approach."

"Roger, Snake, you are cleared closed pattern and gear-up low approach."

Oh boy! I cleaned up the jet, flew a wide arc, and lined up on final for my little air show. Afterburners engaged for max power, and with 40 feet of flame shooting out the rear of my jet, I flew over Mendig's runway at 200 feet, and 400 knots noticing many people from the hangers outside on the ramp watching. The noise of a Phantom at high-speed, max-power, and close-range, is deafening, and very impressive. Pulling up in a vertical climb, I keyed my mic, and radioed, "Thank you, Mendig, Snake is on his way home."

"Thank you, Snake. You are welcome at Mendig anytime, Auf Wiedersehen."

I was all smiles flying back to Bitburg Air Base. I didn't tell many about my adventure as Snake, thinking it best to go low-profile. Over the next few years, I stopped by Mendig to perform my little air-show perhaps twenty times. It was always fun, and I thought how clever I am using the call sign Snake to mask my identity and remain anonymous. That was a little game I played in my mind, pretending Mendig tower did not know what base Snake was from. However, the 6-foot-tall letters "BT" easily read from Mendig tower with the unaided eye on the tail of my jet, identified my Phantom as one from Bitburg Air Base.

Several months before leaving Bitburg for reassignment, our Wing Commander, Colonel Tyler, with his Executive Officer, attended an International Commander's conference. Upon returning, the Exec told the following story to several of his friends and it trickled down through the rumor mill to the Phantom crews in the squadrons.

Mendig's Commander, a German Colonel, approached Colonel Tyler and politely said, "Colonel, I appreciate your pilots occasionally coming to Mendig and flying a low pass over our runway. This is great for our morale, and we get to see close-up the beautiful F-4 Phantom. It's an impressive experience to witness. However, please ask your pilots not to exceed 400 knots and to maintain altitude above 200 feet. They are always welcome at Mendig, Colonel."

Colonel Tyler assured him that "his boys" would comply, politely thanked the German Colonel, walked away, and came unglued. He narrowed his eyes into slits and said to me (the exec), "If I find out who the SOB is that's doing these unauthorized airshows at Mendig, I'll court-martial him."

I thought it best to not go to Mendig anymore. That was a real no-brainer, and I never returned to Mendig, never again used the call sign Snake, and never heard another word about it.

Deeper, I sank into the bottomless pit of the endless search for external thrills and sensory pleasures. But I was a hero and had a Distinguished Flying Cross medal and citation to prove it.

THE DOC

Tapping my helmet gently with my gloved left hand, I nodded my head forward and simultaneously released the brakes. Throttles full forward, then outboard into the afterburner detent, then forward again to max power. I felt the additional thrust as the engine tail feathers opened and the afterburners lit, then retarded the throttles a smidge so that Tommy, the wingman, had a little power advantage to stay in formation. Glancing left, I smiled, seeing his Phantom glued to ours in perfect fingertip take-off formation.

Tiger flight launched from Bodo Air Base, Norway, as two United States Air Force Phantom jets on an aggressor strike mission to inflict damage on the enemy during our NATO exercise war games. It was early morning in mid-March 1976, as we lifted into a beautiful crisp winter morning with calm winds and clear skies. In aviator jargon, the weather was CAVU (Ceiling And Visibility Unlimited).

Coming back on power at 350 knots, I was alert and alive and shared that with Doc as we climbed for altitude. Words cannot describe the beauty and feelings generated by flying a top-of-the-line world-class fighter-jet on a morning like this in beautiful Norway.

Doc wasn't just another back-seat crewmember. He was our beloved squadron flight surgeon. Roger was about my age of thirty and was a real live doctor with MD tagged to his name. Assigned to our squadron of about 50 crewmembers, he participated in our flying and experienced directly what we routinely put our bodies through flying the Phantom. We pulled five or more g's, experienced high altitude pressure changes, spatial disorientation, and other physiological phenomena, as well as personal and emotional issues. Flying in the rear cockpit, he experienced it all too.

Doc trained a bit and was not just a passenger in the rear cockpit. He knew how to operate the inertial navigation system and airborne radar, and thought like a fighter pilot, too. He was part of the crew, not just a few hundred pounds of baggage riding around in the rear cockpit. We were also great friends, and I felt privileged that Doc was flying with me this morning.

Tiger flight, with Doc and me in the lead Phantom and Tommy and Harry in the number two Phantom, was on the blue team in this international exercise. Our mission was, as aggressors, to attack designated Norwegian airfields while evading their defense systems. We would simulate dropping bombs and cratering their runway. We could also attack any enemy military ship either on the North Sea or in a fjord. The potential for having fun was off the charts.

"Doc, I believe we're crossing into enemy territory, so turn on the forward jamming pods and keep the radar on 3-bar sweep 25-mile scope please."

"OK Johnny," chimed Doc.

"Mission Control, Tiger flight of two Phantoms, crossing the fence inbound. Request authorization to attack military airfields and navel targets of opportunity."

"Tiger flight, mission control, you are cleared airfield attacks at your discretion and Norwegian Naval vessels as well. Enemy fighters are in the area and are authorized to engage and defend."

"Tiger flight, Roger, we'll call crossing the fence outbound."

"Roger, Tiger. Mission Control out."

Using silent signals, I sent the wingman to line-abreast ingress formation and dropped down to tree-top level. Smoothly, we blasted through the fjords, up and over the shear walls, rolling back down into the valleys and dales very low and very fast.

"Johnny, I'm checking six o'clock behind us as best I can for enemy fighters."

"Thanks, Doc, and if we're jumped, we'll deal with them before we attack the airfield, which is only a few minutes on the nose."

I couldn't see the airfield, for it was in a small valley on the opposite side of the ridgeline to my left. "Pop-up point in sight on the nose, Doc," I said, and blasted over it. Every cell in my body was in full adrenalin mode as I initiated a 4-g pull-up. Rolling over the top of the hill inverted, there was our airfield with a bonus of two enemy fighters at the end of the runway waiting to take-off. Stabbing the mic switch with my left thumb, I grunted, "Tiger is in for attack,"

"Tiger is cleared to attack," responded the tower.

Touching the bomb master-arm and gun-arm switches as simulation of final arming, I rolled out in a dive, and simulated dropping 6 x 500-pound bombs on the runway. With the bombs gone, I made a small adjustment and aligned my gun to bear on the waiting enemy fighters. "Buuuurrrrp!" I burped into my mask simulating the sound of our 20mm canon, then abruptly initiated a smooth 5 g pull to get-out-of-Dodge.

"Our 6 o'clock is clear, Johnny," said Doc as we watched Tiger 2 pull off his bomb pass and reposition for a south exit of the airfield area.

Climbing through 15,000 feet, my headphones screamed, "Tiger-2's got 2-bandits 2 o'clock slightly high."

"Roger, Tiger-2, tally-ho. Tiger-1's on the left bandit."

"Tiger- 2's on the right bandit," called Tommy. The bandits had just split to take us on 1 vs 1.

But we had a major advantage over the bandits as we were in a favorable stern position. I plugged in the afterburners, set switches for missiles and guns, and never took my eyes off my target. As the bandit F-5 continued its tight left turn, I did too and saw a gun-shot rapidly developing. With 6 g's on our jet, I grunted, "Look left, Roger."

"OK," he grunted, and the F-5 shot across our nose and left side only a few hundred feet away at 500 plus knots. "Buuuuuurrrrp," I hollered simulating the firing noise of our 20mm canon.

"J-E-S-U-S C-H-R-I-S-T," Roger screamed. "THAT WAS VERY FRIGGIN CLOSE, JOHNNY!" I eased off the g-loading, rolled right and reacquired Tiger-2. Checking fuel, we disengaged and dove toward the gray ocean three miles below.

"It wasn't that close, Doc. We didn't hit him, did we? Besides, close only counts with hand-grenades, horseshoes, and dancing." I tried to lighten the mood of our near-death experience a bit. With fighter planes, aggressiveness counts, and had I actually fired our cannon, either we would have stitched his fuselage with 20 mm bullets or sawed off one of his wings. To make a gun kill, one must get close.

We patrolled south working our way out of the war zone, ever vigilant for bandits and other threats. Clearing a ridgeline, we opened to a long fjord and I was struck by the beauty of it all. And there, toward the entrance of the fjord some twenty miles distant, was a Norwegian destroyer, about 500 feet long with perhaps 25 feet from the water to the deck. "Twelve o'clock twenty miles, Tiger," I whispered to wingman Tommy.

"I got 'em," Tommy whispered back.

With the mountains behind us, we were invisible from the destroyer both visually and electronically. "Roger, we're going in at wave-top level to avoid detection. Since our only weapon left is the gun, we'll simulate a strafe run on this boat."

"OK, Johnny. By the way, my altimeter reads fifty feet below sea-level."

"Thanks, Roger, it's obviously off a little but mine says we're still in the air, but only by a few feet."

We flew toward the destroyer very close to the water at 500 knots (575 mph). "See, Roger, the deck guns on the destroyer cannot shoot below horizontal so it may seem dangerous to fly this low, but it keeps us from getting shot from the deck guns."

"Thanks, Johnny, that's comforting to know."

I giggled as that bunch of malarkey just came to me out of the blue. But it sounded good and supported us flying very fast and very low. I loved it down here. Tiger-2 was in perfect formation about 1000' off my right wing as we headed for the ship. We screamed by the destroyer below deck level and I doubt if they ever saw us until they heard us.

Clear of the destroyer, we joined up, safed our armament switches, visually checked each other over, called outbound with mission control, and headed for home. Attacking the destroyer was a lot of fun, but I would have never done that in combat. Our 20mm cannon was not effective against the steel protection of the destroyer. However, it was a great thrill, and I loved thrills.

We brought our Phantoms home, debriefed, and planned for a similar mission the next day. Doc loved the flying, and I loved having him with me. It was win-win all the way.

Author's note: Roger and I retain a deep, fifty-year friendship and I requested his comments on 'The Doc' chapter to include in this book. His unaltered reply follows:

"I honestly thought we could die that day but I trusted in Johnny's skills and was actually exhilarated with what we did. We were playing the role of the aggressor and we definitely were that. In fact, that flight stands out above the hundreds I've had. The experience was similar to one described by Winston Churchill. 'Nothing in life is so exhilarating as to be shot at without result.' I remember it vividly today, nearly fifty years later".

Roger Landry - 10 February, 2023

DELIVERING SUPPLIES TO THE BRITISH ROYAL NAVY

"Ka-BANG!" My head snapped left and filling the open doorway of our flight briefing room was the imposing figure of our Squadron Commander, Lieutenant Colonel Dick 'The Stroker' Cramer, Command Pilot, United States Air Force.

We immediately stood at attention, and I muttered, "Sir?"

He wasn't smiling and his right hand held a thin yellow message flimsy. "Sit down, you guys!" he barked. "I can't even imagine what you did to generate this official exercise message flimsy, but you ARE going to tell me, and you ARE going to tell me the truth. This message is from the Commander of the British Royal Navy aircraft carrier Arc Royal, the flagship of the Blue team that you guys successfully attacked a few hours ago. I'll read it word for word."

Colonel Cramer pulled the message flimsy up to his eyes and hesitated. He stared right through the thin yellow paper and bore individually into the eyes of each one of us. As flight leader, I was sure my life was about to end.

"To the Green team Phantom Tiger flight from the Blue team Commander of the Royal Navy aircraft carrier Arc Royal." Colonel Cramer hesitated for effect, then continued reading slowly, word for word. "Thank you for the much-needed supplies."

We stood frozen in stunned silence for what felt like an eternity.

Then glancing at each other we burst into laughter and back-slapping so loud it took several minutes for us to calm down sufficiently to share our experience with our beloved squadron commander.

"OK, OK, so what the hell did you guys do to provoke this brief message from the Arc Royal to Tiger Flight? Johnny, as flight lead, if you got me in trouble by some shenanigan, I'll have your butt washing dishes for the rest of this exercise."

"Sir, we were just being neighborly and helpful," I replied, then shared our TP re-supply adventure with "The Stroker." He listened attentively, then a big grin spread across his face. Smiling from ear-to-ear, he rose and slowly strode toward the door. Reaching for the doorknob, he hesitated, turned, and faced us. Giving us a thumbs-up, he admonished us with a soft-spoken, "Don't do it again." And that was the end of it. Our Commander knew what we had done and had appropriately reprimanded us.

And that WAS the end of it, until nine years later in 1985 when, well, perhaps best if I share this adventure from the beginning. Please join me now at Bodo Airbase, Norway, Tiger flight briefing room, at 6 am in mid-March 1976.

My squadron of F-4 Phantoms from Bitburg Airbase, Germany, was on the Green-Team of a Tactical NATO exercise conducted in and around Norway and adjacent North Sea area. The Green team also included a squadron of Norwegian Air Force F-104 Starfighters and several other NATO flying units. Our opponents, the Blue team, consisted of several NATO flying squadrons and units of the British Royal Navy including the aircraft carrier Arc Royal with its surrounding escort and support ships. No weapons of any kind were employed by anyone.

The aggressors' mission was to locate and attack the defenders' ships and airfields undetected. The defender's mission was to locate, intercept, and destroy the aggressors before we could accomplish our mission. It was an electronic radar cat-and-mouse game. They compiled scores, and the results of successful and unsuccessful attacks were frequently posted. They encouraged us to be aggressive, but safe.

Molli and I were the lead Phantom crew in our 4-ship Tiger Flight. I briefed the crews about launching our four Phantoms from Bodo Airbase, Norway, remaining below 500' to the North Sea, then flying out across the open water low level at a few hundred feet. We employed a tactical spread formation, maximizing the effectiveness of on-board radars to locate the British fleet.

The idea was to be just high enough for the back-seaters to find the British Fleet with our on-board radars, yet low enough for the ships to not find us with theirs. Since their radars were atop the ship's masts, the lower we flew, the more we blended into the water clutter. We sort of disappeared into the North Sea. Therefore, we flew 100 to 200 feet above the water at 420 knots (500 mph). That gave us a few feet of safety so we would not collide with the North Sea yet hid us from their radars fairly well.

Molli was a master with the Phantom's radar. And he orchestrated and briefed Tiger flight on how he wanted to set up and execute the search patterns for maximum probability of success. Real-time satellite location information and GPS were in the distant future. We were on our own and the success or failure of this mission depended on the skills of Molli and the other Phantom radar jocks using our on-board radar equipment.

Mission briefing complete, I gestured toward the eight rolls of toilet paper and continued. "Each crew take two rolls of TP and put one roll in each speed-brake. Loosen the end a little so it will stream when released, and don't use your speed brakes during the mission. Hopefully, we're going to deliver a gift to our friends on the Arc Royal after our successful mission."

The Phantom's speed-brakes are front-hinged panels on the bottom of each wing that create significant drag when opened into the slipstream and rapidly slow the aircraft. They also make a great place to stow small soft objects like toilet paper or socks for release from the air.

On schedule, Tiger flight of four Phantoms left the coast of Norway, descended to wave-top level, and in tactical spread formation, flew out over the cold dark North Sea. All control movements in the Phantom are very gentle at 500 mph and 100 feet above the gray-black waters. Snuggled into the front cockpit of our Phantom, I glanced inside for a half a second confirming that our aircraft was functioning perfectly, fuel was normal, and we were still going in the correct general direction toward where we thought we'd find the enemy fleet.

"I got 'em, Johnny, about 40 miles, 20 degrees right. That's the Arc

Royal and her convoy," Molli whispered in my earpiece. He was relaxed and had total faith in me as we roared over the North Sea a hundred feet above the water.

"Tiger Flight, we log you inbound and are cleared for simulated attacks on the Arc Royal Fleet at your discretion."

"Tiger Flight cleared for attacks on the armada, all weapons switches are safe," I responded. Oh Boy, I thought, game's on!

We flew multiple attacks, employing our electronic defenses and simulating various weapons delivered on the enemy convoy. We were very successful.

"Arc Royal, Tiger Flight, attacks complete and switches safe, request permission for an over-flight of your ship."

"Tiger Flight is cleared for an over-flight." I wiggled my wings, signaling the three wingmen to join in close fingertip formation and began a gentle long turn for the Arc Royal flyover. We were four Phantom fighter-jets in perfect close formation lined up a few miles astern of the Arc Royal aircraft carrier for a low-level flyover about 300 feet above the carrier's flight deck.

As she slid under my nose, I keyed the mic button. "Tiger Flight! Speeeeed Braaaakes, NOW!" My left thumb slid the speed-brake switch aft, releasing two rolls of toilet paper. Retracting the "boards," I began an easy right turn and gentle climb. Tiger Flight was on her way home.

Other than the message traffic shared by our commander and story swapping at the bar, not another word was heard about Tiger Flight and her mission of re-supply to the enemy. That is until, well, let us just fast forward nine years later to January 1985.

Sharing a beer with a few Royal Naval officers during a NATO exercise in Belgium, I was chatting with Royal Navel pilot Lieutenant Commander Niles Brook. I shared with him the adventure of Tiger flight on that chilly March morning in 1976 out over the North Sea. "And as we lined up on final for our Arc Royal over-flight," I continued. Niles held up his palm and stopped me, mouth open, in mid-sentence. "Johnny, please let me tell the rest of that story," Niles remarked, smiling.

"I was a pilot aboard the Arc Royal that morning and was preparing to launch when I looked astern and saw your four Phantoms approaching. Your formation looked great! Here come four USAF Phantoms about 300 feet above deck in perfect close formation. I can still see it clearly. Then I saw the streamers depart your Phantoms. At first, I didn't know that it was toilet paper, because we weren't expecting you to drop anything. But your rolls unraveled perfectly, and one of them landed very close to me. Then I realized what it was, and I had a great laugh and my respect for the United States Air Force went up off the chart. That, Johnny, was one of the coolest moves I've ever seen in my 18 years in the Royal Navy."

"Thank you, Nigel. That puts a bit of closure on the event and reaffirms that a good pilot doesn't need a gun sight to accurately drop toilet paper from the speed brakes of his Phantom."

STOPPED BY POLICE - THE GUNNERY TEAM

"Hey, Johnny! Congratulations on your selection with Molli for the wing gunnery team."

"Really?" I said, quite surprised.

"Well, they picked you and Molli just yesterday, and I guess you haven't heard the news."

"Nope, sure haven't, but what a fun gig that will be!"

Molli had the highest radar range scores in our squadron from the previous six months, and I was the top scoring pilot. The commander therefore picked us to be the squadron's contribution representing Bitburg Airbase in this important flying event. Excited, we sewed special patches on our flight suits and had our own dedicated Phantom jet with our names painted on the canopy rails. We were in the spotlight for the next two months with special training flights and, finally, the NATO gunnery flying competition. What a wonderful experience!

Molli and I had the skills and we flew well together. One night, I had a few whiskeys and phoned my friend Patti. She invited me over and I went, even though I had an early flight the following morning. Patti was fun, desirable, easy-going, and liked me. Exiting the Base on my return home, I clipped a few of the "witch's hat cones" at the gate maze, and stopped. With a flashlight in my face, the air-policeman asked, "Where are you going, Captain?"

"Just going home, Sargent."

"Please step out of the car, Captain." I was done.

Slightly over the limit, I was driven home. Because I was on the high-profile gunnery team, this incident report went to our wing commander and his commanding General Officer.

Our experience on the team was degraded, and I had brought unfavorable attention to our team. I felt like a fool. Fear was my constant companion, and I frequently looked over my shoulder to see what was coming next. Nothing else ever came. Perhaps I made a lot bigger deal of this event than anyone else.

Molli was my saving grace as he comforted me and helped me hold it together throughout the competition. Perhaps he saw values in me that I could not see in myself.

Competition complete, I reported to the commanding general for punishment from my night with Patti incident. I saluted, stood at attention, and listened. "Well, Captain, you and Molli did well with the flying, and that's reflected in your high scores. The Air force and I are proud of you for that. Do you think you have a serious drinking problem, Captain?"

"No sir, this was an isolated incident, (I lied) and I assure you it will not happen again." The general nodded his head in approval, fined me a few hundred dollars, and dismissed me.

DEE - I MARRIED MY FATHER

In 1976, drinking and partying was a huge part of the fighter pilot experience and officers tended to help each other by minimizing alcohol incidents. Mandatory Friday afternoon "Commander's Call" in our squadron lounge, then Friday night at the officer's club bar, and weekend activities around booze were my norm. I continued to drink for nine more years before another event brought me to my knees and sobriety.

"Hi there, it looks like you could use a refill," I said, smoothing my way toward the attractive girl.

"Yeah, sure could," she said. It was another great party night at the Crystal Palace, a German home rented by several of my Air Force flying buddies in Bitburg, Germany. It was early March 1976, and I led her to the bar and fixed us each a drink. She was attractive, friendly, hippie-looking, and apparently available. Something good might come of this I thought.

Dee and I partied the night away, and in the wee hours of the morning, headed to my place in a nearby village. Home, a nightcap, bed, and finally sleep. Thus began our relationship of ego vs ego. Champagne for breakfast, more bed, more booze, more bed, and I was on a roll.

I knew nothing about her except that she was an American, attractive, and available. We liked the same foods and music, playing guitars and singing together, and both loved the German beers, wines, whiskies, and endless parties. She soon moved in, and I enjoyed coming home to my hippie woman with waiting open arms. We were compatible on the surface, but we never talked in any meaningful way about future dreams, finances, children, or spiritual development. We were all about fun and games. After four months, at thirty-one years old, I felt it was time to get married, so I proposed, and she accepted. In September 1976, we left Germany and arrived at my parents' home in New Jersey to stay for a few weeks to have our wedding.

Stopping one day at a local deli, we scanned the wall menu to order sandwiches. I selected roast beef among the thirty or more sandwich choices from the extensive menu, while Dee chose an odd-ball salami. "I am sorry ma'am, I'm all out of odd-ball salami but I have several other choices that are very similar."

"What, no odd-ball salami? What kind of deli is this?" Dee yelled. The employee was shocked at her loud, aggressive, and arrogant response and so was I. She ranted at the man while I backed away several feet, distancing myself from this mad-as-hell woman. After several minutes, Dee calmed down, made another selection, and we left with our sandwiches shortly thereafter.

I never said a word to her about this because I was frightened of her anger and didn't wish to do anything that might trigger a similar response toward me. I just knew that she would never be angry like that with me and would always be nice and pleasant. After all, I was a very nice man, totally supporting her and she, therefore, had no reason to yell like that at me. Once we left the deli, the pleasant, kind, hippie girl that loved me reappeared and acted as if that entire event never happened. I quickly brushed it out of my mind.

Before our wedding, I witnessed several similar events with Dee becoming angry and inappropriate with people for trivial reasons. A server spilled water on our table once and Dee responded critically, arrogantly, and abusively. Then, in a heartbeat, she turned to me smiling and told me how much she loved being with me and how nice a man I was. I bought it all and never questioned her about her volatile behavior or mood swings. I just assumed that this was the way she was, and if she was nice to me, that's all I cared about. How naive I was.

We married on the lawn of my parents' home and departed for a lifetime of love and bliss. That lasted about two weeks. Dee shortly started becoming critical of me, finding fault with almost everything I did. After our daughters were born a few years later, she began threatening to leave with the children if I did not do this or that. I had very little voice in our home anymore, nor was there any discussion about issues, feelings, or emotions.

Resolution of differences did not happen in our home. Where was the kind, gentle, woman that loved me and met me with open arms just a few years prior in Germany? Where did she go? I did not know. Perhaps if I tried a little harder to please her, she'd be nice to me, I thought. I was continually walking on eggshells, waiting for the next blaming event. It was her way or the highway and to anesthetize the pain in my heart, I drank more.

Dee's degrading behavior toward me reminded me of Dad. Although she was not physically abusive, her frequent deriding remarks were like knives in my heart. She was irresponsible, and blamed everyone else, including me, for the inevitable negative events that occurred in her life. It was never her fault, so there was no reason for her to change or fix anything. I simply could not relate to her behavior. I'd never seen this level of irresponsibility before, and trying to discuss anything, was always met with, "You don't understand, Johnny," or "That's not what I said," or "That's not the way it happened." It didn't matter what it was, there was no discussion, attempt at understanding, or resolution of issues. There was just finger-pointing and anger. I felt trapped and wanted to crawl into a hole and die.

Like me, Dee portrayed pleasantness and responsibility on the surface. She diligently assured our daughters were buckled into the car seats and was pleasant to casual friends and strangers. But she had a basement full of unresolved trauma from her abusive childhood that haunted her.

My part in our relationship was to drink, live superficially, and pretend that all was well. I was emotionally immature, also with a basement full of darkness and trauma from childhood and Vietnam.

My psychic shadow continually haunted me and clashed with Dee's. I was unable, at any meaningful level, to see life through her eyes, relate to her abusive childhood, anger, fears, behavior patterns, and her behavior toward me. There was no way that I could be there for her. Today, I imagine she felt as trapped as I did. Together, we created a life of chaos, conflict, confusion, and pain.

This scenario continued for nine years. My alcoholic nightmare ended on 8 March 1985, when I had my last drink of alcohol and began my journey of sobriety.

STEALING? - BEER DOESN'T COUNT

Every fighter pilot knows that beer doesn't really count as drinking. It's like water to the seasoned drinker and in the late seventies, I was in pretty good drinking shape. My tolerance for alcohol was very high. Since it didn't count as drinking, stealing a case or two shouldn't count as stealing. Hell, it's only water with a bit of alcohol thrown in. Since it was so weak, I thought, it ought to be free.

Those were my thoughts in the late seventies while I was an F-4 Phantom instructor pilot at Luke Air Force Base near Phoenix, Arizona. I rationalized away the dishonesty as I pushed open the door and disappeared into the large walk-in beer cooler at the local supermarket. I immediately grabbed a can of imported beer and popped the top. Guzzling down a cold one, I made a quick survey of the stacked cases of beer and decided which one I'd load on my cart. That cold beer was down the hatch in less than 30 seconds and a minute later, I was out of the cooler carrying two cases of cold beer and gently slid them under the cart onto the lower flatbed section.

My grocery shopping was complete, so I headed straight for the check-out registers. Looking casual and calm, (at least I thought I did) I put all the groceries on the conveyer and moved the cart on through toward the front door. There were no scanners in the 1970s as I recall, and checking out took a bit of time. Making small talk with the checkout person to keep them distracted, I put my bagged groceries in cart and paid the bill. Somehow, I forgot about the two cases of beer under the cart and the checkout person couldn't see them down there. Sometimes, I guess I'm just absent minded.

"Thank you, sir, and thanks for shopping with us!" Off I went at normal speed out the front door and straight to my car. I casually loaded everything, returned the empty cart, and drove home. I figured that if they stopped me somewhere before or after leaving the store, I would just lay it on them that they simply forgot to charge me for the two cases of beer and I'd go back and pay for it.

That never happened and if it had, I believe I would have stopped that game. But I probably did this a dozen times and was never detained, stopped, questioned, or caught. Nothing!

WHAT WAS I THINKING? WHERE WAS MY INTEGRITY? I was an officer in the United States Air Force, sufficiently paid, in my mid-thirties, married, and considered myself honest. Did I not have enough money to pay for my beer? Of course, I did. So, what was going on inside of Johnny?

This is how the alcoholic brain functions. In my mind, it was all about the cheap thrill of getting away with something. My buddies and I could sit by the pool now, enjoying this free beer and laugh at the world for being so stupid to allow even me, a very low level, unskilled thief, get away with stealing two cases of beer. It tasted better because I stole it. I got my cheap thrill fix satisfied from doing this. I felt like I was a world class thief and it felt good, as I recall.

Now, forty-five years later, I reflect on the immaturity, insanity, and total lack of integrity I exhibited by stealing a few cases of beer.

But that is what the alcoholic mind does. This is classic first-floor behavior from the Building-of-Life metaphor shared elsewhere in this book. And what else was I dishonest about? Well, for starters, I drank alcoholically, yet I could not own that behavior. Perhaps the title of this chapter ought to be "Denial in Action."

DAUGHTERS - SARAH AND JENNIFER

Sarah was born at 11:11pm and within a few minutes, while holding her in my arms, she opened her eyes and we shared that initial "welcome to planet Earth" moment. It was awesome. I was a father now and just loved sharing precious early life experiences with Sarah as she grew from her crib to crawling, standing, walking, running, playing, and exploring our exciting world. A year and a half later, Jennifer arrived, and we were now a family of four. I shared with Jennifer those same initial experiences I had shared with Sarah.

I dreamed of being an active father and sharing homework and bedtime stories with my daughters. But it didn't quite work out that way. Dee and I were lost souls without direction or purpose and we had limited communication. My dream of a family and being an active participating father with Sarah and Jennifer as they grew to adulthood lasted only a few years.

The wise know that truth may be hidden, distorted, or manipulated, however, it can never be obliterated. Truth and integrity were all that was necessary, and I did what I could to hold that space and avoid confrontation and conflict with Dee. I didn't have an overwhelming need to be right, get back at, or win every battle. It paid off in the long run as, over time, Sarah and Jennifer came to know us both for who we are.

SOBRIETY - 8 MARCH 1985

Stumbling out of bed, I eased into the bathroom, splashed water on my face and stared into the dull bloodshot eyes in the mirror. I felt awful. Queasy in my stomach, groggy and foggy in my mind, I glanced at the clock. It was 8:15 am, and I was very late for work.

Major John Doerr, United States Air Force was the commander of a small detachment supporting a U.S. Army unit in Southern Germany. What a commander!

I called my deputy and told him to carry on without me today, as I was sick. He complied. I do not even remember going to bed last night. How can I do this to myself day after day?

Dee was out taking Sarah and Jennifer to school and I didn't expect her to return for several hours.

Home alone, I showered and shaved. What do I do now? I'm on a cross. I cannot function without booze, and I cannot function with booze. Fear grew in the pit of my stomach, and I became physically sick. I dropped to my knees and cried. The constant never-ending merry-go-round of my alcoholic life was misery beyond description.

I phoned my boss and told him I was sick and requested time off. He knew what was going on, and was familiar with my drinking habits, my unreliability, and my lack of interest in my job.

"Major, be at your home in uniform at noon. I'm coming to pick you up and that's an official order," he barked.

"Yes, sir," I replied, and hung up the phone. I was terrified of the damage I was doing to my future in the Air Force, to my family, and to myself. Everything was hanging by a thread. I wished life was different, but it wasn't.

I put on a clean uniform and headed for the kitchen. My hands shook as I poured coffee and struggled to hold the cup steady enough to drink.

"I'm a total failure," I screamed, and cried again. Desperate, lost, and scared, a burst of insight came through, and in a flash, I knew that a drink would help. I decided that a little snort of local German Schnapps would fix me right up.

I retrieved the schnapps from the freezer and selected a small shot glass with a little coat of arms embossed on it. It was a gift from a local neighbor to help me make it through the cold German winters. I'm feeling better already just thinking about this drink and the upcoming relief. I carefully poured several ounces of the cold yellowish liquid into the shot glass and swished it around. My entire world was in that yellowish liquid and taking this drink would stop my shakes and ease my fear of meeting the commander at noon. With a few sips of homemade schnapps, I'll be good to go, or so I thought.

Lovingly, I picked up the glass with my unsteady hand and pour it down my throat. It burned slightly on my tongue and I savored the richness and fullness of the homemade drink as it slid down and filled my stomach with warm relief. Instantly, I relaxed. Medicine, that's what this is, homemade medicine that Germans have used to fix ailments and keep out the cold for centuries. It only makes sense for me to do the same. So, while in Germany, do as the Germans do.

Should I have another? If one is good, then two is twice as good. I needed no more coaxing. Slowly, I refilled the glass, and the ritual began again. I raised the schnapps to eye level and stared at the slightly yellowish fluid swirling in the glass. I knew that this "wonderful elixir was my problem fixer." Fear engulfed me and I felt paralyzed. Quickly, I raised the glass and poured the cold fluid down my throat. Slowly, ever so slowly, I lowered the glass. *"JOHNNY, YOU ARE NEVER COMING BACK TO THIS PLACE OF FEAR."*

My heart skipped, then pounded like a bass drum. I heard those words in my mind loud and clear and knew that my life was irrevocably changed.

Relieved and lighthearted, I stood at my bar bathed in serenity, no longer fearing what the commander would do or where he would take me. It just did not matter anymore. A gentle peace and calmness settled over me and I felt loved, supported, and unafraid. Returning the schnapps to the freezer, I sat by the front door, waiting for my noon appointment with destiny.

In that defining moment, my life burst wide open and the desire to consume alcohol in any form was removed. The colonel took me to alcohol detox, followed by a four-week in-house rehab at an American military hospital in Germany. I've never consumed, nor had any desire to consume alcohol since. Like an arrow, I was launched on a trajectory toward an unknown future.

PART II
INTO THE SHADOW

SECTION INTRODUCTION

"Major, you're an alcoholic," said the rehab admittance doctor. "I'm sending you to five days of detox to clean you out a bit, followed by four weeks of alcohol rehab."

So that's what's wrong with me, I thought, and hopefully that's fixable with a bit of work. I felt calm and peaceful. I knew that my old life of drinking and fear was ending, and a new life free from alcohol addiction was unfolding. I was an arrow released on a trajectory toward an unknown future.

It was the eighth of March, 1985, and I was entering an alcohol rehab facility of a US military hospital in Germany. That was the last day that I consciously consumed alcohol. At forty years old, a major in the United States Air Force, and the father of two young daughters, I had the maturity of a twelve-year-old child. I made every life choice since college under the influence of alcohol. With the whiskey bottle gone, my life toolbox was empty.

Into the Shadow is my life adventure of replacing old behaviors that no longer served me, with new ones that did. I was on a journey of filling my toolbox with new life tools.

The following morning, the peaceful picnic ended, and the shakes began. The reality of what I did to arrive here, the quality of fathering I provided for my family, and the emptiness inside my heart settled in.

For several days, I lay in a bed sweating and shaking, wishing I was dead, and had I a butcher knife, I might have used it to end my misery.

Into the Shadow is my life journey from the depths of despair and depression during alcohol detox, till my teacher arrived thirty-four years later in June 2019.

We are all individuals on an earthwalk. Yet at our core, our spiritual center, we are all connected through the energetic web of cosmic consciousness.

Journey with me now through my pain and pleasures, releasing old patterns, gathering new life tools, stretching beyond the comfortable known, and exploring the light and darkness as we walk together *Into the Shadow*.

THE HUMAN SHADOW

The human shadow represents the hidden personality living within every one of us. On the surface, most appear and believe that they are reasonable, good, and kind. However, the shadow contains the parts of the personality that are hidden below the surface and repressed. They are our secrets, our subconscious and unconscious aspects that we keep locked in our darkness, hence, the term *shadow*.

This is where our violence, anger, and hate, hide and reside. The more we repress our shadow, the more destructive, insidious, and dangerous it becomes. As we repress it, we project it outward on others, and it manifests within as neurotic and psychotic behaviors. Simply, it is those pieces of our personality that we find unacceptable, stuff down and hide in our basement, and close the door.

This simplistic explanation of the human shadow is all one needs to know to begin their healing.

Everyone has a shadow or secrets basement where they hide traumatizing experiences that happened to them, and traumatizing experiences they participated in. After a while, denial systems surrounding our shadow form and our secrets don't seem so bad anymore. Soon we may even forget about these traumatic experiences and perhaps even forget that we have a basement containing this darkness.

But even in denial, our secrets still exist and we spend energy holding closed the basement door containing our anger, rage, and fear.

Like the geyser Old Faithful, our shadow will occasionally release some of its energy. It will act-out in ways that are inappropriate or worse and at a time of its choosing. Road rage, violent and explosive responses to minor incidents, and sudden spontaneous eruptions of brutality are all examples.

My shadow pieces formed during early childhood from the brutality of my father, the lack of protection by my mother, and the absence of genuine nurturing from both parents. I feared my father for his violent behavior toward me and harbored anger at my mother for not intervening and protecting me. From those experiences, I learned to fear authority figures, repress anger and rage, relate to women as objects, and distance myself from intimate relationships. I did not trust anyone, including myself.

That was me when I left home for university at eighteen. I did not know that I was dragging along a dark basement full of childhood traumas. I lived in constant fear and anger, wearing a mask with a painted-on smile. My escape from the pain was alcohol. Afraid to express anger, I smiled at everyone and pretended life was OK, all the while seething inside with anger and rage. I avoided conflict at all costs.

I realized only recently that I carried repressed anger and rage toward my mother and that this was why I distanced myself from intimacy and related to woman as objects. On the surface, I was polite, kind, and generous, yet kept women and intimacy at arm's length.

I've never been violent in my life and was afraid to punch someone or get into a fight for fear that they would hit back harder, as my dad did. I projected my fear of my father on everyone.

Fear is the gatekeeper of the shadow basement. To open that door, I had to become friends with my fear. It was an act of courage to embrace my fears and explore my shadow basement.

Dropping bombs in Vietnam was repressed rage released. I saw the whole experience as remote and surrealistic. All sealed up in my trusty Phantom fighter-jet in the middle of the night, in air-conditioned comfort, I was playing a video game, distant from the death and destruction. Based in Thailand, I was relatively safe and experienced few rocket attacks on our base. I had minimal direct contact with the war. But I DID drop real bombs on real people and killed many of them. All that trauma went into my shadow basement and I repressed the Vietnam experience for many years.

The journey to freedom begins in the shadow basement, where we must own our deepest and darkest secrets before moving upward into the light.

The shadow is not all destructive and dark. There is also a "white shadow." These are the positive, creative aspects of our personality. These are our gifts and talents that we discard through negative experiences. Rather than receiving praise for trying to accomplish, I experienced judgement, criticism, and shame because I wasn't doing it good enough.

I was told in fifth-grade that I could not draw well and so my creative artist went into my shadow basement. To protect me from going through that negative experience again, I didn't draw anymore. After I experienced ridicule and embarrassment from my eighth-grade book report failure, my creative writer joined my artist.

Here is Marianne Williamson's piece about our white shadow.

Deepest Fear

"My deepest fear is not that I am inadequate. My deepest fear is that I am powerful beyond measure. It is my light, not my darkness, that frightens me most. I ask myself, who am I to be brilliant, gorgeous, talented, and fabulous? Actually, who am I not to be? I am a child of divinity."

"My playing small doesn't serve the world. There is nothing enlightened about shrinking so that other people won't feel insecure around me. I was born to make manifest the divine glory that is within me. And it is not just in some of us, it is in everyone. As I let my own light shine, I unconsciously give other people permission to do the same. And as I am liberated from my own fear, my presence automatically liberates others." Marianne Williamson

ALCOHOL REHAB

"Of the ten of you in this rehab group, only one will still be abstinent from alcohol this time next year," said the rehab director Captain Kirsten Schmitt. I thought the other nine were wasting their time because I KNEW that I would not drink alcohol again. I didn't know how I knew; I just knew that I knew. This is the "space of knowing."

I paid attention and liked the feelings of becoming responsible and taking ownership of my life. Instead of running away from life, I was learning to walk toward life. I was beginning to go with the flow.

During our third week, we were encouraged to have a barbecue outside on the patio over the weekend and gathered to plan it out. The grill was over there, the charcoal was in a closet, the burgers were in the kitchen fridge, the condiments were in the pantry, etc. Questions arose, "What time shall we start the fire? What about cheese? Anyone want hotdogs?" Nobody made any decisions, so I jumped in and took command to get the project organized. I simply volunteered everyone for a little job. We'd meet on the patio at noon Saturday to enjoy our little barbecue.

Saturday noon arrived and the show began. This wasn't right, and that wasn't where it was supposed to be. Our gathering became chaotic and personalities clashed. "I was supposed to get the ketchup, not you!

You were supposed to bring the buns! Nuh ah! I should have written it down, then we'd know for sure! Oh yeah, you're right. I forgot."

It went on and on. I saw I was the head control nut right in the middle of this drama, wanting everything to go my way and feeling frustrated and angry because people weren't doing what they were supposed to do. Somehow, it came together, and I saw that my controlling personality was contributing to the confusion and chaos. Releasing control is a huge deal, and I realized that my control issues were preventing me from enjoying our bar-b-que.

Alcoholics Anonymous is a program of both doing and allowing. One must do certain things, like not drink, get out of bed and get going in the morning, go to meetings, and work the steps. But early on, I found that if I sat peacefully in any AA meeting with an open mind, I would benefit from just being there. "Just allow the energy of the group to wash over you, Johnny," mentor Ronnie said. "If you drag your body to AA long enough, eventually, your mind will follow." One aspect of allowing is to let others be who they are with total acceptance.

I wrote my parents a long heart-felt letter while in alcohol rehab and apologized for all the anxiety and pain I had caused them and made amends as best I could. They welcomed my letter. Mom wrote that they were both glad I was in rehab, and that they had known for a long time that I had a serious drinking problem. "Oh, by the way," Mom said, "your father was so touched by your letter that he checked himself into an alcohol rehab facility and started yesterday."

As a child, I do not recall ever seeing my father drunk. And Mom and Dad consumed little alcohol at home because they didn't have much excess money to spend socializing. Perhaps Dad slid a bit more into the booze in his sixties after retirement. "Great, Mom!" I wrote, and was optimistic that Dad and I would have common interests now and could support each other's recovery program. I was forty, and Dad was sixty-six.

Four months later, at my parents' home, Dad and I sat over coffee in his kitchen, and I shared, "I love my sobriety, Dad, and life is unfolding in my favor. How was rehab for you?"

"Well, Johnny, it was OK I guess, except I wanted to lose a bit of weight while there, and the scale was just outside the ward. I asked to use it and was told no. The rehab rules restricted me to the ward. And for the life of me, I could not understand why they would not allow me to go just twenty feet down the hall to the scale. It was like a prison that way and I was not permitted to leave the ward for any reason. That's crazy, isn't it, Johnny? I mean, what could it have hurt to just go to the scale and weigh myself a few times?"

I sat in stunned silence. Four weeks in alcohol rehab and this was the primary experience Dad brought home with him. He missed the whole point of the scale experience. Dad hung onto control relentlessly, and my dream of sharing with him the AA steps and principles was not to be. Within a few months, Dad went back to the bottle.

Now fast forward seven years. While visiting my parents during winter, we were gathered for Christmas at my sister's home a few miles away when Dad went back home to retrieve his camera. He shortly returned drunk and spent the evening asleep in Sis's recliner. Mom and I eventually took him home and put him to bed.

The following morning, Dad was hung over, and full of guilt and remorse. During morning coffee, he asked, "Johnny, was I a good father to you?"

"Well, Dad, in many ways yes, but also in many ways no." I shared with him how terrified I was of him as a little boy and although he did many things with me and was a good teacher, everything was always done his way and my way was never good enough and always received correction and criticism. There was no room around him for my creativity to emerge and blossom. I shared how I spent many days cutting the lawn, trimming bushes, and edging sidewalks in continual and constant fear that I was not doing it quite up to Dad's standards. Dad would come home, look around with a critical eye, grab a pair of weed trimmers, and take a few snips around a fencepost. He would then look at me and say with a big grin, 'There, now it's done right!' I shared that I was devastated by his overbearing self-righteous attitude and bear the scars of low self-worth to this day.

"Johnny, when I was a boy, I wasn't big enough, old enough, or good enough to join my older brothers and Pop at work with them in our fields. I stayed home and mucked out the barn." Dad began crying and I felt his pain and saw his wounded little boy.

Mom later commented, "Johnny, that was the only time I ever saw your father cry."

One year later, while visiting my parents, I asked Dad if he recalled how last Christmas he shared that as a boy, he mucked out the barn while his father and brothers worked the fields. I reminded him how that memory touched him deeply and how he cried reliving the experience.

"Well, no, I don't remember that, Johnny, what about it?" Dad replied. During that year, he shoved Little Charlie back into his basement, locked the door, and erased the experience from his memory. And in the basement, Little Charlie stayed till Dad passed about five years later.

I recall my mentor Ronnie's words, "Johnny, we are given a few opportunities during a lifetime to make major changes. When one arrives, don't pass it up as it may be the last."

I'm sad that Dad passed up this opportunity.

HOME AFTER REHAB - INITIAL SOBRIETY

Life after rehab at home was trying. Dee continued to blame, badger, and degrade me for everything imaginable and was not supportive of my positive attitude and new sobriety. She was resistant to discussing our future and seemed to like me better when I was drinking. Not able to process any of my raw emotions, I descended into despair. My two beautiful young daughters were the love of my life, and the thought of being without them was unimaginable. AA meetings were a big help, and I immersed myself in that wonderful twelve-step program. In Germany in the mid-1980s, however, English-speaking AA meetings were few and distant.

One day, I realized I could not continue living with Dee and remain sober. The two were incompatible, and I needed a partner that was in alignment with my new vision of the future. Dee was unwilling or unable to provide that in our relationship. She was unwilling or unable to change. Perhaps it just wasn't her time. Attempts at rational discussion and communication were met with blame, shame, and a stonewalling attitude. We were on different paths and soon I realized that divorce was inevitable. So began the painful separation process.

Before sobriety, I had only a whiskey bottle in my life toolbox and now, with that gone, my toolbox was empty. My emotional maturity level of a ten or twelve-year-old child was completely incongruent with my forty-year-old Major, United States Air Force body. I lived in constant agitation and fear.

With four years remaining in the Air Force until retirement, and a few strikes against me, I was quite certain that my final assignment would be undesirable. I planned to take whatever was offered and ride it out.

Dee suggested that I go visit my flight surgeon friend, Dr. Roger Landry, have him administer a flying physical, then go visit General Normandy and ask him for a flying assignment. "What? Are you nuts? I can't do that!" I said.

"Why not, Johnny? What do you have to lose? You're going to get a lousy assignment anyway. So, go take a chance." She gave me a great gift with that suggestion and I decided to give it a try.

"Hi, Roger, it's Johnny, and I'd love to come and visit you. I'm asking you to please give me a flight physical and hopefully release me for flying duty. Then, I'm planning to go see General Normandy and ask him for reassignment to a flying position."

"Johnny, come on up and we'll see how it unfolds," he said. Roger was a dear friend and my squadron flight surgeon fifteen years prior at Bitburg Airbase, Germany. He loved flying with me in our F-4 Phantom fighter jet. He was a man of integrity, and had moved quickly up the Air Force medical command ladder.

A week later, I had my current flight physical in hand and drove to my appointment with Brigadier General Robert Normandy. Entering his office, I presented myself to the general with a sharp salute. "Hello, Johnny, you look well. Why have you come to see me?" asked the General.

"Sir, since completion of alcohol rehab a few months ago, I'm feeling positive and capable. I've a debt to repay to the Air Force and being a combat veteran fighter pilot, I'd like to do that by teaching these young pilots how to fly fighter planes for my final tour."

"I see, Johnny. Well, I've got your request, and I'll give this some thought. Thank you for coming by," replied the General and I was dismissed. It was very simple and finished in five minutes.

The following week, my friend and former squadron mate, now the assignments officer, Captain Wilkins, called and said, "Johnny, I'm at a loss for words. You have a below average officer's report on the top, an open letter of *conduct unbecoming an officer*, and now I've a note from some Brigadier General to give you a flying assignment."

"Thanks Dick," I replied, and picked one of the two choices offered. Hanging up the phone, I smiled from ear to ear.

Two months later, I went to Florida and checked out in my new airplane, then drove to my final Air Force assignment in southern California. I was amazed at how life unfolds in my favor when I simply allow it, rather than trying to force my will toward some desired destination.

SARAH AND JENNIFER - AFTER SOBRIETY

The Dee-Johnny separation and divorce began a few months after I returned from alcohol rehab and shortly after Sarah's seventh birthday. The dream of being a full-time dad with my daughters as they grew up was shattered. However, they spent their summers with me in southern California. I loved our time together. Playing with children feels natural for me as I relate well with the six-year-old little boy that is the Little Johnny aspect of my personality.

While Sarah and Jennifer were in Massachusetts during the school term, I played long-distance dad from California. I never wrote to them, but Barney, my "house-bear," did. He mopped the floors, washed the dishes, and wrote letters to Sarah and Jennifer with many misspelled words. He just couldn't get his great big bear paws to hit the correct keys.

Sarah and Jennifer loved Barney Bear letters, and every one contained two $5 bills marked "S" and "J" that he stole from my wallet. He said, "Don't tell your dad that I took two five-dollar bills from his wallet." They never did. He even answered my telephone and took messages.

Let's fast forward for a few minutes about twenty-five years to 2012, when Sarah and Jenn were in their early thirties. One day I shared how I wished to reframe our relationship and to clear any unfinished issues between us, real or perceived.

We sat peacefully, with no distractions, and shared a bit of this and that. I asked if they were open to reframing our relationship. "I know you are my daughters and you know I am your dad. I wish to remove the hierarchical component of our parent-child relationship. I see both of you as mature women and equals and that's how I wish to relate to you from now forward. And I request you to hold the vision of me as a mature man, not your father. A parent and child relationship may be hierarchical and many parents misuse and abuse the parent's power. Some parents may intimidate their children and create distance long after the children are mature adults." We all agreed and reframed our relationship to a level playing field.

Then Jenn said, "I have one thing, Dad, to bring up."

"Sure."

"Once, when I was about three and Sarah was five, we were in our bedroom playing. You came upstairs drunk and mad, hollering and shouting, calling us names and saying we stole your car keys and that we had hidden them in our bedroom. You tore our bedroom apart, frightening us, and we ran out of our room crying. Do you remember that, Dad?"

"Hmm, no, I don't, Jenn, I have no recollection of that," and tried to recall any incident like that. Something didn't feel right to me, as I was not hot-tempered or violent, and this event seemed out of character.

After a pause, Sarah chimed in, "Jenn, your memory of the incident is accurate, and it did happen. However, there is one major error in your version of this event. It was Mom, not Dad, that did this and later, when we told Mom how scared we were, she insisted that Dad was the villain, not her. I was older and have a clear recollection that it was Mom that was drunk and tore our room apart. You thought it was Dad, because that's what Mom told us."

I included this event to emphasize the courage it took for the three of us to open our hearts, speak our truths, and share our feelings to clear the past, no matter how uncomfortable or painful. Truth is the greatest gift one person can give another.

DO THE RIGHT THING - EVEN WHEN NO ONE IS LOOKING

I carefully checked my flight helmet and parachute harness, gathered my flight bag, and headed toward the squadron back door, the flight line, and another fun-filled few hours flying the OV-10 Bronco. The last stop was always the washroom. "Take nothing airborne that you can leave at the airport, Johnny," rang the words of flight instructor Rusty from many years ago. I was grateful to still be flying airplanes, now only a few months away from Air Force retirement on the first of February 1989.

The washroom was large and after drying my hands, I crumpled the paper towel and casually tossed it toward the trash can about ten feet away. I knew I missed before the towel left my hand, but headed toward the door, anyway. Alone in the washroom and approaching the door, I stopped, turned, and saw my crumpled towel on the floor, a foot short of the trash can. Had anyone else been in the washroom, I would not have headed for the door, but would have walked to my towel, picked it up, and tossed it into the trash can. I would have done that without thinking, for my ego wanted Johnny to look responsible. I wanted the world to think I lived full time in total integrity. Picking up my trash was the responsible thing to do.

But on this day, I was alone. There was just me and my crumpled paper towel lying near the trash can on the floor. So why pick it up if nobody will ever know? Let the janitor do it, I mused. Focused on my crumpled paper towel, a flood of emotion erupted and flowed through me. In slo-mo, I walked across the room, bent down, picked up my crumpled towel, and dropped it into the trash can. A gentle voice somewhere within whispered, *Johnny, you will do the right thing from your own integrity now and no longer require a police force to ensure that you do.* In that moment, I shifted from being "externally defined," requiring a police force to keep me in line, to "internally defined," guided by my intuition, integrity, and conscience. I passed through an invisible barrier and no longer required rules to tell me what was an appropriate response to any situation.

Shortly, I started noticing minor changes in my behavior. I drove more responsibly with greater awareness and presence. I noticed that I no longer required speed limit signs to tell me what a safe and reasonable speed was. I just did what I felt was appropriate and speed limit signs reinforced that. I knew what was the right thing to do. I also noticed that my desire to engage in activities that were out of integrity diminished toward zero. Lying, at any level, didn't even come up on the options sheet of choices. I learned integrity in that washroom not from a book, but from a personal experience.

Does this mean that I've been a total saint with impeccable behavior since? No, but the infractions have diminished dramatically. I can no longer fool myself and get away with behavior that is out of integrity.

Henry Thoreau is one of my favorite wisdom masters. This paragraph is from his book Walden, which is chock-full of wisdom. And my paper towel experience is reflected in Thoreau's writing.

H. D. Thoreau - from Walden

"Come home each day from afar, from adventures, perils, and discoveries, with new experience, character, and freedom. If you advance confidently in the direction of your dreams, and endeavor to live the life which you have imagined, you will meet with success unexpected in common hours. You will put some things behind, and pass an invisible boundary. New, universal, and more liberal laws will begin to establish themselves around and within You; or the old laws will be expanded, and interpreted in your favor in a more liberal sense, and you will live with the license of a higher order of beings. In propor-

tion as you simplify your life, the laws of the universe will appear less complex, and solitude will not be solitude, nor poverty poverty, nor weakness weakness. If you have built castles in the air, your work need not be lost; that is where they should be. Now put the foundations under them."

I met with success unexpectedly in that washroom, doing a common act at a common hour.

INSTANT KARMA - THERE IS NO FREE LUNCH

Up early one Sunday morning, I headed out the door for my three-mile jog. In my early forties, fit and loving life, I jogged toward the center of town and through a large strip mall. Rounding a corner, I noticed a car parked in front of the self-serve newspaper dispensers. It was 1988, and these dispensers operated on an honor system where the buyer inserts a dollar-bill, the latch releases, and the buyer takes one paper then closes the lid. But this man took the entire stack and put them in the trunk of his car. As I closed the distance between us, I watched him do the same with the adjacent three newspaper dispensers.

Hustling into his car to make his getaway, he glanced over his shoulder and saw me jogging toward him. I raised my fist and gestured to let him know I saw what he had done. He immediately dropped the car into gear, floored the gas pedal, and made an abrupt left turn, cutting across the lanes of the mostly empty parking lot. Glancing back at me with his head half out the window, I again raised my fist and gestured that I saw what he had done. "KA-BAM!" He stopped instantly when his car plowed directly into a twenty-foot-tall heavy metal light post. Apparently uninjured, he jumped out of his car, shaking his fist at me as I jogged around him and headed for home.

I thought about instant karma in action. Once home, I phoned the local police. "Yes, ma'am," I said to the on-duty officer. "I witnessed the man drive his car into the light pole, and I'm glad that you have sent a patrol car to the scene to help. Please tell your on-site officer that I also saw this man clean out all the newspaper dispensers in front of the hair salon and load all those papers in his trunk. Your officer will find the dispensers empty and his trunk full."

"Thank you, sir," she said. "I'll pass that along."

I changed my shirt, grabbed a baseball cap, and peddled my bike back to the strip mall to find the smashed-up car with an open trunk full of newspapers. The police officer had all he needed, so I peddled back home for morning coffee.

That's instant karma I suppose, or at least a quick payback for a dishonest deed. When people compromise their integrity with deeds like that, they create karma that must, by cosmic law, be resolved sometime in the future. It may happen instantly or it may happen many years or several lifetimes later. But it must resolve.

If people understood that they are accountable for whatever they do and however they act, perhaps some would reconsider how they live their lives. There is no free lunch.

SAMMY - THE GROUND SQUIRREL

Grabbing a handful of peanuts, I walked outside behind my garage, where Sammy the ground squirrel and his tribe lived in little burrows. They were friendly, and I enjoyed coming out here in the early morning before driving to George Air Force Base just a few miles away.

I was completing my twenty-years of active-duty service within the next few months and had time to spend with Sammy most every morning. Stooping low, I tossed several peanuts a few inches from Sammy's front door. A little head poked out, followed shortly by a body. Then Sammy emerged and sat on his haunches. He quickly stuffed a peanut into one cheek, then crammed a second peanut into his other cheek.

And there he sat with his cheeks all puffed out and met my gaze. For several minutes, we locked vision and I thought about how simple and basic his life was. He thanked me for the peanuts and I thanked him for coming out and playing the peanut game with me this morning. In a bit, he turned and disappeared down his burrow.

I thanked him again, rose, and headed toward my car for the short drive to work. I thought of the people I would interact with today and other activities I would have from now till bedtime. I giggled at the thought that this exchange with my friend Sammy Squirrel might be the most significant thing I did all day. Thank you, Sammy.

RONNIE

Arriving at my new Air Force assignment in early January 1986, with nine months of sobriety behind me, I visited Social Actions, the Air Force agency that handles alcohol and drug issues, to check-in. Expecting them to know I was arriving; I was surprised to find that they had never even heard of me. The director, however, mentioned that since I completed alcohol rehab almost one year ago, "We'll just call you complete, Major. But if you desire, you may visit our drug and alcohol counselor, Ronnie, down the hall." I went to meet Ronnie.

He was a civilian, about my height, slight of build, bearded, hippy-ish, and reminded me of Willie Nelson. He wore a little skinny necktie with the very skinny back part hanging down longer than the not-quite-as-skinny front part. I silently laughed. I thought, *what's this little Willie Nelson going to teach me?* And he thought, *uh oh, another arrogant fighter pilot!*

Over time, we became inseparable brothers rooted in respect and love. I found an authentic teacher in Ronnie who loved me uncondi-tionally. I listened to everything he said and didn't argue with him. I did what he suggested.

He was a man of few words and he was available to teach anyone that had a desire to learn. His eyes were penetrating laser beams.

Although my follow-on program was complete, Ronnie invited me to attend his two-hour weekly drug and alcohol recovery group. My commander agreed to keep my flying schedule clear for that time, and I immersed myself with Ronnie and his recovery group. The participants were mostly young airman involved in alcohol or drug incidents on or around the base. Ronnie was a skilled group facilitator.

"Okay, Joe, tell me about your AA program. What step are you on?" asked Ronnie of a young airman in group.

"Well, I'm angry that I'm working so many hours and I don't have any free time to go to AA meetings and I'm very pissed-off that I lost my license."

"Enough!" hollered Ronnie. "You're one pissed-off kid all right and you don't have a chance at life or sobriety until you get rid of your anger, which, by the way, you got from your father! Your dad was an angry man!" said Ronnie. It was a statement, not a question. "Wasn't he?" asked Ronnie, looking directly at the young airman.

The airman looked surprised and replied, "Well, yes, he was very angry all the time, it seems."

Ronnie pressed a bit more. "And until you own and diffuse your anger that you've acquired from your father, you haven't a chance at sobriety or a peaceful life."

I was dumbstruck. How did Ronnie know that? The airman hadn't said twenty words and never mentioned his father, and yet Ronnie knew all of this about him and his father. Ronnie always saw deeper into someone than I could and I wanted so much to be like him and gain that level of insight. I bumped him up a few feet higher on his pedestal.

"Hey, Ronnie, you remember the angry airman in group that had all that anger and you told him he got it from his father?"

"Uh-huh," Ronnie grunted, as we enjoyed dinner at the local diner a few days later.

"Well, how did you know his father was such an angry man?"

Ronnie stared directly into my eyes and motioned me to lean across the table, so we were closer. I was going to hear a secret that would unlock the knowledge of the universe for me, I thought. I came to within a foot of his face. He glanced around to make sure no one was watching us or listening to the incredible gift of insight that I was about to receive. Staring like a laser into my eyes, he whispered, "It's always the friggin father, Johnny!"

After a long pause, I asked, "Always?"

"Yes, always. No exceptions." That was it. Ronnie settled back, and we returned to our dinners.

"Naturally," Ronnie continued, "if there is no active biological father, it is the father substitute, male role model, or occasionally a woman." The message was clear to me. My father went from Mr. God to a raging, angry man with a short temper. He had unresolved childhood traumas that he brought forward into our relationship and projected on me. I began to realize and see that there was more to my childhood than I had previously thought. Perhaps I'm repressing the bad stuff and only remembering the good stuff. Hmmm.

A month later, I visited my parents for several days. Upon returning, Ronnie asked me how my visit with my parents went. "It was wonderful! Mom and Dad are the sweetest parents in the world, and I love them very much."

Silence, then he said, "I suggest you take another trip home, Johnny, and this time open your eyes and ears." He turned and walked away.

"Hey wait! What do you mean, Ronnie?" He kept walking and my shouts fell on deaf ears. His words about, 'It's only the father,' seeped into my consciousness.

Several months later, I again visited my parents, this time remembering what Ronnie had told me about opening my eyes and ears. For the first time, I heard their childish bickering and continual cheap shots that they took at each other. I witnessed Dad's anger and constant sharing of negative experiences. I saw my mother's victim-mode mentality, with the constant retelling of every medical issue and hospitalization they've had for the last twenty-five years in vivid detail. It was a never-ending circle of doom and gloom that I had been oblivious to.

Dad could not drive his car more than a few blocks without getting angry and making derogatory cheap shot remarks at other drivers. I saw my mother's denial of his anger. 'Oh, that's just your father's way, Johnny,' and I understood now why I left home at eighteen for university and, other than brief visits, never returned home for very long.

What I believed was normal, healthy behavior, was totally dysfunctional behavior. Seeing the truth of my childhood life was terrifying, and I realized that there was much more work for me to do than just not drink. My life without alcohol was definitely better, but I was waking up to the mountain of work I had remaining to do. 'Johnny, most people settle for mediocrity. Don't be like most.' I realized I had only scratched the surface and my journey of recovery had just begun.

I listened and learned from Ronnie, and eventually joined him for several years for three weekly drug and alcohol recovery groups on our Air Force Base.

Entering the base jail for one of our weekly groups, I asked a young crew-chief during his first week of incarceration how it was in here for him.

"It's horrible," he replied with anger and disgust in his voice.

Six months later, I again asked the same young crew-chief the same question, "How is it in here for you now?"

"Oh, it's not so bad. I kind of like the structure, and the food's good, too." After a while, denial softens a not-so-pleasant experience and the horrible becomes acceptable.

I saw how I was doing this same thing to my early home life. Denial was softening my lacking childhood into something acceptable. I was minimizing and suppressing many of my childhood experiences.

One Friday afternoon, out of the blue, Ronnie asked, "Is a dandelion a flower or a weed, Johnny?" Before I could answer, he said, "Think about it this weekend and tell me Monday." He was gone in a flash.

I read about, studied, and restudied dandelions all weekend without coming to any conclusion. I'll tell him dandelions are flowers because it sounds better than calling them weeds. I'll apply the glass is half-full rather than half-empty theory. This will mean I have a positive attitude and for sure, that's what Ronnie wants to hear.

I had it all figured out. On Monday, Ronnie asked, "Well, what's the answer?"

"It's a flower, of course, Ronnie."

"Nope," he said.

"Weed?"

"Nope."

"Well, it's got to be one or the other, so what gives?"

"Johnny, it's simply a dandelion. See things as they are and don't judge or categorize them based on experience."

"Is a flat tire good or bad?" he asked.

"Bad, of course," I quickly replied.

"You don't quite get it yet, Johnny. It's a flat tire, neither good nor bad, just simply a flat tire. See the world as it is without judgement. That flat tire holds gold somehow. Perhaps the flat tire will remind you to check your tires more often or perhaps prevent you from an accident that was waiting for you further down the road. Just see the world as it is without judgement and that will free up your energy and release you from dualistic mind." Smiling, he turned and walked away.

Ronnie saw more in me than I saw in myself. He was my teacher, and I listened to every word he said. Nearing the end of my twenty-year Air Force career, I thought about applying for a pilot position with a major airline. With my deep-seated sense of low self-worth, I could not see myself as an airline pilot.

"Johnny, you've got the flying skills and personality. Of course, you'll get hired. I already see you in the cockpit of an airliner," said Ronnie.

"Really!" I exclaimed, for I saw myself as 4-foot tall in an airline full of 6-foot pilots. But I gave it a try.

Applying to American Airlines, a question on the pilot application was, "Have you ever been diagnosed or treated for alcoholism?" Surely no airline wants to hire an alcoholic pilot, I thought, and moved my pencil toward the no box. Hold it, Johnny! Your life is now one of rigorous honesty, not convenient honesty. So, I checked the "yes" box, then solicited four letters of character reference and credibility from my squadron commander, Ronnie, and two other credible people. I attached them to my application and included a brief cover letter explaining my alcoholism. Placing an extra stamp on the envelope in case it was near the weight limit, I slid it into the mailbox and pulled up the flag.

Imagine my surprise and joy at receiving a positive response from American Airlines inviting me to their headquarters for an interview. Living in integrity and allowing life to unfold was establishing itself within and around me.

BEST FRIEND OR WORST ENEMY

"Hey Johnny," hollered Ronnie as we approached each other, heading toward the gym for a workout and three-mile run. "There's a guy that will be at my place early this evening for a bit, and I want you to meet him. He's very special and I believe you will benefit from this meeting."

I trusted my mentor, Ronnie, with my life. "OK, Ronnie."

"Great, stop by my house about 6-ish. It won't take long and then we'll go get a bite of dinner."

"Thanks, Ronnie, see ya later." He was gone in a flash.

Opening the door, Ronnie welcomed me and said, "I've asked this special man to wait down the hall and, in a few minutes, we'll go meet him. He can be your best friend or worst enemy, Johnny, depending on your relationship with him." Excited, and uneasy, I couldn't imagine who this man was.

"Let's go." We walked across Ronnie's living room and down the hall. At the bedroom door, Ronnie told me to stop and look into the room. No one was there. "Johnny, he is right behind you." I turned and there he was, staring at me in a full-length mirror.

"Meet your best friend or worst enemy, Johnny," Ronnie continued, "I've learned over the years that no one can do anything for me of real or lasting value. I must do it myself. And how I treat myself sets the course of my life. These are my choices, Johnny, no one else's. Either I treat myself respectfully and set a positive course for my life, or I treat myself disrespectfully and set a negative course for my life. Knowing this deeply in my heart is a major step toward spiritual maturity. I know you understand.

"Everything that's ever happened to you, ultimately, you've done to yourself. You understand more deeply now that you create your own experience. You are your own tormentor, and your own savior.

"Don't waste your time asking anything or anyone outside of yourself to rescue you from yourself or from the situation that you have created for yourself and are currently in. Know that you, Johnny, grow and mature only when you assume full responsibility for every choice you make, no matter what it is. Align yourself with the powers of divinity and the Earth Mother and use these energies to advance forward on your earthwalk.

"Also, when you look deeply, you realize that no one has ever done anything worse to you than you've done to yourself. I suggest you begin by frequently looking with love at Johnny in the mirror and telling him often that you love and support him. This is not vanity. You're affirming yourself and reinforcing that you care deeply about yourself. Doing this aligns you with universal energies and empowers you. You are waking up and recognizing your beauty, talents, and abilities. Honoring yourself is sacred work. Please take this lesson to heart and apply it."

"Thanks, Ronnie, for the powerful lesson." I muttered.

Ronnie's wisdom still rings true some thirty-five years later. This is an important piece. Now go love the man or woman in your full-length mirror.

A BROADER PERSPECTIVE

Totally absorbed in an issue with a former wife, I felt about half alive. I saw only this issue and nothing else. It grew larger in my mind, minute by minute, and I could not shake it off.

Completing my three-mile jog, I stood in the gym's lobby, staring at nothing in particular, when Ronnie approached. "What's going on that's got you so tied up, Johnny?"

"An issue with my former, that's all."

"Well, you look about half dead and your eyes are as distant as the rings of Saturn."

"It's all I can think about, and all I can see right now, Ronnie. It won't go away and I don't know how to get past this. All I can think about is her and this issue."

"Close your eyes, Johnny. I'm going to position you by this wall with the bulletin board." He guided me to a position, then said. "OK, open up and tell me what you see."

"There's a flyer directly in front of me about house-sitting for people on vacation."

"Notice, Johnny, that you cannot see much else, and that flyer is essentially your entire world. That flyer represents your former partner and this consuming issue. Now, I'm pulling you back from the wall a few feet. Tell me what you see now?"

"Well, I can easily see about eight flyers. Some are house-sitting, a few are dog-sitting, and one is from a little girl looking for her lost puppy. The flyer says that half his right ear is missing from a coyote attack, he only has three legs left, blotches of fur are falling out from an old illness, he's hearing impaired, blind in his right eye, and half his tail is missing from a fight with a truck. She says he's very gentle and answers to the name of Lucky."

"So, moving away from your issue even a few feet will reduce its impact on you. Now, Johnny, I'm pulling you way back so you can see the entire wall, i.e., the big picture. Notice how small the original house-sitting flyer is when viewed from this perspective. Life is like this also, Johnny. When I step back from any life issue, it will fade in intensity and perhaps even resolve itself. I'll no longer be consumed by it and I'm free to enjoy the day. Using this tool and practicing this technique allows for a gentler, softer life."

THE I KNOW GAME - LISTENING IN PRESENCE

Ever have someone ask you a question and as you reply they interrupt with, "I know"? When that occurs, I feel like I've been jabbed in the gut with a little pitchfork. Or in conversation, I may share a little and the other person interrupts with, "I know." Another pitchfork in the gut! What's going on? Why do people push people away with comments like, "I know"?

To me, it means that they probably do not know and don't want to know, or I've touched a sensitive nerve within them. This is a knee-jerk defense mechanism used to avoid hearing what one does not want to hear. Egos hate learning something new, hate being wrong, and hate having their nerves touched. So, opportunities to learn and grow are often missed because of the ego. Sad, isn't it? Yet many frequently interject or interrupt with, "I know."

I used to do this until my mentor, Ronnie, painfully pointed it out to me. He began sharing one day, and I made the "I know" comment. He stopped talking. After a pause, I asked, "What are you waiting for?"

"I stopped, Johnny, because you just told me you already know."

To me the "I know" was like saying, "Uh huh!" But Ronnie called me on my words and I realized what I was doing. He then explained why I was doing it. It wasn't complimentary, but Ronnie got his point across and I learned something that day.

Even if I do know what someone is sharing, I'll not say, "I know," for it has an air of arrogance and superiority about it. When someone passes me information or shares something with me, instead of saying, "I know," I now say, "Thank you."

Ronnie taught me to listen in presence. "Johnny," he said, "when someone is sharing, be a present listener. Don't interrupt, don't fidget around, don't shake your head yes or no, don't say stupid distracting things like 'Uh huh' and don't plan your response to their share. Just listen in full presence, make eye-contact, and pay attention. You might hear something, that you would most likely miss if you were being a distraction. Most people that are distractions want attention and that is just another way to get it. Don't be one of them."

"Thanks, Ronnie."

PHANTOM BACKSEATER RICK

The Vietnam air war was raging during October 1972, and I was fragged one night with another F-4 Phantom to fly in search of targets near Quang Ki, in the southern sector of North Vietnam. At our intel briefing, we were told of a Phantom that was shot down in our fragged target area the previous day, and the condition and location of the two crew members were unknown. "Listen up on Survival Radio Frequency and try to establish radio contact with the crew, if possible. They were seen descending in their parachutes near Quang Ki. Perhaps they are in hiding. But if you hear from them, we might send in a rescue mission and get them out of there."

I felt grief and sadness when one of my fellow flyers was shot down. It could just as easily have been me.

Flight lead's Phantom carried high-intensity night flares that allowed us to see ground targets sufficiently on the darkest of nights and visually drop ordnance with accuracy. Flight lead also carried white phosphorous (Willie Pete) marking rockets that emitted a luminescent white smoke on ground impact easily seen several miles away. My Phantom carried 8 x 900-pound cluster bomb canisters, two external outboard fuel tanks, one radar-guided Sparrow air-to-air missile, two Sidewinder infra-red heat-seeking missiles, and one radar jamming pod. My F-4D was a formidable weapon, and I was the perfect man to fly it.

Take-off, join-up, air-refueling, and entry into our target area were uneventful. "Owl 5's dropping down for a look at the Quang Ki Ferry" crackled in my earphones. I acknowledged and watched flight lead's F-4 fade and disappear into the blackness below. The Quang Ki Ferry was nothing like what we might imagine a ferry to be. It was simply a small barge either pulled across this narrow river or powered with a small motor and carried perhaps two trucks and a few people. Not one light was visible anywhere on the ground. I was flying in total darkness on instruments. Willie and I maintained an approximate position over the ground with radar reference to the North Vietnam coastline about twenty miles to the east.

I set up my weapons panel to drop one cluster bomb canister and the dull yellow glow of the weapons station select light confirmed my switch settings. Willie, my favorite GIB (Guy In Back) and I made small talk when I saw two quick bright flashes below me. "There, Willie, on the left." Flight lead had just pickled off two flares. We waited but the sky did not light up as expected, and it was soon apparent that these flares were either duds, or flight lead failed to arm them.

"Goddam it, coming back around for another pass," crackled in my headset and Willie and I both knew that lead had missed an arming switch and released duds. Failing to arm is easy to do in the middle of the night over enemy territory.

I patiently waited at 8,000 feet noting how peaceful, quiet, snug, and safe I felt in my trusty Phantom jet. Shortly, flight lead pickled off two more flares and the area was illuminated in a ghostly white light. My pulse quickened with anticipation. I saw the river area, armed my bomb, checked for a dull green "armed" light and waited. "Nothing moving across the river," crackled in my ears. "I'm moving toward the coast." My heart sank a bit, I safed the master arm switch, checked for the yellow light, and pointed my Phantom toward the coast. I did not personally know the crew of that downed Phantom but remembered that their names were Jim and Rick. We uneventfully completed our mission on other targets and returned to home base.

Fast Forward about fifteen years to the late 1980s while I was enjoying my last Air Force assignment in Southern California flying the OV-10 Bronco. One day at the gym, a Phantom back-seater and I were getting dressed when I read his name tag and it rang a bell of a past distant memory.

"Hey Rick, weren't you in the 8th Wing at Ubon, Thailand in late 1972?" I asked.

"Yup, sure was," he said.

"Did you get shot down near Kwang Ki and spend a few months as a POW in Hanoi?

"Yup, sure did," he said.

I continued, "Well, I was in the 497th Night Owl Squadron and the evening following your ejection, we went hunting for targets at the Quang Ki Ferry. On the first pass, lead forgot his master arm switch and both flares didn't ignite. He flew back over and pickled off two more flares, but the river was quiet."

"Hold it right there, Johnny," (he read my name tag). I waited while Rick stared at me. After a long pause, he said, "Let me tell you the rest of that story. Jim, the front-seater, and I both made it to the ground OK. But the North Vietnamese shortly captured me. The following night they took me north toward Hanoi and I was put on the Quang Ki ferry to cross the river. I prayed we wouldn't be spotted crossing the river by Phantoms flying night missions in the Quang Ki area."

He continued, "When I heard F-4's in the distance approaching, I thought for sure I'd die on that barge. I could not see the Phantoms in the darkness, but your flight lead flew right over the ferry and I saw the two sparks from the flare ejections and thought, 'it's all over.' But neither of those flares lit. I couldn't believe my luck and I heard the Phantom swing wide in a circle and approach again for another flare release.

"Meanwhile, the barge crew hustled us across the river and moored us under some trees along the north bank. It didn't take long for us to complete the crossing and there we sat as the second round of flares ejected and ignited right over us, turning night into day. I prayed that the Owl FAC would not see our little ferry partially hidden in the trees along the north bank, and apparently, he didn't."

Tears came pouring from my eyes as I relived the mission and realized that I was looking into the eyes of a man that I would have surely killed had the first round of flares lit. I told Rick that I had CBU on board, armed and ready to drop on him. We locked eyes for a long time and cried. There are no words to describe this experience.

AMERICAN AIRLINES

Dad was a practical man with lots of knowledge and common sense. He taught me to use my head and think for myself. "Johnny, set your alarm in the morning a few minutes early so you don't have to rush and this will allow you some extra time in case you break a shoelace." Dad had many admirable qualities.

American Airlines scheduled my final hiring interview for pilot at AA corporate headquarters near DFW airport, Texas, at 8 am on Wednesday, February 8, 1989. I arrived at my quarters on an Air Force Base about an hour from DFW airport on Monday afternoon, February 6. Tuesday, the day before my interview, I carefully laid out my clothes, checked the shoelaces, the necktie, the shirt, the jacket, everything I would wear and then drove to American Airlines headquarters to familiarize myself with the route and timing. When I returned to the Air Force Base, I parked my '78 VW camper on a slight downhill to roll-start my bus in case of battery failure during the night. I stacked the cards in my favor every way I could think of and felt relaxed and prepared for this important interview.

Wednesday morning, I awoke, showered, shaved, and drove to the American Airlines Headquarters parking lot. There, I sat in my bus in an empty lot near the front door of AA headquarters an hour before my 8 am scheduled appointment.

Entering the main lobby, I joined three other potential pilots and made small talk waiting for our third and final hiring interview. I felt confident and peaceful.

"Good morning gentleman, I'm Johanna Hartman and I'll be your escort for your simulator session this morning. Let's see, David, David Sodaburg? Humm, David, are you here this morning?" The four of us looked at each other and silently shook our heads no. Apparently, David was not amongst us. Johanna consulted her list and asked, "Johnny are you here?" Smiling, I acknowledged yes. "Welcome to your third and final hiring interview with American Airlines. Let's go fly a simulator Johnny," Johanna said and we headed out of the lobby.

Strapping into the Boeing 707 simulator with retired AA Captain Rick Saunders, we went for a short flight around the traffic pattern and landed. Rick tested my basic flying skills and said, "You passed just fine, Johnny, and I believe that you'll make a fine pilot with us assuming that your paperwork is in order. That'll be taken care of this afternoon with two other retired captains." Flying airplanes has always been easy for me and although I'd never flown a Boeing 707, the simulator experience went well.

After lunch, I entered a conference room and met two retired AA Captains perusing my hiring papers. "Hello, Johnny, I'm Captain John Lawler and this is my colleague, Captain Phil Strom. Please have a seat and make yourself comfortable." Feeling at ease, I sat peacefully as they scanned my papers. Captain Lawler spoke, "Well, Johnny, I see you have over 500 hours of combat time in Vietnam flying the F-4 Phantom. Do you think you can get one of our jets into LaGuardia, New York?"

"Yes, sir," I beamed with a smile. "I believe so."

He smiled as Captain Strom, looking my way, commented, "I've been doing these interviews for about five years and never have I seen anyone claim their alcoholism on their application. I'm guessing others were alcoholic but never mentioned it, hoping we would not find out. You must be solid in your sobriety, Johnny, to be up front and claim ownership as you have. Your level of honesty and openness impresses me. Speaking for both of us, I feel that you're the kind of pilot we want at American Airlines. You'll be hearing from us soon." We shook hands, and I was respectfully dismissed. I felt larger than life and had to duck to avoid hitting my head on the eight-foot-high doorway.

In March 1989, with four years sobriety under my belt and only two months retired from the Air Force, I was hired as a pilot by American Airlines. The "AA" on the front of my uniform hat had a double meaning.

Honesty! There are no compromises. There are no small lies either. Am I in or sort of in? That is the question. Do I wish to live life fully or do I wish to live life part time? I was abstinent for about four years now and it pleased me that my sobriety was sufficiently strong to answer all the questions on the hiring application truthfully. I felt solid.

Sustainment

Sustainment is my key.
With honesty and integrity.
I will Succeed, live spiritually.
For success is my responsibility.

jmb

After one year with American Airlines, I volunteered as the domicile union rep to help our pilots returning from alcohol rehab regain their suspended medicals and return to flying. One day, Mitch, who had been sober for several months said, "I've been fired, and am on way out the door."

"What happened, Mitch?" I asked.

"Well, I had a DUI about five years before American hired me and didn't put that information, as requested, on my initial job application. Getting this recent DUI pulled the FAA back into the picture, and the company discovered that I lied on my application. I'm being fired for lying." A deep sense of gratitude welled up inside me. I had been truthful about my past on my initial job application and he had not. I remembered my self-discussion about rigorous honesty versus convenient honesty. We bid farewell and parted.

"We are only as sick as our secrets," is a little quote occasionally shared in Alcoholics Anonymous, and it's true. Secrets are heavy, require energy to hold and protect, compromise honesty, create fear and distrust, require denial systems, and contribute to negative energy patterns. It was not safe for me to be honest as a child, so I learned how to lie and that became normal behavior for me. Suspicion and mistrust followed. In the Air Force, I was constantly in fear of "someone finding out." It didn't matter what it was they found out because there was always something I did that was questionable. I was constantly edgy and on guard. At American Airlines, I had no secrets concerning my job. Being appropriate and truthful, honoring integrity, setting emotional boundaries, not feeling responsible for the neurotic behaviors of others, all served me well.

The longest journey one can travel is from their head to their heart.

HONESTY - JENNIFER AND THE LEMONADE

The Alcoholics Anonymous Big Book states that, "This is a program of rigorous honesty", and it is. But what is rigorous honesty? There are many levels of honesty and one's honesty depends on how conscious one is.

When I was drinking, I believed I was honest because I wouldn't knock over a Seven-Eleven. And I'd make every effort to locate and return to the owner a found wallet with every dollar still there. That's honesty, of course, but that's easy honesty. It's easy to see and easy to do. That's clear-cut, black and white honesty. However, I wasn't honest enough to own my alcohol addiction.

It took several major life events to crack open my ego sufficiently to allow for a deeper level of honesty to emerge. The path to freedom requires deep levels of honesty.

Sobriety is 5% inspiration and 95% perspiration. Having the courage to be rigorously honest and do my inner work, especially when short-term gratifications are calling, is a tremendous challenge. It's very easy to fall asleep and drift back into yesterday's behavior patterns. I'm learning that I'm worth the effort to move forward.

Our family sat enjoying a lunch at the employee's cafeteria at Chicago O'Hare Airport one afternoon when my nine-year-old daughter, Jenn, checking out the receipt says, "Dad, we have four lemonades here and you were charged for three."

"Well, Jenn, sometimes those things happen but I guess it's OK since it's only one dollar, and the cashier looks busy now. Since there are many people in line, let's just let it go. They'll make it up somehow and it all comes out in the wash, anyway." I went back to my sandwich.

I quickly forgot about this event, until, a few weeks later at 3 am, I sat bolt upright in bed and saw the big lie. Here's my little Miss Honesty holding a mirror for me to see my lack of honesty and integrity, and I dismissed her with a pile of rationalizations.

Over dinner the following evening, I shared my 3 am realization with my family and owned my lack of integrity. I began listening more to my little teachers because of that experience and thanked Jenn for demonstrating honesty to me.

Next trip to that cafeteria, I went to the cashier. "Here's a dollar for a medium lemonade."

"Thank you, Captain, where's your lemonade?"

"I drank it a month ago, good day," and left.

MONSTER BOY

Excited to fly my MD-80 jet, I entered American Airlines operations on a beautiful March morning in 1994. I was the First Officer (co-pilot) paired with Captain Joe Armor. This was our first trip together and I was looking forward to a great trip with him, confident that he was skilled, pleasant, and a great guy to fly with as the vast majority of American Airlines captains were. Checking in at Flight Operations, I grabbed my kit bag, walked to the gate, greeted the gate agents and flight attendants, did my outside airplane preflight inspection, and set up our cockpit. Captain Joe arrived, tossed his kitbag over his seat, settled in and never even looked my way. Very strange!

I never saw a captain act like this, and a knot of fear began forming in my gut. "Before Starting Engines Checklist," barked Joe. Those were the first words out of his mouth. There was no hello or greeting, no friendly gesture, not even a smile. Maybe he's had a rough week, I thought, as I felt the knot of fear in my gut grow.

Finally, Captain Joe turned toward me and spoke, "Here's our crew briefing. When I want your help, I'll ask for it! Any questions?"

"Nope," I replied and felt the ball of fear in my gut expand. Joe and I were both in our late 40s and I knew this airplane well and how to fly it. Why was I so off balance and fearful of Captain Joe? He was tall, square jawed, rugged looking, and dressed in a perfectly tailored uniform. He was a "John Wayne" kind of guy and in an airliner cockpit, the captain has total authority. What the Captain says, goes.

Completing our three-day flying sequence, I was totally whipped. Joe found fault with every little thing I did, even though they were all correct procedurally. Some things were just not done Joe's way. Sometimes, my way was better, but that didn't seem to matter to Joe. Captain Joe allowed only his way in his cockpit.

After only a few legs, it was apparent that I was the accomplished, polished pilot of this crew, and consistently flew and landed smoother than he did. Yet there was not one word of acknowledgment from Joe.

I thought about Joe my first night home and wondered why I could not brush off this painful feeling of "he's better than me." A darkness settled around me as I reflected on our next trip three days ahead.

I sat with these feelings and in a flash of insight, got the clarity I sought. Joe was a frightened little boy in an American Airlines captain's uniform holding the world at arm's length with stiff, stoic, rigid attitudes, manners, and behaviors. He was all bluff and bravado. Monster Boy poured out of me.

MONSTER BOY

MONSTER BOY approaches,
I quiver slightly.
I must face MONSTER BOY now.
I have feared him all my life.

Cold eyes, rigid posture, impeccable uniform,
He appears powerful, confident, commanding.
He barks orders,
I listen, cower, then I pause.

I breathe slowly, calmly,
Easy breaths, I begin to see reality.
My peacefulness, my power, my Self, all return,
MONSTER BOY weakens.

> *I look into his eyes,*
> *I see fear, insecurity.*
> *I hear his shallow voice from deep within,*
> *I feel his hollowness, anxiety.*
>
> *I smile, I know him now,*
> *He shrinks within his Uniform.*
> *I see the frightened child,*
> *MONSTER BOY is no more.*

Three days later, I entered AA Operations and saw Captain Joe across the room. I walked to him, gently put my hand on his shoulder and said, "Hi, Joe, good to see you." He stiffened at my touch and glared at my smiling face. He knew I had him pegged and that his game of intimidation with me was over.

Joe was uneasy and uncomfortable this three-day trip and I met his arrogance and bravado with peacefulness, kindness, and gentleness. No matter how he acted, I remained calm and related to him as the recalcitrant six-year-old child that he was. This trip was much easier for me.

Years later, I connected my father with this event and understood the projection of my fears of Dad on Joe. And it took several more years before I could release my feelings of resentment and fear that I held toward Dad. This experience with Captain Joe was a significant event in my healing and I thank you, Joe, for being a teacher for me.

From the Captain Joe incident and Monster Boy, I saw more clearly why I feared authority figures and understand the tie-in to my childhood fear of my father.

Mom, in her later years, complained about most everything. Somehow, she seemed to think that no matter what she said, those around her would simply suck it up. Pat caught the brunt of Mom's complaining because Pat spent much more time with Mom, in her final years, than I did. Mom took liberties and would say things like, "It's a mother's right to worry," or "I'm your mother and I've a right to ask these questions and say these things." Mom was not about to change.

I began relating to Mom as an out of control six-year-old rather than my mother. This helped, and I didn't feel conflicted if I didn't obey my mother. This tool allowed me to put aside feelings that I was being disrespectful to my mother and allowed me to function around Mom much more easily.

Try it and see for yourself how well this technique works.

MOM AND THE AIRPLANE STROBE LIGHTS

Take-off, climb-out, and level-off at cruise altitude were routine and a lot of fun. I loved flying the American Airlines Super-80 passenger jet. Completing our cruise checklist, I slid my seat back and gazed out the windshield at the awesome view of New York City and the coastline of New Jersey. We cruised smoothly at three quarters of the speed of sound on our flight from Providence, Rhode Island, to Raleigh-Durham, North Carolina.

It was an incredibly clear, moonless, November evening about 7 pm, with a jillion stars visible, wishing us a safe and pleasant flight. Flying has never been routine for me and I was thrilled to be a part of transporting 130 passengers safely to their destination in living-room comfort. I gently touched the control yolk, throttles, and several knobs and switches all within easy reach. I marveled at how our one-hundred-and thirty-thousand-pound jet could fly so safely and smoothly seven miles in the sky. I was always in awe of the flying experience. For me, it wasn't a job, it was a passion, and I always gave it all I had, plus a little extra.

We cruised south along the New Jersey shore a few miles out over the Atlantic Ocean, as the bright lights of Atlantic City came into view. I thought of my parents at home just a few miles inland from Atlantic City when a brilliant idea flashed in my head. "I'm going to go get the forward air-phone and bring it back to the cockpit. Be right back," I said to a smiling Captain Mike Zeidman sitting peacefully in the left seat. I slipped out the cockpit door, swiped my credit card in the air-phone base, and returned with the air-phone in hand. In 1995, we had only two portable air-phones for passenger use on our MD-80 jets. Fortunately, the one near the cockpit was available.

Approaching Atlantic City, I dialed Mom and soon her voice crackled in my ear. "Hello?"

"Hi Mom, it's Johnny."

"Hi Johnny, you sound like you're a long way off."

"Well, Mom, actually, I'm fairly close and getting closer. Is Dad home too?"

"Nope, he's out for a bit tonight."

"OK Mom, here's what I want you to do. Please put on a warm coat and take your portable phone with you out the front door and stand in the middle of the front yard. Don't ask a lot of questions, and when you are there, I've a great big surprise for you."

"OK, Johnny, if you say so."

So, Mom suited up, and within a few minutes, she was back on the phone. "Ok Johnny, I'm in the front yard, now what?"

"Mom, look at the sky directly above Atlantic City and search for the flashing white strobe lights of an airplane moving from your left to your right." I waited a few seconds then asked if she had found it. "Yes, Johnny, I see a blinking white light now and it's moving from left to right."

"OK, Mom, watch that flashing light and count out loud to three."

"One, two, three," Mom counted. I switched off the outside beacon and strobes. "OH, THE FLASHING WHITE LIGHT DISAPPEARED, JOHNNY!"

"OK Mom, count to three again."

"OK, one, two, three." I switched on all the outside lights. "OH, THERE YOU ARE!" Mom exclaimed excitedly.

"Count again, Mom."

"One, two, three. YOU DISAPPEARED AGAIN, JOHNNY. One, two, three. And there you are way over there."

"Well, Mom, we're getting a bit south of Atlantic City, and thanks for playing the airplane-lights game with me."

"Oh Johnny, you are always fooling around, aren't you? I sure hope the passengers didn't mind sitting in the dark while you turned off your airplane lights."

"Well, Mom, I only switched off the outside strobes. I left the inside lights alone, so the passengers were unaffected and didn't know that we just had a little fun with the strobe lights. Well, we're pretty far away now, Mom. Say hi to Dad and we'll chat soon."

"Thank you, Johnny, for flying by and signaling with your lights."

"You're so welcome, Mom."

PLAYING WITH THE CLOUDS

Flying American Airlines Super-80 jets was never work for me. It was my sport. As the captain, when the entry door closed, I was responsible for the aircraft, passengers, and crew of five or six. I used all my experience and skills to give my passengers the safest, smoothest, and most comfortable ride I could. I practiced my flying skills and worked diligently. I was competent and proficient.

A few pilots were lazy and settled for mediocrity. It didn't seem to matter to them how gentle or firm a landing was, so long as it was safe. These pilots didn't seem to care how fast they rolled into or out of a turn, how abruptly they leveled off, or how aggressively they handled the aircraft controls. But it mattered to me and for the five years that I flew with American Airlines as an MD-80 captain, I encouraged my first officers (co-pilots) to hone their flying skills to be the best.

My Air Force Phantom fighter-jet instructor, Rusty, from years past, told me to always fly my jet like I was part of the Air Force Thunderbirds flight demo team. And to fly my jet all the way from the engine start to engine shutdown. 'Don't ever settle for mediocrity anywhere, Johnny,' Rusty suggested, and I didn't. I strove to be a top-notch pilot in the air and on the ground. And I did this in a relaxed, casual manner. I never cracked a sweat on final approach while landing, even in the worst of storms. The most important gauge on the aircraft's dashboard is the fuel gauge and if I had fuel, I had options.

A captain once told me when I was a new co-pilot, 'Johnny, when landing, take what you have at fifty feet in the air, hang on and don't change anything, and you'll have an acceptable safe landing every time.' Perhaps he was right, but I didn't do that. I worked harder in that last fifty feet than most pilots and a smooth, safe landing was my reward. Different strokes for different folks, I guess. I didn't say anything to that captain, and coined an eight-word instruction for a smooth landing every time. "Never, never, never, never, never, never, give up!"

Flying from New York to Chicago O'Hare one afternoon, we were about seventy-five miles from the airport at 20,000 feet. As we started across Lake Michigan on the Pullman arrival, we received a descent clearance. "American one, two, three, descend to cross Fubar intersection at ten thousand."

"Ah, Roger, Chicago American one, two, three, out of flight level two-zero-zero, and cleared to cross Fubar at ten thou," growled First Officer Jasper Saunders. I had plenty of time to make the crossing restriction with a normal descent, but I saw an opportunity to have a little fun. About seven thousand feet below us was a smooth cloud deck, so I immediately hustled down and leveled off just a few feet above the clouds at thirteen thousand feet. The sensation of speed doing 400 mph a few feet above the cloud deck was exhilarating.

"Folks, from the cockpit, I invite you to take a peek out your window. You'll notice that we're hustling right along just a few feet above this cloud deck. It looks like snow covered ground, but I assure you it's not and, in a few minutes, we'll begin a gentle descent right through these clouds and on into O'Hare. Enjoy these sights and thanks for flying with us."

It was awesome. The passengers and crew received a special treat that fine day. After a few minutes, I slowed and began a gentle descent into the clouds. I loved playing with the clouds.

I don't fly airplanes for American Airlines anymore, but I still play with life in a similar way. Having fun feels like the right way to live.

CONTROLLING THE STOCK MARKET

Our pilots reached a wage and benefits contract agreement with the company and were compensated for past wages with stock options. The price of these options was five dollars over the current market value of AA stock. I received my allotment and retained my options rather than selling, for I felt that the AA stock price would rise. And I was correct, as over time, AA stock rose from $25/share, to $30/share, and then to $40/share. As the stock continued to rise, I placed an order to sell all shares at $50/share.

AA stock soon approached my $50/share sell price, and I sat riveted to my computer one day as I watched the price increase through $49.50, to $49.85, then $49.90. It closed at $49.98 per share. I owned 400 shares, and the difference of selling at $49.98 vs $50.00 was only $8. It was insignificant.

The following day, it slipped a little and closed at $49.75/share. I was determined to not sell at anything less than $50/share and so I continued to hold on to my stock options and hold on to my anxiety as well. AA stock began a slow backslide and continued to decrease in value as fuel prices rose, no-frills start-up airlines emerged, and other economic factors came into play.

Six months later, I finally gave up and sold my 400 options at $24.99/share receiving half the compensation that I would have received had I sold at $49.98/share. I was focused on being right and getting every dollar I could out of this deal. Caught in the excitement of the drama, I chose to act from the ego-personality instead of the soul. For six months, I hung onto my misery. Fortunately, I didn't need this extra money to survive. This experience was a divine lesson to relinquish control and practice presence. It was a demonstration of what happens when I act from my personality, not my soul.

After it was over, I laid blame on the stock market, fuel prices, low-fare airlines, and several other external conditions, but never on myself. The truth is that I was the creator of all my misery.

CAN WE CHANGE THE PAST?

When asked, 'Can we change the past,' the vast majority say, 'no way, the past is past and there is no way to change it.' On the physical plane, this is obvious. When someone dies, they're gone. When a house burns, it remains a pile of ashes. When a car crashes, there is no way to undo the accident. This is all true, and until 1998, I agreed that we cannot change the past. But I've learned from direct experience that yes, we can change the past. I'll now share two experiences where we changed the past and the positive effect that those changes had on the present.

In the late 1990s, Bernadette came to me and shared, "Johnny, when I was a fifteen-year-old high school girl, I had very disturbing dreams one night and slept fitfully. I repeatedly saw my mother in the garage sitting in our car, with the engine running, and exhaust directed back inside the car. In my dream, she sat there peacefully and died. I awoke in a sweat at 6 am, ran to the garage, and there was Mom slumped behind the wheel with the engine still running. She had successfully committed suicide. I felt horrible and to this day cannot forgive myself for sleeping through that tragic event and not waking up and rescuing her.

"For twenty-five years, I've relived that event almost daily and experience waves of shame and guilt. I've tried therapy, drugs, and even hypnosis. All have had no lasting effect. Nothing has helped me get past this vision of Mom dying, me sleeping, and the intense negative feelings that come with it. Intellectually, I know I am not responsible for my mother's suicide. However, this vision continues to present itself and undermines everything I do." I agreed to help her.

Bernadette and I sat for a while as a vision formed in my mind. I invited several spirit guides to join us, protect us, and guide us on a journey to revisit that suicide event now twenty-five years past.

I asked Bernadette to close her eyes, take a few breaths, and allow the vision to unfold as our friends guided us back to the garage. Bernadette saw her mother sitting peacefully with the engine running, but still conscious. Then she saw her mother slowly slump forward and die. She observed her mother's blue luminous aura gently separate from her physical body. This time, however, her mother was surrounded by non-physical friends and welcomed to her new home. She was not alone as she was during the original experience in the distant past. Our non-physical friends then guided her mother to her next home. The event had a sense of peace and dignity, and the vibrational energy surrounding her mom's passing was higher than the energy surrounding the original suicide event. Her mother was bathed in love.

Bernadette and I gently returned to our awakened presence and shared how the experience unfolded for each of us. We agreed to hold a sense of sacredness about this event and see how it felt to Bernadette in a few weeks.

Several weeks later, Bernadette phoned and told me that since our experience, no unpleasant thoughts of her mother committing suicide had surfaced and several pleasant memories of her had come through. "And Johnny, this morning, Mom came to me in a vision lying peacefully on a cloud, dressed in white, waving down and throwing roses to me as she floated by."

We changed the energy of a past event and even though the physical event didn't change, the trauma surrounding that event was released. For several years, until contact with Bernadette faded, she continued to tell me that her mother occasionally came to her in dreams and visions in a positive and supportive way. Mother and daughter now shared a loving, supportive relationship.

Some years ago, daughter Jennifer was involved in an auto accident exiting a freeway, and although the cars were banged up, there were no significant injuries. Jenn was responsible for the wreck and six months later, shared that she was traumatized by that event. "Dad, I require excessive space to pass cars or make left turns across traffic. I unnecessarily exercise extreme caution. Driving is uncomfortable for me and even my friends have mentioned that I take excessive and unnecessary precautions."

I offered to facilitate with her an experience where we would revisit the event with the intention of reshaping the energy to a softer, less destructive outcome. She was all in for that.

We sat in silence for a while, and I invited several spirit guides to join us and guide us on this healing journey. We followed our breath and soon became witness to Jenn's car encounter and observed it unfold. We were observers outside Jenn's car and saw her heading for the freeway exit. The other car came into the vision and we watched Jenn's car moving toward the other. But just before they touched, our guides directed Jenn's car away from the other. They did not collide and there was no accident. The distance between the cars increased, and both drove away unharmed. Jenn and I returned to our awakened presence, discussed our experience, and thanked our spirit guides.

Several weeks later, Jenn shared, "Hey, Dad, I haven't been traumatized by driving since we did our little piece. And several of my friends who had previously mentioned that my driving was way overcautious have said that my driving is now "normal" again. I thank you and I thank our spirit guide friends."

Although we did not change the past on the physical plane, we reshaped the energy surrounding a past event which carried through and altered the present. In both illustrations, reshaping the energy around a past event positively affected the present situation. We broke the cycle and the past trauma was no longer carried forward to influence the present.

This is not magic. It is a practical application of cosmic laws. Everything must follow the laws of reality. Once learned, tools like these are available to the spiritual practitioner.

Can we change the past? I say yes. What say you?

THE DRAINBOARD

Facing the twin kitchen sinks in our home, the obvious flow for doing the dishes was from left to right. Standing at the kitchen sink, the table was on my left and the dish storage cabinets were on my right. For about a year after we moved into our home, we cleared the dinner dishes and placed them on the counter to the dishwasher's left, washed in the left sink, rinsed in the right sink, and placed the clean wet dishes on the drainboard to the right directly below the storage cabinets. When dry, dishes were easily put away. This was the obvious way to do the dishes.

One morning while fixing coffee, I noticed the drainboard was on the left side of the kitchen sink. I didn't give it much thought and simply moved the drainboard back to its normal place on the right side. However, the "kitchen manager" informed me that the new way we were now doing dishes was to place the dirty dishes on the right side of the sink beneath the storage cabinets, wash from right to left, and drain on the left side. When dry, we'd cross the sink again and store them in the cabinets on the right. Very strange.

It was totally out of flow, but that was the kitchen manager's vision and if that's what she wanted, then that is the way it would be. I shared that this took more time and energy, increased the risk of breakage, and brought forward every other logical point I could think of that this made no sense of all. From the engineer's perspective, I was right. She simply smiled at me, and said, "This feels right to me, Johnny," and walked away.

I was in the kitchen alone a few days later looking at the kitchen sink area and heard a voice inside say, "Johnny, do you want to be right or do you want to have a harmonious relationship with your wife? Is it critical that the flow of the dishwashing event be logical? Maybe there is something for you to learn here?" I thought of that for a while and realized that a harmonious relationship with the kitchen manager was much more important than being right. It took only a few days to get used to. There were only two of us and we used only a few dishes at mealtime, anyway.

For this engineer, releasing logical solutions and accepting more creative ones is huge. After a few weeks, I didn't think about it anymore. I just did it.

I realized how much energy I've wasted over time judging the way things are done. I used to go to restaurants and observe the servers and their traffic patterns to and from the kitchen and the front counter. Then, in my mind I'd rearrange the coffee percolators and glass dessert storage cabinets to allow for a more efficient flow. It was mindless and I'd compare my way to their way. I always thought my way was better. Then I got sober and that mindless chatter and wasted effort ceased.

Dad was locked into doing everything "his way" and that was the only way to do it around Dad. I saw that rigidity and inflexibility impedes creativity. I was learning how to "go with the flow." I was expanding my logical mind to include my creative mind. The kitchen manager was a teacher for me.

A few years later, I walked into the kitchen to find a few dirty dishes on the left and the drainboard back on the right, just like it was prior to the switcheroo. I didn't say a word to the kitchen manager. Several weeks later, she gently whispered in my ear, "Thank you for being patient with my backwards dishwashing technique. But you were right all along, Johnny. This way is easier and much better."

Not everyone has a logical engineering mind, simple as that. And there is much for me to experience and learn from my mostly unexplored creative mind.

RUSTY VISION

"It sure is a beautiful afternoon to fly, isn't it Johnny?" chimed American Airlines First Officer Becky Wade. We were cruising toward San Francisco International Airport on the last leg of the day. "Bet the sun's going to be just about on the horizon when we land in an hour, Johnny."

"Yeah, that's about right, Becky, and San Francisco is landing west so we'll be staring directly into that huge fireball at touchdown," I remarked, smiling. I began directing my thoughts toward our approach and landing.

The sky was clear and the air was smooth as we descended and lined up for our final approach and landing on runway 28R at San Francisco International Airport.

Approaching the airport, the brilliant red-orange fireball was sitting on the far end of our runway. Becky was right, I mused.

"I told you so, Johnny, she chided, glad it's your landing, not mine!"

I snickered a bit, turned toward her and remarked, "It's just fine, Becky, as today I'm using Rusty Vision, and I'll share that with you later."

Applying Rusty Vision, we continued our approach to a safe, gentle, landing with the giant red fireball parked squarely on the end of our runway.

Rusty Vision was a technique I learned in Air Force Phantom training in 1972. Instructor pilot, Rusty, said, "Johnny, there will be many times flying the F-4 in close formation when lead's airplane will be directly between you and the sun. You will be blinded if you attempt to stay in formation by staring at your normal formation reference points on lead's airplane when those reference points move to the middle of the sun. Moving out of formation is not an option. The Thunderbirds and Blue Angels fly every airshow, dragging the wingmen through the sun and manage to not go blind and maintain perfect close formation.

"When you see the sun's going to be directly in your eyes, Johnny, don't just squint down to restrict your vision to little slits, but move your eyes away slightly and use alternative references on flight lead's airplane to stay in formation until you're past the blinding fireball and can return to using your normal references. It's that simple, Johnny. The key is to prepare and practice. While flying formation sometimes when the sun is not directly in your eyes, select additional references on lead's airplane to use temporarily when lead does drag you through the sun."

Rusty was full of wisdom. I practiced and learned to fly close formation using alternative references on lead's Phantom in place of our standard "wingtip light in the fuselage star." It didn't take long, and it wasn't very hard, but now I could hold close formation even when flight lead dragged me directly through the blazing noon-day sun.

I drifted back to 1972 and remembered when I was one of four Phantoms on a formation training flight over the southern Arizona desert. The sun blazed overhead as Captain Lurch, leading our formation, climbed, dove, and led our four-ship flight in close formation. Several times, I had to use my alternate references to remain stabilized in formation as Captain Lurch dragged me directly through the blazing sun. It was a challenge, but it worked. I did what I had to do and gutted it out. "Johnny, no matter what, do to not fall out of formation. It may feel like you're hanging on for dear life, and you may very well be, but hang on just a few more seconds, then a few more. No matter if it's a blazing sun, thunderstorms, windy, dark nights in thick clouds, or whatever, just hang on a few more seconds and conditions will improve."

Rusty was right, and every time I was dragged through the sun, I squinted a bit, looked away, and stayed glued to lead's airplane in tight formation. I could do it because I had prepared and practiced.

"Overall, that was a pretty good four-ship formation flight for a bunch of newbies," barked flight lead Captain Lurch, concluding our debrief. Lurch was his nick-name of course, and it fit him perfectly. He was tall and angular, had a square jaw, was dark complexioned and hairy. He looked tough as nails and smelled like jet fuel.

Having just returned from a tour in Viet Nam, he was one of our squadron instructor pilots assigned to teach us "newbies" how to fly the Phantom. He derived his name Lurch from his close resemblance to the butler, Lurch, from the TV show The Addams Family of the mid-1960s.

Wrapping up his debriefing, Lurch gruffly asked, "Any questions or comments?"

Newbie Lieutenant Sammy Schmoe, flying as pilot in the number four position, meekly asked, "Captain Lurch, did you have to drag us through the sun so much? I found it very hard to stay in formation when your airplane was between my eyes and the sun, and I thought that maybe you could have been a bit more considerate of us wingmen."

Lurch came unglued. He leaped around the table, grabbed Lieutenant Schmoe by his flight suit collar and held him on his tiptoes one-handed at eye level about six inches from his face. "YOU LISTEN AND YOU LISTEN GOOD, LIEUTENANT. I'M THE @#%^*+^! FLIGHT LEAD AND IT'S MY JOB TO GET THIS FORMATION TO WHERE WE'RE GOING, LEAD THE ATTACK, AND GET US BACK AGAIN IN ONE PIECE. AND IT'S YOUR JOB TO STAY IN THIS FORMATION NO MATTER WHERE I GO OR WHAT I DO! I DON'T #$^*!&@ CARE IF IT'S RAINING LIKE HELL, OR WE'RE FLYING THROUGH THUNDERSTORMS, OR WHERE THE SUN IS OR ANYTHING ELSE. I'M NOT HERE TO BABYSIT YOU LIEUTENANT. IT'S YOUR *^%#$@! JOB TO BE THERE ON MY WING, NO MATTER WHAT. THE THUNDERBIRDS DO IT EVERY DAY. AND IF YOU CAN'T DO IT, THEN I'LL THROW YOUR WIMPY ASS OUT OF THIS SCHOOL AND FIND

ANOTHER PILOT THAT CAN! ANY QUESTIONS, LIEUTENANT SCHMOE?"

"Uhhhhh, no, sir!"

And Lurch put Sammy down gently, walked back around the table and softly asked, "Any more questions or comments?" Not surprisingly, there were none. I was so grateful for Rusty's teachings.

"Out of one thousand feet, three green on the gear, flaps 40 degrees, landing check complete," Becky said.

Glancing over to confirm, I responded, "Three green on the gear and 40 degrees landing flaps, thanks, Becky." I relaxed into my seat to fly the remaining 90 seconds of our flight to touchdown.

And there was the sun, like a blazing brilliant fireball, sitting directly on the end of our runway. Visual reference to the runway at one thousand feet was challenging, and I knew that at touchdown, I'd not be able to see the runway at all through the front windshield. Flying primarily on instruments and glancing outside, I knew precisely where I was, and as we approached the final few hundred feet of our descent, I began using off-to-the-side outside references for alignment and height cues. My Rusty Vision techniques paid off once again, and we smoothly touched down, rolled out, and taxied to the gate. I silently thanked Rusty for his wisdom.

What do *you* do when "life" presents a big giant fireball parked at the end of *your* runway? If you don't know about Rusty Vision, you may not see adequately and either lose control and run off the side of *your* runway into disaster, or continue blindly ahead to be consumed by the unknown. Neither of these outcomes is desirable. Use other references, try other techniques, and explore other possibilities rather than blindly pressing forward doing the same old things and hoping for the best while staring at the fireballs of life that occasionally fill *your* windshield. The fireballs parked on life's runways afford us opportunities to stretch and grow. Become proficient at Rusty Vision.

THE MEN'S ROOM

"Welcome to The Men's Room Workshop - use FIRST NAMES ONLY, and talk about anything you wish except JOBS, POLITICS, AND SPORTS," read the sign by the entry door. I retrieved my name tag and said hi to a few men in the room. There wasn't much to talk about without bringing in jobs, politics, or sports. It was strange to not mention my job as pilot with American Airlines. I loved being known for what I do. Perhaps that association helped me to not look at who I am. Knowing nothing about these men, I imagined they were all doctors or scientists and that I was once again 4-foot-tall Johnny in a group of 6-foot-tall professionals.

So, insecure Johnny made small talk with the other insecure men (but I didn't know that) on opening night of "The Men's Room" weekend. It was Friday, November, 22, 1991. There were twenty men in the room, all standing around with little to say. So began our intensive, experiential weekend workshop that focused on men recognizing and removing the emotional blocks that prevent them from living from their hearts. Over the weekend, facilitators Paul and Kevin guided us through individual and group exercises. We focused on releasing the emotional blocks that prevent men from living from their heart.

As Kevin spoke about opening the heart, and what we would encounter in the next several days, I visualized myself donning a suit of armor. Now I felt protected from the outside world in this suit of thick-plated armor. I opened the little faceplate and smiled. I was ready for "The Men's Room" experience.

We formed a standing circle and facilitator Paul spoke. "Men, when you feel called, step into the circle, surrounded by your brothers, and briefly share what deep experience holds you in bondage. Kevin and I will direct you through an experience that will allow you to participate in your story and guide you to a positive outcome. This will alter the psychological and energetic patterns surrounding this event to release the trauma or at least lesson it."

Chris stepped into the circle and shared. "My father took me to a Saturday afternoon movie theater at about nine-years-old. Once seated, another man came and sat next to me, so I was between my father and the stranger. After a while, the stranger put his hand on my leg and began massaging my leg. I squirmed but was so afraid that I sat frozen in terror as the stranger molested me there in the theater, sitting next to my father, who seemed to ignore my squirming and uneasiness. I was so guilt ridden and shamed that I told no one. Many years later, I discovered that my father was in on the set-up and allowed the molestation. I've lived with the trauma of the molestation, and the betrayal of my father for a long time."

Chris picked men to play his father and the molester, and we set three chairs in a row. Then Chris and his father entered the movie theater and sat down. Soon, the other man entered and sat next to Chris. The other man put his hand on Chris's leg and Chris turned to his father and told him that the man sitting next to him had his hand on his leg. Dad confronted the man, told him to leave, and rescued Chris from this experience. Tears flowed from Chris as he released his anger and rage. The healing was evident.

With Chris complete, I stepped into the circle. I shared that I lacked my father's approval and love and that he was critical, demeaning, angry, and sometimes violent. I shared the "Little Johnny and the Birdhouse" event with the group and picked my father from the men. This father recognized and honored my efforts, told me how creative and beautiful my birdhouse was and how I had many talents and gifts. It was easy, too easy. And although it helped a little, I still carried my childhood trauma for many more years.

Weekend complete, we were encouraged to form a follow-on group and met every other Friday evening at a group member's home. Over time, we created a safe and sacred space for expressing our deep feelings and secrets. We shared not so much the stories of our lives, but how we processed and responded to these stories. We shared at the emotional level and our group became important to us. Feedback was encouraged, but criticism or cheap-shots were not allowed.

Group was a gift to each of us and, over time, we all used the loving energy of our group of brothers to heal and grow. Today, some thirty-two years later, our group still meets occasionally, although there are only a few of us left. The loving strength of our safe group of supportive brothers is an ongoing gift.

Through our group, I met my close brother/friend, Joe. He is a man of integrity and sometimes has the patience of a saint. His wisdom is profound.

Chatting about addiction several years ago, I rambled on and on about how I'm the alcoholic and know all about addiction. After 15 minutes of lip flapping, I finally shut up. Joe looked at me and softly said, "Let's see, Johnny, perhaps I can condense all of this addiction stuff a bit." He looked me in the eye and said," Addiction in three words is, "IT'S NEVER ENOUGH." He was correct. I love Joe.

THE SHADOW WEEKEND

Shadow (Human): The parts of the human psyche that are hidden and repressed where violence, anger, and hate generally reside.

After reading Robert Bly's work, *A Little Book on the Human Shadow*, I realized I would never completely heal until I owned my unseen, subconscious shadow. Bly's book opened my eyes. I saw that I was dragging a bag full of fears, secrets, and creative gifts behind me. Until I emptied that bag and owned my stuff, I'd never be free. I hid my deepest, darkest secrets from myself in that bag. I knew that I had to do my deep inner work.

Attempting this level of work alone, without guidance and support, is dangerous. Engage a trusted teacher, guide, or therapist to assist and protect you when resolving your shadow and doing deep inner work.

I enrolled in a three-day experiential men's shadow workshop in the summer of 1995. The briefing flyer said, "Bring only the clothes on your back and nothing else, not even a toothbrush." I thought this very strange.

Twenty-five men comprised our group, and from Friday afternoon through Saturday early evening, we engaged in several exercises to acquaint ourselves with our shadow secrets. My participation in the Vietnam conflict had yet to emerge. I was still tap-dancing around on the surface thinking that I was doing deep work. I wasn't.

On Saturday evening, I entered the sweat lodge and sat with twenty-five men on the ground around a pit of steaming hot rocks. The little lodge was hot, humid, and full of sweaty men. I was uneasy and uncertain in this confined, cramped space, with no place to hide and nowhere to run. I hated the uncomfortable feelings that arose, but gutted it out as our leader poured more water on the simmering hot rocks. Steam rose from the coals, and my face burned from the hot, muggy air.

A knot formed in my fear-filled gut. It began expanding and panic soon arose. Through closed eyes, I felt the huge knot in my gut rise to my chest and I gasped for air. Visions of bombs exploding and people dying flooded into me and I began screaming.

Softly at first, then louder I screamed, as visions of war flooded my mind. I screamed and SCREAMED and SCREAMED, more and more, LOUDER and LOUDER! The men near me moved away a little as I SCREAMED, SCREAMED, and SCREAMED, over and over. I was out of control and could not stop. Then I cried and cried and cried. Tears streamed down my sweat-stained face as I witnessed bodies of men, woman, children, and animals, being blown to pieces.

This vivid nightmare consumed me, and it went on and on. SCREAMMMMMM, SCREAMMMMM, CRY, CRY. Bodies were everywhere, with blood, guts, and destruction surrounding me. I saw trucks blowing up, men blown apart, and children ripped to pieces. Blood, guts, and body parts covered me in this nightmare. Staring into a man's eyes, just a few feet from me, I watched half his head suddenly explode from a bomb fragment. Splattered by his blood and flesh, he stared at me with his one remaining eye, then dropped to the ground dead. More blood and guts followed, with babies dying, mothers screaming, children crying, and a man plowing a field with his water buffalo suddenly vanished. A pile of human flesh and buffalo guts was all that remained. I was on the receiving end of what I REALLY did in Vietnam. I finally collapsed like a limp rag doll. Strong arms helped me from the sweat lodge and laid me gently on the ground, drained and exhausted.

Then the savage appeared. I knew he was me staring directly at me. Hairy and ugly, he was my monster/werewolf and gazed into my eyes, only inches from my face. I smelled his hot breath of death. I hated him. "THAT'S NOT ME!" I screamed! He spat at me, bared his teeth, growled, and roared, "Leave me in the cellar where I am king." He was now out of the basement, out of his element, and right in my face. I was facing my savage within. He was pure rage, anger, aggression, and destruction-a killer and a murderer. I was looking at death. I was looking at myself.

The following morning, I awoke staring at the hairy, ugly, savage. Escape was impossible, for I knew he was part of me and anywhere I went, he would go too. I knew that if I wished to live fully, I first had to learn to love myself-all of myself, including my savage. I had to own all his hatred and rage and diffuse his energy of death. I realized that much work lie ahead to finish cleaning my basement.

Committed to healing myself, I vowed to keep the savage from returning to the basement. I visualized us in a garden with trees, flowers, and warm sunshine. Determined to teach him to love rather than hate, I began introducing him to the way of beauty. But hate is all he knew, and several times he tried to escape. Grabbing him, I'd bring him back to our garden to continue his transformation from destruction to compassion.

Frequently, he brought the visions of war into my consciousness. When this occurred, I did not push these visions away, but observed the feelings and emotions that arose. Working with savage was terrifying, as the movie of my Vietnam experience played on the screen in the home-theater of my mind. This went on for about one year.

I am responsible for everything I do and the results of everything I do. I volunteered to join the Air Force, volunteered for pilot training, volunteered for fighter-jets, and volunteered for combat duty. I'm the last link in a long chain of people that built my airplane and bombs, maintained the equipment, prepared my aircraft for flight, supported the infrastructure, and cheered from the sidelines as I blasted off on a combat mission. And I alone aligned my gunsight with the target and pickled off the bombs.

I had many opportunities before I joined the Air Force to opt out, but I didn't. Assuming total responsibility for my actions was key to discovering, owning, and diffusing my shadow. If I had not done this work, the shadow would continue to live downstairs and act out in ways of its choosing and contaminate all that I do. One must do this deep work and own their darkness or they will live a contaminated, mediocre life.

It's easy to hang my Vietnam experience on a convenient hook and not take responsibility. Many, or perhaps most, shallowly dismiss their behaviors away. I have heard all the excuses, and so have you. "Somebody's got to do it? If we don't stop them over there, they'll be coming ashore over here. They ordered you to go, Johnny, so why blame yourself?" There are many rationalizations, however, accepting any of these feeble excuses feeds the shadow and supports its work in the basement.

Running from my pain will not heal my soul, nor balance my karma, nor allow me to live a free life. One must clean their basement and own their darkness before they may ascend to the attic and align with divinity. If the basement is not cleared of one's darkness, then we drag that darkness into our present experience. This results in a contaminated life with unpredictable outbursts of inappropriate, sometimes violent behaviors. Road rage is an example of the shadow acting out.

I stayed the course and the results are still manifesting. Everyone has a choice to either live in fear standing on the cellar door holding their demons at bay or embracing their shadow and clearing their darkness. I am not aware of any quick-fix or alternative way to do this work.

Life is not about easy, it's about meaningful. I asked myself, "How deeply do you wish to live your life, Johnny?" How deeply do YOU wish to live YOUR life? Am I content with a mediocre earthwalk with a basement full of trauma using short-term sensory pleasures to keep the demons at bay? Are YOU? Or are YOU willing to run risks and open to a life of freedom and joy? Anything of value requires risk and effort. The bars are full of men and woman wearing cement shoes and standing on their basement door to contain their demons below. Opening that door is an act of great courage. Many that open the basement door are consumed by the demons that emerge. It is risky to do this work with the aid and protection of a knowledgeable guide, teacher, or therapist, and dangerous to attempt this work alone. I encourage everyone to do this deep inner work, but do not explore your basement alone.

Returning home from the shadow weekend, nights became frightening as vivid and frequent nightmares disturbed sleep. I saw bodies blowing up, horribly mutilated faces, with destruction and devastation frequently in nightmarish dreams. But I stayed the course, however, and vowed that I would either get through this or die. This was my experience several times a week for about one year. Life without freedom is not worth living. Then an event occurred and my nightmares began to fade in intensity and frequency. Finally, they stopped altogether.

Healing oneself is a lifelong process and although this shadow weekend workshop was transformative, healing my darkness was not complete until my work with "Teacher" some twenty-four years later brought forward in section III, *"Into the Light."*

Where did the shadow go after I did my work? Prior, perhaps twenty-five percent of my available energy was locked in my basement as rage and hostility (my shadow), with an additional twenty-five percent used by the gate-guard to hold the basement door closed. Much effort was necessary to contain my anger and rage so I wouldn't experience outbursts of aggression. But when my guard was resting, expressions of anger, rage, or worse, emerged. It took a significant effort to control myself.

After I did the work and cleared my basement of darkness, the energy of my shadow and the gate-guard were available for my use. The basement was clean and the gate-guard was unemployed. My warrior energy IS my transformed shadow energy. My light is my darkness transformed.

MR. SONG'S LETTER

Great coffee this morning, I reflected. Settling into my desk chair, I began journaling the events of the last few days. *Not really anything significant going on*, I mused. Then, unfamiliar sensations began manifesting within me. I settled into stillness. A man began speaking to me inside my head. I didn't hear him, like I might hear someone nearby whispering. But his soft gentle voice was clear, and he guided me to the keyboard and dictated the following letter. I was very present, awake, and conscious.

Letter from Mr. Song

Thursday, April 24, 1997

For: Major JC Doerr, United States Air Force, Retired

Hello to you Major JC. I know you were a US Air Force fighter pilot flying the F-4 Phantom fighter-jet based in Thailand in December 1972. With all due respect to your rank, sir, and since you are a civilian now, I will address you as JC or Johnny. I hope you do not mind. I know all about you, probably more than you know about yourself. Please allow me to explain.

This letter differs from anything you have ever received. In December

1972, you dropped bombs on military trucks hiding in my camp at the Disappearing River in North Vietnam. You are a fine pilot, and all your bombs fell on target. However, during that raid, you suspected enemy soldiers were hiding in my little hut and you bombed it into oblivion, killing my wife, our son, and me. I am writing this letter to you, from the spirit world where I have lived for almost twenty-five years now. You have lived with the guilt, sorrow, and shame of your actions for a long time, Johnny, and I will now help you use my spirit energy, and my love, to work through your guilt, sorrow, and shame. You are stuck and I will help you get unstuck. Here is what happened that night. Since I can see and know all from the spirit world, I have full account of your mission. Please allow me to introduce myself and explain.

I was then a young Vietnamese citizen and my name was, and still is, Song. I was twenty-eight years old in 1972 and lived near the town of Dong Hoi in the area you called the Disappearing River in North Vietnam. I was not a soldier and never understood or supported the war that was raging in my country, both in North and South Vietnam, for many years. I was a man of peace and ran a small camp located in this beautiful region. The Camp of the Disappearing River was for boys and young men. It was a camp of peace and I, and my fellow instructors, taught boys and guided them in many activities and arts. Our goal was to allow boys to find themselves in this chaotic world and emerge fully capable, fully developed men. We did this mostly through example and hands-on experience.

One morning in December 1972, twenty-five military trucks driving along the highway toward Dong Hoi turned into my camp, pulled into the park area, and dispersed along the trees. The military leader came to me and told me, he did not request, that he was going to park his supply trucks here during the day to avoid detection and resume his journey after dark that evening. I expressed my concerns, told him I was a man of peace, explained that we had many civilian boys here and asked him to move on. He refused. The trucks stayed all day, and I was concerned that American Intelligence would find out this location and bomb my camp.

The day passed, and I believed I was out of danger as the sun disappeared in the west and the trucks assembled for departure. We were greeted with a beautiful full moon. Soon, the military trucks were ready to leave, and I felt relief. Suddenly, I heard jet fighters and saw some flares over Dong Hoi several kilometers to the east. I knew that the US Air Force was in the vicinity and I wanted the trucks to depart before they were discovered. I tucked my wife and son into our hut and stayed outside to observe. The boys in the camp, fortunately, lived sheltered in secluded caves along the side of the mountain several hundred yards away. I could clearly hear the explosions of bombs near Dong Hoi and I recognized the jet aircraft sounds as Phantom jets.

Suddenly, I heard and felt the earth tremble as a Phantom swooped low over my camp and pulled up into the night sky. I clearly saw the silhouette of the Phantom against the full moon as the jet fighter pulled steeply up and away into the blackness. Two flares ignited directly over my camp and I knew I was in trouble as the trucks were now assembled along the road from my park to the highway.

It was too late to move my family from our little hut to the safety of the caves along the mountain, and all I could do now was hope and pray. The trucks tried to disperse among the trees along the entry road, but they were obvious targets and clearly visible from the air. I heard a Phantom swoop down on its bomb delivery pass and the earth shook as the first bombs fell along the entry road and several trucks, loaded with ammunition and other war supplies, blew up. I knew that the Phantom pilots were good and that they would continue bombing the trucks.

I was horror-struck as bombs moved closer to my hut, my family, and me. Suddenly, I looked up and saw a Phantom silhouetted perfectly by the full moon, diving directly at me and my hut. In its own way, it was a beautiful sight, yet I knew this Phantom was after my hut and I was immobilized with fear. I saw the Phantom begin his pullout and knew that bombs had released and my earth-life here was about to end. The jet screamed overhead, and I saw the blackness of its underside and knew that death was only a heartbeat away. My hut, along with my family, vanished in a blinding flash, followed by another flash 50 feet closer to me, and then a blinding flash. Noise beyond belief, then total silence and peace.

It was over in that heartbeat. My life ended when you bombed my family and me out of existence, Johnny. It has been over twenty-four years since I left your world, and entered the spirit world, yet I see your Phantom silhouetted against that full moon as if it were happening now. I know now, Johnny, that you are ready to receive my gift.

All humans are the same and it is only our minds that make us appear different. You and I are, and have always been, brothers, Johnny, even though you ended my life on Earth. I forgave you the instant I died. Now I write this letter and gift it to you so that you will forgive yourself. You see, Johnny, you are my eyes, my ears, and my mind on the physical earth. I cannot return to continue my earthwalk directly. However, through you, I can. All you need is to forgive yourself for your deeds, own the deaths of your victims, and live your life from your heart. By owning your victim's deaths, you are gifted with their love, their energy, their talents, and their spirits. Victim's spirits are attached to their earth-killers. Johnny, you carry a tremendous amount of spirit energy and love from your victims within you. Your gift from that crazy war is us, your victims.

This is not about punishment anymore, Johnny. This is about forgiveness and healing. This is about you realizing your full earth-life potential and your specialness. You are a spirit home, and that is very special. You are truly fortunate, Johnny, for the spirit love, talents, and specialness of your victims lives within you. All humans who kill on Earth become spirit-homes for their victims and are attached to their energies. You, Johnny, have worked very hard for many years rescuing yourself. You have healed yourself from acute alcoholism and have worked diligently preparing yourself for this moment. You are ready now to realize the gift of spirit-love and energy that is within you.

Only those who seek may receive this gift. Most who die as victims of other humans are not as fortunate as I am. You see, I am very excited, Johnny, that I may realize my earth dreams and goals through you. Are you getting it, Johnny? All your victims forgave you the instant they died. That's the way it works. There is no hate or resentment in the spirit world. It does not exist. It is purged as our spirits leave our physical bodies. Now, Johnny, for us to live on and contribute to the physical world, we must do it through you. You are now accountable to us for your every action, and your every deed. We are inseparable from you. You have no choice in this, Johnny. This is the way it is, like it or not. And I guarantee you that you will like it. Your awakening is happening now as you begin to realize the many friends and gifts that are becoming available to you from Spirit.

Think about it, Johnny. How much brilliance and divinity resides within and around you now? Some of us were intellectual geniuses. Some were talented artists. Some were musicians. Some were talented athletes. Do you get it now, Johnny? We are you; you are us. We live with you. You are our body. We are your spirit. We are an inseparable part of your mind. There is no longer a you and us. We are all the same. That is the way it is from now on, Johnny. I know you are ready.

Johnny, rejoice and sing from the rooftops, for you are now an incredibly *powerful and fortunate human being with a tremendous obligation. We have a special interest in you, for how you conduct your life directly affects us. Should you compromise yourself, we will help you refocus. You have no choice in this, Johnny. This is not up for negotiation. We are no longer with you on your journey, Johnny. We are you.*

We have all dreamed of returning through you to continue our earth path and earth journey. We have returned.

That's it, Johnny, I guess I'm the Spirit spokesperson, and will check in from time to time.

Love - From my Spirit heart,
Song - family, and many friends!

I pushed back from my computer, took a few breaths, and read Mr. Song's letter several times. After a second cup of coffee, I reread his letter again. I could not believe what I read and how this morning had unfolded. I thought that things like this only happen to other people, on TV, or in fairy tales.

A week later, I calmly read Mr. Song's letter to my therapist Paul. At completion, he pushed back in his chair and sat in silence. Finally, I spoke. "Well, Paul?"

He said, "I'm speechless, Johnny. I never encountered or heard of anything like that before." And that was all he said.

Shortly, I began to sense Mr. Song with me and sometimes I'd glimpse him out of my peripheral vision. But I hadn't ever experienced anything like this either and remained skeptical. Doubt and confusion continued for six months until the answer found me.

THE INCA MEDICINE WHEEL

Shortly after Mr. Song's letter, a flyer landed on my desk inviting me to participate in four extended weekend workshops spaced about six months apart, embracing the journey of the Inca Medicine Wheel. Billed as a spiritual journey of personal empowerment, I signed up for the first workshop. It felt right to take part in this sacred experience.

Medicine Wheels are sacred tools that indigenous cultures use to relate to reality. They are integral and embrace the mythology of the culture.

To the native mind, time is a circle with no beginning or end. There is birth, growth, maturity, decay, and death. This is followed by rest and rejuvenation before rebirth. Time forms a circle rather than a straight line. Native minds see no separation. There is no us and them, no judgement of events, and no good or bad. Everything exists as a part of the web of life. Events don't happen to me, events just happen. Also, native mind relates to an animistic world where everything is alive. Since everything on the physical plane consists of atoms, and atoms are energy, everything is energy in one or more of its infinite forms. Everything has a unique energetic signature. Native mind sees life in everything.

First Workshop – The Work of the South

I drove to a Wisconsin Scout Camp for my *Work of the South*.

"When we are in a relationship with someone, energetic threads form that connect us," our teacher, Alberto, began. "Visualize these threads as small luminous energetic strands of blue light," he continued. "Parents and children, partners, siblings, and who we were in our past lives all create luminous threads of energy and attach to our energetic bodies." Alberto spoke at length about how one is influenced and biased by the trauma and drama of others through these energetic luminous threads. People are biased by life events and by other people through these energetic attachments.

I soon saw how much I was caught in my parent's story. I realized I made choices for my life based on how I thought my parents would react to my decisions.

Didn't Mr. Song mention something about how he is attached to me? I re-read Mr. Song's letter to remind myself of how I am attached to my victims with these energetic strands of luminous energy.

"You are truly fortunate, Johnny, for the spirit love, talents, and specialness of your victims lives within you. All humans who kill on earth become spirit-homes for their victims. Victims' spirits reside and live within their earth-killer. Johnny, you carry a tremendous amount of spirit energy and love from your victims within you. Your gift from that crazy war is us, your victims."

Maybe this is what Mr. Song was speaking of! The wording was slightly different, but the meaning was the same. Energetic attachments formed between the ones I killed and me in that crazy war. And he says it's a gift. I laughed and cried. It had been six months since Mr. Song channeled his letter to me, and now I realized that he and what he shared with me was real.

My nightmares of war had subsided substantially several months after Mr. Song wrote me his letter. And several months ago, they stopped altogether. I was waking up. By clearing these energetic attachments, I would be supported by these people. I would stay out of their emotional dramas yet receive their loving support. I was beginning to understand.

Lying in bed that evening, I closed my eyes and Mr. Song appeared to me. He was small, had a white beard, wore a little hat, and was smiling like a Cheshire cat. I instantly liked him and felt his love in return. He spoke, and I heard him. We chatted a while and, doing a few flip-flops, he waved goodbye and left. I KNEW that this was reality presenting itself to me in ways that I could not have imagined just a year ago. I also KNEW that Mr. Song was a "real" person. He now had credibility. Sleep came peacefully.

Attachments are connecting threads of energy that form without thought. They keep us connected to and involved in another's story and drama.

"Our work is to cut the cords of attachment as an act of love and compassion," explained Alberto. "When we cut the cords, we remove ourselves from another's story, and remove them from ours. We free ourselves, and support each other with love without drama."

Cutting the cords of attachment frees me from "story" and I may now have an authentic loving relationship with another supported solely by love, not biased by or entangled in drama, emotion, obligation, and judgement. Mr. Song smiled. Life was expanding, and I loved these new feelings sweeping over me. My world was changing.

Later that evening at our communal fire, we were instructed to breathe an intention to separate with love, compassion, and forgiveness for each person or event into a stick. When ready, each person came forward and submitted each stick to the fire. Kneeling before the friendly blaze, I blessed my father and forgave him for his abuse to me, and apologized for any pain I may have caused him. I did the same with my mother. Into the fire they went with love and compassion. I saw them both in the crackling fire with smiles and love on their faces.

Holding two more sticks, one for Mr. Song and a large stick for all the others, I prepared to release my Vietnam victims. Tears welled in my eyes as I spoke softly to Mr. Song, thanking him for coming to me, for bringing me this gift of love and freedom, and asking his understanding and forgiveness for killing him and his family. He appeared in the fire smiling back at me as I gently placed his stick in the fire. A large ember burst from the fire and landed right in front of me. Gently,

I placed the larger stick into the fire, honoring all the others that I killed, and released them as well. Tears flowed and emotions erupted.

Trust does not mean accepting a "truth" outside of oneself on blind faith without examination, or against inner intuition, the obvious, and common sense. If it feels intuitively right and in alignment with my soul, I'll trust the process. Mr. Song whispered that we were now free of each other's trauma and drama and could now authentically love each other. I slept well that night.

Prior to Mr. Song's letter, reality was limited to the 3-D physical world of length, width, height, and physical time. Opening into spiritual, or non-physical dimensions, was a huge leap. I imagine it is for most. My relationship with Mr. Song challenged all my old beliefs and practices. Spirit wasn't just a vague concept anymore but was reality rooted in experience. I was discarding old limiting concepts and wiping my mind clean of past belief systems.

I knew that rigid, fixed, dogmatic concepts held me prisoner in my self-made prison. Trying to fit new concepts into a mind filled with restricted, limiting beliefs from an old paradigm is impossible. One must first empty the mind to allow new, more expanded, and universal laws to establish themselves within and around you.

Fortunately, as a boy, I was not forced kicking and screaming into a fixed and rigid religious experience. Although there was a Christian base in our family, we went to church only on Christmas, Easter, weddings, and funerals. I also learned to respect and allow others to practice their beliefs without judgement.

For the six months following the first *Work of the South* workshop, I engaged in several fire ceremonies, reinforcing and practicing the art of living freely. Mr. Song supported me whenever I brought him into my awareness. He is a playful man, always smiling, always available, and funny as hell. Stubbing my toe one morning, I swore and there he was, a big smile on his face. He looked at me and said with his infectious smile, "It's a bitch to have a body." His playfulness is infectious.

Shedding the past and cutting the cords means detaching from the trauma and drama of my past and present story. It is an act of love and compassion.

Second Workshop – The Work of the West

The Work of the West workshop, also held at a rustic scout camp, focused on *becoming the spiritual warrior;* the one that has the courage to live in the present moment with no regrets of the past and no fear of the future. Having shed the past, from my work of the south, I was available and open to this experience. One cannot be present when engaged in another's story or dragging a bag full of past experiences.

During a guided meditation, I was shown a past life where I was of great service. I share that experience next.

"Pine scent tingled my nostrils as I observed the darkened native village bathed in starlight. The village center glowed from the huge fire, illuminating the man lying peacefully on the bearskin, radiating love and compassion. His blue aura shimmered around his tired old body and he smiled, knowing his earthwalk was almost complete. He had no regrets. Everyone in the village loved and admired Medicine-Bear as he peacefully passed from this life. It was his time to leave and re-awaken to his more fundamental, energetic nature. I was meeting myself from the distant past. He drew his final breath, and his blue aura slowly rose from his lifeless body.

The aura floated toward me, stopped just a few feet away, and he looked deeply into my eyes. Mesmerized, I asked him his name. He gazed at me and whispered, "I am MedicineBear and I'm returning with you to join you on your earthwalk. You have much to do in this lifetime, Johnny, and I am here to assist." I thanked him and slowly we rose together, and returned to physical consciousness. Awaking from my vision, I felt his presence, and he joined Mr. Song as part of my spiritual family. MedicineBear has been with me ever since.

Over time, I became MedicineBear. He taught me the ways of his people and of being of service to all beings. He is alive within me. I became Johnny MedicineBear and identify more to him than to the physical personality that I assumed at birth.

MedicineBear is always present, and frequently we travel to his village of the Shoshone Nation on the western slopes of the Rocky Mountains in southern Idaho to a time before clocks and machines.

Life continued to expand. Sleep became more relaxed. Nightmares diminished to zero. I had friends on the other side now and found communities with men and women who had experienced similar events. Life became more meaningful. Mr. Song and MedicineBear became my best friends, and were always there to guide and encourage. They are never intrusive, never judgemental, and always supportive. It is pure joy to have this team.

Once, I asked Mr. Song a simple question. He looked at me and spoke, "Johnny, I will never tell you something that you can discover for yourself. Doing one's work is the key to spiritual growth." Mr. Song and MedicineBear have always supported me.

Third Workshop – The Work of the North

This work was to experience *the wisdom and knowledge that may be known, but not told*. Initially, I thought that I'd learn something and be sworn to secrecy. That's what it meant to me. Not so. My clever mind was projecting into the future again.

Alberto held a small stone in his open palm for all to see. He put his hand behind his back for a few seconds and then brought it forward for us to see his clenched fist. "I'm holding the small stone in my fist," he said. "Do you believe me?" Being a clever guy, I thought, well, he's got a lot of integrity and seems like he's telling the truth, and look at those trusting eyes. "All who do not believe me, raise your hand." Five hands go up. "All who believe me, now raise your hands." Five hands go down and forty hands go up, including mine. He opens his fist. No stone. "Belief is mental and is not based on direct knowledge," said Alberto. "With belief, one decides based on accepted communal truths. We want to be a good person in our community, so we believe what the community says is true and simply go along with it. We become conditioned and learn to suppress doubts, questions, and our own intuitive inner voice. We learn that to be accepted in our community, we do not make waves. We may even have knowledge that what is claimed to be true is, in fact false, yet will still support the belief of the community rather than stand in our own truth. Being a non-believer in a community of believers does not work well."

Alberto continued, "But there is another choice other than the polarized responses of duality (believe or not believe). This concept is foreign to most of us and is generally considered unacceptable. It is simply, I don't know. Truth says that if I have no direct experience of something, then I don't know. Truth says it doesn't matter what others say. If I don't know, then I don't know. How simple is that?" That was a huge awakening for me. And I saw that many or most of the truths I have embraced were not truths at all but conditioned beliefs, from what I was taught and told, not from direct knowledge. I concluded that I knew very little.

When a person stands at a podium, perhaps with a microphone and a little reverb, and asks me to accept his or her truth or the truth of the institution as my truth, I run as fast as I can. This is disempowering because the person or institution is asking me to give them my personal power; power of choice, power of reason, power of the heart. If I go along with the crowd, I am giving my "self" away. Don't do it! Think for yourself. Most believe what they've been told and ignore what they observe. There are a lot of slick people and institutions that want you to believe them and follow them. They want your personal power. Don't give it to them. Think for yourself. Notice that in these situations the flow of energy is from me to them. I lose my power and they receive my power.

In my Medicine Wheel experience, the facilitators never asked us to accept anything they said as truth. They encouraged us to question everything. They shared their experience and held space for each of us to experience whatever we experienced. They were true teachers and space holders, encouraging us to go on our personal spiritual journeys of self-realization. There were no tests, no right or wrongs, and no judgements. I was supported, respected, and loved. The energy flowed from the facilitators to the participants in loving and supportive ways.

Staring into my little healing fire on the shores of Lake Michigan at 9 pm during this third workshop, I asked for a sign that spirit was with me this night. Mr. Song appeared. I saw him clearly with my eyes closed. He stood on the other side of the fire and smiled. "Johnny, please come walk with me." In my vision, I rose and followed him beyond the fire into the darkness. We walked a bit and I could see nothing above or below me, just dark empty space. Then one by one I began to see beings around me, some clearly, some faintly, but men, woman, and children, not paying us much attention. It was surrealistic. Mr. Song and I walked in silence for a while and I felt loving kindness.

There were perhaps a thousand people there. Eventually, we

returned to the fire and Mr. Song smiled. I was afraid to ask what I already knew. He said, "Yes, Johnny, you are right, they are the ones you sent to next life (he preferred not saying killed) and they are all here to support you. None are angry, Johnny. You have nothing to fear, and joy should fill your heart."

"How many are there, Mr. Song?"

"One-thousand-and-nineteen," he said. "Johnny, it only matters that you are doing your work, walking your walk, and waking up."

A young Vietnamese girl dressed in tattered and torn clothes appeared. She approached from the darkness and stood at the opposite side of my small fire next to Mr. Song. "Her name is Neiche," he said, "and she will be of service to you in the future." I bowed to her and she returned my bow. They both stepped back away from the fire and vanished into the blackness. I sat alone with my little fire on the shores of Lake Michigan.

It doesn't matter how we wake up, or how much we wake up. It only matters that we try to wake up. There is never wasted effort on the shaman's path. Lighting the healing fire, participating in ceremony, opening one's heart to the unknown, stretching beyond the comfortable, all empower us in unseen and subtle ways to receive the gifts of truth from spirit. One must be open to receive. I remembered from Mr. Song's letter, "Only those who seek may receive this gift." It made sense, for seeking opens the awareness and makes room for the gifts of gold Spirit has waiting for us.

Fourth Workshop – The Work of the East

I returned to camp six months later for the fourth workshop, *The Work of the East*. Like stepping stones, I was shedding the past, becoming the spiritual warrior, learning the wisdom and knowledge that may be known but not told, and now learning how to be of service for all beings.

Any experience that empowers is of great value. When given a choice of this or that, the best choice is the one that invites the greatest personal responsibility and requires the greatest effort.

No one can do another's inner work for them. The serious seeker embraces this knowledge and becomes willing to embrace the pain and suffering necessary to walk through their fire. I tend to avoid cheerleader, pep-rally, or feel-good experiences. When huge throngs sing the praise of a cause (and it doesn't matter what the cause is), it may feel good to join in and the energy generated may be high, but it will not sustain for there is no inner change. In a short time, the good feelings fade and I return to normal with no long-term sustainable change. Will I grow from this experience? Probably not, for no effort was required. These are thoughts to reflect on. It's not what I learn from an experience that is important, it is what I become from it that is important and that is what sustains.

I began to practice the following five principles in my daily life.

1) Non-Judgement: See life events as they are, not polarized as good-bad, right-wrong. Life is non-personal. Engage life non-personally. Live in presence.

2) Non-attachment to Outcome: Release the future. Thinking that a rain storm will ruin your next day picnic creates misery and stress. Go with the flow. Make a plan, then be OK with any outcome. An event that comes off exactly as planned is great. But the one that receives the torrential rain storm will be remembered thirty years later.

3) Non-Engagement: Disengage from confrontation. One is not required to respond to an inappropriate question or an inappropriate event just because it is asked or someone is in your face. If the question or event is inappropriate or irrelevant, choose not to respond. There is no argument when I walk away and disengage. If someone is critical of you, see them as a recalcitrant six-year-old child. Thank them politely and leave.

4) Non-Suffering: Experience the suffering and consider what you have learned or gained from your suffering, Then release it and move on. Don't suffer the suffering.

5) See the world with soft vision, loving eyes. Engage life with compassion, kindness, generosity, and love. Allow others to be who they are.

These principles are tools and I use them daily. Give them a try. They are intuitively true and are gifts for you.

DUTCH & HARLEY

"Well, Johnny, it's about one year until retirement from American Airlines and you've no idea where you wish to live, or what you wish to do," I said out-loud to myself. "What a wonderful opportunity for a major life change." There were many possibilities and I knew that something wonderful would percolate to the surface and reveal itself.

Living alone in my huge four-bedroom, three-bath home, two cars, and all the stuff surrounding me, getting rid of it all excited me. I lived in only four rooms of my ten-room home on a one-acre wooded property in the north Chicago suburbs. It was way too much.

A motorhome drove by one day, and I saw myself sitting in the driver's seat. "That's it!" I yelled. "That's what I'm going to do." The excitement I felt was very similar to the excitement engendered when the sleek silver fighter-jet taxied by me at Bradley field in 1968. I knew that living in a motorhome was my calling.

In the following nine months, I researched motorhomes, toured six motorhome factories, and made my decision. Newmar impressed me, for there was no guard at the entry gate and people entered and left unchecked. Also, eighty-five percent of Newmar's workers were Amish, and these people were skilled craftsman. In May 2004, I went to the Newmar factory and, with the help of a Newmar rep, spec'd out my new coach. Motorhome Dutch (referred to as Dutch from here onward) joined me in August 2004, just a few weeks before my retirement from American Airlines. We were a match from the get-go.

Dutch offered freedom, adventure, challenges, and opportunities that supported my desires while maintaining the comfort of familiar surroundings. Dutch was a key player in the next adventure of my earthwalk.

Some might say that a motorhome is an inanimate object since it has no human or living components, like blood, lungs, or heart. Some might say that a motorhome cannot think, feel, or act on its own. From the physical perspective, this appears true.

A shaman, however, relates animistically to the world. This means that everything is alive. Animism recognizes cosmic or spiritual energy as the deeper, more fundamental expression of reality, imbuing everything. This is not some theory, and anyone, if they do the work, can validate and verify this. Energy supports our physical reality which could not exist without it.

I learned these concepts while exploring the Inca Medicine Wheel. Initially, I hadn't a clue what the teachers were talking about and resisted because their teachings were not congruent with my rigid beliefs. But the door cracked open, and I began experiencing a sense of oneness and connection with inanimate objects like Dutch. It was exhilarating and freeing. I learned from teachers but validated from my life experiences.

After retirement from American Airlines in September 2004, I began traveling in Dutch. I did not wish to tow a car and instead bought a mid-sized 800cc Suzuki motorcycle and mounted it on a lift arrangement attached to the rear of Dutch. This worked OK, but the bike was not big enough and I realized that soon something more suited to my desires would show up.

Stopped at a traffic light in Sturgis, South Dakota in early August 2005, I settled into the seat of my Suzuki cruiser. I'd only had my bike a few months and was waking up "Johnny the biker" within. It had been thirty-five years since my 1970 Honda 305 was stolen and I had hung up my helmet. As I patiently waited, feeling the soft rumble of the engine, a custom Harley-Davidson pulled up on my right and a Big-Dog chopper stopped on my left. I couldn't hear my little engine anymore, and I looked at these motorcycles with a sense of, *I got to get me one of these bad-ass bikes.*

As the light flicked green, both bikes roared off and I sat there, listening and knew that it was in my cards to find Harley, or have Harley find me.

Two weeks later, in Duluth, Minnesota, I entered the Harley-Davidson dealership and knew that the 2006 Soft-tail Deluxe sitting on the showroom floor was, like Dutch, destined to be my companion and share in life adventures. I wrote the check and now there were three in our family.

Going anywhere on Harley is an adventure and requires presence. I am conscious of what I wear and what I take, and I do a little pre-flight before each ride, checking lights and Harley's general condition. Road surface, time of day, and weather all play a major role in longevity with Harley. In a car, riding at night or in inclement weather may be inconvenient and slow me down a bit, but on Harley, darkness and adverse weather present dangers that require vigilance and caution. I travel at least five seconds behind the vehicle in front of me, just in case they straddle a 2x4. With this safety margin, I've a good chance to see and avoid danger.

The head-space of riding a motorcycle is a lot like flying a fighter-jet. One cannot allow laziness or carelessness into the cockpit or on a motorcycle. Harley has taught me to live in presence and not take too much for granted. Pulling onto a country road, twisting the throttle while releasing the clutch, hearing, and feeling his power, all unite me in oneness with Harley. I really get into it. It's a space of non-thinking, no-brain beingness and I'm back in the cockpit of my F-4 Phantom fighter-jet. I love it.

Before I toss a leg over Harley, I envision our ride, and briefly see us going here, then there, then back home, and finally asleep at midnight in bed. I call this "tossing the cocoa leaves." On the rare occasion that the vision doesn't unfold easily, I walk away for a few minutes, shake out the energies, and return for a second try. I've never had it not unfold favorably on the second try. The Cocoa Leaves story as told by a shaman teacher follows.

"We visited a jungle shaman and one of my students was very skeptical and didn't believe that the jungle shaman could see the future. I asked the jungle shaman to toss his cocoa leaves and read what he saw for my skeptical student. The jungle shaman did and said that he saw a terrible car wreck with death. I shared that with the skeptical student, then asked the jungle shaman if he could re-toss his cocoa leaves. The jungle shaman did, and replied that he now saw a terrible car wreck, major damage, and significant injuries, but no death. I shared this with my skeptical student, then asked the jungle shaman to toss his leaves one more time. The jungle shaman did and said that he now saw a near-miss traffic incident, but no accident and no injuries. I told this to my skeptical student, who smiled and smirked, and we were done.

"Two weeks later, after returning to the States, I received a call from my skeptical student who shared that he was recently driving through a very busy intersection in his compact car when a bus appeared directly in front of him. He swerved and stopped with only a foot to spare. Simultaneously, an eighteen-wheeler swerved to miss him and stopped within a few feet of his rear. He sat frozen in his car, blocked fore and aft by huge vehicles. He was shaken but unharmed."

Can we influence the future? Maybe yes, maybe no, depending on one's energy and perspective. Daily, I set intentions and ask for guidance so that I may be of the highest service for all beings.

During a motorcycle ride, one of my non-physical friends might nudge another driver's eyes toward Harley, making us visible where without this "help" that person might not have seen us. Winning the Lotto, however, is an ego thing and it probably won't work. But with pure heart, pure intention, and selfless service, one aligns with the non-physical energies of divinity and anything is possible.

These beings are our angels, guides, helpers, relatives, and others that support our incredibly challenging earthwalk experience. They know how tough this physical road is to travel. Try nudging the future from your heart, not your head, with compassion, love, and service for all beings. And it's a lot of fun too.

FEAR OF THE DARK, THE COAL MINE

I have feared the dark since early childhood. As a little boy, I was afraid of the Bogeyman that lived in my closet and the closet door had to be closed before I could sleep. I wanted the hall light on and slept with my bedroom door open. In my mind, spooks, ghosts, goblins, and the Bogeyman only came out in darkness. A little light kept me safe from these scary creatures. I was afraid to go outside at night alone without the porch light on or carrying a flashlight. I do not remember the genesis of this fear, but spooky movies and Halloween frightened me a lot. I avoided graveyards and spook houses.

I watched several horror movies around twelve-years-old and the frightening images remained vivid in my mind for years. One such movie showed a big old brick college sorority house on a stormy, dark, lightning-filled night. A sister went to the bathroom, lifted the lid, and saw the severed head of one of her sorority sisters floating in the bowl. For years, I hesitated opening toilet lids. I tried to talk to Dad about my fears, but his short, uncompassionate attitude pushed me away. Dad's response to any of my childhood fears was, "When are you going to grow up, Johnny? Real men aren't afraid of the dark." I heard that frequently from Dad about a lot of things. He did not understand and was not there for me in compassionate ways.

Fast forward now to 2008, traveling in Dutch parked at a campground near Elkins, West Virginia. Roger, in the site next to me and I became friends. He lived locally and was the foreman of a coal mine that was temporarily closed because of a methane gas explosion that killed a crew of miners several months prior. Roger shared that methane gas may sometimes be present in coal mines. It is odorless, colorless, and highly explosive. Therefore, methane detectors are abundant and rigid no-flame and no-smoking rules are in place, emphasized, and strictly enforced.

One minor, however, died some distance away from the others with his cigarette lighter lying nearby. The explosion pattern suggested that the catastrophe originated at his location. Roger shared that the mine was now safe, and asked if I'd like to go down in the mine for a closeup experience of coal mining. I decided to use this opportunity to embrace my fear of darkness, small confined spaces, and the unknown. I thanked him and agreed to go.

On coal mine day, Roger and I suited up, signed the IN board, and headed for the entrance. This coal mine was not down in the ground as I had assumed, but horizontal into the side of a mountain. We climbed aboard our little electric locomotive and rode the tracks into the blackness.

There was little head-room, and we ducked frequently to avoid hitting our helmets on the low ceiling. Roger explained the ventilation system and how it pumps fresh air through a shaft to the deepest area of the mine. The released air then always flowed outward toward the entrance. All miners (including us) carried small smoke sticks. When lit, the smoke would always drift toward the mine entrance and safety. "It's a simple, foolproof system that always points to daylight, Johnny!" exclaimed my hero, Roger.

Deep in the mine, we de-trained several times and walked down corridors with only our miner's lamps for illumination. Shutting off our helmet lights, absolute blackness embraced us. Even after five minutes of eye adjustment, I saw nothing, including my hand just a few inches in front of my face. It reminded me of the night blackness when flying over North Vietnam under an overcast sky at midnight.

Flicking on our helmet lights, Roger led me to a wall with a door in it. "We're going into the ventilation system, Johnny, so just follow me through the steel door and keep your back to the wind. It's quite breezy in there." I followed, and we stepped into the inbound air shaft. "Wind is about forty mph," hollered Roger. My light shone on his face and he was grinning from ear to ear. "I designed this entire ventilation system and love being down here working in the mine." I thought I was a little crazy sometimes, but hearing this, I was sure that I was saner than the madman I was looking at. How could anyone love it down here, I thought, but there was no doubt he did.

We rode the electric locomotive into the deepest part of the mine and explored. Roger explained the equipment used, how to extract the coal, and how to transfer it onto the conveyor belt. He showed me exactly where the explosion occurred some months prior. We saw several methane detectors showing that it was safe in the mine.

I felt no fear and enjoyed exploring this unknown world. Roger was so competent and calm in this mine that his ease rubbed off on me.

Occasionally, I checked behind and around a few corners to ensure that we weren't being followed by the Bogeyman. We weren't. Roger said that he and others routinely go into the mine alone. That's hard for me to imagine, yet pilots all alone routinely fly single seat aircraft, in a cockpit half the size of a bathtub, in severe weather seven miles in the sky during the darkest of nights and return safely to Earth. After several hours in the mine, we headed toward the exit and daylight. I thanked Roger for his time and generosity and transferred my name from the IN board to the OUT board.

Rather than wearing a sheriff's badge and a pair of six-shooters to feel like a man, I had embraced a lifelong fear and experienced a deep sense of accomplishment. I sensed my fear of the dark dissolving.

Roger was passionate about mining and loved his life's work. But I could not imagine doing this routinely and was grateful that I was not forced to work in what I felt was a hostile and dangerous environment.

A few days later at the campground, Roger introduced me to his uncle, Joe, a very pleasant, slender, soft-spoken, recently-retired coal-mining man. Roger shared with Joe our tour of the mine from a few days past, and Joe asked what I thought about being in a coal mine. "Joe, I found it very interesting," I replied, "But I probably won't go back again. Once is enough for me."

Joe was also very passionate about coal mining and Roger asked Joe to share his experience in the two-and-a-half-foot-tall mine. "Well,

Johnny," drawled Joe, "I spent several years working in a coal mine only thirty inches high. That's just two-and-a-half-feet from floor to ceiling, or about the height of a dining room table. The mine was only as tall as the vein of coal. To enter the mine, the crew at the entrance rolled onto the conveyer belt lying on our backs head first. When the crew was all aboard, the foreman started the belt and in we rode with the ceiling just inches above our face. If I raised my arm or lifted my head, it was gone, simple as that.

"We rode in about a mile, stopped, rolled off the belt and spent eight hours working in a thirty-inch-high area on our sides, backs, and bellies. We slithered around and ran drills, loaded the conveyer, shored up ceilings, and sent out coal. I've been in three cave-ins but never trapped, at least not for very long. Then, after our eight-hour shift, we'd exit the same way we went in. And you know what, Johnny?"

I was hesitant to ask. "What, Joe?" I whispered.

"I loved it," Joe said with a big grin.

I was dumbstruck. How could anyone love and be passionate about working in a thirty-inch-high coal mine a mile under a mountain? But Joe did.

"By the way, Johnny, what did you do for a living?"

"I was an Airline Pilot, Joe," I said with a grin.

Joe tensed up and looked at me like I was crazy. "You mean you get up there in the sky in an airplane with nothing holding you up and you're not afraid? You'll never get me to go up in one of those things, for sure," he said and meant it too. We laughed and joked around and had a great time together.

Perspective. What is fearful to one is sport to another. I learned a lot from Roger and Joe.

THE HAUNT

Traveling through North Carolina in my motorhome one Halloween a few years ago, I encountered a Haunt. This was a permanent haunted-house attraction in an old brick three-story abandoned school. I thought about my fears of the dark and horror movies and decided to walk alone through the haunted house confronting and releasing old childhood fears.

I bought my ticket from Dracula and entered through the graveyard after sunset. Few customers were at the Haunt that evening and I was alone during my entire walk-through. I paid attention to my breath, feelings, childhood memories, and all the emotions that surfaced. Taking a few deep breaths, I entered the Haunt.

This is only an illusion. It is not real and has no power, was my mantra as I slowly began the journey through the old spooky building. My head snapped left as a bloody-faced hatchet-man jumped from behind a door and stopped inches from my face, dripping blood from his mouth. I didn't flinch, held fast, remained silent and steady, faced him eye to eye, and then slowly walked on. I felt no fear.

I continued through the entire Haunt slowly and in presence. Graveyards, spider webs, and spooky creatures of all sorts came at me during my forty-five-minute adventure. But I made it.

At the exit door, I chatted with a local policeman and he shared that one evening after the Haunt had closed, the alarm system was triggered and he was called to investigate. He entered the Haunt alone and walked through the entire building with only a flashlight. He was the only one there (hopefully) amidst the spooky graveyards, decapitated people, ghosts, goblins, and other horrors. He said he was glad to leave. That would have been very frightening for me, but perhaps now I could do it.

BEYOND FEAR

The sun warmed my skin on this beautiful fall morning and I squinted a bit as Harley and I rounded a gentle bend on the winding country road. It was only 9 am and I was already out on Harley exploring the local Georgia countryside near my campground. A life adventure was about to unfold.

An explosion of brilliant multi-colored fall leaves was everywhere, and I stopped to admire and photograph these lovely creations of nature. A small mailbox pull-off appeared and I braked to a stop, set the kickstand, and dismounted my trusty steed. Walking just a few steps away, I gazed into the morning sun streaming through an ocean of fall leaves in brilliant reds, oranges, yellows, and browns. "Click, click," went the shutter. There were no houses visible as the two driveways leading from the pull-off each went up the small rise then turned and disappeared into thick woods.

Sensing someone near, I glanced left and saw a woman approaching down the drive. I didn't give it much thought. But as she approached, I turned again to greet her and saw that she was carrying a small object in her right hand. Taking a few steps toward her, I said, "Good morning, I'm Johnny, out for a little ride on Harley and was admiring your beautiful trees with the morning sunlight streaming through the leaves."

Then I saw she was carrying a gun. I was dumbstruck! "You better get your &^%#@! ass off my property, pronto." Now I was double dumbstruck as this innocent event went from a friendly photo shoot to facing an enraged woman holding a gun and swearing at me.

"Well, thank you for your hospitality, my friend. I'll be on my way now," I gently replied. Turning slowly, I walked over to Harley, carefully repacked my camera back into the saddlebag, put on my helmet, and tossed my leg over the seat. Without rushing, I started the engine, shifted Harley into first gear, released the clutch, and drove away. I had no sense that she would harm me and was pleased that I did not respond from fear or anger and simply rode off.

A quarter mile away, I stopped at a small Baptist church with several cars parked out front and a half-dozen people milling around. I asked them about the woman at the mailbox up the left drive. "Oh, that must have been Mildred, she does that sort of thing and is deathly afraid of anybody that gets near her property. I don't think she's shot anybody, and we just leave her alone."

"Aren't there laws preventing someone from threatening a stranger and pointing a gun at them for taking a few photos of leaves while standing next to the road?" I asked?

"Mister, this is Georgia and the deep south and that's just the way it is down here."

I scratched my head in disbelief. There was nothing more to say so I cranked up Harley and rode away.

What a way to live, I thought. Here's Mildred, so caught-up in fear that she needs to keep the world at arm's length with a deadly weapon just to feel safe. I was incredibly thankful that I wasn't Mildred.

The following year, a friend and I were out riding Harley on back roads in neighboring Alabama when we stopped to admire and photograph an old barn. Other than a nearby farmhouse, we were alone in our little peaceful world. "WOOOOF, WOOOOF," the deep resonating bark of large dogs startled me.

Turning toward the house, I saw two huge dogs running full stride toward us in attack mode with teeth bared. There was no time to mount Harley and leave, and no place to go for protection. Without hesitation, I flung my arms up above my head and raced full speed directly toward the dogs, screaming and hollering at full volume,

"ARRRRGGGGGGGHHHHH." Immediately the dogs stopped, hesitated a second, then ran full tilt back toward their house. I continued after the dogs for a few seconds, then stopped and strolled back to my friend and Harley. We mounted and rode off.

I responded to both events spontaneously from my heart rather than from my head. I didn't give either situation much thought before acting. I just did what instantly came to me.

As I grow, I have more choices available to respond to life events and you will too. Those people that carry unresolved anger and rage do not have peaceful responses available to life events. They can only respond with anger and rage. After one does their work...softer, gentler, more appropriate responses become available.

KARISHMA

My mentor, Reiki Master, and dear friend, Karishma, is an extraordinary woman. We connected initially in 1998, and she has become a dear close friend and spiritual teacher for me.

It is necessary to have an authentic teacher when one walks the path of the spiritual warrior and ventures on a spiritual pilgrimage. Her patience and guidance over time have proven critical to my inner growth and spiritual maturity. She's been my lifeline and has protected me, sometimes from myself as I've ventured along my path. Being in the presence of a spiritually mature teacher is of great benefit. If I do what the teacher suggests, I benefit; if I don't, I do not benefit. That's very clear and very simple. Either way, the teacher remains unaffected.

In early 2002, Karishma suffered a major health issue that left her seriously compromised and partially paralyzed. Her physical challenges are enormous. Yet I have never heard her complain, or wish life was different-not even once. That is spiritual maturity. She says, "Johnny, as my outer world has contracted, my inner world has expanded." Thank you, blessed Goddess Karishma, for your guidance and love.

Until 2019, Karishma could get around her home and go outside with her walker and wheelchair. But her condition deteriorated and since then, she cannot even roll-over in bed unassisted.

Try lying in bed for twenty-four hours unable to roll-over or scratch an itch somewhere that is driving you nuts. She has lived like that for about five years now yet greets me with a smile and kind word every time. She continues to help me and others with her wisdom and spiritual gifts. She still never complains. Karishma provides an anchor point to help hold the balance of loving energy across the spectrum of the entire planet.

GIFTING

Downshifting and braking Harley for the red light, I stopped a few feet from the homeless man in a wheelchair on the curb. His rumpled Army hat, beard, and little sign made me feel uneasy. He's sitting in a wheelchair right next to me and I'm sitting on my tricked-out, chromed-to-the-hilt Harley-Davidson motorcycle. My ego screamed, *why does he have to sit in that wheelchair right next to me and make me feel so uneasy?* I knew that what I was saying was baloney, but I was silently screaming it, anyway.

I wanted to look at him and yet didn't want to. Slowly, I turned and met his deep-set eyes and asked myself, *how much money do you have in your wallet, Johnny?* I didn't know. *Would you miss twenty dollars?* I thought for a second. *If I don't know how much money is in my wallet, then I won't miss having twenty dollars less than what I don't know I have. Right?* So, I pulled around the corner, parked my bike, walked to the man and gifted him twenty dollars. He politely thanked me and I departed.

Many thoughts went through my mind about the homeless man. Will he use my gift for drugs or booze? Am I supporting his addictions? Why doesn't he go get a job? On and on, my mind raced. Oh well, I thought, at least I gifted him rather than not. I rode off.

A few hours later, I returned through the same intersection and saw the same man, standing on the opposite corner with a different hat, different sign, and NO WHEEL CHAIR. He was miraculously healed, and I felt miraculously scammed. I was angry and mad as hell, blah, blah, blah, and so on.

Then the insight occurred. I saw that I caused my anger and grief not him, because my gift had attachments. A gift is only a gift if given from the heart with no attachments to the outcome. When the twenty dollars transferred from my hand to his, an authentic gift would have been complete. With an authentic gift, it matters not what the recipient does with the gift. Anything else is an ego game. But my ego got involved, and that's what disturbed me.

How I relate outwardly to a homeless person, is similar to how I relate inwardly to a homeless aspect of my consciousness within. Perhaps the homeless aspects within are those pieces of me that are lost, ungrounded, or frightened. The more compassionate I am to my homeless pieces within, the more compassionate I am to a homeless person on the street. If I deny the homeless within, I will ignore the homeless on the street. And if I am hostile to the homeless within, I will be hostile to the homeless on the street. Heal the inner, and the outer follows naturally. The man in the wheelchair was a teacher for me.

My friend-brother, Joe, demonstrated gifting to me several years ago before solid-state memory sticks. Joe loved a certain CD I was playing at my home one day. So, I bought a second copy of the CD and gifted it to him. He thanked me several times.

Six months later, while driving in Joe's car, I said, "Hey, Joe, how about playing that CD I gave you six months ago?"

"Love to, Johnny, but I gave it away." I was stunned. That CD cost me about fifteen dollars and some time to get it for him. Those thoughts instantly ran through my head and I felt a betrayed.

Joe continued, "A few weeks ago, I was driving with a close friend with your CD playing and he absolutely loved it. He asked who the musician was and how I found out about him. I told him all about you and how you generously gifted me that CD. When we arrived at our destination, I put the CD into its jacket and gifted it to him. It was my favorite CD, Johnny, and I played it continually until I gifted it to him. Perhaps he'll gift it to someone else someday."

I was stunned. With a few extra dollars in my wallet, it's easy for me to buy something and gift it. When I gifted Joe the CD, I saw myself as generous, but I was still attached to that CD. Had I known what I learned from the homeless man, I would have been supportive of Joe's actions rather than disturbed even before he shared his story.

Additionally, when gifting personal items, I used to find things I didn't particularly want anymore, gift them, and keep my best things for myself. Joe explained that by gifting your most valued and cherished possessions, you gift a bit of your heart as well. Joe taught me a lot about gifting.

THE MONEY BOX - WHAT'S MONEY FOR?

While riding Harley one evening in northern Idaho, I stopped at the exit of a strip mall next to a family of three sitting by their van. The woman with two children struck me as sincere and in need. The sign over her empty donation box said that they were "trying to get back home to North Carolina," and "we appreciate your help."

I shut down Harley and asked a few questions. The pleasant woman introduced herself as Sandi and said that she had traveled with her children to Idaho from North Carolina several months prior to start a new life. Her uncle in Idaho told her that they could temporarily stay with him and of opportunities for employment in the area. So, they put their few belongings in the van and moved to Idaho. The opportunities didn't work out well, and the uncle revealed himself as an abusive drunk.

After trying to work things out with him, Sandi said she loaded her belongings in her van, grabbed her children and escaped from the crazy uncle while he was out at a local bar. They were returning to their old homestead in North Carolina.

I thanked Sandi for sharing, put twenty dollars in her hand, and asked how much more she needed to get back to North Carolina. She said they had collected a few dollars already but needed about five hundred dollars more for fuel and food while sleeping in their car.

"Blessings my friend," I said and headed for Dutch parked only a mile distant. I have a money box in Dutch. And every few years, I withdraw a rather large sum of cash to restock my money box. This way I have sufficient cash readily available when I want it.

Pulling up to Dutch, I asked myself, *how much is in your money box, Johnny?* I hadn't a clue. *Is there one, two, or even three-thousand-dollars in there?* I didn't know. Continuing, I asked *if there were five hundred dollars less than the unknown amount in the money box, you obviously wouldn't miss it for five hundred dollars less than some unknown amount is also an unknown amount. Therefore, a five-hundred-dollar gift to Sandi and her children won't cost anything and is a freebie. Right?*

Before I could find the obvious flaw in my illogical logic, I retrieved five hundred dollars from the money box, fired up Harley and rode back to the strip mall. I didn't share anything about me at all with Sandi. I simply gave her five hundred dollars in cash, thanked her for allowing me to be of service, and left.

I learned a little more about gifting from Sandi and her family. And here it is fifteen years later and the wonderful feelings of supporting someone anonymously have never faded.

What is money for? Certainly, it is a blessing to have sufficient to live comfortably and many don't have that. To define oneself by their bank-account balance is total ego. The personality wants to hoard money, while the soul wants to use it to help others.

BEYOND COURAGE - GAIL LAUGHING WATER

"Thanks for coming over early Gail," I beamed as I greeted my friend outside Dutch on a clear, cool Florida winter morning in early 2011. "It's a beautiful day for an airplane ride," I remarked, tossing my arm above my head in a sweeping gesture of gratitude to the Gods for this opportunity to fly with Gail in a little single-engine Piper Cherokee.

"I'm not so sure I'm ready for this," Gail remarked. "I've avoided flying all my life, for I have a deep-rooted fear of flying, or rather, crashing. This is difficult for me Johnny."

"Well, Gail, you can call it off anytime between now and our take-off roll down the runway. We'll carefully check over everything together inside and outside our airplane in slo-mo. Please remember that you have the final say and if you wish, we'll put her back in the chocks, and go have coffee, no questions asked. How's that for a deal?"

"Well, it sure couldn't be any fairer than that. I'll tell you right now that I've carried this flying fear for a very long time, but perhaps this is the day to release it."

"Deal!" I said and acknowledged her trepidation with a gentle pat on her shoulder.

We fired up Harley and rode light-heartedly to the small airport and parked next to the flight-line. I love this little airport, with its friendly ambiance and wonderful staff. "These airplanes are my flying family, Gail."

"Gosh, Johnny, are we going in one of those little, small ones?" she whispered nervously as we climbed off Harley and walked toward the airplanes.

"Absolutely, Gail, and that little red and white Piper Cherokee over there is our trusty steed today," I said pointing toward our airplane.

"She sure looks tiny and flimsy to me, Johnny. I'm not so sure about this," she remarked.

"Well, let's go look her over, Gail, and I'll show you how she works."

And we did. We poked around inside and outside, and I explained everything to Gail about the flight controls, their functions, how safe flying is, and what would happen in the unlikely event that the little engine failed while we were airborne.

"Wouldn't we plummet straight down to earth?" she asked, a cloud crossing over her face.

"Not hardly, Gail, we'd glide just like a glider plane does and find a little field, golf course, or road to land on. And the area around here is very safe for flying as there are no mountains, few obstacles, and plenty of open fields, golf courses, and roads to land on. Also, from a thousand feet up we can see the Gulf of Mexico to the west and easily identify the coastal towns. So, it's very hard to get lost, too."

I smiled as Gail noticed how flimsy and thin the skin of our little Cherokee felt compared to a car. I remarked that structural strength, not skin strength, is necessary in an airplane as there is little chance of someone ramming us at a stoplight. We laughed and giggled as we completed our thorough preflight of the Cherokee's airframe and engine.

We said a little blessing of thanks and gratitude for the beautiful day, our wonderful flying friend "Cherokee," and aligned our energies of gratitude and playfulness with those of divinity. We visualized our flight from engine start, through take-off, flying, landing, taxiing to the ramp and engine shut-down. I helped Gail into the right seat, strapped her in, then climbed into the left seat and closed the door.

Together, we then thoroughly checked all the instruments across the dashboard, ensuring that everything was in order and that all was ready for flight. I noted with pleasure her interest, and that she seemed more at ease. I felt honored that this courageous woman trusted me to take her airborne for this potentially life-changing adventure. Although she was still apprehensive, Gail told me to continue and was ready for engine start.

We fired up Cherokee's little engine, taxied to the run-up area, and went through our pre-takeoff checks together. "Doors closed and locked, flight controls checked, trim set for take-off, mags checked, mixture rich, fuel selector on both tanks, flaps up, runway clear, and we're ready to go, Gail."

"And so am I," she said quietly letting out a heavy sigh and gently touching my arm. I pointed our little Cherokee straight down runway 32 and gently pushed the throttle all the way in. Feeling normal acceleration and noting all gauges in the green, we rolled a short distance to a gentle lift-off into a clear, bright Florida winter morning. Out of the corner of my eye, I noticed Gail's little smile.

At one thousand feet, I again glanced right and now saw a bigger smile spreading across her face. She's enjoying this, I thought. Shortly, she pulled out her camera phone and began taking photos, grinning from ear to ear like a giddy little girl.

Our flight was pleasant and uneventful, and forty-five minutes later we parked our Cherokee, deplaned, and stepped lightly back on to the ramp.

"Johnny, as we started our take-off, I felt my fears falling away. It was like they were glued to the ground. Once airborne, my fears faded and I was free to enjoy this wonderful flight. Thank you so very much."

"The pleasure was truly mine, Gail," I remarked. I was filled with joy.

Subsequently, Gail Laughing Water has flown fearlessly on several commercial carriers. The courage one must find to walk straight into one's fears, real or imagined, is enormous. It's akin to standing in the face of an emotional tidal wave and holding that stance at all costs, down to the wire and beyond. Gail could have called off our flight anytime up to take-off. But she stood her ground, trusted her gut, and KNEW that if she were to live on the free-of-fear level of consciousness, she had to do this; she had to embrace this fear.

When one unwaveringly faces one's fears head on, the fears weaken and dissolve. The energy required to hold onto them is freed and available for one's use as desired. There is no way around doing this work. Blessings, Gail Laughing Water, my courageous friend.

April, 2021, Florida. I sent the draft of this chapter to Gail for accuracy, comments, and any subsequent experiences she wished to share relating to our Cherokee flight in 2011. I was particularly interested to know if relief from her flying fears had sustained. She graciously edited the manuscript and included the following comments:

I am Gail Laughing Water, and it pretty much happened just as Johnny described it. I even had a chance to pay his experience, strength, and kindness forward about three years later. A friend of mine had passed suddenly and her husband had been diagnosed as legally blind the year prior. They lived on the easternmost seaboard of Maryland. He wanted to grant his wife's wish to have her ashes spread in the ocean off the coast of California where her family still lived and she had grown up.

I drove down to Maryland and became her husband's seeing-eye guide on the many flights it took for us to get to the west coast and back. Our first flight was aboard a small twin-engine prop plane that held about eighteen passengers. It was a little bit bumpy—ok, a very bumpy ride that early morning, heading over the bay toward Dulles airport where we changed planes to a much larger commercial airliner.

But had it not been for my friend, Johnny MedicineBear, and his quiet strength and coaching those few years previous, I would still live in the shadow of my fear of flying.

I will always be eternally grateful to him.

SYNCHRONICITY

Do you have a sense that Spirit, through your guides and angels, is taking care of you in subtle supportive ways? Or are you one of those that believes that something awful is just waiting to happen to you sometime before the sun goes down? Perhaps, you feel like you're being punished for some minor deed or perceived infraction of some rule. Wouldn't it be nice if we could exert some influence on what comes our way? Well, we can. And that's a fact, Jack! You don't have to do much or change any of your core beliefs to make this happen.

Forty years ago, I was very skeptical about the spiritual realms of reality because I didn't understand nor have the awareness to even meaningfully relate to Spirit. Today I have an appreciation for the underlying energetic or spiritual components of reality that support our physical experience, and yes, we do have an influence on what comes into our field of view. If I'm constantly complaining about life, rarely grateful, excessively critical of myself and others, judgemental to the extreme, living on auto-pilot, and not caring if I hurt others or not, I'll attract unpleasant experiences into my life. But if I'm compassionate, loving, and caring, and care about others and how I interact with them, I'll attract uplifting and more pleasant experiences into my life.

And that is another fact, Jack! I attract into my experience people and events that match the energies that I put forward.

Riding Harley several years ago in Minnesota, I happened by the Duluth International Airport. Near the entry road was a Phantom jet-fighter on a pedestal. I stopped, shut Harley down, dismounted, retrieved my Canon camera and took several photos of this fine display. I thought of the many times I'd flown the Phantom and pleasant memories returned in a flood of emotions. *Thank you, Spirit for this wonderful moment,* I mused and repacked my camera and tossed my leg back over Harley.

Twisting the ignition switch, I was greeted by silence instead of the usual whir of the fuel pump and the illumination of a few status lights. I stuck my hand over the headlight and it was also off. I switched the ignition on and off a few times but Harley was totally dead. *Humm.* So, I dismounted and took the seat off, revealing the battery and a fuse box. All seemed in order. I checked the battery cables and they seemed tight to me. Not knowing much about the electrical system on Harley, I guessed that a main protection fuse had blown. So, I scratched my head and gently whispered, "I could sure use a friend now that knows this bike, to get me on my way."

Within two minutes a couple pulled over in a small pick-up truck and asked, "What's wrong with your bike, my friend?"

"Well," I said, "I'm Johnny, and I shut her down to take a few photos and now she's dead as a doornail."

"I'm Tony" said the nice man, "and my wife, Chris, over there in the truck and I ride. I work on Harleys a lot. Let's take a look at your battery terminals. Sometimes even when they seem tight, they lose continuity and the whole system shuts down. I've got a 10mm wrench in my truck. I'll be right back." He's back in thirty seconds, takes a few twists on both battery terminals and says, "Give her a try now."

I turn on the ignition and all of Harley's lights illuminate. I smile, check for the neutral light, ensure the kill switch is off and squeeze the starter. Harley fires up in all his glory. "Tony, I cannot thank you enough for your kindness." I pulled out a twenty-dollar bill and pushed it toward him.

"No thanks" Tony said, "Chris and I are on a little vacation for a month or so and I'm just here to help."

"You are a kind man, Tony, and this is how one act of kindness engenders other acts of kindness. I'll pay this gift forward."

Tony went back to his truck, smiled at Chris, and slowly they drove away. As he pulled out, I read the sign on the side of his pick-up: "Tony & Chris's Harley-Davidson Motorcycle Service, Lutz, Florida." Wow! Harley breaks down, and a kind motorcycle mechanic drives eighteen hundred miles complete with a lovely assistant and tools and fixes me up for free. Now that is synchronicity at its finest.

Events of this nature happen quite frequently when we are aligned with the energetic. This is not luck, and it cannot be explained for it is outside of the physical realms. Perhaps events like this happen to you also, but if they don't, try aligning yourself with the positive energies of spirit and the earth and let the energies of nature work for you. May the force be with you.

I KILLED MY DAUGHTERS

During May 2015, I spent several days in Amarillo, Texas parked in an RV repair shop fixing a few minor issues with Dutch. Harley and I explored Amarillo and the local countryside. Several miles northeast of downtown, I happened upon the *Wat Lao* Buddhist Temple complex and rode Harley into the parking lot for a look around.

Graciously welcomed into their dharma hall, I sat peacefully before the beautiful altar, which included several life-size jade Buddha sculptures. Peaceful energy was pervasive and I felt at ease and at home.

Resident monk, Master Sam, welcomed me, blessed me, and tied a small ribbon around each of my wrists. He invited me to sit peacefully in front of the beautiful altar. I did.

As I relaxed, the altar began to sway slightly. It was a mystical journey. The altar softened and became a window into my past. I saw many people in the background moving and walking around. They were luminous in appearance, and I knew they were the ones I killed during my missions in Vietnam.

A young pregnant woman pushed through the throng and worked her way to the front of the crowd. She stared directly at me. Clothed in a tattered, worn dress, she stretched her hand forward reaching for me when poof, a puff of smoke appeared and she was gone. I knew I had killed her on some mission in Vietnam. Several minutes later, she reappeared and pushed her way forward through the crowd again. And again, she reached for me when poof, another puff of smoke appeared and she was gone again. A third and fourth repetitive event followed.

Sitting in silence, I allowed this vision to settle, then returned to normal consciousness. Bowing silently to the Buddha and Master Sam, I slowly walked from the Dharma Hall. At home, I untied the two ribbons and placed them in a safe place.

The young girl vision stayed with me and several days later I shared this experience with my insightful mystic teacher-friend Karishma. She listened patiently and asked several questions about dates. "Yes, Karishma, I flew the Phantom in Vietnam in 1972 and 1973. Sarah was born in 1978 and Jennifer in 1979."

"Johnny, I've tracked the karmic threads and the young pregnant girl that came forward with her arm stretched, reaching for you was your daughter, Sarah. Her unborn baby was your other daughter, Jennifer. That is how they died in their previous incarnation."

How bizarre is this, I thought? If a fortune teller had told me before sobriety that I had killed my daughters in Vietnam, ending their last physical life, and that I would someday learn this while visiting a Buddhist temple in Amarillo, Texas, I would have scratched my head and walked out the door thinking this guy was crazy. But today, I welcome this knowledge to heal the wounds of yesterday.

Four months later, Sarah, Jennifer and I sat together in Dutch and opened a sacred session. "I wish to share a significant event with you two and ask you both to listen without interruption to completion. Then we can chat about it."

I shared about the Amarillo Wat Lao Buddhist Temple, Master Sam, the sacred altar, the sacred blessing, and vision I had with the beings I saw at the altar. I shared about the young pregnant woman in the tattered dress that came forward several times with outstretched arms, only to disappear in a puff of smoke. I shared about my conversation with Karishma and her tracking of our karmic connections.

We sat in silence for a while, allowing this story to settle. Finally, Jennifer looked at her sister, Sarah, and said, "Mom?" We laughed and hugged. I am very grateful for the closeness of our family. And apparently, we've been a family for at least two lifetimes. I gave each daughter one of the yellow ribbons and tied them on their wrists.

GIFT EXCHANGE WITH DAD

Being with Dad about a month before he passed was a gift for us both. He was a mellow man now, living with Mom at home and sleeping in his own bed. But Mom and Dad were getting old and wearing out. They had limited time remaining.

I sat by Dad's bed one afternoon and asked him to join me in breathing together. This was easy, and we simply synchronized our breaths. The constant, "Why Johnny?" questions ceased, and his doubting mind was quiet. He was getting close to releasing his physical body back to our Earth Mother.

I asked spirit to please join us and support us. We sat in stillness, breathing and doing nothing. After a while, we concluded our breathing time together and closed our space. Dad opened his eyes and said, "Johnny, I've no idea what you did, but I am not as afraid to die as I was earlier this morning."

Spirit gave us a beautiful gift a month before Dad passed.

DAD'S PASSING

I leaned toward daughter Jennifer at my father's funeral and whispered, "Jenn, I feel Dad's presence in this chapel, and I sense that he's up there in the front right corner by that window observing us." She smiled at me and squeezed my hand as if to say, 'I feel him too, Dad.' Reverend David Parker rambled on for a while, then offered the family and friends an opportunity to share. I walked toward the front of the church, pulled out my old ten-hole blues-harp Hohner harmonica and played a little jig called "Lumps in the Pudding." That was Dad's signature song that he learned from his mother and taught me to play when I was about four-years-old. I've been playing the harmonica and that jig forever, and when we meet, I'll be glad to play it for you, too.

Dad took me flying at thirteen in a little airplane that he and a few of his buddies rebuilt. When he passed, I was in my late fifties and a captain with American Airlines flying the MD-80. Dad was my first flight instructor.

I loved flying for American Airlines and to me it was never work; it was my sport. I loved wearing my uniform, walking through the terminals, setting up the cockpit, interacting with the passengers, and flying these marvelous airplanes.

After 9/11, the rush to launch on-time relaxed a bit, and I took a few minutes to play "Lumps in the Pudding" on my harmonica for the passengers on nearly every flight. I made this little forty-five second concert part of my welcome aboard chat. Passengers and crews alike complimented me on the little show. "Folks, we don't have a fancy sound system on our Super-80 aircraft, but I've brought along my little ten-hole blues-harp harmonica that my father and grandmother taught me to play when I was a little boy. Here's a quick tune I learned from them many years ago." Without fail, there was clapping and maybe a whoop or holler. The stress and tension of travel and flying dropped away with "Lumps in the Pudding." Flying for me was total pleasure.

After Dad's funeral at his home in South Jersey, I returned to the Chicago area and sensed Dad with me around my home. I set out Dad's ring and his father's pocket watch in a special place and Dad and I chatted. I loved having Dad around, and for several weeks, I strongly felt his presence.

We chatted about my childhood, his childhood, our home, and some of the significant memories that we shared together. He said that if he could have, he wouldn't have treated me so harshly and would have played with me more when I was a boy.

Dad didn't have a playful childhood and became the man in his parents' home at about sixteen. He refused to bring a girl home until they added an indoor bathroom to his parents' small house. Apparently, his father and older brothers didn't mind using the outhouse and pushed the bathroom project aside. So, Dad designed and built the indoor bathroom in his parent's house on his own.

Even though there was only a twenty-six-year age difference between us, Dad was about a hundred years older than me. He was from a different generation.

Our time together after his death was beneficial as I came to understand why Dad treated me as harshly as he did. I forgave him for his brutality, but releasing all my anger, rage and resentments toward him required another twenty years of work. It took time with my spiritual teacher, shared in the third section (*Into the Light*) of this book, to resolve my anger and rage toward Dad.

DRIVING TIPS

This may seem like a strange place to find a chapter about driving tips. However, I believe there is much to gain from observing one's own driving patterns and the driving patterns of others. I was fortunate to have Dad as my driving instructor, as he had a ton of common sense, good practical ideas, and emphasized safety above all else. He instilled in me driving behaviors I've applied and passed on to my daughters.

I've got Dad now on a spiritual hot-line, live, and direct from the land of next-life. "Hi Dad, please share all the wonderful driving tips you passed on to me so many years ago."

"Sure Johnny, here we go."

"When you come home, don't just switch off the ignition, jump out, and abandon your car. Consciously shut it down. Turn off the wipers, headlights, and radio first, then switch off the ignition. Pay attention and listen for any unusual sounds. If something amiss is discovered, note it and fix it before you use your car again.

"When you next return, do a little "pre-flight" as you approach your car and take notice of anything unusual, like new oil on the floor under the engine, or perhaps she's listing slightly to one side. Investigate and correct if necessary. Don't drive away in a compromised car that's not 100% road ready if possible.

"All should be quiet as you insert the ignition key. Switch the ignition key on first and listen for unusual sounds for a second or so before you crank her up. And always start your car at idle with your right foot lightly on the brake, not the gas. After she starts, listen for any unusual sounds or noises for a few seconds. If you hear something, investigate before you drive off. You might detect a condition that, if not rapidly corrected, might grow into a major repair or fail into something dangerous. Most of the time, all will be well and it's easy to slip into complacency. That's understandable, so just be present as you approach, get in, and start up your car.

"Let your car run at idle for about a minute before you give her any throttle. This doesn't mean you can't move, for immediately after engine start you can drop her in gear and you're on your way. Just don't give her any gas for the first minute to allow your engine to warm a little and lubrication to flow freely. The colder the weather, the more important this is.

"Keep your registration and insurance card in an envelope over a visor or in the glove box and include a $20 bill with it. You might forget your wallet and find yourself short of cash at the pump or convenience store check-out. When you get home, replace the $20 before you take off your coat or you will surely forget to do it later. Then when you next need that $20, it won't be there and you've compromised your system.

"While driving, if possible, always leave yourself an 'out' to one or both sides.

Ideally, you will have safe space in front and behind your car as well. The unexpected always happens unexpectedly.

"Imagine driving on a multi-lane hi-speed freeway when the car or truck on your left inches toward you. If there is a car on your right, you've no place to go. Don't let yourself get boxed in like that if you can avoid it and do not cruise side-by-side with another vehicle for any distance, if possible. This allows you an escape route, if necessary. Be aware of where you are in your local surroundings and strive to be in the safest, least vulnerable place.

"Leave an absolute minimum of two seconds between you and the vehicle in front of you while cruising along. Even in heavy traffic, don't be badgered by aggressive unconscious drivers pushing you to close the gap in front of you to any less than two seconds. That's YOUR safety margin. Let them pile up their cars while you continue on your merry way.

"Leave five or more seconds between you and the vehicle in front of you if you're on a lightly traveled high speed road. Always drive in the least vulnerable space you can find. This means stay as far away from other vehicles as possible. If you're driving ten seconds behind a vehicle, you've room to relax a little and enjoy the scenery. Even if the vehicle in front of you hits a brick wall, you'll be able to safely stop and avoid the wreck. But it you're trailing less than two seconds behind the car in front of you, chances are, no matter how vigilant you are, you'll become part of the pile-up if that vehicle initiates a foot-to-the-floor panic stop. Additionally, if their brake lights are inoperative, or you are distracted even for a heartbeat, you won't know what happened until you plow into the vehicle in front of you. Spread that distance even further if you're trailing a motorcycle, for any collision with a motorcycle is probably a death sentence for the biker crew.

"Don't make the car in front of you your primary focus, either. Glance at them, then look at what's going on a quarter mile, half mile, or even farther ahead. You cannot do this if you are driving aggressively or on someone's bumper. But you can, if you're five-plus seconds behind the car in front of you. This way, you can anticipate what is coming toward you in the next minute and hopefully eliminate unpleasant surprises. You might notice someone weaving excessively or driving very slowly and develop a little plan to deal with them before they fill your windshield.

"If you are on a four-lane road gaining on the car in front of you and decide to pass, don't wait until you're directly behind them to change lanes. Give them some room and switch to your passing lane at least a tenth of mile away. And always change lanes slowly. Ease out of your lane into another, just in case you've not seen a car hiding in a blind spot over your left shoulder. Hopefully, they'll have time to warn you or move out of your way. If you aggressively change lanes, any safety margin is reduced to zero.

"Approaching busy intersections with multiple lanes, expect the surrounding cars to make last second lane changes. They may be unfamiliar with the area and realize that they are in the wrong lane to go where they want. Without looking around, they'll head for the lane they need and hope for the best. Give them room, allow them to go, and perhaps you've avoided a wreck.

"If you're approaching an intersection and are planning on making a left turn across traffic and have to wait a bit till traffic clears, stop in the middle of the intersection where you will begin your turn with your wheels roughly straight. This will prevent you from inadvertently being shoved into on-coming traffic should you get slammed in the rear. Wait patiently and don't inch forward. Stay positioned without moving till traffic clears then go, turn, and accelerate normally. Don't jump hard on the throttle. Engines tend to stall or fail during rapid throttle movements more often than during cruise use.

"If you inch forward every few seconds while waiting for an opportunity to turn across on-coming traffic, then you will make the drivers of the on-coming traffic nervous. Everyone that sees you move, even one inch, won't know if you are going to continue moving or if you will stop in the next inch. So, STAY PUT till you are ready to turn across traffic. The "inching forward" guideline applies also to wherever you are stopped and waiting for traffic to clear, like turning onto a highway from a stop sign.

"Suppose you are holding at a STOP sign to make a left turn across traffic onto a street. The car approaching from your left is signaling to make a right turn onto your street. As this car approaches, you glance right, see that it's clear, and pull out in front of the car that's signaling a right turn onto your street. 'WHAM!' You get smashed in the driver's door at speed by the car signaling the right turn.

"As the dust settles, you note that his right turn signal is still flashing but obviously he didn't turn. 'I'm sorry,' he says, 'I had no intention of turning. I must have failed to turn off my right signal after I passed a car a mile or so down the road.' It is very easy to leave a turn signal flashing for miles without the driver's knowledge.

"Regardless of who is at fault, could you have prevented this mishap? Absolutely. The only thing you know about another car that has a blinker light flashing is that the blinker bulb works. Anything else is an assumption. As that car approached from your left, signaling a right turn onto your street, you must wait till he slows and begins his right turn. Then, it is safe to pull out in front of that car. Even if the approaching car wants to turn right onto your street and has the blinker on indicating his intention to turn, he may have a last second change of heart, snap off the blinker and accelerate right into your driver's door. Finally, take your time and don't be rushed by nearby aggressive drivers.

"Johnny, if you ever start to skid on water or snow, loosen your grip on the wheel and gently turn into the skid. That means, whichever side of your car the rear is skidding towards, that's the way to turn your front wheels. Don't turn a lot, just a little. Also, if you are having a terrible day and are about to skid or run off a road, try to stay conscious and look at what is filling your windshield. If you've a choice to collide with either a telephone pole or a tree, take the telephone pole. You'll bash up your car, but utility poles snap easier and are much softer than trees. Big trees are deeply rooted and have little give. If you're heading for a 3-foot diameter mature oak tree, you're probably done for. Give this some thought now, Johnny, and refresh yourself occasionally so that if the time should ever arise, you'll know from instinct exactly what to do. The real-time panic stop or emergency is not the time to review what to do.

"Suppose you're driving at highway speed on a busy two or four-lane highway approaching a railroad crossing. You are familiar with this crossing and occasionally are stopped by the flashing red lights and the lowered gates as a high-speed train roars by. But if the warning signals are not activated, does that mean that it is 100% safe to drive across these tracks? No! Does the train engineer know if the gates and lights are functioning properly? Should the activation mechanisms fail, a warning signal is sent to the engineer in the approaching train. However, getting a high-speed passenger train or long heavy freight train stopped may take over a mile. And the system that warns the engineer of the gate and lights failure may also fail. I'm suggesting that one use caution when approaching railroad tracks.

"Slow down and look as far as possible both ways up and down the tracks for approaching trains and don't cross the tracks until you've cleared left and right sufficiently that you won't be hit by a high-speed train. Few people do this but several thousand people are injured or die each year from grade crossing accidents. Don't be one of them."

"Thanks Dad, I wrote all your suggestions down and they will go into a book soon that may help people."

"Great Johnny, thanks for checking in."

I'll add one more to Dad's list that is very important. Driving is an impersonal experience, so please take nothing that happens out there personally. Just see events as "happening" not "happening to me." Never get angry at anyone or anything. And if someone cuts you off, or flashes you the bird, you can exacerbate the situation and do the same or worse back to them with a string of obscenities, and aggressive, dangerous maneuvers, or you can diffuse the situation by smiling and not taking it personally. Wish them a nice day and be grateful that you're not their life partner. Aggressive people use the highways to dispel and dissipate their anger through hostile behaviors at whoever is in their field of view. Stay detached, let them float on by, and contribute to your safety and the safety of all.

Another afterthought. Here's the scene - I'm driving on a two-lane high speed, open arterial highway near Nowhereville, Montana, and can see for miles in every direction. There is not one car or truck in sight. Then, way in the distance, I see five little black dots on the road coming toward me at high speed. Shortly, they sail by. "Whoosh, whoosh, whoosh, whoosh, whoosh," and then they are gone. Five cars with minimal spacing between each car all jammed dangerously close together. They race by as if coupled together in a little train. Then nothing again for many miles and many minutes.

Why do people choose to drive so dangerously close to each other, rather than spreading out to a safe distance? Nobody in their right mind would follow dangerously close to the car in front of them and stay there for miles and miles when the option to spread out, increase the safety margin, be less vulnerable, and enjoy the ride is right there for the taking. Initially, I could not understand this. But now I have a theory.

Some people live in the fast lane all day, every day, dangerously close to disaster and so this is normal behavior to them. Some feel that if they are not pushing the edge somehow, they are not quite alive. Some just must be first or ride the leader's bumper dangerously close, to feel good. And some find a thrill in knowing that disaster is in their field of view and only they can prevent a catastrophe. Different drivers embrace aggressiveness differently.

And some drivers are just totally in the dark. Some rationalize their aggressive driving with words like, "That's the way dad drove, and that's what I learned and so that's how I drive." They never question the safety and look at other options. They blindly drive right on the bumper of the car in front of them when there's only the two of them on the road.

These people are unconscious, for common sense whispers, "Leave a lot of room in front of you, sit back, relax, look around and enjoy the scenery. After all, you and the few other cars around you are the only cars on the road."

This is rural Montana and if you trail the car in front of you by ten or more seconds, you'll obviously increase your safety and be less vulnerable to mishap. And you'll still get there at the same time.

Anyone can drive a safe distance back for a few minutes, but aggressive drivers cannot sustain a safe distance back and will creep up on the car in front of them unless they constantly remind themselves to stay back.

I've noticed over time that my driving has become more mellow from doing my work. As I release aggressiveness, let go of control, and care about the safety of myself and others, I become more passive, laid-back, and enjoy the scenery much more. What about you?

MOM AND GINNY JAGUAR

My mother was a sweet woman with a genuinely loving heart. On the surface, she presented a warm and positive demeanor, but she worried a lot about life events that really weren't worth worrying about. She saw the glass as half empty rather than half full. Mom was deeply concerned about what others might think of her and our family, and spent a lot of time worrying about these perceptions and the unknown future. As an adult, it was challenging for me to be around her for long periods. But I lived distant and wasn't with her daily.

Pat lived close to Mom and Dad and shared with me how difficult it was for her to deal with Mom. I suggested that she see Mom not as her mother but as an out-of-control five-year-old child. "Pat, you wouldn't be triggered if a five-year-old was ungrateful or inappropriate to you, would you?"

"Well, no, I guess not," replied Pat.

I continued, "You'd ignore the comments and move on. Do the same with Mom." I found that this is a wonderful way to deal with parents or other elders that are ungrateful and/or inappropriate.

In our dysfunctional family, all four of us assumed roles very early on that never changed or matured. Dad was the tyrant. It was his way or the highway. Mom was the peacekeeper/enabler, excusing Dad's abusive, controlling behaviors. Pat was the warrior and stood up for herself, sometimes defiantly. Dad backed down several times facing Pat. I was the victim and received the brunt of Dad's rage, never daring to challenge him or his authority. I was deathly afraid of Dad.

We all congealed into these final forms very early and our family dynamic seemed carved in stone. Nothing changed until very late in life, if at all.

One afternoon, when I was home with Mom, she mentioned she would love to talk to Grandmom (her mother) and tell her how sorry she was for being such a bad daughter. Mom was in her late seventies and her mother had passed twenty-five years prior. I couldn't imagine what Mom might have done to warrant such feelings. So, I pressed a bit and asked, "Mom, please answer yes or no to these simple questions."

"OK, Johnny."

"Did you ever run away from home?"

"No"

"Did you ever get suspended or expelled from school?"

"No."

"Were you ever arrested?"

"No."

"Did you ever do drugs?"

"No."

"Did you ever come home drunk?"

"No."

"Did you ever steal anything more significant than a penny candy?"

"No"

"Did you tell any major lies to your parents?"

"No."

"So, what did you do, Mom, that makes you a bad girl? Perhaps you didn't make your bed a few times?"

"Well, I guess I wasn't such a bad girl after all, was I, Johnny?"

Mom had a great big heart and she loved her mother a lot. "I just wish I could talk to Grandmom. I miss her a lot," Mom shared.

"Well, Mom, maybe we can work something out. Please lie back on your bed here, take a few breaths, close your eyes, and very shortly a beautiful black Jaguar cat will come to you. Gaze into her emerald green eyes, please. Her name is Ginny."

Mom did and Ginny took Mom to visit her mother. I sat near and soon Mom stirred as she returned from her journey.

"Johnny, Ginny took me to the ocean and there was Grandmom on the beach. She saw us and we talked and hugged and it was wonderful. She loves both of us very much."

Subsequently, Mom and Ginny went to the beach and visited Grandmom frequently. It was a wonderful gift to me to be a part of this experience with Mom and Ginny Jaguar.

I lived a distance away and phoned Mom every few days in the morning. Mom occasionally shared that Ginny took her to the beach to visit Grandmom the night before. I was thrilled to hear Mom talk about visiting Grandmom on the beach.

I phoned Mom one morning. Ring, ring.

"Hello, Johnny, how are you today?"

"Well, Mom, I'm fine except I've got a filling that fell out and I'm going to fix it myself."

"Really, Johnny. How are you going to do that?"

"Well, I've got a do-it-yourself dental repair kit and I'm about to drill out my tooth then fill it with goop from my home dental repair kit. Just a second, Mom. It'll only take a minute to finish drilling out my tooth."

I held the phone near the coffee grinder and pressed the button. Grrrrriiiiiinnnnnnndddddd. "IT HURTS A LOT, MOM." Gggggrrrrrrri-iiiinnnnnnnndddddddddd. "ALMOST DONE, MOM." Gggggrrrrriiii-innnnnnndddddddd. Silence. "There, Mom, now all I have to do is fill my tooth with goop."

"Oh, Johnny, that must have hurt. You're a very brave soul."

I chuckled and then told Mom that it was the coffee grinder and I was just having fun with her. She got it, laughed, and said, "You haven't changed a bit since you were Roy Rogers coming down for breakfast a few years ago."

I guess she was right.

RESPECTING THE GODDESS

During the years 2000 through 2004, just prior to retirement with American Airlines, I facilitated several spiritual workshops in my home. Mostly woman attended my small workshops. I found that, like playing the guitar at the fraternity house in college, I was the center of attention. I enjoyed being center stage.

Women were drawn to me and trusted me. I found it easy to be in a woman's favor and sometimes used healing experiences and workshops to become personally close. I did not do this on a conscious level with intentional deception, manipulation, or malice. It just sort of happened. But it did happen.

Everything was consensual, of course, but there was a sacredness and responsibility that I, as the facilitator, failed to honor. A facilitator's responsibility is to set solid boundaries and honor them. It is the facilitator's responsibility to maintain the sacredness of a sacred experience.

I can see today what I could not see twenty years ago.

THE WARRIOR'S CREED - THE WIMP'S CREED

Sitting in deep thought one afternoon, the "Warrior's Creed" jumped out of nowhere. It was the late 1990s, and I seemed to be in a creative mode. As the "Warrior's Creed" blossomed to completion, I thought of the yin and yang, the plus and minus. Shortly, the "Wimp's Creed" flowed out. I offer them as gifts and tools for your spiritual journey.

The Warrior's Creed

Everything I do, think, say, feel, or imagine, either enhances or diminishes me. As surely as one linear earth-time second displaces the previous, always, with every breath, either I move forward or backward, expand, or shrink, gain, or lose-never stagnant.

Emotionally, physically, intellectually, and spiritually, never two breaths in a row, even while sleeping, am I the same. Therefore, I regard each moment as a precious gift, perhaps my last, constantly aware of everything. Yes, everything!

Engaging life fearlessly, fully aware, fully accountable, is the Warrior's Creed.

jmb

The Wimp's Creed

Everything I do, think, say, feel, or imagine, always diminishes me because I'm a wimp. As surely as one linear earth-time second displaces the previous, always, with every breath, I move backward, shrinking from personal growth, responsibility, and ownership, always losing-always stagnant.

Emotionally, physically, intellectually, and spiritually, always, with every breath, even while sleeping, I regress. Therefore, I regard each moment as routine, not caring if it's my last, never aware of anything. Believe me, nothing.

Engaging life fearfully, never aware, never accountable is the Wimp's Creed.

jmb

Most focus on the lighter and brighter aspects of their personality and disregard or deny the darker side. I did. I loved seeing the kind, considerate, generous, and talented Johnny, and had no interest in my darker aspects. I didn't want to acknowledge my flaws.

In my local AA group, there is a chart on the wall listing *Character-Assets* on the left and *Character-Defects* on the right. Character-assets, and character-defects, are discussed in detail in the twelve steps of Alcoholics Anonymous. Love, kindness, compassion, and honesty, are assets, while anger, dishonesty, unwarranted pride, harboring resentments, are defects. It's pretty much common sense.

I looked at that chart for years and one day realized that I cannot have assets without defects. The assets and defects complement each other and are on opposite ends of the same energy thread. I must understand and appreciate dishonesty to know honesty. The genesis of the character assets are the character defects.

It is vital to appreciate that as I am loving, for example, I may also be unloving, as the darker side of love lives within me. Doing my inner work has dissolved much of my unloving energy and that energy is available for my use as I desire. Doing the work frees up energy and shifts me closer to center balance.

The "Warrior's Creed" poured out easily and is all about the light. I visualized the *Taijitu* (the Buddhist Yin-Yang Symbol) which symbolizes the light and dark of everything. One cannot have a shadow without a source of light. The "Wimp's Creed" followed, and I realized I was both the Warrior and the Wimp. For every aspect of light in me, there is also a mirroring aspect of darkness. It may not be apparent, but it's there. Shining my light on my darkness illuminates and diffuses that dark energy.

When I was a young boy, my father berated me. There was a song, *If I knew you were coming, I'd have baked a cake*. Dad would put in different words, "If I knew you were coming, I'd have pushed you back." Then he would laugh and continue with, "Here comes Johnny, the flower of the family, a blooming idiot." He'd laugh louder and walk away.

As a child, I also smiled and laughed, but it always hurt. Every time Dad did that, another little sliver of Johnny went and hid in the basement.

"Your father didn't really mean that, Johnny. He's only joking," Mom would say, rescuing Dad and downplaying the whole incident. "You must respect your father, Johnny, he's working hard, and blah, blah, blah." I heard that same degrading piece over and over and Dad's laughter rang in my ears for years.

Sometimes I'd visualize myself in my Roy Rogers Sheriff's outfit, pull out my pearl-handled pistol and let Dad have it. But I did not directly say anything to Dad about how hurtful his behaviors toward me were.

One day, I realized that when I diminish, degrade, or put myself down, I'm doing to myself exactly what Dad did to me as a child. My six-year-old Little Johnny would run and hide and it would take hours to find him and bring him back home. I did this mostly over small stuff, like bumping my head or dropping something. When I do these things now, I avoid the automatic responses like "that was a stupid thing to do." I slow down, rub the bump on my head, and move on.

Today, I am conscious about what I say to myself and how I respond to myself. It matters how I treat myself. "That was stupid. What's the matter with you, Johnny? That was a dumb thing to do," are past responses that rarely surface.

It took time for these behavioral responses to diminish, but they did. Today, it is rare for me to respond degradingly to myself. And when I do, I don't say, "That was a dumb thing to say." I observe what I did or what I said and simply let it go. Be the warrior, not the wimp.

THE MIDDLE PATH – NON-DUALITY REALITY - AND MORE

Most of us live in a duality paradigm. Duality engenders polarization and separation. Duality means this or that, us or them, right or wrong, good or bad, etc. Spiritual practices, however, embrace beginner's mind-the mind of innocence-the uncluttered, unconditioned mind before thought. This is the mind of a newborn child. It is the mind of non-duality, the mind of presence.

Before sobriety, my reality was total duality. I knew nothing else. Duality requires much energy to sustain, and one is always in conflict. Whatever I chose to believe, created an opposing view. I rationalized and justified my behaviors constantly. I compared myself with others and defended my rightness just because it was mine, not because it was righter or better than the other. I was a rat trapped on the endless wheel, always beginning, and ending, on the starting line. Trapped in duality, I used enormous amounts of energy going nowhere. I lived a contracted and depleted life distancing myself from those with different views.

The "Middle Path" poured out one day. It expresses the more fundamental reality of non-duality.

The Middle Path

My psyche was so polarized, judging everything in sight;
Good or bad, white or black, even left or right.

I found that I was always drawn between some two extremes;
And felt the need to choose between one of them, it seems.

Judgemental mind, pulled apart, I was always torn in half;
Then a gentle voice deep inside whispered, "Try the Middle Path."

A great Idea, I felt relief, no longer must I choose;
For The Middle Path is always right, there is no win or lose.

The need to make a choice has passed, I feel so very wise;
With conflict gone, my mind is clear, I see with loving eyes.

And in all my years of choosing, and judging all I see;
I'm pretty much convinced today, I've really been judging me.

Now no longer polarized, I feel that I am free;
And my journey down The Middle Path is where I wish to be.

jmb

The "Middle Path" invites one to live beyond the dualistic mind. It is seeing reality as it is, not as our dualistic mind presents it. Clarity is the space beyond duality.

Our conditioned thinking is deeply ingrained. However, a sustained effort for a few weeks will loosen old habits and invite a deeper, richer life.

See reality as it is. Do not judge, compare, try to change, or wish reality was different. Observe from witness mode and you will release yourself from the bonds of duality.

Karishma shared the following metaphor of duality. "Visualize yourself, Johnny in a children's playground sitting on one end of a see-saw. The further out you are from the center, the higher you will go and the rougher the ride. The rough-ride space of duality is living on the end of the see-saw. The closer you are to the center, the smoother the ride and the nearer you are to balance. Sitting astride the center, you will gently rock back and forth a bit as the ones at the ends significantly move up and down. The center is the space of balance and non-duality. That is the space of peace, joy, and freedom.

Use this visual and the "Middle Path" as tools to aid you in moving toward a non-duality reality.

"All The Same" expresses my oneness with everything else. Trees, fish, bears, birds, rocks, water, air, and humans are all created from the same earth elements. Therefore, everything is a child of the earth. I embrace this brotherhood and sisterhood oneness paradigm.

We are here as an expression of life in our physical bodies only for a short while. But where did I come from? Who was I before I was born into this body? Where do I go and what happens to me when I leave my body? These are questions I wish to explore and get a sense of before I release my physical body. It is in my best interest to explore these questions while alive. Waiting to die and hope that reality will be revealed to me after I take my last breath is foolish. As one explores the path of the Spiritual Warrior, they raise their vibe and that's the pay-off. Go exploring.

I was told as a child that I ask too many questions. In Sunday school, I heard that, "There are some things that God knows and little boys can't know." I figured out later that a vague answer like that meant that the teacher did not know the answer and didn't want me to know that they didn't know. Vague generalities like, "You will go to heaven if you are a believer," may lure in the gullible, but the spiritual warrior seeks spiritual truth and does not fall prey to these shallow promises.

There is comfort belonging to a community of believers and it is very easy to relax and join the crowd. Many succumb to comfort and "easy." They just seem to melt into the crowd, not make waves or ask questions, and lead a rather nervous mediocre life.

But is truth being shared and taught? What about the many outside the community that ascribe to a different story? These are tough questions asked by few. It takes courage to be a believer but it takes much greater courage to be a seeker of truth.

Consider the energy flow. When I take part in any experience where the institution expects me to accept their truth as my truth, I am lowering my energetic signature. I am giving away my personal power; my power of choice. The energy flows from me, the participant, to the authorities or institution. It is energy-depleting and shuts down my inner voice.

I did this at home with my parents. I kept quiet, tried not to ask too many questions, and just went along with the program to be a good little boy. This happens in many religious experiences. We learn to listen and accept without question what we are taught and told. If we are good enough at doing this, we may even receive shallow rewards.

But we pay a big price in energy depletion. We distance and disconnect our personality from our spiritual core and lower our vibe. We become separated from ourselves. We become sheep, going along with the crowd, blindly following the leaders, and distancing ourselves from ourselves.

Authentic teachers guide and support. They point the way for the student to find their own answers. Teachers do not provide answers. No authentic teacher will ever ask you to accept their truth as your truth. They will encourage you to do your deep inner work and find your own way. An authentic teacher will never offer a reward for doing what they suggest or a threat if you do not do as they suggest. Use caution when you are with a person or institution that promises rewards if you follow them or threatens you if you do not follow them.

We are "All the Same" for we are all an integral part of the fabric of reality.

All the Same

Life and death are all the same,
The differences arise alone in my brain.

My earth, life and death, began the same time,
And are separated only in my mind.

As cells of my body age and decay,
They are replaced by new ones each day.
So, the process of dying is necessary,
And I'm truly thankful for the death of me.

Allowing life to be death eliminates fear,
And allows me to realize my warrior.
It's not about daring and bravado you see,
It's all about spiritual bravery.

Like eating and eaten which are the same,
For someday I'll become something's dinner again.
All this food I've consumed, I've a great debt to pay,
And will do so at death with my body's decay.

I now stroll my earthwalk with certainty,
With no need of promise or guarantee.
I know life and death are all one,
And I am a part of the earth and the sun.

It's great comfort to know that I'm part of this cycle,
To glimpse and appreciate life's natural miracle.
It's all so simple and All The Same,
When I live in my heart and not in my brain.

jmb

"Morning, Johnny, looks like a beautiful morning for flying," grinned First Officer John Christensen. I smiled in return. We made small talk in the layover hotel lobby as our crew gathered and we departed for Albuquerque International Airport. I loved my job flying the Super-80 aircraft as an American Airlines captain. It was a marvelous company to work for with excellent people and top-notch equipment. I had the best flying job in the world.

Being straightforward and honest with American Airlines during my hiring experience, they knew of my alcoholism, my rehab experience, and my volunteer work with our company pilots that had completed alcohol rehab and were reestablishing themselves as productive pilots with the airline. Chuckling, I looked at the silver AA symbol on my hat badge over the visor and smiled at the double meaning of "American Airlines" and "Alcoholics Anonymous."

Flight planning, preflight, boarding, and engine start this early morning were all routine and enjoyable. Dawn was just breaking as we taxied from the terminal to the approach end of Runway 08. Takeoff this morning would be eastbound toward the mountains and into the rising sun. An unusually strong sense of gratitude and euphoria filled my heart.

"American 123, Albuquerque Tower, winds calm, Runway 08 cleared for takeoff," crackled through my headset.

"Roger, tower, American 123 Runway 08 cleared for takeoff," John acknowledged. Easing the throttles forward, I felt the power build and we slowly accelerated toward the mountains on runway 08. At 135 knots, I eased the yolk aft, felt the nose lift gently off the runway, and we slipped gracefully into the cool morning air. The aircraft was an extension of me.

We climbed to altitude, settled into cruise mode and shortly thereafter I scribbled "Just for Me" on the back of our flight-plan.

Just for Me

I become one with my universe every moment I am alive. This is my reason for being. There is no other. I am so fortunate for this awareness.
As I turn onto my runway and push the throttles of my forty-million-dollar jet plane forward, I know in a heartbeat the real purpose of it all. It is clear and makes perfect sense.
One hundred thousand employees of my great company, tens of thousands who designed and built my marvelous aircraft, hundreds of caretakers who graciously prepared my machine for flight, my colleague sharing my cockpit, my cabin crew a few feet aft, and my passengers joining me this special morning.
All are here at this moment ...JUST FOR ME!

My aircraft and I become one with each other and join my sky as we gently lift ourselves into my morning.
One with my sunrise,
One with my morning clouds,
One with my mountains,
One with my earth,
One with my universe.
It is happening as it should, as always...JUST FOR ME!
Five billion years of everything exists every moment, JUST FOR ME!
This is my great gift.

I cannot make these experiences happen. I can only be present and available when energies align and the magic unfolds.

The Moment

I live only in the present moment.
How I lived in past moments determines my life now.
How I live now determines my life in future moments.
Today I will continue or terminate yesterday's progress.
Today I will cultivate or destroy tomorrow's dreams.
I alone make this choice, every moment.
I'm sure glad it's my choice.

jmb

DREAMS - VISIONS - PERSONAL JOURNAL

Dreams and visions are messages from somewhere beyond the personality; somewhere beyond our 3-D physical world. They are beyond thinking. I listen and pay attention to dreams and visions and value these messages.

Dream and vision experiences provide insight and guidance toward the future and validation of past work. In 1993, I started journaling feelings, dreams, and visions along with significant events. Although I do not write daily, I write frequently about life events and the emotions and feelings that arise.

I use my journal as a tool. Perhaps some of my experiences will resonate with similar experiences you've had. My dream interpretations are mostly my own with some occasional guidance from therapists and friends.

I've tried to preserve the integrity of the original entries and leave them close to the original writing. Some may be a bit rough around the edges.

Journal Entry - 24 December 1993

*** VISION *** My organs called a meeting of all my body organs to be held in the center of my chest. Every organ came to this grand pow-wow. My heart, lungs, liver, spleen, skin, bones, nose, and eyes all came. Every organ was there and they were seated in a big circle. In the center of the circle was my brain. All the organs told the brain that they were angry at brain and that brain was no longer in charge. The brain had screwed things up badly for way too long. My liver was really pissed-off and gave the brain hell for pouring all that booze on him for many years. The liver said, "You damn near killed me with all that whiskey." The liver was furious.

The conversations went on as every organ gave the brain hell. My kind and caring heart, recalled how he skipped beats because the brain drank so much and my stomach gave him hell because he shoved in food that wasn't necessary. My bones gave him hell for keeping me a few pounds overweight and my lungs gave him hell for making him work harder than they had to.

My brain was told that it was no longer in charge and from here on, it was a servant working for the organs. The brain was no longer king and I am no longer subjected to an out-of-control brain.

Brain input is now minimal and if there is any thinking to be done, the organs will request the brain's services when needed. The organs stuck a name tag on the brain. It said, "Maytag Repairman" because, like the Maytag guy who never gets a service call, my brain might never be called on again. The brain can just sit around now twiddling its thumbs waiting for a call for action that may never come. I laughed a lot about this beautiful vision. *** END ***

Journal Entry - 27 February 1994

*** DREAM *** I am in a very large office building with perhaps seventy-five floors. The building is very tall but not fancy, with brick on the outside and plain vanilla halls, walls, and doors on the inside. It looks a bit like the Empire State Building. I'm on the ground floor and want to go up to the sun deck on the roof.

There is a large crowd of people waiting for this elevator. Several elevators stop, but all are full or there is room for only a few people. I'm too far back in the line to get on. Eventually, I look around for an alternative way to get on an elevator. I walk down into the basement and call an elevator from down there. I'm the only one in the basement so when an elevator finally shows, I'll be able to get on and ride through the crowded first floor.

The basement is large, dark, dank, and gloomy. In this old building, the basement is oppressive. When an elevator finally arrives, it is different than the elevator that stopped on the ground floor. This elevator is a small cage with wire sides and no floor. I have to strap a harness around my waist to keep from falling instead of standing on a floor. I strap in, and hang onto the side. There is another man about my age also riding this elevator up. He assures me that this is a safe elevator to ride all the up to the roof sun deck. He chooses, however, to climb up through a little door in the ceiling and rides the roof of the elevator. He tells me that this elevator takes a different route than the regular elevator that stops on the ground floor.

I am now alone in this elevator cage and the other man is sitting on the cage roof a few feet over my head. His legs and brown cowboy boots are dangling near my head. Away we go and the elevator leaves the building and goes outside and up the side of the building suspended only by one thin cable. I am afraid, but not terrified or panicky. Sometimes, I close my eyes for looking down is frightening. We are now a long way above the ground. I tell myself to enjoy the ride and look around because this is a unique elevator ride. I look up more than I look down. Looking up at the cable swaying above me, I see that we are going to connect with a long metal beam hanging way out over the side, like the beam of a parachute-jump ride in an amusement park.

The guy riding the roof is still with me and enjoying the ride. He's calm as he is apparently a veteran elevator rider. Although a bit frightened, I hang in there. The cage goes up and up, swaying in the breeze and finally after a long time, we arrive at the top and the elevator stops. The roof station is like a ski lift terminal at the top of a mountain. Getting out of the elevator, I am given tickets to go back down whenever I wish. I drop my tickets on the ground and they land in three piles, with about five tickets in each pile. Immediately, one pile blows away over the edge. A young boy retrieves the other two for me and gives them to me. Now I have limited tickets to return. I feel as if I am in another world, not on a roof or the sun deck of a building. I am many miles up and I can see the edge of the sun deck. However, I cannot see the earth below. Looking around and feeling light and free, I see that there is now no roof to this building. It is sort of like heaven as I envisioned heaven to be from my Sunday-school days. The other man is gone and I am alone. Everything is bright, clear and clean. Then I woke up.

*** COMMENTS *** This powerful dream is a metaphor for the ascension of my consciousness. To go from the ground floor to the top floor, I must first go down and clean my basement. Once complete, I may then ascend to the rooftop.

I am all the components in this dream: the building, the elevator, etc., and I believe the other man was my therapist Paul (he wore cowboy boots). He was a guide in this dream and helped by pointing the way and supporting me. This dream validates my work. *** END ***

Journal Entry - 4 March 1994

I remembered Mom saying, "Johnny, you have a face that only a mother could love." I heard that many times from early childhood until perhaps forty. It was degrading to me and I didn't like it.

I never found the courage to tell my dad that I felt belittled with his degrading comments, I just asked him to stop. Dad's standard answer to my requests of, "Please don't say those things to me," was, 'Can't you take a little joke, Johnny?' So, I learned to keep my mouth shut and suck it up.

Journal Entry - 8 March 1994

*** DREAM *** I was swimming with a group of men in an ocean. Sharks were in the area and occasionally a shark showed up and ate somebody. The sharks randomly picked a man, attacked and, in a flash, ate him. Swimming in shark-infested waters was dangerous and men died.

I was very concerned and afraid that I would be eaten. But I kept swimming as the other men were also doing. I was never attacked and no shark ever got close to me. I saw several men get eaten, but they were all behind me and I could see none of the details of the shark attacks. I was frightened but kept on swimming. Then I woke up.

*** COMMENTS *** I am swimming in shark-infested waters in my life and need to move on rapidly to get to a safer place before I get picked off by a shark. Doing deep inner work is not for the faint of heart and some die along the way. *** END ***

Journal Entry - 10 April 1994

Recently, Sarah and I went together to our evening session with therapist Paul. Sarah spoke about her fear of thunderstorms. Then Sunday night, we had a big thunderstorm and Sarah spent the night on our bedroom floor. Monday morning, I asked her to find courage to look at and embrace her fear of thunderstorms when it hit me that I have a lifelong fear of the dark. I'm asking her to look at her fear and guess what? It's time for me to look at mine.

During our previous session with Paul, Sarah shared that when she was a little girl, Grandmom (my mother) and my sister Pat told Sarah she shouldn't be afraid of a thunderstorm because, 'That's little kid stuff.' If Sarah heard that from my mother, I could only imagine how many times I must have heard that or similar from both my parents. 'You shouldn't be afraid of the dark. That's little boy stuff.' As a little boy in Mom and Dad's house, my room was on the second floor at the end of the hall. It seemed like it was half a mile from my bed to the hall light switch. So where did I go when I was afraid of the dark or thunderstorms, or whatever else I was afraid of as a little boy? I never went to Mom and Dad's room for comfort, and I don't recall ever going to Pat's room, either. So, I guess I just knuckled it out and today at forty-nine I'm still afraid of the dark.

Therapist Paul told us we will have to be our own parent on this one. For Sarah, he suggested that when a storm approaches, turn on a small light or a little music, or perhaps go to the kitchen for milk and a cookie. Something other than coming into our room and being with us. And for me, I need to walk outside and see that it is OK, and take Little Johnny with me and show him it is safe and meet the monsters face on. MONSTERS ARE ONLY IN MY MIND!

Then I gave Paul my "Monster Boy" poem, and he held it to his heart. He felt honored, and I told him of my dream about swimming in shark-infested waters. Paul told me that doing deep inner work is serious business, and dangerous, too. He said that some people go crazy when uncovering the secrets of their deep subconscious. I commented, "You mean perhaps somebody might find out that they killed somebody or something like that and not be able to deal with it?"

He said, "Right!"

It reminded me of the many missions I flew in Vietnam that I've never dealt with. I hope that I don't go crazy when I do. He told me that the dream means that I am swimming in my subconscious and so are many others and some get picked off by sharks and don't survive this journey.

Journal Entry - 16 May 1994

*** DREAM *** I am in a western setting and being held hostage by a robber. The robber is behind me with his gun over my shoulder, looking around my head. I am the shield. There are two other robbers near us, both with pistols. The robber behind me shoots one of his fellow robbers and, just then, someone enters from the right side. The intruder just came out of nowhere, like out of the shadow. The intruder held a pistol in each hand and he fires each gun once with deadly accuracy. I am witnessing this scene as the cameraman looking through the camera. I see myself, and the others like actors on a stage. I am at my present age of fifty.

My rescuer wore a white hat, and I could not see his face or the lower half of his body. However, he was quick with his guns and deadly accurate. He shot the robber holding me and I knew he would not hit me, although the robber he shot was very close to me. Although I was in great danger, my rescuer never hesitated for an instant and killed the robber behind me, as well as the other remaining robber. "Blam Blam," and it was all over. Then I awoke."

*** COMMENTS *** The message is telling me to kill whatever is holding me hostage and get on with my earthwalk unencumbered. I am me and the rescuer of myself as well. I am the cowboy in the white hat. I must kill the robbers, those pieces of me that are holding me hostage, and free myself. This was a powerful dream with a powerful message. *** END ***

Tonight, I shared my dream about the robbers with therapist Paul and he told me that all the people in the "Robber Dream" are some part of me and I am rescuing myself from myself. I am rescuing the soul from the clutches of the ego/personality. He told me I am my own worst enemy. Paul told me that the reason that I hear Little Johnny all the time now is that Little Johnny is no longer afraid to come out and be heard.

When I was a little boy, Little Johnny was pushed back deeper and deeper and every time he would come out, Dad or Mom or someone hurt him. After a time, Dad's voice and other destructive voices were so ingrained in me, that I could not turn them off. I imagine that when I was drinking, Little Johnny would say, "That's enough, Johnny, take me home." Fat chance he had of being heard. So Little Johnny came through in this dream because he's learning that it is safe to do so and that's what the "Robber Dream" is all about. I am rescuing a part of myself from myself.

Journal Entry - 26 June 1994

*** DREAM *** I am at an "Enlightenment Center" housed in an old stone monastery or abbey. To grow and move toward my enlightenment, I must climb out along a ledge with only a loose and rickety metal railing to keep me from falling. I go out on this ledge many stories up, repeatedly, every time saying this is my last time out on this dangerous ledge.

There are many corridors in this monastery, and I am frequently lost as I wander through the halls. Then I go out on a ledge again, swearing that this is my last time to do this as it is very dangerous and I have come close to falling several times.

The corridors are always empty and lost again, I wind up in the dark basement. Then, up from the basement and out on a ledge, I go again. Every time I come back inside from hanging over the edge of the ledge with the flimsy railing, I'd swear I'd never go out on a ledge again. But soon, I'd be out there again. Also, parts of the flimsy railing were missing, making it even more dangerous.

*** COMMENTS *** I feel wonderful about this dream as it is validation that I am doing deep inner work. I am risking my life to get to a higher place. The monastery is me and I'm going into my dark basement and doing deep work down there. Then, up I come to go out on a ledge and risk my life to do work out there. The ledge is a visual of taking risks and venturing into the unknown. *** END ***

Journal Entry - 30 April 1995

I staffed a "Men's Room" weekend workshop and had a breakthrough during our check-out this afternoon. The weekend was a powerful experience for me from the beginning, and I felt close and available to the twenty-four participants. On Sunday morning, we did an exercise about shame, dirt, and secrets. I did not know what shame was until this morning and now I have some idea of how much shame I am carrying. I know for sure that I have much work to do in this area. I stepped into the center of the group and shared my shame.

I said that I was a coward, and that I stuff my anger, and do not talk about this very much. Another man then stepped into the center and spoke about killing someone. I reflected on my 196 combat missions in Vietnam. Carrying about 8,000 pounds of munitions on my Phantom jet each mission, I dropped about 1.5 million pounds of bombs. That's a hell of a lot of explosives to drop on the Vietnamese people, and I have never yet shed one tear over this. I have never felt the guilt or shame of dropping all that ordnance on targets in Vietnam. I have never felt any grief, sorrow, remorse, or any emotion about destroying Vietnam or killing the Vietnamese people.

I have completely shut out my killer, my slayer, my executioner, my aggressor, my SAVAGE. I have sealed myself in a suit of armor called a denial system. During our completion check-out, I told the remaining men there that I had dropped all these bombs in Vietnam somewhere and I had never shed one tear or expressed any remorse.

I cried uncontrollably for about thirty minutes supported by the remaining men. I am so grateful that they were there for me to grieve. Leader Paul told me as I cried, that he saw a man now willing to do his work. Leader Kevin told me that he trusted me more now, for I have opened the door to my dark side. I saw my golden heart growing and illuminating my shadow basement. It was a start.

*** COMMENTS *** I've opened the basement door now and have released a bit of my shadow. This is work that must be done with the support of a skilled therapist, mentor, or group. Doing it alone is dangerous because guilt and shame released may be overwhelming and lead to suicide. Johnny, use caution when doing your deep inner work. *** END ***

Journal Entry - 2 April 1996

(One year has passed since I opened the door to my shadow basement holding the ghosts of the people I killed in Vietnam.)

It's 10:50 pm, and I was so depressed earlier today that I called for an emergency session with my therapist friend, Paul. He told me not to go to work tomorrow, so I called in sick for my trip. I am non-functional. I feel dead inside and have felt dead, depressed, trapped, and alone for about three months now. This has been a very trying time for me.

Paul told me I am not only trapped externally, but trapped internally as well. My trip to my parents' home and time with Mom and Dad stirred up a lot of stuff inside. I feel like a child around my father. At home, Dad saw that his granddaughter, my daughter, Sarah, wasn't smiling as we strolled through a mall, so he sat her down and told her that, "Everybody is sad because you aren't smiling." So, she's supposed to smile no matter what, just like I have been doing all of my life. And now, it is catching up with me and Little Johnny isn't smiling anymore.

Paul told me I have every right to be enraged at my parents with the crap that Mom and Dad laid on me. It's no wonder I was afraid to miss the ball playing shortstop in little league, or to miss a note playing trumpet in the school band. And I was never mad because I wasn't supposed to ever be mad or show any emotions. I was supposed to look good all the time. Paul told me I came into his office today in great pain. I am the Little Johnny piece of me today and Little Johnny is very depressed, very angry, very sad, and very empty.

Paul reminded me that I have spent my life trying to make Little

Johnny happy with booze, cigarettes, sex, food, and flying fast airplanes. Now, Little Johnny is telling me that none of that works anymore. I talked about my feelings of being trapped and how I would like to leave my wife and move into a small home by myself. I could let people in when I wanted and when they get too close, I could ask them to leave. I do not know if I can sustain a long-term relationship with a woman. I do not know if I can or want to stay with Marcia.

Paul reminded me I am trapped internally, the same way as I am trapped externally. I am a frightened little boy. Sometimes I tire of this stuff and the words of my brother-in-law ring out, "Why rock the boat when everything is OK?" The difference is that I know everything isn't OK. Paul told me to stay in the pain and see what happens. I will do that. My heart aches.

Paul said to sit in my pain. That's my lesson for today. Sit in and stay with the pain. I must go through it, not around it. I've been avoiding this pain for twenty-three years but my journey through this pain is my path to freedom. Recovery is what I'm trying to do. Recover the me I do not even know. No wonder I am in such pain and feel depressed. At least I am feeling the pain and acknowledging my depression. I guess that is good. I know in my heart that I need to be right here and I need to feel this pain and that eventually I will come out some place else in a better place, or else I won't survive. In either case the pain will cease. I know the message is, *"Do not anesthetize myself with anything or I will stay in this pain forever."*

Little Johnny is really getting pissed off at me for forcing food down his throat. Adult Johnny and Little Johnny are both aspects of me. I am feeling the pain of my childhood that I avoided growing up. As a child, I was not nurtured and not cared for in any real sense. True love and safety were missing. I have not felt this "growing up pain" for fifty years and it is surfacing. I'm feeling and acknowledging it. I almost want to make a vow to never act-out again, however that is pointless as I have done that about a thousand times before and it never works, nor will it ever work. I need to stay in this pain and the changes will come. From this pain comes strength! So here I sit. Tomorrow, I will sit in my pain again and allow it to diffuse.

It's now 11:16 pm and will sleep with a pad to write my dream messages. Perhaps one is coming tonight. This trapped, non-functional state has been going on for about three months and Paul tells says I have every right to be enraged about my lacking childhood.

I have a lot of trouble being angry and expressing anger. I know nothing about rage. I have a feeling that this is a direction that I need to go. Little Johnny is full of anger and rage. **RAGE, MAN! RAGE!** The thesaurus says rage equals fury and wrath. I need to roar like a lion and do some of that "manly" stuff. Know what I mean? Good night!

Journal Entry - 12 May 1996

It's 6:23 am and I am up early, troubled by overeating from last night. We went to Milwaukee Roadhouse last night for a big dinner and then I had a peanut butter snack at about nine and then at ten-thirty I had a piece of cake. If that isn't insanity, I do not know what is. It is unimportant to me today when I say, "Why do I do this to myself?" So, I'll re-word this into a statement. I KEEP MYSELF DISCONNECTED AND DISTANT FROM MYSELF. I UNCONSCIOUSLY OVEREAT, EVEN THOUGH I KNOW THAT MY LIFE WOULD BE ENHANCED GREATLY BY LOSING 30 POUNDS.

It does not matter what I say, do, promise, or vow, my relationship with food remains unconscious. I have not changed this behavior and I continually feel depressed. Here's why (as if I really know): some years ago, I was not depressed about my weight and life because I did not know better, because I lived shallowly. Now I do know better and engage life from a deeper center of consciousness. It is a struggle, for I am holding myself accountable, at least at some level.

I was depressed last month and I am now because I am unwilling to take care of myself. Since I am the creator of my experience and I don't like my experience, then it's natural for me to be pissed off at myself. But that just depresses me more and I act out again to feel good. Down the rabbit hole I go. I am doing it all to myself.

In less than three weeks, I go on the shadow weekend workshop "Birthing Your Shadow." The crux of the weekend is for me to lay claim on my shadow-the disowned, denied and forgotten parts of me that I don't want to see and that I project on others. A master said that, 'If I do not bring forth what is within myself, that which I do not bring forth will destroy me.' (Maybe I can bring forth that part of me that is so unwilling to heal myself.)

I don't do well with rage. I do not know how to appropriately vent rage, which is repressed anger. Here's my chance to get in touch with those hidden aspects. Right now, I am frightened and feel awful. I've had headaches for about three or four weeks now and I feel lousy about that. I need to sit, count my blessings, and get on with my life.

Journal Entry - 18 May 1996

*** DREAM *** I am at American Airlines Headquarters attending a luncheon with many captains and our CEO. It's normal for the CEO and captains to have lunch together and the conversations are casual as we mill around waiting for the luncheon to begin. I remembered talking to another captain who recently checked out, and he said that these luncheons are always fun. I chat briefly with our CEO and we exchange pleasantries, and not much more. It all feels shallow to me. Then there is silence, and I become uncomfortable during this protracted period of silence.

There are some children at this luncheon and I enjoy hanging around and playing with the children. Someone comes to me and tells me to stop playing with the children, grow up, and sit with the others at the luncheon. But I continue to play with the children as I prefer the children to the pilots and company officers at the dining table. Then I woke up.

*** COMMENTS *** I liked the feeling of being around the children much more than the feelings of being around the grown-up pilots and company officers. I guess I'm just a child at heart, or as perhaps I'm drawn toward honesty and integrity. *** END ***

Journal Entry - 20 May 1996

*** DREAM *** I am walking along a road in Germany carrying a gigantic sword which is broken into three pieces. I wish to get to a town and find a place to get my sword fixed. A car stops, I get in, and we head toward a town. I'm sitting in the back seat and ask the two men in the front where I can get my sword repaired. The passenger tells me they will take me to a sword repair place.

Both men in the front seat are strangers to me, and the passenger is a very big man. He looks at my broken sword, then forcibly grabs my arm and clutches it tightly. As he twists my arm, I scrape his arm with my broken sword and he releases me. The driver stops and I get out of the car, but am not yet near the town.

The car drives off about one-hundred feet and abruptly stops. Then the big man that grabbed my arm gets out and menacingly comes toward me. I take a defensive stand with my broken sword, and he stops and backs off. He returns to the car and they drive off. I then walk into town and find a shop that fixes broken swords. It is a clear day with lots of sun, yet there is a chill in the air and a wintry feeling. Then I woke up.

*** COMMENTS *** This dream feels very empowering. I'm learning how to protect myself from bullies and stand up for myself. It's a great dream. It's validation of inner work. *** END ***

Journal Entry - 8 June 1996

*** DREAM *** I am the overseer of a huge tapestry along a wall of a museum. It is rather dark inside the museum, but this tapestry is well illuminated by lights. There are many portraits and pictures of outdoor scenes on this very long, seemingly never-ending tapestry. I am to propose and recommend changes to improve this tapestry. I look at many new portraits and many new scenes and then recommend changes. The new tapestry will have some of the old scenes but many new ones.

Suddenly, a whirling mist or fog rolls in and when it dissipates, the new tapestry is on the wall, with many new scenes that I had envisioned all in place and finished. I am pleased and people come to admire this new tapestry. Some tell me they have seen many attempts to change the old tapestry, but all have failed except this one. Compliments abound as people admire the new tapestry with the new beautiful scenes.

*** COMMENTS *** I am changing my tapestry and this dream is validation that some scenes in my life will remain, and some will be discarded and replaced with new beautiful scenes. It is a marvelous dream. *** END ***

Journal Entry - 21 July 1996

*** DREAM *** I am in my rather flimsy house and working at my computer. It is bright daylight and I am home alone. Suddenly, I look outside and see a tornado approaching a few miles away. Dark gray clouds move in and I see the funnel spiraling up only a short distance away. I am confused and do not know what to do or where to go. There is no safe place to run and no safe place to hide. I don't think that my house will survive this tornado. I wait inside my house, watching the tornado approach. I thought about running outside, but not knowing which way the tornado would go, decided it was best to stay in my house and ride it out. Just before the tornado hit, I woke up.

*** COMMENTS *** I was frightened and scared and saw my world out of control and me in great danger. But I faced the tornado and did not panic. I simply waited out the storm and was ready to let the chips fall where they may.

This is exactly where my life is right now. Therapist Paul says that my house is me and I am also the person in my house. Perhaps my house is my physical body. I am very frightened today for my life because I am afraid that I will punish myself for the deaths I directly caused in Vietnam.

I understand what therapist Paul meant when he said that "shadow work is dangerous and some don't survive." However, I know that not doing this work and not embracing my shadow is also dangerous and will result in living a life only half alive. If I am to have a meaningful life with purpose, free of pain and addiction, I must walk through this fire. And I WILL do whatever it takes to walk through this fire and emerge on the other side in freedom. Or I will die trying. *** END ***

Journal Entry - 12 August 1996

*** DREAM *** I am traveling back to college in my old VW Bus. I picked up a hitchhiker and together we drive to the college campus. I don't recognize the campus as it is rainy and gloomy, and the streets are hillier than I remember. I look everywhere but cannot find a parking place for my bus. Finally, I park the bus at the edge of the campus and walk with the hitchhiker to help him find his destination on campus.

I don't know this hitchhiker person, and in my dream, I am in my early '50s, not college age.

After I leave the hitchhiker at his destination, I look for my bus and cannot find it. I search everywhere and walk all over the campus, up and down hills and through many parking lots. But I cannot find my bus nor remember where I parked it. Nothing seems familiar. Finally, I see a VW bus at the far end of a parking lot and think it is my bus. I run toward it. As I approach, I see that it is a similar VW bus, but not mine. I am extremely frustrated, angry, and pressed for time. Finally, I wake up.

*** COMMENTS *** This is metaphorically where my life is today. I am in a gloomy place, frustrated and lost. I am the bus, and I am also me in this dream. It is like I cannot find myself and am looking for myself. I will keep walking and looking and doing my work. Eventually I'll find myself. *** END ***

Journal Entry - 15 August 1996

*** DREAM *** I am in a military command post exercise yet was not even aware that there was an exercise going on. The exercise is just beginning and as I check into the command post, I find out that I am the Division Commander. There is only one person of higher rank and he is in a headquarters far away with the other division.

I do not know where the other division is and everything around me in this dream-scape is my division under my command. I am standing outside when we get attacked by nerve gas. I first run and then realize that I am the Division Commander and feel frightened and incapable of handling this great responsibility.

Then something happens to me and I feel empowered and capable. I put on my gas mask and proceed toward my HQ tent to get organized and start commanding. I know that when I arrive in my HQ tent, I will assume command of my entire division. I ask someone where my HQ tent is and they point and say, "It's right over there, Commander." I head toward my HQ tent without reservations or doubt, and suddenly I feel like a take-charge commander. I begin to act like a commander and start thinking of strategies and planning. I am now capable and in charge of the division.

*** COMMENTS *** I feel I am ready for life changes. This dream is perhaps a sign and I know I can take charge of my life, making good solid decisions in my favor and that my life is going to turn out just fine. Nothing is better than being in command of one's own life. I feel a lot of excitement about this dream. *** END ***

Journal Entry - 13 September 1996

My deepest shadow is my stuff from Vietnam. The men in the shadow reunion workshop honored me. One man said that he honors me for flying combat missions in Vietnam, but even more for how much inner work I have done since then, trying to heal.

Shallow people go to the bar and get drunk to drown out the inner voices and forget what they did. And for many years, that's what I did. Not anymore. I am no longer one of those men and the more I dig out of my shadow basement, the more I reclaim myself. For me, there is no turning back and either I will free myself from my prison or I will die trying. This is what shadow work is all about. One of the great philosophers said, "An unexamined life is not worth living." I am examining my life.

Journal Entry - 25 October 1996

I must find the purpose for my suffering. I must understand the meaning of my suffering. Finding the purpose and acknowledging my suffering is accepting it. This is part of ownership. My participation in Vietnam and my suffering today is part of my divine plan.

It's not clear to me, but I trust as I continue to walk through my fire, it will become clearer to me. My suffering will diminish and hopefully end. I know in my heart that I will never be a true healer until I heal myself. It's that simple. So, I ask myself to find the meaning and purpose of my suffering. This is deep shadow work.

I have connected all of this with those I killed in Viet Nam. I am suffering their wounds. This is my penitence. This is my grieving. Now the next step is to become a healer of humans. However, in order to be effective, I must become a healer of Johnny. Somehow, as I write this, I feel that much more will be revealed to me.

*** COMMENTS *** Re-reading in 2022 my journal entries from 1996, I realize how much I minimized the visions of death and destruction that appeared to me in dreams and visions. I recall vividly many nightmares, visions, and disturbing thoughts and woke-up many times in the middle of the night sweating and shaking from witnessing bombs exploding and people being blown to bits from my bombs. These frequent nightmares are lacking in my written journal, probably because they were too painful to write about. Today, in 2022, I can talk, write, and read about Vietnam without an emotional pull. I retain the history, but am no longer triggered by these events. I can safely acknowledge these dreams and visions without emotional participation.

Journal Entry - 30 November 1996

*** DREAM *** I am home visiting Mom and Dad and go out for a while. Dad did some remodeling of his house and he also remodeled himself. He rebuilt the garage while I was gone and when I returned, he showed me his work. It looked good and I was pleased. The garage was three feet longer and there were lots of fresh 2x4s around the inner wall. I could smell the freshness of the new wood.

Also, Dad lost a lot of weight and he looked great. He was thin, handsome, strong, kind, and gentle to me when I returned. I admired him a lot and was very fond of him. I was glad and proud to be his son. He was the father I always dreamed of. I loved being this beautiful man's son. He was working in his new garage without a shirt and his skin was golden brown and glistening in the sun.

*** COMMENTS *** I love this dream. It is wonderful seeing my father like a Greek God. I admired and loved him. I cherish this dream and will carry this image of Dad with me. This is very significant, as this is healing our relationship. *** END ***

Journal Entry - 19 February 1997

I accept jobs and do things for others that I do not wish to do. Example: Jenn, was here at Christmas and put some stuff in a box from the basement. I was going to ship the box to her when I realized Jenn did not pack the box well and there was no shipping label on it for Fed Ex.

I became angry with Jenn for just throwing the box into the basement and expecting me to do all the rest of the preparation. When I confronted her about this, she told me I was really clear to her, and I told her to just put the box in the basement on my workbench and that I would pack it and ship it for her. She told me exactly where the box was in the basement and she was correct.

So, this is what I believe happened. To be her friend, to be liked, and to be a nice guy, I automatically, or unconsciously, assumed a task for her *that I really did not want to do* (she could have done all the prep herself), and then promptly forgot that I offered my services to her. A few weeks later, I went into the basement and was angry with Jenn that she had left a task for me that she could have done herself.

This pattern of me offering my services, helping people, or assuming a responsibility for someone else, causes problems for me. If I do not truly wish to do something for someone, then don't offer to do it. I don't have to be abrupt or rude, just straightforward, and direct. Also, I don't have to make an excuse as to why I am not willing to do something that I don't wish to do. As an example, let's say that someone says, 'Join me for dinner Wednesday, Johnny.' If I don't want to do this, then I might say, "Thanks for the offer, however, I'll pass." And then just let it go. I don't want to lie and make an excuse like, "Oh I can't because, (fill in anything)." Here are a few steps for guidance.

1)Listen, then pause and allow, don't react, wait, then respond.

2)Recognize when I am being asked to do something that I truly do not wish to do.

3)Do not volunteer to do something that I do not wish to do. Do not assume an unwanted responsibility.

4)Recognize when one of these situations develops and hold a boundary. Terminate the issue before it *becomes* an issue.

I watched Dad help people all his life, even recently, and then resent doing what he was doing to help them. He resented the people for asking him, and he even resented the people that he/Dad, of his own volition, volunteered to help without them ever asking. How nuts is that? Dad's comment was, "They shouldn't have asked me to do it." Now that's personal responsibility, eh?

Journal Entry - 23 March 1997

*** DREAM *** I am a prisoner in a prison, which is more like a house on the inside. There are people around me that are hostile and violent and want to kill me. It is very surrealistic and I am a fit man of great strength and power. I'm standing in a room when suddenly a huge circular saw blade cuts through the wall from the outside. I'm watching from the inside as the blade, about six-feet in diameter, comes through the wall. Parts of the wall fall away and the saw blade is cutting the wall like it was paper, with pieces of wall flying everywhere. The prison is being destroyed. It's a very scary place and I run out of the room carrying a squeeze bottle of "Powerful Mist."

When I squeeze the bottle, a mist sprays out that is deadly and kills anyone who is trying to harm me. When sprayed, they drop and dissolve on the floor. I fight my way out, using the mist to kill several attackers who are after me. Eventually, I am alone when a beautiful woman with great powers comes toward me and I feel my heart melting and my power draining.

She pushes me and I fall to the ground on my back. This woman stands over me, straddling me, and I spray my mist at her, but it has no effect. She stands over me, laughing and taunting me, and is about to drive a knife through my chest. Meanwhile, I'm spraying my mist at her with no effect. I believe I am going to die.

My vision tunnels and I begin to lose consciousness. My magic mist is powerless on her. Suddenly she drops off me as if struck with a bullet and I regain my strength and look up into the face of this beautiful woman. She is smiling at me and tells me that everything will be OK now. She helps me up and I rise to my feet. The day is bright and light and I feel free. I don't know who she is or where she came from.

*** COMMENTS *** All the people trying to kill me are pieces of myself. They are aspects of me. My addictions that are killing me are the men that came after me that I killed with the magic mist. I have the inner strength to kill off the demons with my own power, and in this dream, I kill them one at a time with my magic mist. My willingness to give my power to a beautiful woman who is about to kill me is also clear. That's been an ongoing scenario for a long time. Only when I give up the fight, do I win. The beautiful woman is the "Goddess" energy within me. My Goddess then becomes my friend. She is compassion and love. I am embracing my divine feminine energy, my Goddess energy, my energy of compassion, love, caring, and creativity. What a powerful and beautiful dream. *** END ***

Journal Entry - 30 June 1997

*** DREAM *** I am flying missions in Vietnam in my Phantom jet. I'm feeling very strong, WITH NO fear, and I volunteer for missions that are extremely dangerous. I return from a mission and learn that an F-105 got shot down and the pilot is missing in North Vietnam. I volunteer to go on a rescue mission, even though it is very dangerous with only a minimum chance of success. That doesn't deter me and I am in a bathroom and look at myself in the mirror. I am my age today, yet powerful, fit, handsome and fearless. My squadron mates tell me I am crazy to go on this mission, but I have no fear and want to go. The squadron commander does not let me go because it is too dangerous. I look again in the mirror and see myself as I just described myself. Then I wake up.

*** COMMENTS *** This was a powerful dream and I saw myself as I wish to be. I had no fear of the commander or the mission, and I felt capable of doing anything. I could have flown this rescue mission and not only survived, but I would have also been successful. I would have found the downed pilot and somehow rescued him.

This dream was so powerful that here it is now seven hours after waking up and I still see clearly the man in the mirror. *** END ***

Journal Entry - 12 May 1998

*** DREAM *** I am living at Mom and Dad's house, but they are not home at the moment. However, there are many people around and it is daytime. Somehow, the house catches on fire and everyone hollers, 'Fire,' and runs outside. I am in the study trying to call 911, however, the phone line is dead. I go outside and see that the fire is on the outside of the house only and the fire is only along one side of our house. The fire is just on the surface, and the walls seem to be structurally intact. Also, the house and yard appear larger than they actually are, and the entire scene is surrealistic.

The house is now engulfed in flames, yet nothing is burning. Now there are flames all along the ground at the foundation of the house. I try 911 from the garage phone but cannot get through. I run to the neighbor diagonally across the street. A car blocks my way as I cross the street, however, I run across the street in front of the car and it stops.

The neighbor says, "So and so's basement flooded all the way up so it is full of water."

I ask, "How's he doing?"

Neighbor says, "Quite Well!!!...get it? Like a well full of water? Har Har!"

I run into his house and call 911 and I still see the fire along the west foundation of our house, but the house has not burned. Perhaps a gas pipe has burst, and that is providing the fuel for this fire. The fire company answers and in a clear voice, I say, "My house is on fire," and I tell them our address.

They say, "Got it, be right there!" That's it and I woke up.

*** COMMENTS *** I feel like my internal house and foundation are on fire. I hope that this is a sign of impending major change. I'm shaking the foundation for a change, perhaps to build a new house. *** END ***

Journal Entry - 12 June 1998

*** DREAM *** Many are inside the kitchen of a huge restaurant and want to escape. We are going to escape by flying away in a magnificent airplane. The people board this airplane and, although I am not the pilot flying, I am close to the front of the passenger cabin. The plane is a convertible, open cockpit type, only much larger. The pilot blasts off and we are barely airborne, flying below the power lines strung across city streets. We are flying very low. The pilot plows through the power lines and hopes that the nose will cut the wires and we will be OK. So, he pulls up right into the lines and I look forward and see us plowing into a dozen power lines and they begin to stretch and hang around the nose of our airplane. Up we go and the lines finally break loose. The sky now is becoming navy blue, then black, because we are flying so high. We're on the edge of space.

Eventually, all the power lines fall free and we are now up in space. The sky is absolutely crystal clear and black and all objects are very clear and I see perfect details of even the most distant objects. I see the moon and the edges of craters and other details with absolute perfect resolution. Stars and planets are like objects in my backyard. I see all of this while we are flying in our marvelous open-cockpit airplane. I am on the right side, about a row or two back from the pilot. It is like sitting in a roller coaster car, open and with everyone's hair blowing in the wind. After a while, we roll over and start back down to earth, which is a very long way below us. Our planet is beautiful and green as we come back down. Suddenly, we are back in the restaurant kitchen.

*** COMMENTS *** I felt apprehension while flying below the power lines just after takeoff before we blasted up through them and into space. Then, once through the power lines, I felt free and excited. I believe I am on a journey and will break through my restraints and experience life with more awareness and clarity. It was a wonderful dream. *** END ***

Journal Entry - 14 January 1999

I spent Tuesday evening with Kathy on my layover. She looks great with the same perfect body that I so clearly remember from ten years ago, when we knew each other in the Air Force. We had dinner at her place, chatted, and sipped tea in front of her fireplace. It took a lot of restraint to not reach for her hand and touch her. She is so desirable but she feels miles distant from me and holds that distance.

I am physically attracted to beautiful, sexy woman, and feel my power ebb when I am near beautiful and desirable woman like Kathy. I lose my "self" and feel my energy drain. I go into an out-of-control mode from desire. I'd love to have Kathy here with me in my home. But being very honest, I want her here on my terms, which means closeness when I want it, how I want it, and then not to deal with her and her feelings and emotions when complete. Then when she does something, I disapprove of (like just being Kathy) I can send her home and hang the termination responsibility on her. That is not honest and certainly not a genuine relationship. If I am in this mode with any woman, I have no hope of a real loving relationship with them. It would last only a short while, with no fulfillment or heart connection. Perhaps I'll see Kathy again.

Journal Entry - 3 February 1999

*** DREAM *** I am a pilot flying in the Air Force and a select few of us have learned how to fly without an airplane, like Superman. Taking off was the hardest part, and I struggled every take-off to get airborne. But once aloft, I flew effortlessly and had plenty of reserve flight energy to stay airborne and maneuver as I wished.

One beautiful day, another pilot and I were to fly a mission without airplanes. We both wore Air Force flight suits, and I had a knapsack on my back. Fortunately, there was a strong headwind, so taking off wasn't difficult. We flew along a beautiful river and I, showing off, swooped down, clipped the top of a small hill, and lost all my lift. I crashed into a river, but was unhurt. My knapsack broke off as I hit the water. The river was very clear and I could see the bottom.

My buddy made a few passes over me and I signaled I was OK and off he went to complete the mission alone. A cabin cruiser approached, and I swam toward this boat for rescue. I felt great; the weather was great, and the water was clear and cool.

*** COMMENTS *** I am flying higher by myself, i.e., without external help and seeing deeper into my consciousness. It was a positive dream. *** END ***

Journal Entry - 30 March 1999

*** DREAM *** I enter a deep dark cellar fraught with danger. There are strange human-like creatures here and I see them as I begin my descent down the stairs and along hallways into the basement. A man-like creature comes toward me and throws a knife at me in slow motion. I grab it in mid-air and toss it hard at him. The knife strikes him blade first, and he drops to the floor. I don't know if he is dead or wounded, but certainly he is disabled.

I continue down deeper and deeper and encounter more strange creatures and all that I engage, I defeat. Finally, one comes from behind a partition and he tosses a knife at me. I see it coming and am not fast enough to defeat or deflect this knife. It strikes me and I drop to the floor as my lights fade. Then I woke up.

*** COMMENTS *** I awoke frightened and disturbed by this dream. It was very unsettling and emotionally draining. I slept restlessly. In my current life, I am in my basement now engaging all my demons that live there. That is what I did in this dream and perhaps the knife that struck me was telling me I am to die and leave my body and the physical world. Perhaps my mission or purpose on this earthwalk is complete. I will take this dream to my Sacred Mesa tonight and sit with it.

Perhaps I have a demon in my basement that I must meet. That is what I will do tonight. Perhaps the message is that I have more deep shadow work to do, which might mean my death. Very unsettling because it's dangerous to do deep shadow work, and it's also dangerous to not do deep shadow work. Have courage, Johnny. *** END ***

Journal Entry - 20 May 1999

My friend Jean channels and facilitated a chat with Mr. Song and me. I asked some questions, and he told me some things. "John, lighten up on yourself. You have learned much and have grown much. Be nurturing, not critical, and be present." I know old patterns are in play here and that Mr. Song's "lighten up" message was about me beating myself up about everything.

Mr. Song focuses on the major work, not the small stuff. In fact, take care of the major issues and all minor issues will fall away. He sees the big picture. Jean tells me we have scripts to follow, and I was playing out my role in this earthwalk drama. My mind calls me a killer and as I move deeper into spirit, this will hopefully soften and ease and I will find peace. "Lighten up" now has a deeper meaning than focusing on shallow issues. The more I live in spirit, the softer my eyes, the clearer my earthwalk is and the more I lighten up. Thank you, Mr. Song and thank you, Jean.

Journal Entry - 29 June 1999

Good morning. I had a very close psychic friend share the following insight with me yesterday. *We are all here to work through pieces carried in from our past lives. My work this lifetime is to embrace my Savage, or Killer. It is about me making peace with and moving beyond the savage.*

Journal Entry - 4 July 1999

I arrived home last night at about 5 pm after my last trip as first-officer (co-pilot) with American Airlines. I flew with AA Captain John and he allowed me to fly most legs. He honored me by telling the passengers that it was my last trip as a first-officer. He told the passengers that I was about to upgrade to captain and shared that I was a Vietnam veteran fighter-pilot and how fortunate American Airlines was to have me flying their airplanes. It was very special and from his heart. Thank you, John.

Journal Entry - 6 July 1999

I tried to drop or trade a three-day trip using normal means and was unsuccessful. Exhausting all normal channels, I went to Chief Pilot Steve in operations a week before the undesirable trip and asked him if he could help me drop it. Without hesitation, he told me to consider myself off that trip and that he would make it go away somehow.

I expected to have it converted to personal vacation days, however, it was dropped with a code I was not familiar with. I called crew scheduling and was told that my trip was dropped with pay. I called Steve, and he said that the Chief Pilots agreed to remove me from my trip with pay as a little token of their gratitude for the ongoing work I do for the American Airlines Alcohol Monitor program. How about that? Don't ask, and ye shall receive! Thank you, Chief Pilots of American Airlines.

Journal Entry - 8 March 2000

It's 5:22 am and fifteen years ago on this morning, I had my last drink of alcohol and began walking toward life instead of running from life. Last night I had a little dream about drinking and being drunk.

*** DREAM *** I am in the Air Force and going on temporary duty. I am attending the in-brief on Sunday prior to Monday's flying. I listen to the briefer talking on and on about how to fly the Phantom and bomb at the local gunnery range. He's rambling on about gunsight settings and all the stuff I already know. I'm champing at the bit to leave and go to the bar for happy hour. He finally stops and all the pilots go to the bar and order up some drinks.

Later in the dream, we have a big party and I, along with many friends, get roaring drunk. The next day everyone meets for brunch, and I'm hung over as hell, yet I go there and all I can think about is having a drink to feel better. I absolutely need a drink to function and realize how much energy it requires to function when in this drinking mode. I awoke at 4:15 am and I was so grateful that it was only a dream. I am sober and alive and very functional.

*** COMMENTS *** It was a very appropriate dream, as today is my fifteenth sobriety birthday.

PART III
INTO THE LIGHT

SECTION INTRODUCTION

"I can't see! I can't see!" I not only can't see, but I don't understand either and I want to run fast and far. Having vision but living in darkness is very uncomfortable. Teachers illuminate darkness so that those that seek may embrace their suffering and journey into the light.

Within a few days of "Teacher's" arrival in mid-June 2019, she established new guidelines and our relationship shifted from supportive friends to teacher and student.

I was moving out of my comfort zone and into unexplored territory. There was nowhere to hide and no reasonable options available other than to stay in the pain and trust, or run away, again, from myself. It was excruciating at times, and I felt like I was dying. And parts of me were.

Just being around her stirred my soul and challenged me deeply. It took a while for me to realize that my uncomfortableness had its roots in my suppressed and repressed anger, rage, fears, and loss of control.

I had never been full-time with a spiritual teacher before, and felt off balance and uncomfortable around her. Old behaviors, old habit patterns, and old ways of doing things weren't working out well anymore and had to go. Even my beautiful Motorcoach Dutch and Harley-Davidson motorcycle lost their top priorities and went to the back burner. Much of how I lived my life was headed for the trash can and would be discarded.

Teacher served divinity, and repeatedly said, "It's not personal for me, Johnny. I've been called to be here as your teacher by the Divine. This is sacred work."

Being super-sensitive to energies, she requested for her comfort and protection that in this book, I hold her in sacred anonymity. So, with great reverence and respect for this selfless being, I refer to her simply as "Teacher."

Into the Light is my life journey from Teacher's arrival in mid-June 2019, till the completion of this book in December 2023.

I invite you to walk with me through my experiences, discoveries, pains, sufferings, challenges, and pleasures with an open heart and an open mind. Hopefully, you will relate, be challenged, and grow. *From Savage to Shaman* is not a story or adventure book, but a transformational tool to help you move beyond your darkness, through your shadow, and "*Into the Light*."

THE BEGINNING

I parked Dutch at Hoover's Campground and RV-Park near Ashland, Oregon, in mid-June 2019, and once again, Donna, the owner, offered me her military discount and the premier spot at her park in exchange for a ride around the local area on Harley. She also knew that I was a hobby photographer and asked me to photograph her campground and even take a few portrait shots of her as well. I jumped at the chance to exercise my passion for photography and, of course, I accepted. It was great fun to be with my friend that I knew from a dozen previous visits to her campground. Life was full of pleasures.

My first day there, Teacher sent me a note saying that she was heading toward Ashland, Oregon, and asked if I might want to share a re-acquaint and catch-up visit. I agreed, and a few days later, she arrived at Hoover's Campground in her van.

My time with Teacher began casually when we initially met at a spiritual center about ten years prior. Our time together always had a sense of playfulness and lightheartedness that was exhilarating and pleasurable. We subsequently maintained a peripheral friendship that was rooted in respect. I looked forward to spending time with her as our few prior encounters were always pleasurable and supportive.

Back in late, 2008, at the spiritual center where we first met, she asked if I would contribute a few chapters about my Vietnam flying experiences to include in some future book of hers. I was all-in for that and honored to be a part of her project. Nothing more ever came of that request.

Life was pleasant upon her arrival in Ashland. I was sober now thirty-five years, owned Dutch and motorcycle, Harley, had significant friendships, engaged in meaningful and pleasant activities and was healthy. I was approaching my seventy-fifth birthday. All was well, and I looked forward to daily activities like exploration adventures on Harley, photographing whatever came into my viewfinder, and doing a little walking and a few stretches to maintain health.

But I continually sensed an unpleasant undercurrent of "unfinished business" that I couldn't, or didn't, want to address. I was consistently a bit over ideal weight, resisted deep intimacy, and had an underlying fear of authority. I avoided long-term relationships with woman and didn't trust them. I rationalized that away, saying, *perhaps I'm just not destined to have a partner this lifetime.* And perhaps I'm not.

When I sat in stillness focusing on intimacy, I felt fear creep in and knew that I was afraid of deep relationships with woman. I readily gave away my power and felt inferior to physically attractive and/or strong, accomplished, independent woman. I knew this, yet deluded myself into believing that "all was well" and rationalized these feelings away. I retained a fear of my father and projected that fear on anyone that was in a position of authority or perceived authority over me like a police officer. This led to controlling behaviors.

I didn't have a structured meditation practice, and although I established one many times, the practice usually lasted only a few days. Not sustaining is a common thread in my life. I begin enthusiastically, lose momentum, quit, and begin again. However, the pleasures I experienced, along with my established denial and rationalization systems, allowed me to live a relatively peaceful and enjoyable life.

I was content making minor changes, digging deeper here and there, dabbling in this and that, and denying the uncomfortable undercurrents. I knew that there were a few rough edges to Johnny MedicineBear, but *hey, everybody has rough edges, and nobody is perfect.* But I was to discover that my rough edges were just the tip of an iceberg and much unresolved shadow energy lay below the surface.

She was intelligent, independent, and conscious, with similar interests as mine. But I soon discovered that below these apparent attributes, there was an authentic spiritual teacher guided by divinity. Fully appreciating this took months.

A few days after her arrival in Ashland, Oregon, she said, "I received guidance from Spirit, Johnny, about a new book project we will co-create."

"Great," I replied with a smile.

"The book project will be titled *From Savage to Shaman,* and this spiritually inspired and spiritually guided book will be about your life experiences. The three sections are Into the Darkness, Into the Shadow, and Into the Light.

"This book will be a tool intended for everyone, civilian or military, woman or man who suffer from depression and live in their darkness. Military veterans who return from war and entertain or attempt suicide will easily relate to your story, Johnny. Everyone will be able to find themselves in this book and hopefully use the healing tools offered. We will create it together, Johnny."

"OK," I agreed, totally clueless about what this would entail.

"But first, I will help you clear your unresolved shadow. This is necessary for you to authentically create and write from your heart and soul, not your ego-personality."

"OK," I replied, not understanding but agreeing anyway.

"As your teacher, I am establishing strict boundaries from here forward."

"OK," I whispered, again confused and now a bit apprehensive. I had several questions and was clueless, but agreed to do whatever she requested and required. I knew that this was necessary for my spiritual growth. Her presence was an unexpected opportunity.

Much changed. Chanting mantras and sitting meditations became the first activities of the day. Group or session periods, under Teacher's guidance, probed the depths of my inner psyche and invited repressed energies to reveal themselves and surface. Playing the stereo ceased, and we lived mostly in silence, with no extraneous conversation and no physical contact. Even the generally accepted, 'good morning' greeting or small hug stopped, and my humming, singing, whistling, and Native American flute playing all ceased to allow space for introspection and inner exploration. It was very quiet in Dutch. Occasionally, we watched relevant documentaries and videos, or listened to audio clips of masters all directed at spiritual growth. I was learning how to be silent and listen. At seventy-five, I learned I don't have to argue, always be right, or have the last word.

And so began the journey "Into the Light."

ROUND AND AROUND I GO - WHERE I STOP, I DON'T KNOW

Here is my life from a few years past. Perhaps yours is similar. Sleep is challenging and restless with dreams that I usually can't remember. I always sleep better after "a few" or even better than that when "half-in-the-bag." I'm always busy, or at least my mind is always busy. I cannot shut off my inner voices, sit still, or be silent for very long. My mind will not leave me alone. I focus on this or that project, some shallow activity, a mindless social event, or another dumb TV show. But it's always something that doesn't truly make a whit of difference long term. My life IS a continual series of never-ending sensual distractions.

Damn, they did it to me again. Why don't people just lighten up? They've got my number and are picking on me. I'm sure it's their fault, not mine cause I'm very reasonable and generally right too. Why can't they see that?

Time to rearrange my closet, and make it "better." I move something that's been in the same place for years, to a "better" place and soon forget where I moved it too. When I next go look for it, I'm surprised that it's not in the place I've kept it forever. Oh yeah, I remember now that I recently moved it and don't remember where I moved it to. Then, I mercilessly criticize myself for being so stupid.

I straighten up my tool shed and do the same thing out there. I reorganize files, defrag my hard drive, or go wash my car again.

Sometimes when I'm not in the compulsive "doing" mode, I slip into the passive "not-doing" mode and just "chill out" for about six months and nothing gets done.

Should I have a drink? It's almost noon, and one beer won't affect me much and I can relax this afternoon. Nice nap. Where did the afternoon go? Whoa! It's almost five, and time for a drink.

I wish I could get that song that plays continually in my head to stop. I'm sick and tired of it. Interesting! I've heard it a million times and still don't know the words.

I deserve another drink tonight. It was a tough day, and if you had my stressful job, you'd have another, too. Great idea! I'll just have one more so I can really relax and enjoy myself. "Ahhhhh, that's much better."

Uh-oh, overslept again. Oh well, I guess I should have gone home earlier last night, but I was having way too much fun and found so much in common with my new friend on the next bar stool. After all, both our names begin with J and that's surely a sign from heaven. Hope the boss doesn't see me sneaking into work through the break room.

Another day and the cycle of insanity begins all over again, with endless mind chatter, endless distractions to hide the internal chaos, and endless denials that there is something wrong. It's everybody else's problem, but mine. If only they would understand, or change, everything would be just fine. The Merry-Go-Round goes round and round. This is how I lived my life and many currently live theirs, albeit, some perhaps more than others.

Almost everyone is addicted to alcohol, drugs, food, work, power, shopping, gambling, tobacco, sex, exercise, sweets, coffee, chocolate, diet sodas, etc. Those addicted are on the Merry-Go-Round and it never stops. The only options are to sit on the horse going round and round, up and down, forever, or get off.

Please place yourself in this story with honesty and courage. Make a resolve right now to get off your Merry-Go-Round and step into the unknown, into the unexplored, into new adventures, and into freedom and joy.

EARTHLINGS

A week after her arrival, Teacher and I together watched the 2005 documentary *Earthlings* about humankind's economic dependence on animals raised for food, pets, clothing, and entertainment. It graphically presented the violence and cruelty inflicted on these beings by the industry that supplies the meat, fish, eggs, and pets for our animal consumption, animal clothing, and domestic living pets. The brutality, cruelty, and disrespect for these beings was overwhelming.

As I watched a man slitting the throats of live cows hanging from meat-hooks by their hoofs, I saw, in slow motion, metal fragments slitting the throats of Vietnamese people from the exploding bombs I dropped from my Phantom jet in Vietnam many years ago. I watched the entire documentary, crying uncontrollably.

At completion, I cleaned out my fridge, freezer, and pantry of all animal products and have sustained a vegetarian, and mostly vegan, food plan ever since. This diet transformation occurred not from any verbal oath, vow, or commitment made by me fueled only by an ego-resolution, but because of the loving, supportive energy of Teacher that allowed for an internal transformation to occur. I didn't "do" anything. I just stopped resisting. Over time, I realized that just being in Teacher's presence was a gift.

Cutting into a steak today would be akin to cutting into my arm. Separation between animal-beings, the Earth Mother, and me diminished. Without Teacher's supportive energy and guidance, this shift in diet to vegetarian and vegan would not have occurred.

I FELT the pain and suffering inflicted on those defenseless animal-beings and FELT the pain and suffering of our Earth Mother by the unconscious behaviors of her children. And none of this destruction is necessary as the overwhelming evidence supporting totally plant-based nutrition is readily available.

It also brought to consciousness the pain and suffering I inflicted on my "earthling" brothers and sisters in Vietnam by my unconscious participation in that war. This was the genesis of the deep work required to diffuse this energy.

Over time, the desire to consume meats, fish, and other animal-based foods has faded. This is transformation that happens in the presence of an authentic Teacher. It is transformation by Grace.

BABY AND SWEETHEART

We traveled north from Ashland, Oregon to several campgrounds, staying a few days here and a few days there, with me driving Dutch, and Teacher following in her van. The daily routine included mantras, meditations, a bit of walking, a few stretches, group/session, and writing the beginnings of this book. Initially, the focus was on me becoming conscious of old behaviors, fixed habit patterns, and my inflexible ways of doing things. She guided me to observe, acknowledge, and release some old detrimental behavior patterns.

As example, I frequently addressed woman casually as "sweetheart" or "baby" and never thought of it as demeaning or degrading. I viewed sweetheart and baby as terms of endearment and friendliness, and to me they were. I was challenged by Teacher about this and realized that perhaps, just perhaps, I'm making assumptions, asserting my ego, and subtly projecting anger on woman by taking these casual liberties. It never crossed my mind that my casual behaviors might offend a woman.

She suggested I find more appropriate and respectful ways to address women. Initially, I resisted and blew this off as insignificant. I didn't want to change and thought that Teacher just didn't understand.

But that didn't last very long and shortly I softened a little and realized that she was right.

I learned to be clear and respectful in conversations with anyone regardless of gender and stopped referring to women as baby or sweetheart. I found that a simple hello and thank you worked just fine and noticed uncomfortable feelings arising when, occasionally, "Thank you, sweetheart," Johnny emerged. Perhaps my casualness with woman was my personality pushing against them and keeping them at arm's length.

This change has sustained. And when occasionally little Johnny jumps out and refers casually to a woman as sweetheart, I do not demean or criticize myself. I simply acknowledge the event and let it go. It may seem trivial, but progress is a series of small steps.

LEAH

We met in Alcoholics Anonymous in 2014 and over time developed a deep, supportive friendship. Leah was on fire with her sobriety and recognized aspects of me that resonated with her. She asked me to be her spiritual guide and teacher and I accepted.

Teacher, I thought, what does that mean? Well, a true teacher doesn't really teach anything. The teacher points to the path they have traveled and guides the student in their own self-discovery.

Over time, I appreciated that Leah was as much a teacher for me as I was for her. Initially, some of her behaviors disturbed me as they bumped against my unresolved issues with the "Goddess." I didn't like it.

When we met, I still had unresolved issues with "the feminine," especially my mother, but was not aware of this. When I felt disturbed by some of Leah's behaviors, I pointed my finger at her and blamed her for my uncomfortableness. I was really running away from myself and my unresolved issues.

After Teacher arrived in Ashland, Oregon, in mid-June 2019, I told Leah that I was departing on a spiritual pilgrimage with a spiritual teacher that she did not know. I emphasized I needed to detach and separate from her and hoped that she would understand and support me.

Not sure of where my spiritual pilgrimage would take me or when I would return, I was brief and gave few details. It was challenging to present this to Leah and harder for her to understand, as we both enjoyed our frequent chats and the comforts of a deep friendship. But all communication had to stop for me to stay focused on my work with Teacher.

Perhaps Leah saw it more as I, her trusted friend, was simply running away.

The quality of an interpersonal relationship is not determined by how little one displeases the other, or how kind one is to the other, but how truthful one is to the other. The foundation of a healthy relationship is based on truth, regardless of how painful it may be to share truth.

Many would lie rather than share a truth. I did this for years. *I can't tell her that, what would she do if she heard that from me?* These were excuses I used many times in my distant past. A relationship built on that level of communication is not a loving-relationship. It is an interpersonal battle of the egos.

Leah and I were both uncomfortable from this separation experience, but with time processed our feelings and emerged more deeply connected. Sharing truth with a supportive friend is reserved for the spiritually mature.

Upon returning from India in late January 2020, Leah and I reconnected. I shared my entire experience with her. We recognized the growth we had both experienced by not running from, but staying in and working through our discomfort and feelings. Our friendship deepened rather than disintegrated into a finger pointing match, each blaming the other for the relationship's dissolution.

TRY THIS, TRY THAT, NOT THIS, NOT THAT

Trying unsuccessfully to open a webpage with a slow internet connection, Teacher leaned over my shoulder one afternoon and said, "Try this, try that, no try this, that won't work, try that." I became frustrated and felt like a scolded child as I attempted to accommodate her, while being pleasant and polite. Fear and anger crept in, and my "happy space" dropped to zero.

"You just destroyed me," I said in a voice laced with anger, "with your badgering belligerent attitude."

She persisted. "How about trying that and clicking over there?" She ignored me and continued with her pushy "know-it-all" comments. I caved-in and saw myself as a little boy with my father standing over my shoulder lecturing me on how to do something while totally ignoring my efforts and feelings. It was my unresolved issues with my father and the projection of him on Teacher that was the fundamental problem.

"How can I destroy you?" she asked?

"Well, I guess you really didn't destroy me. You just destroyed my happy space," I replied.

"How can I destroy your happy space if it's a solid, happy space? No one has the power to destroy your happy space if you are in presence," she continued.

"You weren't very nice or pleasant to me," I responded, defensively.

"That doesn't matter. Many people are not nice or pleasant. It only matters that you gave your happy space away. I didn't destroy it," she said.

I continued, "You turned into my father, and I saw Dad, not you, leaning over my shoulder scolding me. You were just the trigger, I guess, and that's why I went to fear and anger."

"Your response was rooted in unresolved trauma from your childhood, Johnny. It manifested in the projection of your father on me. Had you resolved that trauma, you might have responded with 'OK, I'm on it, please go sit down. I'll work this out alone and if I can't get it, then you may try.' That would have taken care of the whole event.

"But neither you nor anyone else can do that till they have resolved their childhood traumas. These traumas will continue to surface and contaminate your life until you take your last breath, if not resolved. Few realize this, and fewer still do the required work. Now that you see it and understand it, it's up to you to move through it."

I began to appreciate how extensive my controlling behaviors were. I could not maintain a happy space anywhere other than in a Johnny MedicineBear controlled environment. So, I attempted to control just about everything. When I couldn't, I went to fear and anger while wearing a smile so others wouldn't know that I was "out-of-control."

While in a car, I was uneasy not being in the driver's seat. I resisted going to unfamiliar places and even tried to sit in restaurants with my back to a wall. It takes a ton of energy to control one's environment.

Needing to control and not being in control always leads to suffering. And, once in control, attempting to retain control also always leads to suffering, for eventually control is lost. Therefore, the being with unresolved trauma strives to control their surroundings to remain comfortable. They are doomed to a depleted life of fear and suffering.

But now I knew either I do the required inner work, or live an unfulfilled mediocre life of fear and suffering, occasionally enjoying sensory pleasures to ease the pain. Also, until complete, Dad, in many forms would continue to appear in my life and create additional opportunities for me to resolve childhood traumas.

THE WORK OF BYRON KATIE

Teacher introduced me to "The Work of Byron Katie," and guided me through multiple sessions using Byron Katie's worksheets as a base. We worked through judgements and life experiences using her "One-Belief-at-a-Time" worksheet, and the "Judge-Your-Neighbor" worksheet. An internet search of "Byron Katie - The Work" will guide you to her website. This resource was of great value.

"I am nothing but a dirtball," I muttered while sharing about a long-ago painful event.

Teacher said, "Use the One-Belief-at-a-Time worksheet, Johnny, and then we'll go over it together."

With low self-worth brought forward from childhood, I identified deeply with unworthiness. Dirt-ball seemed to fit well. Using Byron Katie's worksheets, I saw that the perception of myself as a dirt-ball, was a projection of my unresolved childhood traumas carried forward. The worksheet guided me in transforming these negative perceptions into positives. I am a dirt-ball only when I believe I'm a dirt-ball. I'm referencing who I am from the long ago past. Teacher made a sign that hung on the wall for months. It read, "I am not a dirtball. The truth is that I am a being of light and love in service to all."

I suffered a lot from lack of knowledge of reality and holding onto past perceptions tenaciously. This is classic victim mentality.

THE BUILDING-OF-LIFE

This metaphorical narrative helps me relate to my behaviors and the behaviors of others. It came from a book by one of my favorite wisdom people, Vernon Howard. I encourage you to read it slowly and deliberately. The floors of the building refer to levels of human consciousness.

I walk into a city and see the Building-of-Life before me, decide to stay awhile, and conduct my life's business here. I enter on the first floor, set up an office space, and begin conducting my life's business. Being at street level, I can't see much of the outside landscape.

Here on the first floor, phone calls are frequently not returned, people are short-tempered and agitated, and things occasionally disappear from my desk. It's loud and chaotic here, with an atmosphere of competition, narcissism, dishonesty, and aggression. People don't cooperate with each other very much and there are many disputes and many cliques. I am constantly agitated and guarded. It's a trying place to live and requires much effort to get anything done. Addictive people occupy the first floor or below. There is little or no peace and serenity to be found here. I begin to wonder if there are other floors in this Building-of-Life.

I go searching and way off in a corner, I discover a door that doesn't look like it's used very much. It's hard to open and squeaks on its hinges. Opening the door, I find a dark steep staircase heading upwards. I climb, and, after a long arduous effort, emerge at a higher level. I know this floor is higher for I can see much more of the outside landscape. So, I set up my office on this level and find that here most phone calls are returned, people are more pleasant, things don't disappear from my desk very often, and it's calmer, quieter, and more peaceful. I like it here. Pleasantries are the norm here, and I accomplish much more with less effort.

After a while, though, I begin to wonder if there are still higher levels in this Building-of-Life and again go exploring. Off in a secluded corner, I find another door that also squeaks on its hinges from lack of use and behind it, another dark steep stairway leading upward.

Once more I begin the climb and after another long arduous effort, emerge at an even higher level. From here, I have a very broad view of the outside landscape. So, I set up my office on this level and for the first time, I experience safety. Work is effortless here, requiring only minimal energy. Communications are clear, people are authentic, creative, and spontaneous. This community is like family. Nothing disappears from my desk and gifts occasionally show up. I'm at home here.

I decide to return to the first floor and tell my friends what I've discovered about this Building-of-Life. Using my magic key in the magic elevator, I descend to the first floor and emerge into the chaos.

"Johnny, where ya been?" asks a friend.

"Did you guys know that there are higher levels in this Building-of-Life where it's much more pleasant and less chaotic?" I share.

"No way, this is all there is, Johnny."

I begin to share with my friends about my experience and the higher levels that I've discovered. My friends show little or no interest and look at me like I'm nuts.

"Johnny, we're going for a burger and a beer, to shoot some pool, and watch the drag races. Care to join us?"

I thank them for the offer and politely decline. Alone, I call the magic elevator and return to my upper level.

The Building-of-Life is a metaphorical expression of awareness and consciousness levels. As one does their inner work (the long arduous climb), their awareness and consciousness expands. The world changes for these few, for they now source from a higher level of consciousness.

Here are a few truths about the Building-of-Life. First, everyone believes they are on the top floor. Second, no one can relate to a level higher than the level that they occupy. Third, one may expect nothing but first floor behavior from first floor people. Fourth, every ceiling and floor is a one-way mirror. One can look through the floors and observe the activities of the lower levels below, but one cannot look through the ceilings and observe the activities of the higher levels above.

Few realize that higher levels in the Building-of-Life even exist. Of those few, only a few search for and find the door to the stairway. Of those few, only a few open the door and begin the climb. And of those few, only a few persist until reaching a higher level. And it is a rare soul indeed that returns to find the second, third, fourth, and more doors to continue their spiritual pilgrimage resting on their current level as necessary.

Be one of the few.

RELATIONSHIPS - PARTNERSHIPS

Do you have a loving, supportive relationship with your partner, or an ego-personality-centered relationship of compromise and conflict? Are you partnered with your soulmate, or are you partnered with a teacher? One's relationship includes all personality aspects, including the unhealed hidden traits, known or not. Most people are unaware of their hidden personalities and their dark side. Paraphrasing Robert Bly from his book, *A Little Book on the Human Shadow*, he said that, 'As one marriage takes place in the chapel, another simultaneously takes place in the basement.' The marriage in the basement is the joining of the unhealed or shadow aspects of the participants.

What many believe is a loving, supportive relationship may be a comfort and convenience relationship. Both partners enable each other's unhealthy behaviors, while blaming the other for the issues that occur. Partner A allows B to drink excessively, or release anger and rage, while partner B allows A to eat excessively, or work to extreme. Each stays in such a relationship to avoid doing their own inner work. They are constantly pointing the finger of blame for their own problems at the other and focusing on the other's faults.

After resolving addictions and compulsions, one becomes available for a higher-level relationship. Heal oneself and one's relationship improves. The relationship with one's partner cannot be any healthier than the relationship one has with themself.

Nothing other than healing the hidden personality will yield permanent results, for the source and solution of one's problems lies within.

One attracts into their life everything-good and bad, pleasant, and unpleasant. This includes every being and every event, without exception. Whatever is going on, you asked for it, and the universe brought it to you.

There are two options when one realizes that their relationship is chaos and something must change. First is to place blame externally for one's current misery. *He, she, or they did it to me. It's their fault that I'm so miserable.* Second is to face the problems head-on, take responsibility, and heal the trauma living in the basement.

The ego will never run out of excuses and ways to create chaos, as the ego wants to always retain addictions and place blame for one's misery out there. It does this to keep itself alive and actively employed. Since the ego identifies itself AS the individual, it never gives up without an intense and relentless struggle, for it sees release of addiction as the death of itself. It requires total commitment and courage to hold the line in the face of an avalanche of addictive desires. But that is necessary in order to transcend any addiction. The ego must die to allow for the expansion and expression of the soul. Freedom lies on the far side of addiction.

Once one's traumas are cleared, then one is available for a loving relationship with a healthy partner, since one now has a loving relationship with oneself.

It's possible, of course, that both partners "wake-up" simultaneously and support each other on their upward journey. But this is rare, as usually one begins to climb and the other remains in the current space. One expands and one resists expansion. The relationship then moves further out of balance and dissolves or continues in deeper confusion and chaos.

"When faced with the choice of changing or proving that there is no need to do so, most get busy on the proof." (anon)

ADDICTIONS

Brother-friend Joe and I bantered around, discussing addictions one day. With twenty years of continuous sobriety, I saw myself as an authority on addiction and I ranted and raved about this and that and finally, after a while, stopped.

Joe said little during my share, and finally he said, "Let me wrap up your whole discussion, Johnny, in three words. Addiction: It's never enough. That's all there is to it." Joe was right on target and I pass Joe's wisdom on to you, my friend. If unsure if you have an addiction, be brutally honest and watch your behavior. If "it's never enough," most likely you have a problem.

Even a small leak in a ship, if not repaired, will continue to grow, compromising the hull's structural integrity. The ship will become weighted with water, sluggish, and less responsive. If ignored, the ship will eventually sink.

We are all ships on the sea of life, responsible for our own structural integrity. Compromising ourselves puts a little hole in the fabric of our psychic ship, and compromises our structural integrity. If one ignores this compromise, the tear will continue to expand. A small compromise today invites a larger compromise tomorrow.

Giving up cravings/desires repeatedly, each time swearing off and saying, "this is my last," always results in failure. Shortly, one caves in and repeats the old behavior. Perhaps the compromise is small at first, but soon one is back in full-force.

Alcoholics Anonymous is full of people who have traveled this road repeatedly. This also applies to other addictions like chocolate, diet sodas, midnight snacks, watching endless news, or desiring power over others.

What's the way out? How do I spring the trap and release the cravings, desires, and addictions for good? The only way is to rise above the compulsive behaviors-to elevate consciousness. And as you grow, desires will fade and dissolve. This cannot be accomplished with reference solely to the physical planes, for the mind that wants to discard these behaviors is the same mind that supports them. It requires a deep resolve to become a Spiritual Warrior, a seeker of truth, and embark on a Spiritual Pilgrimage. Practicing mindfulness, as in sitting and walking meditations, brings one back to presence. Few are successful at this straight away, as it is new and foreign to most. Be gentle and never judge or criticize yourself if you are not at first successful. Being hard on yourself in any manner is counterproductive and will lower your energy and resolve. Your ego will encourage you to judge and be hard on yourself, as this weakens your resolve for success. As one's resolve weakens, the ego will re-assume control and encourage sensory-pleasure escapes. The ego is always trying to please, using short-term sensory pleasures to "keep one happy." These surface, shallow, short-lived activities are always followed by neurosis and suffering.

When we confront the ego and hold the line, facing an avalanche of compulsions and desires, the ego weakens. Eventually, the ego gives up and dissolves. This allows space for the soul to emerge. The less ego, the more soul. And with more inner space available, spiritual/soul guidance will naturally arise from within.

The loving support and guidance of an authentic Teacher is essential for spiritual growth. Being in Teacher's presence with a deep resolve to heal, allows for the dissolution of deep trauma. That trauma holds one in unhealthy cravings and desires. Once healed, past traumatic events will no longer trigger anger, rage, or worse.

Today, I may revisit my childhood without unpleasant emotional responses.

Teachers are everywhere. Look in recovery groups, support workshops, authentic spiritual experiences, and in the non-physical as well. But having a teacher means nothing unless one has an unwavering desire to shed addictive behaviors and compulsions. One must follow the authentic teacher's guidance.

This is not work for the faint-of-heart. As one grows and expands, the foundation of one's life crumbles. One might find out that what they thought was a solid rock foundation was really a flimsy cardboard look-like-rock foundation. From the pile of rubble, a new more solid YOU will emerge on a rock-solid foundation.

Shedding an addiction takes enormous courage. Here is the secret of success for you to accomplish just about anything. The secret of success is eight words long.

"NEVER, NEVER, NEVER, NEVER, NEVER, NEVER, GIVE-UP!"

When the going gets uncomfortable, keep on trucking. When the going gets tough, keep on trucking. When the going gets painful, keep on trucking. And when you feel you cannot go one step further, take a few more steps, then relax. The infinite wisdom of divinity will challenge no one beyond their capabilities.

LYING AND DENIAL

When one lies, one knows they are lying. One is conscious of what they are saying. With lying, one speaks falsely. One observes a brick wall, then tells another that the wall is wood. That is lying. Lying and deception were the worst infractions in indigenous societies and were punished severely. It was more serious to lie than to kill or steal.

When a native person killed another, it was generally for a rational reason and somewhat acceptable to the community. It involved only a few people, and was quickly dealt with. Native cultures didn't have many casual, impersonal, or random killings.

Stealing was often a demonstration of one's bravery and ofttimes after the steal, the item was returned to the original owner. Lying undermines a community's integrity.

The Scout, also known as the truth-bearer, demonstrated unquestionable integrity. Scouts were the eyes and ears of the community and searched for the best hunting grounds and safe routes for the people to travel. They spoke only truth, did not embellish, and reported exactly what they saw. They communicated with spoken words, voice inflection, body language, and physical gestures using body paints and personal objects such as knives, bows, and arrows.

When a scout returned from a mission, they ran to the village center and conveyed their message to the entire village as a sacred dance. They then sat with the chiefs and elders to share the details of their experience. Rarely did a scout embellish or compromise truth. If they did and were discovered, they were dealt with quickly. Everything in indigenous societies was sacred.

Today, lying and dishonesty has become the norm. Dishonesty, however, slowly erodes the structural threads of the fabric that supports the integrity of a society. In our de-personalized industrialized western culture, when one lies, even if challenged, it creates doubt, and soon becomes accepted as truth by some. We've moved from a time when speaking truth was the norm, and one's word was accepted as truth, to the barrage of lies we experience today that undermine our culture and create chaos.

We are besieged with lies in many forms on many fronts, from the crib to the coffin. Commercials and marketing presentations by the mega-millions, for example, are all lies in one form or another. It is challenging to distill truth today from the barrage of available and easily obtainable information. Many have become Masters of Deception, and perpetrate an attitude of, "I lied, so what! You can't prove I did. I got away with it and that's good enough for me. I'm the winner." Personal integrity has become a rarity.

So, what does one do? One must be responsible and accountable to themselves. When one is centered in their soul, they are centered in truth. When one is centered in their personality, they are centered in deception. Speak from your soul and you are speaking truth. Speak from your personality and you may be speaking deceptively, for the personality has ulterior motives. It's that simple. Shedding the personality means shedding the ego. This allows for soul expansion where one may live in truth and integrity. Every time one speaks truth, no matter how painful, one benefits.

Denial is a defense or coping mechanism that allows one to believe something is true when it is not, or to believe something is not true when it is. And there are many shades of in-between gray to this very simplistic straight forward explanation. Denial may also appear as a buffer, allowing for a slow integration of horrific events into one's psyche and the ability to function in the face of these horrific events. Denial may prevent one from suicide.

My participation in Vietnam was supported by my denial of the reality of war and what I was REALLY doing. The savage lives in denial. I justified and rationalized my bombing missions with thoughts like, *better to stop them over there than on the California coast*, or, *somebody's got to do it*, and perhaps the craziest one was, *I'm here to help the Vietnamese people*. My denial systems, along with the support of Jim Beam, Jack Daniels, and Johnny Walker, kept my mind from seeing my bombs exploding, killing many people and destroying Vietnamese villages. Without my denial system, I could not have functioned as a combat fighter pilot.

After sobriety at age 40, my deeply entrenched denial systems allowed me to wake up slowly to the horrors of my direct participation in war. Had I seen a clearer reality of my war experiences earlier in my sobriety, I may have realized too much, too soon, and might have become one of the suicide statistics. Denial helped me to slowly own my shadow by acting as a buffer, so that the shock of reality was dampened and not experienced as a tidal wave of trauma.

Imagine standing below a dam and opening a huge valve to drain a lake. You are directly in front of the drain discharge pipe and the water will be released directly at you. The lake is your consciousness and all your deep, dark secrets lie toward the bottom of your lake. If one allows the water to release slowly at first, one can withstand the pressure and cold from the release. One may become very uncomfortable but can deal with it. One must keep at it, continually draining water and staying uncomfortably wet and cold as the lake drains. Eventually, the lake will empty, and one is now safe from the dangers of their deep, dark secrets. And they are out of danger of the dam bursting and receiving the full force all at once of their deep, dark secrets. When one has released and experienced all the water from their dammed-up lake, the anxiety of dying from the failed dam is no more. One may now dismantle the dam and plant a garden in the fertile soil of the empty lake bed.

The lake is a metaphorical expression of the space where one's deep secrets and shadow energies reside, hidden from view. It is created in one's mind by the denial systems (the dam) and is delusional. One builds the dam to contain one's "Shadow Lake." One builds denial systems to contain one's deep, dark shadow secrets. And the mind keeps its dark secrets (shadow energies) hidden from view, hidden from your conscious mind, deep in the lake. Everyone, with few exceptions, has a shadow lake held at bay by one's personal dam (denial systems).

Most are completely unaware of their lake and their dam, but it is there. It takes major effort and energy to maintain one's dam and contain their personal lake full of stuff one doesn't want to look at or deal with. Nightmares, grotesque thoughts and visions, desires to watch and/or direct participation in violence receives its energy from the depths of Shadow Lake. If one's dam bursts, the deluge of released water (shadow energies) will instantly kill them (suicide).

Some become aware of their lake and might observe the surface from above, deluding themselves into believing that all is calm and quiet at Shadow Lake. However, there is much going on below the surface in the undercurrents and depths where the deep secrets reside, hidden from view. Occasionally, one's damn (denial systems) will spring a leak and with tons of propelling pressure, manifest in violent outbursts like road rage, or physical violence/abuse to others or self. Life, with a lake full of unresolved shadow, is a life of confusion, chaos, and fear.

Do not do this deep work alone. It is suicidal to go swimming in one's lake or attempt to drain one's lake and dismantle the dam without the help and guidance of a true teacher. When one embarks on the Spiritual Pilgrimage, one must have an authentic teacher/guide to point the way and insure one's safety. The teacher is the safety net and will know how much water and pressure one can withstand when the drain valve opens. Too little and progress is too slow; too much and one may not survive the onslaught.

'The unexamined life is not worth living,' said the Greek Philosopher, Socrates, and I wholeheartedly agree. With proper support and guidance, I implore you to face your dam, crack open your valve, experience your shadow, and venture forward toward freedom and joy.

CONTROL - GUIDANCE

What is control? What is guidance? How are they different? Alcoholics Anonymous taught me that I have no control over people, places, and things-only myself. Before sobriety in 1985, I tried countless times to control my addictions, behaviors, and emotions with no sustained success. When I gave up trying, sobriety happened. In the giving-up, perhaps my ego cracked open sufficiently to allow my soul to illuminate and sobriety occurred. One must somehow dissolve the ego to create space for the soul to shine. The soul will never shine while the ego is in control. Therefore, it usually takes a major life-changing event to sufficiently loosen the ego for the soul to illuminate. It must happen this way as the ego will never, on its own, relinquish control. It will use every trick in its massive bag of deceptions to retain control, for it views giving up control as giving up its own life.

Control is ego-power. It is power over someone or something. Guidance is the voice of divinity speaking through the soul.

The ego always wants the being to be comfortable and happy. So, the ego, in its never-ending quest for comfort and happiness, uses short-term sensory-pleasures to achieve its goal and tries to control everything. It creates the supporting denial systems and resulting delusional world surrounding the being so that one may feel comfortable, relaxed, important, and in-control. As one's ego becomes the more dominant source of reference, it grows in strength, reveling in its own importance. Soon, the ego becomes the principal identity of the person. As the being continues to function from the ego, the soul fades and may eventually be lost.

The ego desperately attempts to stay within its "comfort zone" and rejects reality outside of this. Known, accurate information and the clearest logic is stubbornly refuted by the ego, for it sees acknowledging information or events outside its comfort zone as relinquishing control. That is akin to relinquishing its own life.

Winning is everything to the ego and it will lie, cheat, steal, and rationalize its inappropriate, dishonest, aggressive, and sometimes violent behaviors away as necessary. When the dust of an ego battle settles, it will again go hunting and soon engage in another event. This cycle is continuous if the ego is the primary center of the being. Most humans source from their ego.

The being centered in ego will always meet with resistance from other ego centered beings. Hence, battles are endless and continuous. They are fraught with frustrations and dangers, emotional highs and lows, pains, and pleasures, and always end where they began—on the starting line. There is no finish line in the ego race and no winners.

Many believe that the 3-D personality that speaks, experiences pleasure and pain, feels emotions, and engages life in the physical realms is all that they are. Even though they may have heard of their soul, many or most humans have no meaningful relationship with their soul.

The ego attempts to control that which it has no control over. It wants to look good in the eyes of other people. It's a losing battle, but the ego doesn't know this. Ego centered people continually speak of their greatness and importance.

Control is a paradox. When one relinquishes ego-control and allows the soul to shine, physical desires lessen. The ego, pretending to be one's friend, is the very thing that prevents one from true peace, freedom, and joy.

When the soul begins to shine, the being receives soul-guidance and support, and is now in the flow of divine energy. The ego must move aside for the soul to emerge.

The high road is to ignore the ego and act on soul guidance which is available from within 24/7 for everyone-no exceptions. Imagine perusing a menu and having the urge for the hamburger, fries, and milkshake. But alternatives like salads, veggies, and other healthy choices are available. The ego says, 'One more burger, fries, and shake will taste so good, and you deserve it.' The Soul says, 'Eat healthy, you're worth it. Your body will love you, and at completion of this meal you'll feel wonderful, and not compromised.' It's always my choice. Do I listen to my ego or my soul? Who's in charge here? Who's in control? Soul guidance will always point one toward long term beneficial decisions.

Most of the choices from soul guidance are not in alignment with the ego's desires. Therefore, one's choice of following the ego or the soul is critical, for it determines one's quality of life. I emphasize that the ego must release for the soul to emerge. There is no room in the house for both to peacefully co-exist.

Anything one does, guided by the soul, will be of long-term benefit. Acting from ego, however, may lead to short-term sensory pleasures, but will always be followed by neurosis and suffering. One gets nowhere by following the ego with its repetitive attempts to make one happy supported by delusion and denial. Who I listen to is my choice and my choice alone.

How does one get to the space where ego control releases, even a little, and soul guidance emerges? Begin by witnessing yourself with no attempt to change anything. Simply observe. Visualize stepping back from your body and observing yourself from a small distance. Visualize the exercise with the menu. Notice what you say, what you do, how you act, all without judgement. Just witness. You must be brutally honest. You soon note that the ego is always choosing sensory pleasures, softer easier ways, and comfortable alternatives, requiring you to compromise your integrity to sustain from your ego center. But soon broader possibilities and options will begin to manifest. Your soul will strengthen and expand. You are becoming the Spiritual Warrior. Let others follow their ego. Be your own hero and go with soul guidance. You're worth it.

JUDGEMENT

Do you judge the outer world and wish you didn't? Read on. Here's the problem and the fix in a few short sentences.

Judgement is ego. Judgement is duality. Judgement is energy wasted. Judgement keeps one trapped in the lower vibes. Judgement binds one to unconsciousness. Judgement destroys one's happy space. Judgement prevents one from engaging higher levels of awareness. Judgement holds one hostage.

Why does one judge? Because judgement of "out there" is a projection of one's judgement of "in here." It is a projection of one's inner consciousness outward. That's all there is to it.

Want to stop judging? Do the required inner work necessary to raise one's consciousness to a higher level-the level above judgement. When one ceases judging oneself, when one becomes loving and accepting of oneself, internal judging ceases and one will cease judging out there.

How does one do this? It's simple. Practice equanimity, compassion, loving appreciation, and acceptance of everything, no matter what, with every breath. That's all there is to it. There is no other way. The end. jmb

TRAVELING ON - GODDESSES & MANTRAS

"Johnny, I've more guidance," said Teacher. "Goddess Dhumavati has come through to work directly with you and help loosen your deeply entrenched ego and shadow fixations (sensory pleasures and desires). Dhumavati is the seventh of the ten Tantric Mahavidya Goddesses, and is associated with the inauspicious, the darkness of life obscured by smoke. She's usually portrayed as an old widow with a winnowing basket in a horseless chariot or sometimes riding a black crow." This sounded very strange to me as it may to you. I had only a vague idea about Hindu Gods and Goddesses, nothing more.

"Thanks," I whispered and left it at that, at least for now.

As a young boy, I heard much about God and religions that I could not relate to. Nor could I understand how anyone could speak of people and events from the distant past and know without doubt that what they were saying was, in fact, true. Hearing truth from trusted authorities left me conflicted, for what they told me could not be validated or verified.

The adult authorities in my life seemed confident that they knew what they were talking about. Yet their message didn't stand up the test of simple logic. Mom said, 'Jesus is the only perfect person who ever lived.' How did she know this? She wasn't there when he was alive, nor was anyone else that is alive today, so how did she or anyone else know this? How did she know that there are no other perfect people alive today? There are many people on the planet and even Mom didn't know them all. And is Mom suggesting that he never got into trouble as a boy? He never swore? He never came home a little late? He never stole a cookie from the jar and said he didn't? I asked Mom about these things and she said, "You just don't understand Johnny, he was perfect and that's all there is to it.' Mom had a way of tap-dancing around direct questions with vague, evasive, soft-peddled responses. 'Oh Johnny, you ask too many questions,' was one of her favorites. 'Just accept it and be a good son, like the other boys in our neighborhood.' She obviously didn't know the other boys very well.

The church spoke a lot about God, of course, and I asked several times what or who is God? Not receiving a relatable answer or practical guidance pointing toward the answer, I eventually drifted away from the established church. God, for me, remained some nebulous being or energy that created everything in a week and lived somewhere out there. As a boy and young man, I was not introduced to the journey inward with meditations or other techniques that encourage awareness, centering, and presence. Over time, I slowly opened to the inward journey and began exploring my inner space.

Dhumavati and the other Gods and Goddesses of the Hindu traditions are not separate beings even though they are referred to as Gods, Goddesses, or Lords. They are spiritual aspects of divine consciousness. They are aspects of The One. Dhumavati is an aspect of delusion and destruction and is a fierce destroyer, including dissolution of the ego. If one is to become spiritually conscious, one with God, or embrace the Christ consciousness within, one must dissolve the ego. A spiritually mature person will not be Christ-like on Sunday and a tyrant on Monday. My intention is to share sufficiently so that you, dear reader, may relate meaningfully to this journey, and not run. If you are truly determined to improve your condition in life, embrace the soul and become a Spiritual Pilgrim. The ego must dissolve for the soul to shine.

Practicing my Dhumavati mantra every morning aligned me with her energy of dissolution. The intention was to dissolve, or at least loosen my ego. It took a while, but eventually it happened.

HAVING FUN - EXPERIENCING JOY - BALANCE

Johnny MedicineBear loves having fun. I enjoy pleasurable feelings and simple activities like riding Harley and bantering around with friends. There is nothing wrong with engaging in these activities unless activities like these become my life's focus. Then I'm engaging life solely from my personality and ignoring my soul. If I am riding Harley to escape from life, seeking thrills by racing around purely for fun, then this activity is not in Johnny MedicineBear's best interest. If I'm riding Harley aware of the smells, sounds, and sensations around me, then I'm riding in presence and nurturing my soul. It is always desirable to live in presence.

The ego/personality is focused on short-term sensory pleasures while the soul is focused on presence. It is challenging to listen to the soul, ignore the ego, and act on the soul's intention. This does not mean that I cannot enjoy the short-term sensory pleasures of the physical earthwalk. It means, however, that I must be honest with myself and know what I am doing before I do it and not engage in self-deception and denial.

Writing this book is hard work and requires discipline. But the joy experienced brings warmth and feelings of satisfaction that sustain. My heart and soul are engaged in this work. Occasionally, I take some time off and go for a fun-filled ride on Harley in presence. It's engaging in the best of both worlds.

Do not lie to yourself about what you are doing. If one goes to the gym two hours every day and spends one hour in the steam-room and one hour at the juice-bar, they will experience few sore muscles, little growth, and are wasting their time. If they tell their friends that they regularly spend several hours at the gym and just don't seem to get anywhere, they are lying to themselves and living in delusion and denial. But if one uses the equipment, runs the track, and enjoys a steam and juice on their way out the door, massaging a few sore muscles, they are nurturing their body and soul.

The physical, mental, emotional, and spiritual aspects of an individual are all interrelated. As one exercises one area, all other areas are also affected. One cannot work on the physical without affecting the others. This goes both ways. Lallygag around for a year with little or no physical exercise and one's mental, emotional, and spiritual expressions also deteriorate.

GLACIER PARK

We parked for a week in a familiar campground at the western edge of Glacier Park, Montana. Camp owner and dear friend, Zhavanya, welcomed us and gave me a choice spot to park Dutch and explore this beautiful area. This is a favorite summer stop for me. This year with Teacher, however; it was pure torture. Holding myself accountable for every action and every thought, was agony. There was no playful bantering, no background music, no singing, no sightseeing, nothing other than writing this book, chanting mantras, meditations, reading spiritual books, listening to spiritual audio clips, and other inward journey experiences. It also meant no wishing things were different, no dwelling on the past, and no dreaming and fantasizing about pleasant future events. Doing this 24/7 was excruciating.

Living in presence is impossible from the personality. And eliminating distractions to allow for a glimmer of presence is challenging. My life before Teacher was a continual stream of pleasantries and distractions. I didn't see it that way till Teacher arrived, but it quickly became obvious that with few exceptions, I lived my life engaging in one pleasantry after another.

"Let's go ride Harley through Glacier Park today, Johnny," Teacher suggested. My heart lifted, not so much from the idea of experiencing magnificent Glacier Park, but of just breaking the daily challenging routine and easing my inner pain. I wanted to escape from my misery, to control my environment, to eat what I wanted, to say what I wanted, to act as I wanted, to go where I wanted, and yet I knew that experiencing this pain and suffering was necessary. "Great," I said, and an hour later, we left on Harley for our "ride through the park."

Teacher lived in presence. "What is it like to live in presence?" I asked her a few days ago.

"One cannot describe the experience, Johnny, any more than one can describe what 'wet' feels like to one that has never experienced wetness. One must experience presence to relate or understand it."

One cannot directly relate to a consciousness higher than the consciousness they are. This is illustrated in the Building-of-Life metaphorical story found elsewhere in this book. "I live in presence, Johnny. My mind is not trapped in the past and the future. It is here, right now, in full expansion in this space of presence. This is the space of creativity and oneness with all. I don't "think" about what I will do next. Life just naturally unfolds. When you, Johnny, consider what you want to do next, where you wish to travel next, or what you want to eat next, you base your choices on past experiences. If you enjoyed something, you'll likely do it again, and if not, you'll likely not do it again and choose something else. That applies to what you eat, the people you associate with, what you read, what you watch, everything.

"Most live from this dualistic mind of past and future. The contracted dualistic mind is not open to creative energies or presence. As you endure your pain and suffering, Johnny, you are loosening the vice-grip that your ego has on you, and your soul and creative mind will begin to emerge. How this occurs is different for everyone and one does not know when, how, or even if it will happen. But the only way to higher consciousness is to do the inner work. I see your soul, Johnny, and it's screaming to get out."

We launched off on Harley with Teacher riding in presence and me riding in total misery. For about six hours, we traveled through Glacier Park, mostly in silence. She said nothing, and when we stopped for breaks, she spoke little and maintained her distance. Teacher basked in bliss and I seethed in misery. I wanted to dump her, or trade her in for a "friend" that would put her hand on my shoulder, whisper a few words of encouragement in my ear, and tell me how much fun she was having riding with me through magnificent Glacier Park. None of that happened, and my mind continued unrelentingly, wishing life differed from what it was.

Teacher spoke of detachment. "I'm detached from others, events, and even my body. I live in 'witness mode' Johnny, detached from the ongoing dramas, pain and sufferings of the physical experience. Being detached, I'm not caught in any of life's dramas that are continually unfolding everywhere on the physical plane. Not wanting life to differ from what it is, I'm not a slave to the emotional field. Therefore, I continually experience freedom, joy, and bliss regardless of the surrounding dramas."

Learning this intellectually is the first step, of course, but integrating this comes with expansion to higher levels of consciousness. Riding Harley through Glacier Park with Teacher and wishing she was someone else so that I could "enjoy this experience" as I wanted it to unfold, is an example of how I create my own suffering. My ego wanted so much for "things to be different than they were," that I could not, even a little, disengage, and remained locked in misery the entire trip. I was a million miles away from the loving energies of Harley, Glacier Park, and Teacher.

Teacher knew of my misery yet never, for this event or any other where I was experiencing suffering and misery, offered sympathy. She held the space for me to suffer and experience the suffering safely. Teacher knew what I was going through and where most "friends" would offer sympathy, she steadfastly refused and held the line.

I've gone to sympathy with friends while they were experiencing emotional pain. "Oh, you poor thing. Uh huh, I see, oh that's too bad, blah, blah, blah." And when it was over, I was drained, energy depleted, and angry that I gave away my time listening to my friend rant and rave. This is what most people do because it's the best that most people can do and it's all that most know how to do. Does it help the situation? Not one bit. In fact, it is detrimental as it delays one from doing their inner work. Listening in sympathy to a friend rant and rave is akin to giving a drunk another drink. However, most can do no better, for that is the only available response on their level of consciousness.

Teacher is pure love. No matter how miserable I was, no matter how angry I was, no matter how much I swore, no matter how loud I shouted, Teacher never gave an inch. She held the mirror for me to see myself unwavering every moment we were together. Rather than respond to my rage with anger, she reflected love. It's very unnerving to rage and shout at someone and have love returned.

There were also times we screamed at each other. However, Teacher was screaming from learning and love, while I was screaming from anger and rage. It was necessary for me to engage in these shouting matches with Teacher as she was the mirror for me to experience out-of-control Johnny MedicineBear, raging. Her energy supported the dissolution of the savage aspects of Johnny MedicineBear. No matter what I did, how I acted, or what I said, she always remained in presence and responded from love.

A true teacher can provide a willing student the opportunity to grow the soul. No other teacher can provide this experience. There were times of course, where I was grounded and we engaged in mature, meaningful conversation. Almost daily, we did session/group work. These were learning opportunities, not shouting matches. But when I was angry and things weren't going my way, Teacher held a very firm line.

GROWING UP

"When are you going to grow-up, Johnny? When are you going to get rid of your stuffed puppy, Johnny? When are you going to stop acting like a little boy and start acting like a man, Johnny?" Over and over, I heard these and similar phrases during my child, teen, and adult years.

What does "growing-up mean?" I watched my parents (particularly my father), and their friends, and wondered when "growing-up" would happen to me. I thought I'd no longer play, laugh, or ride my bicycle. Someday I thought I would simply morph into a stiff, stoic, rigid, business-only, no playing-around man. It was frightening. I believed that one day child-like behaviors would cease and grown-up behaviors would begin. I would one day wake up and be a man. It didn't seem to matter what I wanted, for I believed growing-up was an inevitable life experience. I was "expected" to become a man someday with a family and responsibilities. There was no room for a playful, childlike Johnny MedicineBear in that scenario.

Many adults have lost their inner-child. These people are all business. They obsessively retain trivial personal secrets that are killing them, wouldn't be caught dead sleeping with a stuffed puppy, and are much more concerned about the outer ego-self appearances, and "what others think," than they are about their inner soul-self and what they themselves think. They are out of touch with reality and what is going on. Many cannot relate in any meaningful way to their inner-child and are consumed by ego-appearances and addictions.

But what does it really mean to grow up? It has little to do with the ego and outward appearances, and everything to do with the inner soul. And it applies equally to woman and men alike.

Most childhood activities and games cease or fade from lack of interest as one matures, while others grow into forms of adult activities appropriate with age. Childhood games mature into age-appropriate activities, and playing and playfulness continue, expressed in more mature forms. Music, visual arts, and constructive projects are adult expressions of one's playful and creative childhood games. When one separates from their childhood and discards their childhood behaviors and memories, they also discard their childhood creativity. A home designed and built by a loving, childlike, playful individual has its origins in that child's playhouse or dollhouse. Such a home is a soul-creation imbued with the energy of its creator.

While flying for American Airlines, I was sometimes asked to share about my job. I'd reply that, "This company gives me a front-row window seat in a forty-million-dollar jet plane, fills it up with gas and nice people, and says, 'Johnny, go take-em for a ride.' That's not work, that's play." It doesn't mean that I was irresponsible, lackadaisical, or immature. It was casual and fun-filled 'play' for me and I am at my best in a relaxed, stress-free environment where creative thoughts and actions flow easily. One day, flying with a stiff stoic captain, he commented, "Johnny, flying an airliner ain't no game, you know."

I thought a few moments, then replied, "To me, it is." And it was.

If our inner child dies as we grow-up, our childlike ways of engaging life also die. Life becomes difficult, heavy, drudgery, and it requires hard work to accomplish most tasks. It takes tremendous effort to juggle appearances, secrets, and lies (of commission and omission), with very little energy left to accomplish anything creative. Our dreams seem further away and our only option is to try harder. Engaging life in this mode is torture, self-inflicted.

Don't let your inner-child die. "Little Johnny," my very active six-and-a-half-year-old, goes on walks, rides bikes, sings and dances, and engages life playfully. This is not running from or escaping from life, but of engaging life naturally as it unfolds through the inner-child. Nurture your creative energies and don't think that anything is "stupid," no matter what. Go sleep with your stuffed puppy and remember something that you "gave up" when you "grew up." Now relive that experience again. And if your inner child is absent, these activities will invite him or her back home. Growing-up is about being complete, having all aspects of yourself available, and loving every part of yourself. The very activities that the stiff and stoic would never do are the very activities that the stiff and stoic must do to grow-up. Being childlike keeps one in the natural flow of life.

THE BLACK HILLS MOTORCYCLE RALLY - STURGIS, SD

I parked Dutch in the same spot at the same campground I'd parked at for every previous Black Hills motorcycle rally I attended. Sturgis, SD is home of the world's largest motorcycle event. Every year in early August, about 250 thousand "bikes" and 500 thousand bikers journey here for a ten-day non-stop mega-party.

During my ten previous rallies, I rode Harley through the beautiful Black Hills of southwestern South Dakota, found little out-of-the-way gems to explore, and photographed the non-stop stream of bikes, bikers, and oddities that drifted across my viewfinder. Sturgis is a real "slice of life" with every imaginable "motorcycle," and people from gentle non-biker curious tourists to the heavy-duty motorcycle clubs. Every year, I'd snap zillions of photographs of everyone and everything. This year with Teacher, however, it was very different.

I wasn't there to have fun, chill out, take a ton of photos, and ride Harley through the Black Hills merely for enjoyment. This year, I was on my "Spiritual Pilgrimage." I was experiencing how challenging it is to break habit patterns and stay in presence. I was experiencing how challenging it is to "hold the line" in the face of a tidal wave of desires. But this is the only way to move forward. There is no simple, easy way to "do one's work."

Teacher shared, "Johnny, when you engage life from your ego-center or personality, you are constantly chasing desires, and are rewarded with short-term sensory pleasures only. These pleasures never sustain and are always followed by an emotional hangover. They do nothing to raise one's core vibration. There is never any long-term positive effect gained from an ego-centered activity.

"Engaging life from the soul-center," Teacher continued," brings peace, freedom, and joy, which sustains and raises one's core vibration. To lessen ego-desires (addictions), one must be brutally honest and willing to do whatever it takes to clear unresolved shadow energy patterns. This means going into your basement and bringing every secret, no matter how small, out of the darkness and into the light. Freedom requires a clean basement. This work is not for the faint-of-heart, which is why few do this work, Johnny. But there is no other way to attain emotional and spiritual freedom.

"Most seem content to live a mediocre life of shallow sensory pleasures constantly seeking refills. Only a few stretch, sacrifice, and do the required work to experience life from the deeper, more fundamental soul-self."

It was our seventh week since Teacher's arrival and from my journal, I paste the following entry.

Journal Entry - August 2019

Teacher guides me, holds space for me, supports me, loves me, encourages me, and holds me accountable for everything I think, say, or do. She prepares all the food, does all the food shopping, and set up a vegan/raw food kitchen with a food processor and dehydrator in Dutch. We watched several pertinent documentaries, and she shared several of her relevant life experiences with me. She was spiritually guided to come here and wake me up for this book project. She brings Master Baba, Lord Shiva, Goddess Dhumavati, and other high spiritual beings with her. She's also introduced me to Byron Katie's "Judge-Your-Neighbor" and "One-Belief-at-a-Time" worksheets. She's done this in presence with love, asking for nothing, and sleeping every night on the couch wrapped in a quilt.

This morning she asked, "Does this couch pull out, Johnny?"

"Well, actually it does," I replied, feeling stupid for not having thought of it before. Being so independent of each other, with each drifting to our sleep-places when it's bedtime, I totally forgot that the couch pulls out into a larger bed. I opened the couch smiling but feeling REALLY STUPID. After all, Dutch is my home and when one of my daughters visit, I always open the couch for them at bedtime. The larger bed was a significant upgrade in the accommodations. Most would have at least remarked, 'I wish you had opened the couch when I arrived, Johnny.'

But Teacher simply smiled and said, "Thank you, Johnny." That's emotional maturity.

Having Teacher with me full time was an opportunity, and I was waking up even though I sensed little inner movement. Today was day fourteen of a no-food, juice-only fast-cleanse and day twenty-one of an internal-organ-cleanse using natural supplements. Desires and cravings were lessening.

Writing on my computer one day, Teacher asked me a simple question. It was no big deal, yet I was triggered, disturbed, and felt angry, which quickly shifted to deep sadness. I began crying, which soon deepened to uncontrollable tears and weeping. I was jealous that Teacher lived in bliss and presence and I lived constantly in easily triggered emotional turmoil.

"Johnny, you are blocked from your deep anger and rage and shifting your emotional response from that anger and rage to sadness and crying. This is a denial/survival technique which is preventing you from accessing the root of your deep anger and rage."

"Well, maybe," I replied, startled.

I thought I was past all that with my father, as I feared him more than I was angry at him. After all, he wasn't emotionally available for me because he wasn't emotionally available for himself. I understand that and knew that he kept everyone at arm's length. I feared my father and I've projected that fear on authorities outside of myself, like police, bosses, etc., and the Monster Boy pilot from American Airlines.

As a young boy, after dad strapped me with his leather belt, Mom would come to soothe my wounds and rescue me. She'd hold me, and tell me that everything would be OK, Johnny. Then we'd go to the kitchen for a little treat. Mom was very kind to me that way. She was my savior and rescuer.

"Did your mother ever put herself on the line and step between you and your father to protect you, Johnny? Did she ever stand up to your dad and tell him to hit her instead of you? Did she ever tell him that if he ever hit you again, she would take you away or call the police for his brutality toward you?" Teacher asked.

"Well, no, she didn't!" I blurted. And in a flash the dam burst, and I saw my mother as a terrorized victim that never defended her young son from his tyrant father. She was a coward, and passively watched Dad brutalize me.

"ARRRGG," I SCREAMED! I jumped up, threw my arms in the air, ranted, raged, swore, and beat my couch and pillows into oblivion as I pounded Mom and Dad into dust. Teacher stepped away as I released half a century of pent-up rage at Mom for her BETRAYAL and Dad for his BRUTALITY! I shouted, beat, and pounded Mom and Dad till exhausted. Teacher held the space for me to safely release this deep rage.

Spent, I lay on the floor, emotionally drained. Suddenly, some life-long issues popped into clarity. I knew now why I didn't trust women, why I resisted intimacy, and why I ran from affection and love. I knew also that this release would not have occurred without the presence, support, and love of Teacher.

The first step in healing is recognizing that there is something that needs healing. The next step is to muster the willingness to do whatever it takes to heal those pieces. There is a significant level of danger and risk involved when doing deep work and I strongly suggest that this level of work be done with a trusted teacher or therapist. They will ensure your safety. Many suicides have their genesis in one's hidden secrets.

This is an example of how denial systems protect. Had I realized Mom's betrayal before Teacher, before my protector, before my safety net was in place, I may have "gone off the deep end." Spirit works in wondrous ways. And when it was time, the veil lifted, and with willingness and work, the deep dark secrets dissolved.

Releasing trauma elevates one to higher spiritual levels. They move toward freedom and joy. It's simple. The more inner work one does, the more trauma one releases, the less baggage one carries, the lighter one becomes, and the brighter one's light shines. One sheds the victim archetype and assumes more responsibility for their life.

SAFETY - SAFE TO LIVE, SAFE TO LOVE, SAFE TO SHINE

Safety is huge. I feel safe in Dutch, and he protects me from the worst of storms and keeps me safe from out-there threats. But what about in-here threats? How safe is it in-here, in my physical body and in my mind? That's a more fundamental aspect of safety, and it is the one that matters the most. We are never any safer out-there than we are in-here, because out-there is an outward projection of in-here. I'll explain why out-there is generated from in-here and why you create your own reality.

Everything we see, smell, taste, hear and touch is an in-here interpretation of energy in one of its infinite forms received through one's physical sensors from out-there. The human body is a multi-sensory receptor, and the brain interprets the electrical signals sent to it from our physical sense organs.

Reading this page, do you see the page? Most would say yes, for it appears obvious. But do you? No, you do not. One does not "see" the page. Nothing is transmitted from one's eye to the page and returned with the image of this page imbedded in or on it. One does not look out-there and see this page.

It works something like this. Light radiation from external sources reflects off this page. When the eyes are turned toward this page, some of that reflected light passes through the eye's lens, and stimulates the sensors at the back of the eye. Electrical signals are generated from the stimulated sensors and transmitted via the nervous system to one's brain, where they are interpreted and presented in visual form as this page. What you see is your interpretation of reflected light energy. You don't see the image of this page out-there, and import that image to your brain. You create the image of this page "in-here," in your brain, from energy received. You create your reality.

The clearer one is inside, the clearer one sees reality. The fewer filters one looks through, the less dirt on one's lens, the clearer one sees. Reality and truth are the same. Therefore, angry people see an angry world, and gentle people see a gentle world. Also, it explains why several people viewing the same landscape may have unique interpretations of the scene. A painter viewing a forest may see his or her next canvas. A musician may see his or her next musical creation. A businessperson may see his or her next money-making project. And a child may see his or her playground with friendly trees and animals. This is good news, for it puts you in the driver's seat of your reality and life experiences. This is why one's work is always inward and why life just gets better when one does their inner work.

One might wonder why at sixty-years-old, resolving childhood trauma is important. But resolving and releasing internal trauma of any sort affects both the inner and outer worlds. After completing inner work, one might notice how peaceful and loving they feel in-here, and that their out-there aggressiveness, fears, or other projections have diminished. Life out-there will flow easier after completing inner work.

It was not safe for me to live, safe to love, or safe to shine, 50 years ago, when I was flying combat missions in Vietnam and drinking alcoholically to silence the screaming inner voices. It wasn't safe inside at all and the daily multiple enemy threats I faced out-there were projections of my in-here enemy threats. If I'm living on the edge out there, it's because I'm living on "the edge" in here.

Therefore, one's work is always inward, for the outer world is a continual non-stop movie of our inner dramas. Those that live with inner chaos, fear, and confusion will engage life from this center and create an outer experience of chaos, fear, and confusion. Those that live with inner peace, joy, and freedom will engage life from this higher center and create an outer experience of peace, joy, and freedom.

Do not waste your time trying to make the outer world better or safer. Allow the outer reality to unfold in witness mode, and observe without judgement. Then, with great courage, tell yourself that "this outer world I'm witnessing is my inner world projected outwardly." And if you don't like what you see, have the courage to do something about it. Just witness, allow, and know that from witness mode, you are slowly diffusing inner trauma. Do this work from your heart, not your head.

Safety - Safe to Live, Safe to Love - Safe to Shine, is realized by doing inner work. One becomes safer in proportion to the amount of trauma recognized, diffused, and resolved. The world out-there is as safe as the world in-here. So, focus and commit to resolving internal traumas and discover the beauty of your safe haven within.

IF I SPOT IT, I GOT

If I spot it, I got it. I've heard this mentioned many times in the rooms of Alcoholics Anonymous. There is much truth in this catchy little statement. People, places, things, or events that I am uncomfortable being around, is because the energy patterns created by these people, places, things, or events, bump against similar energy patterns within me.

I may dislike a man in my AA group because that man reminds me of my father. It may be his voice, mannerisms, physical body, or something else. But they trigger something in me that is unresolved and I become uncomfortable. When this occurs, most are unaware of why they are uncomfortable around this person and simply avoid the individual.

But that doesn't either solve the problem, or advance me forward. Avoiding the problem is like putting a band-aid on a sore. The band-aid is a temporary fix and helps keep the sore clean while the body builds the scab and does the work of healing the wound. Without the body's help and healing abilities, the sore would continue and never heal, no matter how frequently I bandaged it and I'd never be free of this chore. When one avoids doing their inner work, nothing gets fixed, nothing changes, and the problems remain.

When I feel uncomfortable with some external stimuli, I know that

I have inner work to do to bring into balance that piece of me that is uncomfortable. So, if I am uncomfortable with a man in my AA group, as example, I will sit peacefully, and ask for clarity on why I am uncomfortable. I can do this several hours later when alone. As the answers come, I heal that piece.

Just such an event occurred with me during my employment as pilot with American Airlines. I share that experience in the chapter titled, "Monster Boy" found in the second section of this book, *Into the Shadow*.

Perhaps reading this chapter is making you uncomfortable. If so, it's time to go to work. Being uncomfortable is therefore a gift, as it is inviting one to do their work and pointing to where their efforts need to go.

PHYSICAL AND NON-PHYSICAL REALITY

The non-physical expression of reality is all existence that is not physical, i.e., all that is beyond length, width, height, and physical time. Here are some of the many names relating to non-physical reality. The world of spirit, the world of energy, the energetic, life-force energy, divinity, God, Great Spirit, angels, spirit guides, ghosts, apparitions, auras, chakras, and energy fields, are all names for attributes, beings, or expressions of the non-physical. The non-physical is all existence that is not in physical form.

It is essential to relate meaningfully to non-physical reality, for the non-physical is more fundamental and supports the physical. One cannot exist in physical form without the underlying non-physical support. However, one can exist in the non-physical without a physical form. If one believes that the 3-D physical reality is all that there is, and nothing exists beyond, there is little hope for experiencing long-term freedom and joy. The best one can hope for in this case is an anxious life of competition and fear, constantly chasing short-term sensory pleasures to relieve inner chaos, confusion, and pain. Ultimately, if one truly believes this option, one then ceases to exist when the physical life expires. One's life is a frightening existence of constant anxiety and fear.

One must open to a broader, more expansive conception of reality to soften the personality and realize one's soul. A sort-of, wishy-washy, or vague conception of the non-physical will not do.

There are many experiences that offer vague, shallow, and empty explanations of God, Heaven, Angels and Spirit, asking the practitioner to have faith and to believe. These practices are not primarily focused on or encourage the inward spiritual journey, self-realization, self-exploration, and expansion of consciousness. They encourage one to believe what is taught without question. They generally promise a reward if one does what they suggest, and threaten with punishment if one does not do what they suggest.

But if you deeply wish to be whole, free, and joyous, an appreciation of the non-physical from direct experience is a must. One does not need to take a stand for or against anything. The master sees all reality just as it is, without duality, and without judgement. Do the same. And one does not need to become a master to know that they are heading in the right direction. Any effort without bias will bring guidance and awareness that feels authentic and withstands the tests of logic, common sense, and the obvious.

Most believe what they believe not from rigorous examination and self-exploration, but because that's what they've been taught and told since early childhood. These beliefs become so deeply ingrained through constant repetitive conditioning that these people will blindly follow their leaders even into acts of violence and worse. This is the genesis story of many wars.

Followers are on a cross between embracing the accepted truths of their faith or opening their hearts to a more expanded truth, irrefutable logic, common sense, and ultimate reality. One makes a choice to remain in their flock or expand into freedom. This is difficult as the flock rarely accepts and support those who explore beyond the perimeter fence. So, one becomes a troublemaker of sorts. And it is pointless to move horizontally to another flock, as the same experience generally occurs there as well.

So, elevate the awareness upward and rise above all flocks. Limitations will fade and dissolve and one will experience freedom and joy. One is not judging the flock as right or wrong, one is realizing its limitations. This is the authentic path to the Living-Christ, the Living-Buddha, and all Gods and Goddesses.

Here's an example of irrefutable logic that many cannot see:

The parents of newborn identical twins Abraham and Benjamin both die within a few days of the twin's birth. Abraham is adopted by new parents of fundamental religion "A" and Benjamin is adopted by new parents of fundamental religion "B." The twins are separated growing up with no contact with each other. These two religions are very different, have a history of war with each other, and regard each other with distrust and suspicion.

At age eighteen, Abraham and Benjamin are reunited for the first time since birth. They are both so deeply conditioned into their respective religions that they cannot peacefully coexist. Each regards the other as an enemy, not a brother. They are suspicious and distant of each other and they hold each other at arm's length. They don't trust each other. Each is absolutely convinced that his religion is the one and only way to heaven and salvation and it is his duty, supported by God, to open his brother's eyes and show him the truth. Each sees themselves as a child of God, and each sees himself as right.

Had the boys been swapped at birth and raised by the other's parents, each would have been conditioned in the other's religion and felt exactly as the other does right now. One might think that this clear logic would spring the trap and dissolve their differences, but that doesn't generally happen. Denial systems prevent one from embracing irrefutable logic, the obvious, and clear truths. The ego senses the impending loss of control, feels threatened, and resists by all means possible. The ego minimizes, rationalizes, trivializes, and lies to retain control of the personality for it sees loss of control as the death of itself.

This same scenario, on a national or global scale, creates cultural and religious separation and plants the seeds of war. The only way out is to rise above this consciousness.

Our industrialized society worships the intellect, the ego, and money. Those with no or minimal sense of their soul generally have huge egos to compensate. When one has no or limited soul awareness, they receive limited or no spiritual nourishment and love. To compensate, the ego focuses externally for sensory pleasures, power, and control over others to fill the void. The ego works overtime and is never satisfied. Egos love new things, love to control, love to feel good with sensory pleasures, and thrive on excess. However, there is never a moment's rest, peace, or joy, as the ego is constantly refilling the personality's fun-bucket. When one's ego is challenged by truth, it will attempt to convince the personality that the challenge is hogwash to retain control. The ego desperately wants to be in charge.

In 1990, I sensed truth in the concepts of oneness in all creation. On the 3-D physical plane, the molecules that comprise my physical body were in rocks, plants, animals, and humans before I was born. All elements and molecules have existed for billions of years in all expressions of physical life. Therefore, I am comprised of many things that have lived before me. This truth allows for oneness with all creation.

There is also non-physical memory. This memory is a key in regeneration. Imagine a small cut. Within a few hours, the bleeding stops, and the healing begins. A few weeks later, the cut is totally healed. From memory, new skin has grown and replaced the damaged skin perfectly. There are billions of skins on the planet, yet every skin cell in my body has divine intelligence to replicate my skin exactly. This is an example of the underlying divine intelligence that supports our 3-D physical reality. It doesn't make mistakes. It's empowering to know that one is supported on their earthwalk by this underlying intelligence that is ultimately pure love. Some may call this divine intelligence God.

KNOWLEDGE AND KNOWING

Many say that they know something when they mean that they have knowledge of something. Knowledge is intellectual. Something read in a book or told to us, sometimes reinforced with words like "truth," "for sure," and "without a doubt." Knowing, however, arises from inner experience. Knowledge may become knowing if it withstands the tests of authenticity, validation, logic, common sense, and the obvious. If, over time, knowledge fails any of these tests, then it ought never be accepted as known fact or truth.

Suppose one is in an unfamiliar city and wishes to go to the library. Not knowing where the library is, one asks a local person and receives directions. One now has knowledge of where the library is. Following the directions, one arrives at the library. Now one knows where the library is.

For the spiritual pilgrim, the seeker of truth, there can be no confusion and no mistaking the two. It is delusional to claim knowing when one only has knowledge. It takes great courage to validate, verify, and authenticate from experience what is presented. Questioning does not mean opposition to. Questioning means seeking deeper truth and understanding to validate and verify. To the seeker of truth this is the only way. It is a huge step toward spiritual maturity to differentiate between these two concepts and not confuse or interchange the two. Simply put, knowledge is gathered externally, while knowing arises from within. That's the difference between knowledge and knowing.

WHAT DO I DO WITH THE S.O.B.S

Most have a few SOBs in their life. SOBs seem to just somehow show up. And there are a few in every community that can't get along with others, pick on people, can only see things their way, and refuse to compromise or cooperate. They are all fear-based people with an agenda rooted in control and desire for power over others. They might be the president of the Home Owners Association or a co-worker that constantly antagonizes, pulls pranks, endlessly gossips, and refuses to respect personal property.

A bully is another name for an SOB. Bullies love shoving their weight around and relish the feelings of "power." This is the perceived power of a political position, not the authentic power of a person. Bullies identify themselves totally with external power, for they have little or no internal strength and integrity. They hold the world at arm's length, letting no one close to their heart. They fear and resist love and affection.

Confronting a bully is pointless. No matter how solid one's position may be, with irrefutable facts and crystal-clear logic, the bully will turn things around and point the blame at the other. SOBs and bullies are first-floor, low-vibe, irresponsible people. They are never wrong and will argue you into the ground.

The way for me to diffuse issues with SOBs is to not focus on their words, attitudes, and behaviors, but to focus on my response to their words, attitudes, and behaviors. They are trigger people that are illuminating sensitive or fragile areas of self. This is usually where one keeps their buttons. SOBs seem to find the buttons and push them, sometimes over and over.

In Shamanic traditions, the spiritual warrior has no enemies for they have no need of enemies. This truth applies to SOBs and enemies alike. From that, I may conclude that if I have SOBs in my life, I have need of SOBs in my life. As I heal myself and assume ownership of my words, attitudes, and behaviors, I will no longer be affected by the SOBs.

When I feel resistance toward another, it means that something about their words, attitudes, and behaviors is bumping against something within me. This realization is uncomfortable. However, once embraced, options become available. As soon as I feel tension building, or the hair on my neck beginning to stand straight, I open my handy SOB bag of tools and apply them.

Here are some tools for your SOB tool bag.

Tool number 1. Don't take whatever is going on personally. The SOB doesn't care about you, they just want your power. But they only receive the power that you give them. As challenging as it is to do, take a few breaths and remain neutral.

Tool number 2. Go to witness mode. This means to detach from the person or event. Step out of your body and retreat about 6 feet away. Observe yourself and the event non-personally.

Tool number 3. Disengage. Do not strike back and do not respond to questions if you can avoid it. If you must reply, answer only relevant questions without emotion. If you engage with anger or judgement, you've lost your higher space and are giving your power to the SOB. You are now down on their level and the ego battle is on full force. Since the SOB lives in the world of ego battles, they will spar you to exhaustion and you will lose.

Tool number 4. Protect your inner child. The little 6-year-old aspect of yourself that resides within doesn't understand grown up behaviors. The child feels the pain of the jabs, barbs, insults, and unjust actions. The adult must protect their inner child. Reassure them they are safe and that you, the adult, will keep them safe from SOBs no matter what.

Tool number 5. Take the higher road and see the SOB as a misguided being with a soul. If you look through the personality and see their soul even a little, you will sense how damaged and needy this person is. Compassion will replace fear and anger and you will begin to distance yourself from these toxic beings. Be thankful that you are not their life partner (hopefully).

Eventually, the SOB will realize that they are getting very little power from you and are wasting their time. They will find easier prey to harass. They always go after the most responsive to their behaviors (the angry ones) and the weakest (the fearful ones).

FOOD

Shortly after viewing the Earthlings documentary and removing all animal and animal products from my diet and living space, Teacher began preparing raw organic meals for us in Dutch.

As a child, our family ate mostly meat and potatoes with a cooked vegetable to round out our meal. Sometimes there was iceberg lettuce, local tomatoes, or cucumbers for salad. This is what I experienced in my youth and Mom and Dad merely passed on what they knew. I didn't realize the nutritious, delicious huge diversity of foods readily available until I was in my early thirties. I thought lettuce was iceberg lettuce and that was all there was to it. I didn't know about romaine or red-leaf, and I obviously paid little attention observing the large varieties of foods available in food stores. I always bought iceberg lettuce because that's what I always did.

As a boy, I hated spinach because it was stringy, tasteless, watery, and only came in cans. I ate it because Popeye the Sailor ate it and he had huge arm muscles. We never had raw spinach leaves in place of iceberg lettuce.

That loosened a bit in my early thirties and changed a lot when Teacher arrived. I was open to the thoroughly enjoyable wide variety of raw-food dishes she lovingly prepared for us.

I grew to love raw plant-based foods. With Teacher, I also learned to eat in presence, paying attention to this sacred act of receiving nourishment and life-force energies from the plants that were becoming me.

When I consume a carrot, its energy merges with mine as it passes through my energy and the carrot receives a gift from my more complex and higher vibrational energy. The carrot will return as a slightly more evolved carrot next trip around. It works something like that. It feels right to me.

When an animal is killed, its life-force shortly leaves its body. Packaged, refrigerated, and frozen meats are dead foods. They contain empty calories and contaminants with perhaps a bit of nutrition. This is dead food with zero life-force energy. If the animal was brutally slaughtered, and it probably was, the slaughtering trauma is present in the meat and transferred to the recipient upon consumption.

If we desire an apple from a tree, ask and receive permission from the tree for one of its apples. Pluck it, thank the tree, and consume the apple in presence with gratitude. That completes the cycle. The tree gifts you an apple, and you gift the tree gratitude. And a live apple is loaded with "life-force" energy. Live food, respectfully gathered and consumed, is very beneficial for the giver and the recipient.

Consuming dead foods, has a dulling effect, while consuming live foods has an enhancing effect. Dead foods remain stagnant within one's body and contribute to disorganization, trauma, and disease. The benefits of a plant-based raw or slightly warmed foods diet are enormous. This is easily confirmed with a casual internet search.

The new food processor arrived along with the five-rack food dehydrator and several other kitchen utensils and gadgets. Dutch became a first class rolling raw-food kitchen. The Vita-Mix blender and Breville juicer completed our kitchen. It felt good to not participate in the pain and suffering inflicted on the many thousands of animals caught and slaughtered daily for human consumption.

My body was becoming healthier, and perhaps the aging process has slowed a bit. Raw food is alive with vibrant life-force energy, that is not available in dead or cooked foods. It's as simple as that.

It feels good to not participate in the needless brutalization and destruction of animal brothers and sisters.

A CHIPPED BOTTLE MAY HOLD PURE WATER

Some discard teachers because the teachers are not perfect, have faults, or exhibit a few rough edges. They focus on the teacher's shortcomings, judge them as not qualified, and are therefore not receptive to the teacher's wisdom. If one will have as teacher only a being with no faults, they will probably wait a very long time for a teacher to appear. Teachers are human, and few have no faults.

Authentic teachers are spiritual warriors rooted in truth and integrity. Along the way, they pause and share their experiences and wisdom with others. It's unnecessary for a teacher to achieve perfection before they can share their wisdom and be of service to others. Connect with these people and learn from them.

My mentor Ronnie had a few rough edges, but he had a compassionate heart and was very skilled at group therapy. I learned from him and saw his roughness as part of his personality. His roughness made him a great teacher and was necessary for him to be effective in group. Many benefitted from his rough personality.

The ego doesn't want us to move forward and will look for reasons to discard a qualified teacher. Just as a bottle may have a small chip on its surface, a teacher may have a few rough edges on their surface as well. Do not allow your teacher's imperfections to prevent you from embracing their wisdom.

THE JOURNEY CONTINUES

Journal Entry - 12 August 2019

We left Sturgis, SD this morning and I drove Dutch almost 400 miles to Summit, SD with Teacher following in her van. Last night, I slept fitfully and realized that I have spent my life looking for pleasure, love, and everything else, outside of myself. I used sensory pleasures to "feel good" and avoid doing deep inner work. It's devastating to see how outwardly I was focused. I feel hollow today like there is nothing inside. I cried again like I do just about every day. Yesterday, I wrote thirty Byron Katie "Belief Worksheets" for the things that arose from Saturday's Lily Pad entry. I hold a sacred vision to be of service to humanity and all creation.

Teacher is very sensitive to energies and communicates with Lord Shiva and other non-physical beings. I feel in the dark and inadequate around her. I feel like I don't have a clue. I must stay the course. Remember that you are beauty and grace and love, Johnny. Honor yourself for walking the path of the spiritual warrior as far as you have gone. Stay open to expansion. Stay the course and focus inward.

Journal Entry - 13 August 2019

I listened to Master Osho about how flies are attracted to fetid meat while avoiding sandalwood and how men are machines without souls. Anyone that operates at the ego level is a machine, controlled by the contracted mind.

I can feel every little pull that drags me from my center. There are no small compromises and everything I do or don't do counts.

I awoke this morning early feeling dread and uneasiness. I walked to Lake Superior beach after meditation and did Medicine Wheel opening ceremony to strengthen my connection with the Earth Mother below and divinity above. I blessed the lake, all creation, and noted how freely the seagulls flew above me. My intention is to stay in witness mode and ask for guidance from my Soul.

MEDICINEBEAR'S TERRORIST GROUP

MedicineBear's Terrorist Group

There's a terrorist Group alive in my mind,
They won't leave me alone when all appears fine,
They drive me insane; I've already gone blind.
This Terrorist Group alive in my mind.

My Teacher arrived a short while ago,
And Said "MedicineBear YOU GOTTA GO,"
I shouted and screamed, "No Way and Uh Oh,"
MedicineBear's me, and I'm running the show.

A scream from the left, my minds gone awry,
This terrorist group is powerful stimuli,
Threats are exchanged, and bullets do fly,
MedicineBear screams, "I don't want to die."

The battle keeps raging all day and all night,
Nobody is wrong, and nobody is right,
Many bodies lay dead, what a horrible sight,
And MedicineBear's caught in a horrible plight.

Finally, one day screams cease in my mind,
MedicineBear's found peace for the first time.
Terrorist group is no more, no one whined,
MedicineBear's head's now clear for guidance divine.

THE PERSONALITY LOVES NOISE - THE SOUL LOVES SILENCE

Journal Entry - 27 August 2019

This morning, the rainbow shaman card appeared, which is the essence of the spiritual journey-crossing over the rainbow bridge of limited ego-mind to the full realization of one's essence. It portends that the end of the storm may be near and to not give up. This morning also, Teacher read a poem that came through to her mentioning the rainbow. It's auspicious.

I am recognizing how much I mirror my father's controlling behaviors and see how I also have unresolved anger and rage. When triggered, I feel deep anger and rage even if I don't act on it. I also see some of Dad's behaviors in me. Several friends have recently mentioned that they have witnessed and felt self-righteous ego from me. Of course, that was news to me. But now I am inspired to move forward. This is a gift.

Yesterday, I asked Teacher a simple question that was not relevant to our dialog and she pointed out that when I do this, it's JMB the ego-personality that wants to assert himself. She said, "Ask yourself, where is the thought or question coming from? Is it coming from your personality or your soul? If it's coming from your personality, don't ask it, for your personality is always of the ego. It is always self-serving and wants to look good, feel good, and be important. This may be very subtle, but it's there. If it's coming from your soul, then ask it.

By asking, you are honing your awareness of where your consciousness is centered. At any moment, are you centered in your personality or in your soul?

The personality is uncomfortable with silence. As silence lingers, the personality may come forward and ask an irrelevant question to break the uncomfortable silence. It will create a little distraction or disturbance to disrupt. Therefore, most engage in incessant pointless chatter. The personality always wants to feel important, so the disruptions and questions asked might be geared to inflate one's ego.

To clear the mind of chatter, I must resist and eliminate pointless small talk at even the subtlest levels. This pointless chatter comes from past behaviors. And no matter what I do or how I act, never berate, belittle, demean, or diminish myself.

Teacher said, "Johnny, your soul is screaming to come forward. Remember that you ARE NOT your father, and when you 'act like him,' it is YOU acting out, not your father. And you are not possessed by your father, either. You carry shadow energy patterns resulting from your childhood, and these, with work and support, will dissolve and release."

REVISITING THE F-4 PHANTOM

I flew the F-4 Phantom fighter-jet in the 1970s while serving as a pilot in the United States Air Force. Recently, I asked, *what spoke so strongly and compelled me to go fly this front-line fighter-jet in the military in combat? Why did I give up my safe office job to engage in this very hazardous and dangerous occupation?* I wasn't drafted and didn't have to join the military, I volunteered. *Was it dedication to duty? Was it love of country? Was it the thrill of going very fast? Was it the feeling of power from piloting this awesome aircraft, loaded with missiles, bombs, rockets, and a cannon?* I don't know the answer, and perhaps there is no definitive answer. But the question stirred up some thoughts.

The Phantom was big, with the canopy rail several feet above my head while standing on the ground. I could pound anywhere with my fist on the skin of the aircraft or even with a hammer most anywhere with no damage or even leaving a mark. The Phantom was hard as steel and incredibly strong. The wings, only 38' 5" wide, supported its maximum takeoff weight of 58,000 pounds and at fighting weight could sustain an 8.33 g loading. In high-g maneuvers, the wings routinely supported loads of around 250,000 pounds, or roughly the weight of a rather large airliner with 200 passengers on board. The Phantom was an awesome aircraft.

But what happened to me when I climbed the ladder and strapped into the cockpit, fired up the engines, and flew this airplane? Flying the Phantom was exciting and stirred in me the same emotions that playing Sheriff Roy Rogers did as a little boy and the thrill of flooring my V8, fifty-seven Chevy. I became someone or something else when I strapped on my Phantom. Fears, cares, and worries dissolved when I stepped into "Phantom space." I morphed into another being and was expanded into a super Johnny-MedicineBear for the time that my Phantom and I were one. I was in "Phantom world" and there was no separation between us. The Phantom was our body and I was our brain.

My Phantom spoke to a more fundamental, more primal component of me. Perhaps it resonated with my caveman. The outside modern world, with all its rules, confusion, and chaos dissolved when I merged with my Phantom. Flying the Phantom stirred in me feelings of power, control, invincibility, and strength. The same primal feelings arise today, perhaps at a lesser level, when I toss my leg over Harley's seat, fire up his engine, feel and hear his power, and launch as one on another adventure. Riding Harley speaks to and nurtures my caveman. Fifty years ago, this primal feeling was so strong that I lost my "self" in the seductiveness of the Phantom experience.

The desire to fly the Phantom required me to establish a denial system that I lived in and supported. I forgot what war was - what it REALLY was. I pushed aside all thoughts of people suffering and dying. And I minimized and pushed aside thoughts of death and dangers to myself and the effects my actions had on those close to me. Sheriff Roy Rogers did the same thing. As a boy, I didn't give thought to the reality of shooting someone, and I didn't give thought to that when I signed up with the United States Air Force, either. I used external stimulus, the caveman component, to fill the voids inside left from my lacking and abusive childhood. I was not aware of this in the 1950s, '60s, or '70s, but I have strong sense today that this is why I did it. I felt manly, felt valuable, felt mature, felt all grown up, and tried to fill the holes left from my childhood traumas. The caveman component is important, and perhaps there are ways to experience this more primitive energy other than destructive behaviors like war.

Football, as example, has a caveman component. Some may get injured, but few die. I suspect that the same dynamic applies to the attraction of muscle cars, racing machines of all sorts, and perhaps guns as well. And today, I suspect that some don't feel complete unless they are packing a weapon.

I do not carry a gun, for I have no need to carry a gun. I have no need to carry a gun, for I have no need of protection. I have no need of protection, for I have no enemies. And I have no enemies for I have no need of enemies. It doesn't matter if you agree with this paragraph or not. It is true.

Freedom arrives only for those that have resolved their fear, anger, and rage. Please be conscious of your "caveman" component and address it wisely. The "cavewoman" exists equally alongside the caveman.

RELIGION AND SPIRITUALITY

Religion: A particular system of faith and worship.
Spirituality: Focusing on the spirit or soul versus focusing on material or physical things.

What's the difference between religion and spirituality, if any? Why do so many fiercely defend and follow their religion even though the total membership of that religion is a minority of the world's population? Why are so many so sure their religion is "right"? Casual observation shows that most seem to follow the religion of their family and culture. It's what everyone in their community has always done and what they have been taught and told to do. Does that make it right or the best? Why are so many so disrespectful, guarded, and afraid of other cultures and religious practices?

These and other similar questions stir thoughts and emotions that either encourage one to ignore these thoughts and contract deeper into their religious practice or shed their religious practice and become a spiritual pilgrim - a seeker of truth.

Religions are bounded. Spirituality is unbounded. Religions are exclusive. Spirituality is inclusive. Religions focus on external rules of morality. Spirituality focuses on intuition and consciousness. Religions offer rewards for compliance and punishments for none-compliance. Spirituality offers neither rewards nor punishments. Religions create separation and inequality - us or them. Spirituality encourages oneness and unity - all are equal.

There is perceived safety in a religious organization and community where everyone embraces the same basic beliefs. But what does one do when an original idea or thought outside the acceptable norm occurs? It's easy to find oneself out of favor for being a rebel or troublemaker if one expresses thoughts considered unacceptable.

One may observe this in the treatment of LGBT+ people. Parked in Dutch for a short rest in a church parking lot while traveling one afternoon, I was preparing to depart when the pastor knocked on my door. We chatted casually for a few minutes, and I thanked him for the lovely rest spot and told him I'd be on my way very shortly. He then asked if I belonged to his church. I told him no and that I didn't belong to any church. He began to quote verses and made suggestions of how I might improve my chances of going somewhere pleasant when I pass from this life. I listened patiently, then asked him directly if he and his religion supported a woman's free choice concerning her physical body, including her choice about abortion. He said no, that abortion was unacceptable and that all unborns have a "right to life." I then asked him if he and his religion supported LGBT+ people and their right to choose their sexual preferences. He said no and that LGBT+ sexual preferences were unacceptable. I asked what he would do if the unborn that he saved from abortion, now fifteen years old, discovers that they have same-sex preferences? Would he now discard this soul because they didn't conform to the accepted views and beliefs of his religion? He stared at me for a few moments, and at a loss of words, turned and walked away. His external rules of morality put him on a cross of which there was no answer or escape. External rules tend to do that.

The question might arise. Do I conform to the accepted norms and toss my outside-the-box thoughts and questions into the trash? Or do I address these thoughts and questions? It's challenging to walk the rocky road of the spiritual pilgrim. But nothing of value is ever easy. What's the goal and purpose of this earthwalk? Am I here to be a good boy accepted by my community and conform to their accepted norms? Or am I here to grow, expand, and relate to reality at the highest levels possible?

What's the payoff for me, by walking the "rocky road of the spiritual pilgrim?" After all, it is easier to conform, sit in the middle of the pack, not make waves, and feel the comfort of a community of like-minded people. The spiritual pilgrim will sense the shallowness of this level of comfort.

There are some "truth seekers" however that find truth within the ranks of religions. They are the shining lights within the fold. Mother Teresa was one of them.

I experienced acceptance and comfort while sitting on my familiar barstool with my familiar friends tossing down my familiar drinks in my familiar bar night after night. I thought they were my closest friends, and if I complied with the accepted norms of that little club, they were my friends. I got along with everybody and everybody got along with me. But when I got sober, they left, for they didn't like me when I didn't comply to the rules of "the drinking club."

Religions are the same way. Tell your church leader that you've joined an Ashram or Zen Center, practice daily sitting meditations, and that you realize that Buddha, Mohamad, Lord Shiva, and others also have the energy of divinity similar to the Christ. If your leader encourages you to continue and broaden your spiritual journey in this way, stay on board. If your leader says you've gone astray and tries to convince you to "return to the fold," you have a challenging choice to make.

Observe the energy flow of any organization or community. In most religious experiences, the participants are expected to accept the truth of the institution and/or leaders as their own truth without question. One is expected to behave in certain ways and follow the accepted norms. Accepting something as truth from an external source disempowers the individual. It shuts down one's inner voice. Participants in such a community are encouraged to conform, not make waves, silence their inner voice, and become one of the fold. They may be told that their rebellious voice within is some demon or devil trying to temp them. These institutions do not support or empower the individual. Rather, the individual gives their power to the institution. The energy flow is from the participants upward to the institution. The participants eventually lose their ability to see clear logic and reason. They are now sheep blindly following their leaders.

In a sacred fire ceremony, however, the leaders or facilitators hold the space and support the participants. There are no expectations and no judgements. It is as it is. Spiritual work encourages expansion of consciousness, not contraction and conformity.

Don't confuse the teacher with the goal. Teachers don't teach, they point the way. They encourage participants to fully experience what they encounter on their journey. They are guides. If one wants to find the North Star and does not know where it is in the night sky, ask a teacher that knows the night sky to point to the North Star. Following the teacher's arm, locate the North Star. Once found, one no longer needs the teacher. Do not confuse the teacher's arm pointing to the North Star with the North Star. The path is not the goal.

Organizations encourage and even demand compliance. I'm suggesting to use one's own mind, and one's own intuition. Find one's own path, explore one's own soul, and experience one's own freedom. The foolish believe what they are told and discard what they observe. The wise believe what they observe and discard what they are told.

When one follows rules, one relinquishes freedom. And where there are fixed rigid rules, there is always conflict. Consider a man in Poland in 1939 concealing Jewish friends in his home when the German Gestapo bangs on his door and asks if he is harboring Jews. If he follows "the rules" and tells the truth, his friends will surely die. If he lies, he's committed a sin. He's on a cross. What does he do? If one suggests that the rules don't apply here, it's obvious in this case what to do. But where does one draw that line when rules apply or not apply? There is no simple answer to this situation if one follows external rules. One is in conflict. However, if one follows their heart and inner guidance, the answer is simple. The man tells the Gestapo that there are no Jews in his home and hopes for the best.

The same question arises when a young maiden, beaming from ear to ear, comes and asks if one likes her new dress? One may think it's the ugliest dress in the world, and could stress out over how to answer this question from this excited young maiden that clearly loves her new dress. When one is conditioned into looking outward for guidance to moral questions of truth, one shuts down the inner voice. We rely on "the rules" for answers rather than our own inner-guidance. If we do this long enough, we no longer have an inner voice, or we don't trust or listen to it. We learn to "not trust ourselves."

What is the proper response to the young maiden's question about her new dress? Look in her eyes and see the love and sparkle, excitement for life, and tell her how beautiful she is in her new dress. That's the high road.

Relating to divinity through any rigid system is akin to observing the heavens at night from your living room through a skylight. Only a small area is observable and the skylight may need cleaning. Step outside where the entire heavens are visible and observe all that is. One then gets a sense of the "big picture," and is free to return to the living room, knowing that there is much more than what is visible through the skylight.

Imagine others around the world observing the heavens through their living room skylights and seeing only a small slice. Can you see the arguments arising when two, three, or more are absolutely convinced that they see "all that is" through their living-room skylights? It doesn't mesh with what the others observe.

If everyone steps outside and observes the heavens without constraint, over time, everyone will see all that is. Exclusiveness will diminish and we may merge into a world community of supportive brothers and sisters.

BELIEF AND KNOWING

As a young boy, I was expected, to "believe" things that I did not and could not validate as true. I assumed that what I was taught and told was true and that was all there was to it. To remain in favor, stay out of trouble, and "be a good little boy," I accepted these beliefs and didn't question. For obvious reasons, most young children do not question their parents about such things.

The few times that I did, as I recall, I was admonished and so I learned to "keep my mouth shut" and simply go along for the ride. These were the concepts and "truths," presented by my parents, my teachers, and my clergy. As a young boy, I trusted these people. I couldn't imagine that what I was being told was anything other than absolute truth. My parents were Mr. And Mrs. God, my teachers were the wisest in the world, and the minister knew God personally. That's how it unfolded for this young boy. So, I believed it all and shut down my questioning inquisitive inner voice.

At Sunday School, I was told "truths" that left me uncomfortable. It was during this time that I experienced the "Middle of the River" vision shared in the first section (*Into the Darkness*) of this book.

As I matured, I thought about things like, *is there anyone alive that knows first-hand that what I'm being told in Sunday School class is true?"* Nope! I recall playing a child's party game where a story was told to one child who whispered the story to the next. That child passed it on to the next, and that continued all the way around the room till the last child shared what they were told. It was great fun to hear how different the final story was from the initial. I thought about how many languages, translations, revisions, and alterations there have been to sacred texts and I questioned their validity and authenticity. The older I became the more I questioned.

But I was supposed to have faith that what I was taught was truth. Even as a young boy, something about the whole church experience felt shallow and incomplete. It didn't feel quite right. I thought about my Jewish friends Matt and Mark that lived a few doors away that were being taught a different story as truth.

It is spiritually mature to question. Questioning does not mean opposing. It means exploring in depth the validity and authenticity of whatever is offered. The wise trust what they observe, not what they have been told. The fool trusts what they've been told and rejects what they observe.

Belief is the intellectual act of accepting as truth, something that cannot be substantiated or validated, and lacks tangible evidence.

It is a lot easier, however, to believe and have faith than to be a seeker of truth. The spiritual pilgrim is a seeker of truth and they tend to upset the applecart in religious institutions.

Suppose you are the Guru of Water and have spent a lifetime learning through experience all about water. I, knowing nothing about water, climb the mountain to visit you, for I wish to learn all about water. After a long arduous climb, I arrive and ask you to please share with me your knowledge of water. Can you tell me what water feels like, or what it tastes like? Nope. You can share some of its properties and aspects, and liken it to this or that, but you cannot share what a direct experience of water is like. It is impossible. Words fall short of a direct experience. So, you, the wise Guru, instruct me to fill a bucket with water, and put my hand in it. I now know from experience what wet is. A true teacher doesn't teach, they provide a space for the student to acquire knowledge from direct experience.

This is knowing. We know only what we've directly experienced.

Accepting as truth that which is not directly experienced is disempowering. It lowers the vibe. Belief shuts off the questioning inner voice and puts one on a cross of sorts. Do I listen to my questioning inner voice, or do I listen to the outer voices?

Walk the path of the spiritual warrior and question for validity. Be the spiritual pilgrim, the seeker of truth. Belief or knowing, the choice is yours.

PERSPECTIVE

It's important for me to keep life in perspective as I travel along my earthwalk. I, Johnny MedicineBear am significant, and yet I am also insignificant. Sometimes, I feel larger than life and sometimes I feel quite small. It's all about perspective.

Until a few thousand years ago, our planet was considered by most to be the center of the universe with the stars, sun, and planets orbiting the earth. As better measuring instruments and techniques developed, the concept of solar systems, stars, star clusters, galaxies, clusters of galaxies and an ever-increasing sense of the size of the observable universe emerged.

In 2023, astronomers estimated that there were more than one-hundred-billion stars in the Milky Way galaxy. Using modern optical space telescopes and other measuring techniques, astronomers also estimated that there were approximately four trillion galaxies in the observable universe. Multiplying these two numbers together suggests that there are 4×10^{23} or 400,000,000,000,000,000,000,000 stars in the observable universe. That is an unimaginable number. To get an idea of how large that number is, astronomers suggest that there are more stars in the universe than there are grains of sand on all the beaches and deserts on the earth. Also, there are more stars out there than there are cups of water in all the oceans on the planet.

Additionally, detection of exoplanets (planets outside our solar system) has become common. Current estimates are that of the one-hundred-billion stars in our Milky Way galaxy, there are one-hundred-and-forty-billion planets orbiting those stars. That's an average of about 1.4 planets per star. And approximately three-hundred-million of these stars have earth-size planets orbiting in the habitable-zone (not too close/too hot, and not too far/too cold). Opportunities for life to develop throughout the observable universe seem quite common.

Looking into the microworld, I wondered how much of our physical world is solid matter and how much is empty space. Today, scientists know that an atom has its mass concentrated in its center nucleus and the rest of the atom is essentially empty space. So, I asked, "What percentage of an atom is mass?"

An example offered said that if a hydrogen atom was the size of the Earth, the nucleus would be a solid 600-foot diameter ball at the Earth's center. Six hundred feet is approximately one tenth of a mile and it is four thousand miles from the surface of the Earth to the center. Therefore, the size of the nucleus is approximately 1×10^{15} of the total size of the atom. That's 1 divided by 1,000,000,000,000,000. That's a lot of empty space. There may be other sub-atomic particles in and around the atom, but for this comparison, I've only considered the major components. Our universe is overwhelmingly empty space.

The physical universe is unimaginably large with gazillions of stars and planets and simultaneously unimaginably empty. There is plenty of room for radio waves, light waves and all kinds of particles and radiation to travel without bumping into things.

Allowing myself to just bathe in this knowledge puts my little dinky life in perspective. Our planet may be the only one we know for certain that sustains life, but the possibilities for life on other worlds can no longer be ignored or dismissed.

Also, physical, spiritual, and cosmic laws are ubiquitous. They work the same everywhere. What works on the Earth also works on the hypothetical planet, "Zonk," somewhere out there in our vast universe. Odds are that the universe is teaming with life in one or another of its infinite forms.

The intent of this chapter about perspective is not to encourage a conceptual discussion about the size of the universe or whether life exists beyond our own planet, but to plant the seeds of the incredible expanse of our physical universe that leaves me in awe and open to all possibilities. I encourage you to loosen the shackles of rigidity that may bind you to fixed rigid ideas and concepts of the creation, sustainment, size and scope of the physical and non-physical universe and the life that it supports. Be open to all possibilities and keep life in perspective as you fully participate day by day in your earthwalk.

TRUST

Who do I trust? Do I trust my friends, especially the ones that say, "Trust me?" Do I trust myself? What do I do if a sacred trust with a brother-friend or sister-friend is broken? Let's explore trust.

I trust myself most of the time and yet sometimes I don't trust myself. At least I know when I'm being honest or not. There are a few rough edges about Johnny MedicineBear that occasionally violate my self-trust. These are small issues, but by acknowledging these small broken pieces, I move toward healing them.

The level of my trust aligns with the level of my consciousness. If I embrace first-floor lower-level consciousness, I embrace first-floor level trust. The personality, not the soul is the primary source of reference at this lower level. Trust, commitment, honesty, and integrity are on shaky ground with first-floor consciousness.

Trusting someone on the first-floor is a gamble. This is where addiction resides and all addicted people are unpredictable, unreliable, and dishonest. All addicted people will compromise truth and integrity to act-out their addictions. They will lie if necessary to deny and protect their addictions. They frequently sell out themselves and friends. When an addict says, "Trust me," no matter how sincere they truly are, it will not sustain.

When two people of first-floor consciousness engage in a discussion, it generally ends up in a shouting match, with each pointing the finger of blame at the other. That's first-floor consciousness in action.

I've a brother-friend that I've known for over 30 years. We connected in a men's workshop and have attended many men's groups together. He told me many times that 'you are my closest man-friend, Johnny, and no matter what, I'll always love you and be in your life.' I said the same things to my friend and meant every word, and so did he.

Several years ago, he severed all communication and activities with me without explanation. Calls stopped, e-mails stopped, and visits stopped. What happened? His life circumstances apparently changed, and so did he. At least that's all I could wrap my head around.

So, what did I do with this? There was nothing that occurred between us, no incident, no argument, nothing happened that I am aware of. But something did change.

Forty years ago, I would have driven myself crazy trying to figure it out. My mind would have gone in circles imagining different scenarios about this and that. But today, I can simply let it go. It doesn't matter how he relates to me; it only matters how I relate to him.

If my friend were to phone today, I'd say, "Welcome home, brother." There's no betrayal here, or broken promises. There is only life unfolding as it ought to. My inner child, Little Johnny, that is the essence of my creativity and divinity, was initially hurt. But with a little time, he healed. On the physical planes, one cannot ever rely on another with 100% certainty.

Many children have had the unconditional trust that they gave their parents, relatives, teachers, and religious leaders, severely compromised. It takes a ton of inner work to heal sufficiently and allow a supportive, loving relationship with another human being to blossom. It takes a ton of inner work to sufficiently trust and open one's heart, again, and allow oneself to love. I have great respect for those who have walked this path and have transcended their anger, rage, and resentments.

I've learned to trust Spirit 100%. When I'm sick, I know that there are gifts in my illness that are nuggets of gold that cannot be acquired any other way. That's why I'm sick, or at least one reason I'm sick.

When life gives me a flat-tire, I'm given an opportunity to grow and expand. If it's not clear, then I must look around a bit till I discover the gold. Sometimes, I just need to be peaceful and let the nuggets of gold find me. I know they are there or I wouldn't be having the experience. This is trusting 100%.

Johnny MedicineBear, the personality, doesn't like flat tires and I feel the initial resistance when one shows up. But over time, I've learned to trust Spirit and sure enough, the gold is always there.

I trust that your heart is open and, if not, that you have found gold nuggets in this chapter to help you open your heart and embrace your earthwalk experience.

(Additional thoughts.) My long-term brother-friend that went absent for a few years is back. We reestablished communication and have spent time together and routinely chat on the phone.

Sometimes, one needs time on their own and to let friends go without explanation. The spiritually and emotionally mature welcome the friends back with an open heart when they reach out. I am grateful that my friend returned.

TRUTH

I flipped on my receiver and tuned into the "Truth Radio" station. Is it truth? If there is an agenda behind any broadcast or conversation, it is contaminated and biased. It is not truth. Truth is pure.

Did my parents parent truth? Did my teachers teach truth? Did my preachers preach truth? What is ultimate truth? These are tough questions and deserve attention.

The Building-of-Life metaphorical story shared elsewhere in this book is a working tool. It is about consciousness levels. The more awake and aware one is, the higher the floor of consciousness they occupy. Our ability to recognize and embrace truth is the same as the floor we occupy in the Building-of-Life. That is our current state of consciousness.

First floor people lack awareness and do not relate to truth very deeply. Some will knowingly claim obvious lies as truths. Be wary of unconscious first floor people.

Spiritual truth will look the same regardless of how or where one finds it. Spiritual truths will be true across the entire spectrum of spiritual paths and religions. Truth is truth under all conditions.

Truth may be found in a child's smile, a fragrant rose, or a pile of trash. One may have to look around a bit, for the outer wrapper surrounding truth may appear different. But that's only the wrapper holding the truth. One must be able to see through the outer wrapper. If you feel conflicted and believe that truth exists only in selected places, or for selected people, then you have not yet discovered truth.

Truth is inclusive and ubiquitous. It is found everywhere and applies equally to everyone. If truth is not in your viewfinder today, then expand your view. This means that you must take a few steps up toward a higher level of consciousness. This will take effort and time. But there is no other way to establish a deep relationship with truth.

TAP-DANCING

By late August 2019, Teacher and I had traveled together for about ten weeks and Dutch was a little "Zen-Center or Ashram." I was focused on the inward journey, maintaining presence, being mindful of all activities, practicing meditation, and writing both my personal journal and the beginnings of *From Savage to Shaman*. It was very peaceful in Dutch with few distractions, minimal mindless chatter, and no playful bantering. It was also very quiet as all soft background music was switched off. This summer's travel was not focused on sensory pleasures and having fun, but engaging in our spiritual pilgrimage.

The inner work was intense, and I cried almost daily from processing childhood traumas and Vietnam war experiences. Most nights, I slept poorly either lying awake reliving horrific events or experiencing unpleasant dreams and visions. Some nights, I cried continuously for hours releasing sadness, guilt, and shame. But I did not run away and stayed the course.

Teacher spent her time supporting and holding space for me and working on her own projects.

Journal Entry - 29 August 2019

This morning, after meditation and my walk, I returned to Dutch and noticed Teacher sitting peacefully on the couch in meditation posture. I instantly felt fear and became overly cautious of my movements and tried to not make any noise and disturb her. I turned on the coffeepot, hoping that it would not make any noise, but coffee pots have voice and this one gurgled, spit, and sputtered. Shortly, in silence, she placed a mat on the living room floor and began her yoga practice. There is not much room in Dutch and I felt like I was being crowded and became more uncomfortable. My energy contracted, and the fear increased. I tapped-danced around, afraid of making any noise at all. I felt myself sliding into a place of deep fear, shrinking smaller and smaller. I carefully poured my coffee, added the honey, and by now was almost terrified of disturbing her. I was trying to be quiet from fear, not from an authentic space of just trying to be respectfully quiet.

I stepped into the bedroom and sat gathering thoughts and feelings. Perhaps, for the first time, I could differentiate between being quiet from fear and just being respectfully quiet while still functioning from presence. I saw my old patterns of living in fear of my father and his judgements of my behaviors playing out this morning in Dutch. I began to realize that it is OK for me to be who I am.

As a boy, I lived in constant fear of disturbing Dad in our home and it played out this morning in Dutch. I realized my projections were the source of this fear, not Teacher's meditation and yoga in our common living space.

Here's my new practice. When fear or anger arises, STOP, breathe, and ask, where is it coming from? What is the source of this fear? Ask for and focus on my highest guidance in this situation and act on this guidance.

Don't just let it happen, be a victim, and brush it off. Don't just do the tap-dance and pretend all is well. One will never wake up if one constantly plays the victim. So, if I rattled a cup this morning getting my coffee, then so be it. If Teacher absolutely required silence to work her program, she could have gone outside or at least discussed it with me.

I can try to be quiet and respectful, but that's about it. I must remain in a space of presence not fear, and be guided by source, not ego. Do not make choices and act from the victim mode of fear. Any response that I make to any situation while in fear-based victim mode will be laced with anger.

I've lived in these old fear-based patterns much of my life. I tried not to disturb people because I want to be liked. I've been kind and generous to people because I want them to like me. I've tap-danced around issues because I don't want to make waves. This space means that I must be fair, clear, and unafraid. Thank you, Teacher, for bringing this experience to me so that I could absorb the lesson and grow.

MY SUICIDE - KILLING PARTS OF MY EGO

My salvation is a suicide of sorts; not of the physical body, but of components or aspects of the personality. By personality, I mean the physical body, the emotional fields, the ego, and the mind. It's rather complex, yet we don't need to understand a lot about it to relate and initiate positive change.

Why would I want to kill off a piece of myself? It is because the very thing (the ego) that sees itself as a bringer of pleasure is the very thing that is blocking me from living in freedom and joy. It's a paradox. Ultimately, one's ego is the obstacle in the path of spiritual expansion.

What is the ego? What does it do? And why do I want to destroy parts of it? The ego is a non-physical component that brings to our awareness the challenges we need to embrace and transcend. It creates obstacles on our path of spiritual expansion, presenting us with opportunities for growth.

The ego wants to remain in control and will lie, cheat, and steal to accomplish this. Being in control feels very positive to the ego and it loves to tell others how important I am, how beautiful I am, how talented I am, and how smart I am. The ego is self-centered vanity.

When life events go south, the ego places blame externally. It is generally in "survival mode" and functions out of fear. It sees loss of its power and control as its own death. The ego repeatedly encourages short-term sensory pleasures to relieve life's self-created sufferings.

My ego constantly justified my alcoholic drinking. It rationalized and dismissed away immature and irresponsible behaviors with hollow laughs, shallow words, or a wave of the hand. "You don't understand! If you were me you'd do the same thing! Go away, I'll change when I'm ready now leave me alone!" I used these and other excuses repeatedly to hold myself in a contracted space.

Spiritual expansion is required to transcend addictions. It cannot be done from the ego, for the egoic mind that claims to *want out* of the addiction is the same mind that is holding one *in* the addiction. One may experience short-term relief, but the relief will never sustain. This is why "swearing off" always results in failure.

I relentlessly resisted sobriety even with several wrecked cars in the junkyard and two young daughters at home relying on me. But when one steps free and rises above addictions, the need and desire to "act-out" fades and the ego's rock-solid grip on the personality loosens. In the loosening, space is created for the soul to emerge. Divinity shines through these cracks and the soul begins to establish itself within. Other destructive behaviors and addictions feel these positive effects and loosen as well. Soul-light begins to illuminate areas that were in prior darkness.

Heal one addictive behavior and all addictive behaviors are positively affected, perhaps only a little, but nonetheless affected.

The ego senses these changes and entrenches itself deeper, creating tempting, enticing, and seductive scenarios to draw one back into the darkness of addiction. One must resist and "hold the line" in the face of an avalanche of addictive temptations and sensory pleasures. After a time, the ego will lose traction, loosen, and eventually give up. Nobody wakes up some morning and says, "I believe I'll quit drinking alcoholically for good today," and succeeds. If it were that simple, there would be no need for Alcoholics Anonymous and addiction rehabs.

Anything of value requires effort. As one focuses on sobriety and resists temptations, desires, and cravings, they strengthen their connections with their soul.

When I align myself with divinity, I will receive help. This is not because God likes me better than someone else, or I asked favorably. It happens because I align my soul with divinity. Intention is the energy behind the words. This is doing the work.

When I pray, I believe it matters little the words I say. But the intention and energy that I put forth with my prayers does matter. If I'm sincere and humble, my prayers will resonate with like energies and be returned with kindness and love. If I mechanically recite a known prayer that I've said many times without intention or thought, I'm wasting my time. I get out of my prayers and meditations what I put into them.

It takes spiritual work and effort to embrace and transcend addictions. This is the path to spiritual freedom.

Until the obstacle on the path is faced, embraced, owned, and diffused, it will reappear as an obstacle on the path.

The ego trying to protect, will place blame for one's misery externally. And it may suggest a trip to the bar to relieve the tension and misery. The stronger one's ego, the more effort is required to obtain the freedom that lies on the far side of addiction.

ASKING A REASONABLE QUESTION

This morning, I asked Teacher a reasonable question, but she didn't respond reasonably, and I got angry. She requested me to search for something for her on the internet and I agreed to do it. Then I asked her for additional guidance and clarity about the search. She avoided my question, and said, "You already know the answer, Johnny," and that was it. Instantly, I felt the distance between us grow. After all, she asked me for help, I didn't volunteer, and it would have been very easy for her to simply answer my question, I thought. Instead, she continued, "Don't ask that which you need not ask." I wanted to just smack her.

"Why does everything have to be such a hassle with you?" I asked. "I'm trying to help you and you're resisting and making it difficult. Since you've probably searched for this before, why not just help a bit and give me a hint?" But by now, my interest in helping her was gone, and I sat at my computer staring at her while my mind rationalized and found reasons I ought to just tell her to do it herself, then go for a walk and regain my composure. I was getting angry, and yet, just a few minutes ago all was well. Now, with her here fooling with me, I thought, my happy home-space is totally disrupted.

She ignored me and continued typing on her laptop while sitting like a Buddha on the couch. "Do you want my help or not?" I asked, laced with anger?

"Of course, I do, Johnny, that's why I asked," she calmly replied, and continued to type. No suggestions or help came from her, and I uttered a few obscenities under my breath and walked out the door. The hell with her, I thought, focusing all the while on how she was so unfriendly and uncooperative to me and noticing how calm and detached she was to my little "hissy-fit."

I cooled down a bit and after a while returned, more open and available. She invited me to sit and share what occurred during our exchange. "You asked me to do something for you, which I agreed to do," I said.

"That's correct, and then what happened?" she asked.

"Well," I continued, "I thought since you knew more than me about this search, you could have made it easier for me by providing a little guidance."

"Then what happened?" she asked.

"Since you refused to help me help you, I thought you were being very self-centered and didn't much care how your inconsiderate actions were affecting me." Then the light bulb illuminated.

After a long pause, Teacher said, "I see you understand now, at least a little."

"Yes, I believe I do," I said. "I must take responsibility for my state of being. It was all about me wanting you to act how I wanted you to act. You were supposed to respond to my request for help the way I wanted you to. You, not responding like I thought you ought to, offered me an opportunity to get mad and angry at you. I remember a teacher suggesting that we practice non-attachment to outcome, but I didn't do a very good job of that this morning. And being critical of myself right now, I'm not practicing the non-judgement principle, either. It's a challenge being with you."

"Maintaining presence is impossible for most when someone doesn't respond as you think they ought to respond. And you could not maintain presence this morning, Johnny. It is truly OK to ask for help so long as you are OK with any answer or lack of answer. Had I not felt your immediate anger toward me, I would have helped you as this lesson would have not been necessary. But that was not the case today. Be aware that when someone's response is not in alignment with your desires, just stop, even in mid-sentence if you must. Then breathe, pause, and retain or return to presence before you act. Go to "witness" mode and see your ego-personality-self from a few feet away, detached, and separate. Witness your personality and your behavior from your soul's eyes.

"Your response of anger and separation this morning has its roots in unresolved trauma. There's still work to do there, Johnny. Every time a similar situation like this arises, embrace it as another opportunity to go into witness mode and observe, rather than allow yourself to revert to anger. The witness mode response invites your unresolved shadow to diffuse and dissolve at least a little. Also, please remember that our time together is not personal and that I'm not here to "be your friend" as it is with most interactions between people. I'm here as your teacher and to make the most of our time together.

"You are showing up and doing the work Johnny, and that's what is required."

JOHNNY'S LILY PAD - DARK JOHNNY

Journal Entry - 10 August 2019

During morning meditation, Teacher softly said, "Find a vision of pure joy, Johnny."

I was immediately transported to a lily pad floating on mirror-smooth water, with both my grandmothers sitting with me. It was very peaceful. After meditation, I stepped outside, and the vision continued.

While sitting with both grandmothers on my lily pad floating on a pristine mirror-smooth lake, the lily pad began rhythmically rocking. It was gentle at first, but soon increased in intensity. This is very strange, I thought, and dove into the crystal-clear water to investigate.

Under my lily pad, a large, dark, intimidating man loomed. I sensed he was some aspect of me. "I'm Dark Johnny, and I'm doing you a favor, thank you very much," he said. "You never want to be caught asleep when danger comes knocking, do you? And it will come, you know!"

I told him how I enjoyed my calm, peaceful lily pad and asked him to stop disturbing me with his antics. He ignored me, turned, and began to swim away. I swam after him, caught him, and dragged him back. Kicking and fighting, I pulled him out of the water and onto the sunlit lily pad. "Sit with me and my grandmothers," I said, and he did. He knew I would not allow him to swim away and escape. He resembled me, but appeared rougher, more haggard, unkempt, tired, edgy, and fearful. He reminded me of sluggish tar.

"I'm here to keep you vigilant and on your toes, Johnny, so that you won't be surprised when trouble comes knocking," he said. "So, I continually disrupt your sleep, peace, and calm, to keep you on edge, ever ready and prepared for the unexpected." I listened as he continued, "And I constantly remind you of deep ingrained beliefs that were imprinted in your mind during your formidable childhood years, mostly from your father. These beliefs I hold true. It is for your own good that I do this, Johnny."

"What beliefs?" I asked.

"I'll go over my list, which may not be complete, but it'll do for now and it's in no particular order. These are your core beliefs that I have constantly whispered in your ear for a very long time."

- You snooze you lose.
- The harder you try, the better the results.
- Men don't cry.
- Never show weakness.
- Be a man. Be strong. Be stiff, stoic, inflexible and rigid.
- Look tough, it's all about perception and appearance.
- Do men's things like sports and hunting, not woman's things like cooking and sewing.
- Hunt, fish, display your guns and trophies and hang them on the wall for all to see.
- Brag about accomplishments, so everyone will know how great you are.
- Install outdoor floodlights around your house so burglars will rob your neighbors, not you.
- Always put yourself first, you are the most important person on the planet.
- You are number one and everyone else is less than you.
- Get rid of childhood mementoes, it's time to grow up,

- Take cheap shots at people, then laugh it off. It'll keep them off guard.
- If punched in the gut, take it like a man, and never show pain, even if it hurts like hell.
- Sleep with one eye open. Expect trouble.
- Don't trust anyone, especially foreigners, strangers, women, and children.
- Treat everyone with suspicion.
- No one is as smart as you.
- Real men aren't afraid of the dark.
- It's a dog-eat-dog world.
- Use a firm grip when shaking hands. It shows strength.
- Be aggressive and intimidating, for it shows you won't tolerate any BS.
- Never be loving, gentle, kind, or passive, for it shows weakness.
- Dominate conversations.
- Never listen to others, and be critical of what they say. Interrupt often.
- See criticism and advice as a personal attack.
- It's OK to lie when necessary.
- If caught in a lie, deflect attention away with a bigger lie or place blame on someone else.
- If nobody finds out, it's not a lie.
- Dress assertively to show strength, not weakness.
- Never show fear.
- Smile even when disturbed or angry.
- Be unemotional and stuff all feelings into a box, then set it on fire.
- Emotions are for girls and sissies. Manly men don't feel or show emotions.
- Get the first punch in.
- Never admit wrongdoing, and lie to support it if necessary.
- Gut it out, never be a candy-ass.
- Gentle people are cowards.
- Don't trust anyone that doesn't drink.
- Spiritual growth is BS.

- If I'm not aware of it, it doesn't exist.
- Men are superior to woman.
- Be the "man-of-the-house" and keep the wife and children in their place through subtle threats and intimidation.
- People different than you are inferior.
- Everybody is out to get you.
- Tell people you carry a gun even if you don't. That'll keep them off guard.
- The world is a dangerous and fearful place.
- Never admit that you don't know something, just pretend that you know everything.
- Never ask for help.
- Control of people, places, and things will make you happy.
- Small and short people are cunning and devious and out to get you. Watch out for them.
- When you've got someone down, keep kicking till you finish them.
- There is a terrorist hidden behind every tree.

I listened as Dark Johnny (my inner voice) shared my deepest imprinted beliefs and knew that it was time to untangle these dark energy-patterns and reestablish my inner space. I spent the day looking deeply and intently at each belief, sitting patiently, and allowing each illusion to dissipate and dissolve. Being brutally honest, I asked, "Is this belief true? Is it serving me and others? Is it aligned with my soul's intention?" One by one, I observed my responses as I held each belief to my heart then released it, allowing its energy to diffuse. This took all day.

I noted that the surrounding water was mirror-calm and thought it strange that my lily pad, while rocking, made no ripples on the smooth lake. Dark Johnny's antics affected only me and my lily pad. My rocking lily pad was a projection of my inner turmoil generated by false, hollow, self-centered beliefs. I was the source and cause of my pain and suffering.

I sat with Dark Johnny as he softened and began to enjoy our peaceful lily pad. Eventually, he merged into me and Dark Johnny is no more.

Most everyone has an inner Dark Johnny that focuses on negatives and failures, and views the world as threatening and frightening. But freedom, peace and joy lie on the far side of harmonizing one's dark inner shadow beliefs. I encourage you dear reader, to gently observe your behaviors and beliefs, perhaps using Dark Johnny's list as a guide and clean out your basement of shadow energy patterns that hold you hostage in your self-made prison. Rewards are generally felt very early on and acts of kindness will begin to spontaneously arise.

AFRAID TO GO AND AFRAID NOT TO GO

Journal Entry - 13 September 2019

I awoke this morning experiencing a lot of fear about our upcoming travel to Europe. There are many unknowns and our journey will be a pilgrimage, not a vacation. A pilgrimage is a journey, often to an unknown or foreign place, where a person goes in search of new or expanded meaning about themselves. It is a journey of introspection and sacrifice. The challenging outward journey reflects the challenging inward experience. This may lead to a personal transformation. When complete, the pilgrim returns to normal daily life.

There will be no sightseeing, no bantering around, and no tourist-attraction side-trips. We will concentrate on mantras, meditations, and travel in presence. Teacher said that "we have to get out of Dutch, Johnny, for you are too comfortable in this familiar space for deeper growth." So, out of Dutch we will go, and where, how far, and how long, I don't know. I am uneasy. I'm afraid to leave the comfort of my familiar home. I'm also feeling a deeper fear of allowing this opportunity to pass and not go.

This travel is an opportunity that will probably not happen again in this lifetime. I can stay in my comfort zone, call the whole thing off, remain as I am, and tell Teacher to go home. But that doesn't even feel like an option to me. So, I will go and embrace fears of traveling into unknown and uncharted waters.

This happens with new jobs, new relationships, new this, or new that. But I'm seventy-five years old and content with my retirement life. I'm in good health, but don't have the desire, drive, and stamina that I did at age 40 or 50. I feel like I'm on a cross with fear of going and fear of not going.

I heard from silence, "Your greatest fear is not of going on this pilgrimage, Johnny, but of not going, and passing up this opportunity to move forward on your earthwalk. You are the spiritual pilgrim, so pack your bags and get on with it." At that moment, I committed to doing what Teacher suggested, without question, and moved forward with our plans for our spiritual pilgrimage.

It is a big deal to simply be and allow life to unfold. I was learning to trust the process of life and so it was quickly decided by Teacher that we would move out of Dutch and begin traveling about mid-October 2019.

The next morning, we went to look at new Mac Computers to replace Teacher's outdated laptop. We were also on day five of a juice cleanse, consuming only water and juice for a week or perhaps ten days. The entire experience of being with Teacher is the greatest challenge I have ever faced and I frequently want to run away and call it quits. I want to eat real food, listen to rock 'n roll, ride Harley and leave this torture that I'm enduring right now. But I am terrified of not continuing my spiritual journey. It is the right thing for me to do no matter how painful it is or becomes. I am also jealous that teacher is happy and in a blissful state while I'm riding in her car next to her in pain and misery. I ask myself, *why am I feeling so much pain? Is it that I'm in healing mode, peeling off deeper layers of protective onion skin, shedding denial systems, and releasing anger and fears?* Being with Teacher invites and allows deeper energies to surface. She holds the space for their dissolution and I endure the pain and experience it happening. As we ride, I sit in silence.

We participate together in all that we do. Teacher is not on the sidelines saying, "Juice-cleanse for you, Johnny," meanwhile consuming real food. She's in the experience and walks every step of the way with me. Raw food, body cleanses, session work, worksheets, and watching relevant videos and documentaries are all done together.

She is like the Master who was sitting peacefully when a woman and her son approached. The woman said, 'Master, please tell my son that sugar is not good for him and to stop eating sugar.' The Master replied, 'Please bring your son back to me in one week.' The woman left and returned with her son one week later. The Master said to the son, 'Sugar is not good for you, son. Do not eat sugar.' The woman thanked the Master then asked him why he didn't say that to her son last week. The Master replied, 'Because I have not eaten sugar for one week.'

THERE IS NO SUCH THING AS FAILURE

Some seem to regularly experience setbacks, disappointments, and "failures" of one sort or another in their lives, while others seem to frequently "luck-out" and have a smoother road to travel. How can there be no such thing as failure if one wasn't chosen for a job, or laid-off from a job while others were retained? Failure is a part of life, and you may be one that routinely seems to get the "short end of the stick."

We've all heard, or perhaps said to ourselves that, "Failure follows me everywhere. Why does it always happen to me? I never win the drawing or door-prize, yet my friend, Sarah, always seems to hold the winning ticket." We've all been there and done that. Some even have the T-shirt to prove it. Let's now explore why there is no such thing as failure.

Everything, without exception, in all dimensions of reality, is vibrational energy in one or another of its infinite forms. This is not a concept or theory-it is a cosmic fact. All seekers of truth come to this realization somewhere during their journey. If you have not yet received this knowledge, please make room in your awareness for the possibility that it is true. Do not oppose this.

Everything has a vibrational signature, which is the resultant vibrational energy of all that comprises the being or thing. Many are unaware of their vibrational energy fields. But awareness and acknowledgment of their existence is extremely important. Our resultant vibrational signature emits outwardly, and the universe responds and returns to us life experiences that vibrationally match what we emit. Our vibrational receiver is tuned to a similar frequency as our vibrational transmitter.

The frequencies of dishonesty, deception, manipulation, abuse of power, control, harming others, harming self, fear, anger, rage, and other similar responses are low. The frequencies of compassion, caring, understanding, generosity, responsibility, truth, inclusiveness, service, love, and similar responses are high. Therefore, when one engages in low vibrational activities, one emits a low vibrational energetic signature, and the outer world returns low vibrational experiences. These come to us in a variety of unpleasant events and unpleasant people.

When one engages in high vibrational activities, one emits a high vibrational energetic signature and the outer world returns high vibrational experiences. These come to us in a variety of pleasant events and kind, compassionate people. The immutable cosmic laws of reality assure us we will receive what we emit. This cosmic law is very simple and easy to relate to.

What about the failure part? From the ego, painful and undesirable life events are failures and are met with negative responses. From the soul, painful and undesirable life events are opportunities for growth and invite spiritual expansion.

What one calls "failure" always contains a gift. The cosmic laws of the universe bring us events and experiences that reflect what we need to learn for spiritual growth. If an event occurs where one experiences disappointment and pain, one has choice of response. One can get mad or angry, run away, blame God or someone else, or they can embrace the experience, find the gift, and expand emotionally and spiritually.

Disappointments and pain are necessary in one's life, for they invite spiritual and emotional growth. Without suffering, there can be no "soul-growth" for the suffering loosens the ego sufficiently to allow the soul to expand.

When growth is realized, that form of suffering is no longer necessary, and the events that brought that suffering forward will diminish and eventually disappear. One notices that as one becomes more loving, generous, and kind, their "friends" also become more loving, generous, and kind. It's cosmic law.

We suffer failures in many forms because we "choose" to fail. One's ego wants short-term comfort and pleasure, while one's soul wants long-term growth and expansion. And soul-growth is a fundamental reason for this current earthwalk.

Does one learn from winning the lotto? The soul learns little, but the ego loves it, for now it may gloat and brag. But does one learn from losing? Yes, for one now has an opportunity to "learn" how to responsibly deal with the pains of failure. That is the gold.

If one crumbles their losing ticket and angrily tosses it into the trash exclaiming, "I never win and there's always a dark cloud hanging over my head," they invite another failure, for they have not learned how to cope. But if one has knowledge of cosmic laws and realizes that they, and they alone, invite failure, they may use this experience to grow.

Here are a few suggestions that I offer you to deal with "failures."

- Be conscious when failure occurs. Go to witness mode and observe yourself. Do not judge or attempt to change behaviors. Observe and do not criticize.
- After you've cooled down, challenge yourself with these thoughts. Am I willing to do the required inner work to create a revised me reflecting more soul-intention and less ego? I've been responding for years like this but now I have tools to use for transformation. What am I waiting for? Let's get on with it.
- Live a conscious, less ego-centered, more soul-centered life. Live in presence.

The ego blames failure on external circumstances. It views unwanted and disappointing events as failures and encourages acting-out addictions as compensation for one's failures. The ego avoids personal responsibility and blames others. From the ego's perspective, there is such a thing as failure, for it's never the ego's fault.

The soul, however, knows cosmic law, and it attracts these "failures" into one's life as opportunities. So, from the soul's perspective, there are no failures. The choice of viewing an event through the ego or through the soul is yours.

This is not work for the faint-of-heart, but the only way out is to do the work.

SUCCESS HAS ITS GENESIS IN FAILURE

The previous chapter said, "There is no such thing as failure," but this chapter says that there *is* such a thing as failure. Confusing? The ego judges some life events as failures, but it is from these events that the seeds of success are sown.

At Rutgers University, I was required to complete two semesters of English composition for my undergraduate Bachelor of Industrial Engineering degree. I hated writing and resisted it with every cell in my body. It was 1962 and writing did not come naturally to me, or at least that's what I thought. Writing was not my long-suit, and the only thing that I resisted more than writing, as I recall, was asking for help. Not asking for help caused me much grief of my own making.

I showed up for first semester English comp class and remember feeling angry about the requirement to complete two semesters of English comp. As an engineering student, I believed that I only had to know math and science, not sissy things like writing. Failure of my eighth-grade book report still haunted me.

I remember little about the actual English comp classes, assignments, or exams. But I remember receiving Fs on several papers, and my anger blinded me to the reality of the situation. Too embarrassed to tell even my roommate of my failures, I held them secret and stewed in the failure juices. I was a wreck. To ease the pain, I drank beer and blamed the professor, the system, and life. I was incapable of asking for help and working it out.

Why did I resist help? Why the unflinching, "I can do it myself" attitude? Well, Dad never asked for help. He was my hero and I wanted to be just like him. I wasn't conscious of this, but from the wisdom of time and years of inner work, it is clear today why I responded to my English requirements as I did.

The "I can do it myself" attitude also prevented me from asking for a few guitar lessons. I quickly learned to strum simple chords and easily played folk songs for the Saturday night fraternity house party gang. But I never learned how to finger pick, play bar-chords and several other basic guitar-playing skills that I could have mastered with a few lessons and a little practice. I was beyond asking for help.

I responded to everything like that. I was not open to new ways or changes to the old ways, and no one was going to tell me how to do something. Reflecting on my late teens and early twenties, I see today how rigid my attitudes and behaviors were.

So how did this problem resolve? First, nothing changed until sobriety occurred at forty-years-old. Sobriety invited, nay, *required* inner work. And as I did the inner work, I began to see how these old behavior patterns were restraining me and preventing me from realizing my potential. It was a breakthrough when I first asked for help.

I began to see my father for the man he really was and gently lowered him from the pedestal I had him on. The stranglehold I had on myself loosened. I lightened up on myself. It wasn't necessary for me to know everything and do things perfectly. And my way didn't have to be right. I relaxed and allowed life to unfold rather than pushing and shoving my way through it. As I became easier on myself, life became easier on me.

Can you see yourself in this chapter? If you do, the way out is to release the trauma that holds you in your own prison. See parents for who they really are. Honor their positive qualities and dismiss the negative ones.

Today, I know that I am not my father. I don't have to do it like Dad did. And today, I wrote this chapter peacefully and in presence, without fear, judgement, or intimidation.

DEEP WORK

Journal Entry - 14 September 2019

This morning, I was agitated and emotionally off balance as Teacher and I sat in group-session about 8:30 am. She kept asking, "What is behind your agitation, Johnny?"

Eventually, I acknowledged that I see myself as a murderer and killer. Dropping bombs on the Vietnamese people was percolating to the surface again. I felt depressed. Curled up in my lounge chair, I cried for several hours. Teacher sat opposite, holding space, and guiding me here and there, through this and that as I wailed and wept uncontrollably.

Then a very graphic vision manifested. I saw myself grab my big black handled kitchen knife from the cutlery drawer. I saw myself standing behind myself, grabbing my head from behind and holding the big kitchen knife to my throat. I saw myself pulling my head way back and slowly slitting my throat. I saw myself forcefully pulling my head further back till it was attached to my body by only a thin strip of neck skin. I saw the blood and color drain from my head.

I tensed and rose from the chair heading for the cutlery drawer only a few steps away. Teacher rose also and started toward me. We stood face to face only inches apart and locked eyes. That broke the spell and we both realized that the actual throat slitting would not happen today. The current suicidal danger was, for the moment, checked.

I slumped back into the lounge chair and realized that my deepest secret was that I was a murderer and a killer. I saw that all my controlling behaviors, all my addictions, all my acting-out, and all the other ways that I've held the world at arms-length, have been necessary to keep hidden from myself this deepest darkest realization that I am directly responsible for many deaths-that I am a murderer and killer. Until now, I could not have owned or even looked at that deep dark piece of me, for had I acknowledged this prior to today without Teacher's support and guidance, I may have carried out the throat-slitting vision. I felt the tension in my body drain and my muscles slowly relax. I understood that my suppression and denial systems sustained over time were necessary to keep me from realizing the truth of my participation in Vietnam.

Teacher penned a large note and hung it on the wall in plain view. "I AM NOT A MURDERER OR KILLER. THE TRUTH IS THAT I AM A LOVING BEING OF LIGHT IN SERVICE TO ALL." "Johnny, this is your mantra and repeat it over and over. Never forget that you are a being of light and love not a murderer or a killer." I didn't yet understand, but I was feeling relief and the current suicidal visions and thoughts had subsided. I made this my daily mantra and focused on seeing myself as a "being of light in service to all."

Teacher continued and reminded me that everything is energy in one of its infinite forms, including not only physical objects and beings, but emotions, behaviors, and thought patterns as well. Everything means everything, no exceptions.

War is karmic energy. It is the energy of cause and effect playing out. Participation in war is an agreed upon event. The killers and the killed, at some fundamental level, all agree to participate in "wargames" before the shooting starts. One may ask, "Why would one agree to participate in war and agree to kill or be killed?" From our 3-D physical perspective, war makes little or no sense. But on higher planes of reality, it does make sense or it wouldn't happen. One experiences energy patterns during war that cannot be experienced in any other way. These are necessary to experience for one's evolution. So, from a higher perspective, war is necessary, and war makes sense.

It's a leap of faith to entertain the possibility that this is true. If you are resisting these thoughts, please allow room for the possibility that this is truth.

The energy patterns experienced from killing an enemy in war differ from the energy patterns experienced from a conscious pre-planned murder. Similarly, the energy surrounding an aggressive football player hitting an opponent on the opposite team with all he's got differs from the energy surrounding the bully/aggressor attacking an unsuspecting victim. There's an agreement and understanding that those who participate in football will hit hard, and will be hit hard. There's no such conscious agreement with the aggressor and the victim. Football, however, and other violent sports have similar energy patterns as war.

I began to realize that I was a participant in the Vietnam War Games, not a brutalizing murderer in it for self-serving reasons. Like a player on the football team, I was a fighter pilot on the American War Team. And just like the football player all decked out in his uniform ready for battle, I was the fighter pilot all decked out in my flight-suit, ready for battle. They are both energy patterns playing out, friend and foe dancing cheek-to-cheek on the karmic stage of life.

My ego loved the thrills of combat, loved dangers faced, and loved the adrenalin rushes. I loved the ribbons and medals, loved to drink to the enemy destroyed, loved to honor those that didn't return, and loved to glorify war, singing songs of praise and bravery. My ego loved seeing myself as better than the enemy and believed the chaplain when he blessed our airplanes launching toward Vietnam loaded with bombs and rockets. One must be "all in" if one is going to participate in war or football. One cannot have second thoughts or entertain feelings of compassion, love, and caring for the "enemy," when one is launching into the blackness on a stormy night heading for targets in North Vietnam, or on the scrimmage line waiting for the center to snap the ball.

One cannot simply repeat the "I am not a murderer or killer" mantra and expect that suicidal feelings and thoughts will disappear. They dissolve when one's vibrational energy and consciousness rises above the level of suicidal thoughts. As one's vibrational energy rises, suicidal and other destructive thoughts fade.

There are dangers present, however, when one plumbs their basement and finds demons lurking in the deep shadows. Please have a trusted, knowledgeable guide and teacher with you to assist and protect. Do not attempt to do this work alone. This is deep hard shadow work fraught with dangers. I am aware of no other way out. You are not alone as I walk with you in support as we travel together into the light.

Everyone's experience is unique doing deep shadow work. Your efforts and results doing this work will be different, perhaps very different, than mine. Honor your journey inward, exploring your depths regardless of how it unfolds. Be gentle and patient with yourself. Expect pain, frustration, and setbacks, for without them this work would be too easy and your challenges insufficient for you to retrieve your hidden gold. Insights, visions, and relief will come when you are ready to receive them; not before. Any effort in this area is never wasted.

The inward journey will test you to your limits and beyond. Know that Spirit is aware of your pain, your efforts, and your desire to rise. Remember that one makes little progress at the gym if the dedicated two hours a day are spent in the steam room and juice bar. To realize gains, one must exert effort, use the equipment, run the track, and work up a sweat. Spiritual work follows these same principles and progress comes only with effort. Effort will raise your vibration to levels above your traumas and pain. There is no win or lose, and no effort is ever wasted. Everything unfolds in divine order.

I felt the residual effects of this deep work for months following the "slitting my throat with the kitchen knife" experience. I wish to re-emphasize the seriousness and real dangers of deep inner shadow work. I stress again, **do not do this work alone**. Find an authentic teacher to guide, support, and ensure your protection and safety from your own destructive behaviors that will probably surface doing this work. You will be vulnerable and fragile, so expect emotional turmoil and stay close to your support team. Do not go it alone.

One week after the throat slitting session, I was driving Dutch to our campground near Asheville, NC with Teacher following in her van. I began crying uncontrollably. The tears poured out, and I pulled off into a rest area, parked Dutch, crying and wailing. Teacher came into Dutch, sat near me, and held supportive space as I released more trauma.

After arrival in Asheville, we went to a local Indian Restaurant for our evening meal. As the food arrived, an overwhelming sense of sorrow and despair enveloped me. *Why should I enjoy this wonderful meal while those I destroyed lay dead?* I thought. The tears flowed, the sobbing began, and my arms became heavy. Within a few minutes, my arms were so heavy that I could not lift the fork to my face. Try as I might, the fork with food would come no closer than a foot from my mouth. I returned the fork to the table and sat in silence. Tears of sorrow and remorse flowed for 30 minutes as I sat and sobbed. Teacher understood and allowed me to cry and experience the release. A wise teacher is essential in one's healing efforts. Eventually, the visions of the dead and dying lessened, and I ate a little food.

That night, I dreamed I was attacking a Vietnamese village flying my Phantom jet-fighter. A man was tied to a pole in the center of the village. This man, hated by the villagers, had killed many locals and I was instructed to strafe him with my 20-millimeter on-board cannon.

I rolled-in, placed my gunsight on the man tied to the pole and watched him grow as I tracked in closer for the kill. Squeezing the trigger, I saw that it was ME in the center of my gunsight. I gasped in shock and shouted, "DIE, YOU NO-GOOD SOB."

I squeezed the trigger and saw my body twitch as the slugs struck home and "I" splintered into fragments. Flesh, blood, and bone flew in every direction as I roared over the dead man now hanging mutilated and limp on the pole in the center of the Vietnamese village. "That man deserved to die," I screamed, and made another strafing pass on the mutilated body, tearing him further to shreds. I climbed away and pointed my Phantom toward home.

Sorrow, anger, rage, hatred, and loathing, all must purge and release for the soul to shine through. And when that happens, it will be at a time and a way of its own choosing. One cannot retain darkness within and authentically walk in the light. The darkness must release for the soul to shine.

Teacher explained, "Johnny, you destroyed an aspect of your ego.

You killed that piece of your ego that was tied to the post. That piece of you that dropped bombs on people and rationalized its behavior away with lies, distortions, denials, and delusions is dead. Your killer that holds you in your prison of hatred, anger, fear, grief, sorrow, sadness, guilt, remorse, and shame was strafed into oblivion by you in your vision. That aspect of your ego is no longer with you, and you've experienced a payoff for doing your work, Johnny. It was "real" and although it didn't actually happen on the physical plane, it did happen on the energetic planes. That aspect of your ego is gone now. There is room for your soul to shine through.

"To heal, there must be room for the light to enter. Your ego, which clings desperately to its life, and clings desperately to Johnny MedicineBear and sees itself (Johnny MedicineBear) as the best of the best in everything, must release. Those aspects of you that you strafed and killed in your vision are aspects of you that are now dead and gone. It's all good, Johnny. You will never kill again, for that energy is no longer alive within you. And it would have been suicidal for you to have explored this area and attempted to do this work alone."

I am incredibly grateful for my Goddess Teacher that guided and supported me while I plumbed the depths of my deepest secrets and healed.

Three months later, at the SWAN Ashram in southern India, the 3rd generation pundit astrologer, seer, and medium, told me that my hatred, anger, rage, and sorrow surrounding my participation in the Vietnam war was reduced to zero, and that all suicidal tendencies were gone.

Please stay the course, and know that your path to freedom will be revealed to you when you are ready to receive.

UNRAVELING JUDGEMENT

Listening to YouTube talks while driving, I heard a piece of wisdom from Matt Kahn on unraveling judgement. He shares simply in a very gentle way. This is from one of his talks about the five steps to unraveling judgement.

1. Nothing is stupid.
2. Everything helps everything.
3. If it could have been any other way, it would have.
4. What weakness is this helping me strengthen?
5. Thank you.

A search on YouTube for Matt Kahn, "unraveling judgement," will bring this piece forward. I found it helpful.

MOM AND DAD - WHO THEY TRULY WERE

Recently, I began loving my parents and appreciating who they truly were. Until returning from India in January 2020, I focused primarily on my parent's shortcomings, faults, inadequate parenting skills, and lack of spiritual awareness. But that's changed, because I've changed.

We respond to life at the level of our consciousness. From early sobriety until just a few years ago, I viewed my parents from victim mode. I focused on their faults rather than acknowledging their gifts, because that is how I focused on myself. It can be no other way. Even though I was aware of their positives, I could not stay focused on those qualities, for I could not stay focused on my own positive qualities. I projected my insecurities and fears onto my parents. This is irresponsible behavior. I simply blamed my shortcomings on them. This is victim mode mentality. And I was unaware that I was doing this.

As I healed, I began to see my own positive attributes and beauty. As I lightened up on myself, I simultaneously lightened up on my parents. I began to see the gifts that Mom and Dad brought to me.

Yes, Dad was hard on me, and Mom didn't protect me from him. But that no longer matters, and today, I appreciate the personal sacrifices and hardships that my parents endured for my sister Pat and me.

It's true that Mom and Dad parented the best they could, and I knew that in my head for a long time. But that didn't lessen the pain in my heart until I healed myself sufficiently to rise above resentments that I carried toward them. It took time and inner work to genuinely love myself and that allowed me to genuinely love my parents.

It's worth the effort. For as I do my inner work, the outer world becomes softer and gentler.

DREAM - THE FUNERAL PYRE

Journal Entry - 01 October 2019

I dreamt I am in a foreign land with strange people. Many are milling around and I ask what's going on. "We are having a large funeral pyre over there very shortly," commented a local native. Interested in the local customs, I walk closer.

The wood pile is the size of a small shed. By observing the lavish clothing and expensive jewelry worn by the people, I guess this funeral is for a noble person. I wait and watch.

Soon, a man torches the woodpile and sets it ablaze. The fire lights up the area and I now see the man lying on top of the woodpile, calmly waiting for his body to be consumed.

Suddenly, I levitate above the fire and see that the calm man lying on the woodpile is ME smiling through the flames as my body is consumed. I was peaceful and knew that it was my physical body that was burning and being consumed, freeing my soul. I smiled and watched and as the fire burned down. Then I descended back to the ground and walked away.

Burning the ego to allow the soul to shine is my work. This dream portends my journey forward, releasing the ego. It is a positive sign.

Dreams are insightful messages from the deep self, or spirit, that are of great value and importance and ought to be acknowledged.

I encourage you to journal your dreams, and notice how they feel to you. I do not try to "figure them out" as they are not literal but metaphorical and poetic. They are pointers toward the path and validation of my progress.

THE GREATEST PSYCHOLOGY BOOK OF ALL TIME

Most parents read the greatest psychology book of all time to their children before the children can read and when bedtime was no later than 8 pm. To this day, I cannot read this little book without my voice trembling, tears flowing, and emotions percolating to the surface.

The *Little Engine That Could*, by Watty Piper, is a classic children's book and was read to me when I was a little boy. I loved it and today still love it as it continues to have a powerful effect on my life.

I am every player in the story. I am the toys on the train. I am the children on the other side of the mountain. I am the train itself, and even the mountain that must be conquered.

I am the passenger engine that pulled the little train loaded with toys into the yard. My job was done and being unwilling to go the extra mile, I disregarded the pleas of the little toys to pull them over the mountain and headed for the roundhouse and rest.

I am the big freight engine that refused to pull the little train of toys over the mountain, because pulling a load of toys was way below me.

I am the tired, rusty old lazy engine that saw failure in everything and felt that it would take too much effort to pull the little train over the mountain. So, I headed for the roundhouse chanting, "I cannot, I cannot, I cannot."

And I am the little blue engine that, although small, saw success in the effort to pull the little train of toys to the children over the mountain. The little blue engine was compassionate and loving and put the children and their needs before her own. She chanted, "I think I can, I think I can," all the way up the mountain. Nearly exhausted, she crested the hill cheered on by the toys on the little train. Easing down the other side, to the laughter of the toys, she chanted, "I thought I could, I thought I could, I thought I could."

What a story and as I write this my eyes are moist. So which engine am I today as I go out in the world to play and engage life? The choice is mine. Sometimes when I've much effort to exert, I remember this story and my mantra is, "I know I can, I know I can, I know I can." Thank you, *Little Engine that Could*.

SPIRITUAL WORK IS YOUR LIFE'S WORK

Do not delude yourself even for one second by thinking that I am different than you. My path may appear different, my life experiences may appear different, and I may appear different. But, like you, I have issues, I suffer, I make choices, and I receive consequences for my choices. And like you, I engage life either from my pleasure-seeking personality, or my spiritually oriented soul, or somewhere in between.

If you are struggling or stagnant on your spiritual journey, know that this is part of the process and that your struggle or stagnation is necessary. Impediments to progress are necessary components of the spiritual journey.

Spiritual progress is not a steady climb, like walking up a gentle slope. It is intense work, with pain and suffering, sweat and tears, interspersed with periods of rest. Everyone on the spiritual journey moves forward a bit, rests a bit, then continues onward.

Meaningful spiritual work is much more intense than listening to pleasant sermons, engaging in shallow meditations, or dancing and singing around community bonfires. It is discovering, embracing, and healing our deepest darkest secrets and fears. This is everyone's life's work. Most never do it. And of the few that start, the majority quickly return to the sensory pleasures enjoyed before the spiritual journey began.

The path toward spiritual maturity and freedom is through our pain and suffering. Some go on a spiritual pilgrimage, but travel only a few feet beyond the starting line, enter a holding pattern for a while, then give up. They return to full-time participation, seeking sensory pleasures and shallow distractions.

Most are unaware that they have a hidden component of their personality containing their deepest darkest secrets and fears. For them, there is nothing to fix, nothing to change, and nothing to heal. Life is just fine as it is. Some say, "I'll find out what it's all about when I die." This is a major mistake for our earthwalk is our opportunity to move toward oneness with the divine by doing our work. Any effort exerted on the spiritual path is never wasted.

The guard at the gate of our shadow basement where our secrets reside is fear, and we must become friends with our fears to enter our shadow basement. Fear is a very deceitful and clever component of the personality. Fear will stop at nothing to convince you to leave well enough alone and not enter your shadow basement of secrets.

But one's gold and freedom are found in that basement of secrets. We must move through the guard's resistance to go mining for our gold.

Don't settle for mediocrity. Embrace your fears and go do your deep work.

US OR THEM - PINK FLOYD

Journal Entry - 4 October 2019

Teacher and I watched the concert-movie *Us or Them* with Pink Floyd one evening at a theater in downtown Asheville, North Carolina. The "Us or Them" theme of duality, separation, and right/wrong is the story of my life and many other's lives as well.

Scrolling behind the band were graphic scenes of the Vietnam war with bombs exploding and people being blown to pieces. I was deeply moved and affected. I watched and saw "my bombs" killing those people. I sat trance-like, didn't make comments, or wish it was different. I just sat in witness mode and observed. It was me killing those people. I was numb. We drove home in silence.

Upon returning, Teacher asked, "Where are you, Johnny?"

I lied and said, "I'm fine and will go to bed now." (That was the guard at my shadow basement door responding, not me)

"Where are you, Johnny?" she repeated.

"I said, I'm OK and just want to go to bed."

"Where are you, Johnny?" she repeated for the third time in a strong authoritative voice.

I exploded! "I'M *&^%$# TIRED OF ALL THIS CONSTANT

BADGERING, AND I JUST WANT THE WHOLE *&^%$#@ THING TO END, SO LEAVE ME ALONE. I'VE HAD IT, I'M @#^&$%& DONE," I screamed.

She remained patient as I yelled obscenities at her, at the world, at everything. After a bit, she grabbed me and pounded the center of my back, releasing more suppressed rage and anger. It jerked me back to the present. I soon felt my body relax and slumped into Dutch's lounge chair, exhausted. I was totally spent and sat for an hour, whimpering. Finally, I went to my bedroom and fell into a restless sleep.

That night I had the following dream:

I was a monk in a Buddhist Monastery with many monks all wearing brown, very plain, rough, utilitarian, hooded robes that looked and felt like burlap bags. I was simply one of many all looking exactly alike. I asked a monk why everyone was gathering in the dharma hall. He replied that, "The Master is going to give a dharma talk."

"May I go also?" I asked?

He smiled and said, "Of course, because you are the Master."

In disbelief, I walked to the dharma hall and was invited to sit on a little raised platform where everyone could see me and I could see everyone. I stepped up and sat cross-legged. I smiled at all the hooded monks, and they all smiled back. I knew that these people, all looking just like me in their brown robes, were the ones that I killed during Vietnam.

I loved and respected these people and felt their love shining on me. Then, they all began to glow and illuminate with a beautiful bluish white luminescence. I was now seeing them as light beings, not simply physical humans. I saw their auras and their souls. I realized that we not only all looked alike, but were all beings of divine light, and were all connected. We were all children of divinity.

It was an awesome dream and perhaps portends that my Vietnam horror is ending.

This dream encouraged me to continue my spiritual pilgrimage. It was a sign that energies are shifting and old patterns are releasing. I must persevere with my work, especially when obstacles are present and suffering is experienced. When I am facing obstacles, I am facing opportunities. Don't quit. When the going gets the toughest, that's the time to push on a little harder and move on a little further. Relief and rest will eventually arrive.

LIVING LIFE CLOSER TO THE BONE

Journal Entry - 5 October 2019

I'm at my desk in Dutch this Saturday afternoon about 1:30 pm with Teacher sitting on the couch, writing on her computer. My life differs from what it was last year. Conversations are sacred, meaning that we do not jabber and joke around. There are few pleasantries as pleasantries are unnecessary sensory pleasures. I feel Teacher's support from her actions, more so than from her words. Saying, "I love you," as example, seems superficial and unnecessary between conscious beings.

I am content to be here. No, it's more like I'm enthusiastic about being here. There is a part of me that resonates deeply with this experience. It's not about feeling good in the general sense that I've always used these words. Previously, feeling good meant that I was on a little high from some sensory pleasure. I may have shared a delicious dinner with friends or had chocolate cake with vanilla ice cream. But what was a good meal in the past? It was all about flavor and ambiance. Today we are eating healthy, live, raw, plant-based foods that taste delicious and feel good to the body long after they've been consumed.

There's no hangover or judgement about eating unhealthy foods as

I've experienced in the past. I've learned to enjoy the flavors and tastes of live food.

Also, I don't seem to eat as much and yet I'm totally satisfied. The meals that Teacher prepares are the most satisfying I've ever had. Her raw mashed potatoes, created from raw cauliflower, cashew nuts, and olive oil is delicious. The desire to eat cooked mashed potatoes, drowned in butter with sour cream and other condiments has faded. I have no desire to eat animal flesh at all. I never thought that this would happen, but it has.

We live in Dutch for days without music on the stereo. I never thought that would happen either. I observe my past behaviors in others without judgement of them or myself. All judgements are self-judgements.

I've written the beginnings of the *From Savage to Shaman Book* and am deeply engaged in this endeavor. I never thought I could or would write a book, but it is happening. I've cried a ton of tears releasing childhood, Vietnam, and other traumas. And I've cried a ton of tears FOR Little Johnny, FOR my Vietnam friends, FOR my parents, and FOR our precious Earth Mother. I find myself more peaceful and moving toward aligning my earthwalk with my soul's intention. I have purpose in my life today.

With few exceptions, from about age twenty-five forward, my life was one pleasurable event after another. All I did it seems was move from one party to the next and enjoy the good times.

I've heard over and over, "Thank you for your military service, Johnny" and "Johnny, you deserve to have your beautiful Dutch and Harley. You worked hard for them." The truth is that I was an immature twenty-four-year-old when I joined the US Air Force in 1969, and all I wanted to do was go fly fighter-jets, drink whisky, and party hardy. I cared little about anything else except having a good time.

Rewarding, good-paying jobs seemed to just drop in my lap. I never thought I worked hard. From age twenty-four till retirement on my sixtieth birthday, I flew airplanes, and that was never work. Flying was my passion and my sport.

I know that many work incredibly hard, hate their jobs, and are rewarded very little. Many have worked much harder than me and have been rewarded much less.

When I am of service, I feel a strong sense of purpose in my life. I'm alive in this body.

Last November, I completed my usual six-month summer travels in Dutch towing Harley in the trailer. Returning to Florida, I reflected on my summer journey. It was lots of fun. I took tons of photos, enjoyed many tasty meals, went for many pleasant Harley rides, and thoroughly enjoyed myself. Yet I felt that my summer was superficial and something was lacking.

Did I delude myself? At the end of the summer, was I more spiritually mature than when I left in the spring? Nope! Did I appreciably grow and expand my consciousness and awareness? Nope! Did I acquire new spiritual tools or experience anything significant? Nope! Was my travel purposeful and meaningful? Nope! But it was lots of fun, just like my whole adult life has been.

And beneath all the superficial fun, I have felt a slight undercurrent of uneasiness. The emotions that surface when I am not distracted by sensory pleasures are fear and anger in one form or another. To suppress those undesirable emotions and remain comfortable, I controlled and manipulated my immediate environment. I always wore a smile and pretended everything was all right. While I was doing this, I did not know that I was doing this.

When the fun eased off, I went for more fun to cover the deeper feelings. Johnny MedicineBear continued spinning round and round slightly out of control, deeper and deeper into the hole.

To be clear, the highs and lows of 2018 were much less than the highs and lows were thirty, twenty, or even ten years prior, but they were still there. Since I have no desire to drink alcohol, and clearly see the progress in my life, I deluded myself into believing that I was solidly sober and my work was complete. This year with Teacher, I learned that there was still much more work left to do.

I often wondered why I was never in a deep loving relationship with a woman. I knew that the reasons were inside, but instead of doing the deep work, I'd go after another superficial, shallow relationship which in short order would dissolve into a finger pointing separation and termination. That has stopped! Teacher called it the Merry-Go-Round game and said, "Either get off and do your work, Johnny, or stay on and leave this life with much unfinished business and without ever realizing your soul's intention." That was her message in so many words right from the start in mid-June 2019. She also said that, "My work with you is not personal. I am here by divine guidance, and there is a divine plan for you, Johnny. The *From Savage to Shaman Book* Project is a big part of that plan. It's your choice what you do with this life."

I got off the Merry-Go-Round and stepped into the unknown. It's only been three months since Teacher arrived, but I'm seeing progress and moving out of my nightmare. Is it fun? By my old definition of fun, it is not. It has little to do with sensory pleasures. But my body and mind are shifting and changing. There is progress from inner work around the divine feminine, my parents, the Vietnam war, and addictions. I'm walking a path toward spiritual freedom. It may not be fun, but it is deeply rewarding.

I'm leaving much behind as I move forward. I see old behavior patterns, old ideas, old physical attachments dropping off without remorse. The future is an open experience, not planned from the past, as I've always done. The old pattern was, if I did it before and liked it, I would do it again. That leaves nothing for creativity. I do not know where my life is going today, and as I allow the future to unfold and release attachments and desires, I become open to a future of infinite possibilities.

"It's neither hard nor easy, it's simply necessary," I remarked while talking with Teacher this afternoon. And I recalled mentor Ronnie's emphasis on eliminating polarized words like good and bad, right, and wrong, and hard and easy. Ronnie said, 'Find words that accurately describe what you're trying to convey and use them, Johnny.'

Today, as I write this chapter, it is roughly two years since I returned from India and completed my spiritual pilgrimage with Teacher. Reading this chapter, one may conclude that there are no longer any sensory pleasures in my life at all. One may feel that a person either walks the spiritual path or eases pain and suffering with sensory pleasures. There is a third option that becomes available only after one has done deep work.

Can I today enjoy an ice-cream cone, or watch a mindless TV show? Yes. But today, these sensory pleasures are simply sensory pleasures. I am not using them to ease pain and suffering. When I engage in these activities today, I do so in presence, and fully enjoy the experience. On the surface or to the unaware, it may appear the same as it was for me 20 years ago. But once my basement was cleaned, I became free to engage life doing whatever I wish without guilt, shame, or remorse.

Please use the tools found in this book to assist you in discovering your gold and finding your freedom.

HI-HO, HI-HO, IT'S OFF TO EUROPE WE GO

Three months into our spiritual pilgrimage while traveling in Dutch, Teacher suggested that we move forward by changing the home surroundings. That meant that it was time to leave Dutch and continue our work somewhere else. She said that I was too comfortable in my familiar motorcoach and that a greater challenge was necessary. So, Teacher asked for and received guidance of how and where to continue.

We journeyed for a week to the Neem Karoli Baba Ashram in Taos, New Mexico. This was a warm-up for our upcoming time in India. We were now on divine-time, not clock time. That meant that events happened when it was the proper time for them to happen not when Teacher or I wanted them to happen. One cannot be on divine-time and be in their head or logical brain. Divine-time is a time of allowing. An example of divine-time is the opening of a flower. It occurs when all is ready, and not when I or anyone else wants the flower to open. It is about allowing

After Taos, we flew to Dublin, Ireland, and stayed in small hotels for about a week in several Irish villages. Our next stop was the isle of Mallorca off the coast of Spain where we rented a house for one month. Finally, we flew to the SWAN Meditation and Yoga Retreat Center (an

Ashram) in Goa, India and participated in several programs for about two months.

We were not tourists. We were on a spiritual pilgrimage. That meant that every breath I breathed, every thought I thought, and every action I did was done in mindfulness and presence. There was no bantering humor, no joke telling, no sightseeing and very little photo-taking. This endeavor was an opportunity for me to engage reality from my soul, rather than my personality. It was continuous hard work.

SITTING IN A CHAIR

"Johnny, tomorrow," said Teacher, "beginning at 8 am, sit comfortably in a chair and don't get up, other than potty breaks, for anything. Have water available, but no food, no reading, no distractions. Don't sleep, just sit without movement for eight hours in a chair. Sit in presence with an empty and open mind. As thoughts arise, do not engage, but observe from witness mode and allow them to float through. Notice your body, and where discomfort arises."

"OK," I said, and I did.

At 8:00 am the following morning, I sat in the comfortable living room chair in my hotel room alone and with no radio, TV, phone, iPad, or other distractions. Within a few minutes of sitting, my mind started to race, question, and distract me from presence.

In witness mode, I observed the world around me, but did not engage. In witness mode, my emotional field is detached from the experience and therefore, I should remain unaffected. That's how it works in theory, and with practice, perhaps I'll move closer to that space. But I'm not there and it takes reminding and trying to stay in and reap the benefits of witness mode.

A song began to play repeatedly in my head. I just listened to it, acknowledged that it was there, and tried to ignore it. That didn't work, and the song repeated and repeated, again and again. I acknowledged it again and again, but the song would not stop playing.

I envisioned a CD player and repeatedly hit the stop button, but the song kept playing. I opened the lid and extracted the CD, but the song continued playing. After a while I screamed, "STOP, DAMMIT." But the song played on. I threw the CD against a wall and stomped on it repeatedly and destroyed it. The song played on. I felt my anger arise, as the song played on. I did not move from my chair nor try to distract my mind with other thoughts. I sat in silence with the song playing over and over in my head.

Focusing on my breath, I thanked the song for bringing this challenge to me. I became friends with the song and saw it as a gift not a detriment. When my attitude changed from pushing it away to allowing it to play, the song slowly faded and soon stopped on its own.

Perhaps the message of the song experience is to be accepting of life events that arise without judgement or wishing life was different. Perhaps, it means to live in alignment with, *and not*, in opposition to life. Previously, songs would frequently play repeatedly in my head, but that doesn't happen very often anymore. I believe that I had to experience head-on the discomfort of this unpleasant energy pattern for it to dissolve and dissipate.

Other than a few potty breaks, I sat for eight hours straight in a hotel room chair. Spiritual growth opportunities arrive in many strange ways. It was uncomfortable, and challenging, but I did it. Perhaps I learned something that I could not have learned any other way. I grew a bit and perhaps I'm a bit more present in the everlasting now.

CASUAL BANTERING HUMOR

I noticed during my time with Teacher how much I love to banter around and play simple mindless games with people. This is fine perhaps with children, but I noticed that I frequently assume this bantering playful posture also with adult people that I have just met, casually know, or spend little time with. I never gave it much thought before and simply dismissed away this aspect of my personality, rationalizing it aside with thoughts like "that's just who I am," and "I can't do anything about it." I never examined this behavior before, but I'm seeing how counterproductive constant or inappropriate bantering is.

In my case, it was a defense mechanism to keep the world at arm's length. I'm not speaking of casual playfulness, once-in-a-while joke telling, or wearing a genuine smile. I'm speaking of always bantering around, making light of everything that's going on, responding to a meaningful question with casual humor or trying to keep it light when someone is having a crying-their-heart-out moment.

As example, this light-hearted bantering along with unnecessary chatter came out often in a café. I always introduce myself by first name to the server, which is fine. I still do this with a friendly greeting included in the exchange. But prior to Teacher, I'd share with the server which local campground I'm staying at or a little about Dutch or Harley. It's like I wanted them to know that I was a bit different or special than the regular patrons in the café. If I ordered something with cheddar cheese, I'd sometimes ask if they could sub the cheddar with feta for "feta is betta than chedda." This worked especially well on omelets, salads, and pizzas. That didn't always happen, of course, but I had several other light bantering cuties in my bag to use at the café. I had a compulsion to be cute, tell a joke, or something to create a little center-of-attention event.

Teacher suggested I simply be polite, friendly, straight forward and brief. The server doesn't need to know where I'm from, how long I'm staying in town, or get drawn into a little bantering feta-betta-chedda exchange. This unnecessary chatter added confusion to the ordering dialog, sometimes contributing to misunderstandings and incorrect orders.

That was my ego, wanting to be recognized and using the superior position of the customer to force myself a bit on the server. Since I was the customer, I had a control advantage. I was always friendly and personable, but bantering took up additional time and some of the server's energy. It wasn't helpful, and it was certainly unnecessary.

This was the first time I saw this behavior pattern in a mature light. Today, I practice letting the bantering go and am more present with servers in the ordering exchange. I am more present for life. It seems like small stuff, but it's not. Anything one does to discard mindless behaviors and reduce "lip-flapping" chatter is positive and a big deal.

My inherent personality is outgoing and friendly. That's who I am. The aim is to not stop being outgoing and friendly, but to be *appropriately* outgoing and friendly. Ask appropriately and respond appropriately. And if a pun jumps out or a feta-is-betta-than-chedda moment develops, it will just happen and we'll all laugh together.

At a restaurant a few years ago, a spontaneous act of kindness from daughter Jennifer arose while sharing a seafood dinner. Lovingly and with much fanfare, she offered me the last crab on the serving platter, saying, "It's yours, Dad, I never want to be shellfish."

IT'S ONLY A MUSHROOM

"Look at those magnificent mushrooms, Johnny!" I exclaimed to the universe as I stepped from Dutch this morning into gorgeous, brilliant sunlight. In the rough grass a few feet from the door, was a patch of mushrooms that were just little tiny umbrellas but yesterday. It rained last night and now a whole family of perhaps twenty-five beautiful wild mushrooms were living where a few days ago there wasn't a trace. I marveled at how rapidly they grew.

A little visual formed and I reflected on my early teen years when I was working with cousin Frank in his landscape business. While cutting grass, I wished I could avoid mowing down wild-flowers, mushrooms and other little plants that grew randomly in lawns. I didn't want to mow them down, but I was to make the customer's yard look like a world-class country club. Frank mowed down everything, including mushrooms and wild-flowers. He would say, 'It's only a flower, Johnny,' or 'It's only a mushroom.' He was the boss, and I'd say, "Blessings to you, Mr. and Mrs. Flower," and "RRRROOOOOMM-MMM" down they went. The mower chute would exhale a little breath of perfume amidst the minced flower petals and green grass clippings. I wanted desperately to be strong, and manly, just like my big cousin Frank so I did what he did without question.

"ONLY A MUSHROOM!" I SCREAMED this morning. "Are you

nuts?" Mushrooms have life-force, vitality, healing properties, and so much more. I cannot even begin to appreciate the energies and intelligence that imbue mushrooms. *It's only a mushroom, what a great theme for a book,* I chuckled. And today, that theme is this chapter in your book.

I looked deeply into the mushrooms and saw their complex cellular, molecular, and community structure. I saw their DNA, intelligence, and organization. I saw the carbon, oxygen, nitrogen, iron, potassium, and other basic elements that, along with intelligence and life-force, created these beautiful beings. I laughed as I viewed myself composed of these same basic elements with a similar cellular, molecular, and community structure. Mushrooms and humans drink the same water, breathe the same air, and consume foods all originating from the same soil. "I'm a mushroom!" I giggled and realized how true that is. From that perspective, the mushroom and I are the same.

I looked deeply into the soil that gifted the mushroom its nutrients and supported its life. Soil comes from all that has ever lived and passed. I saw many trees and plants, bears, deer, and birds that over thousands, no *millions* of years, have lived and passed, creating the nutrient rich soil supporting these mushrooms. I saw the entire history of the earth in the soil and how this little mushroom family is an essential piece of the delicate web-of-life. Every cell in my body also came from the same soil and is also an essential component of the delicate web-of-life. The mushroom and I can both trace our physical genesis to a common point-the genesis of the planet Earth.

I saw the water necessary to promote and sustain these mushroom beings and me as well. I saw the air that we both breathe and reflected on the evolution of our atmosphere into what it is today. I saw the iron and other heavy elements necessary for life and the super-nova explosions that birthed these heavy elements long before the Earth was born.

I saw the timelessness of time and the interconnectedness of all life right here in my little yard in these marvelous mushrooms.

The contracted mind observes shallowly, categorizes, analyzes, judges, identifies, names, and endlessly talks like it knows. The mature mind gazes deeply and reflects on its true nature. Those that say, don't know, and those that know, don't say.

If I can see myself in a mushroom, I can also see myself in every human being on the planet.

I will never harm any being that is my brother or sister. And as I see myself in all beings, distance between us diminishes. Every being becomes my brother and sister. Separation vanishes.

The entire universe exists in every mushroom.

MARY AND THE WEB OF LIFE

Recently, a friend who is just five years shy of her hundredth birthday, and I casually chatted and laughed and giggled over nothing significant. It is a pleasure to check in with Mary occasionally to just be with this spiritually mature, loving woman of ninety-five. She is a medium, healer, and first-class spiritual warrior with an active, compassionate personality and spirit. Just being near her is a gift and I cherish my good fortune to have her close to me.

"I don't think I'm of much value anymore, Johnny, as I don't get many callers and spend a lot of time alone. I'm just sort of hanging around." I don't recall her words exactly but that is the flavor of our conversation during February 2023.

"Mary, you are of great value just by being alive. It is you and other conscious beings like you that are holding together the fragile web of life. You don't need to do anything, Mary. Just being spiritually mature, alive, and conscious is sufficient.

"You and other conscious beings are the anchors helping our fragile and stressed-out planet retain its fundamental life-force integrity." I elaborated a bit more for Mary, "Light-Beings, like you, Mary, are the anchors that absorb the shocks of the unconscious activities of the masses. We help hold the oceans in balance, while others, through thoughtless actions, are polluting them and destroying the fish. We don't need to think about this as it plays out on its own. We are there for the trees, the animals, the waters, and the soil. Hopefully, there are enough of us to stop the current downward trends and nurse our home back to vibrant health."

"Thank you, Johnny," Mary chided, and we hugged, giggled, and laughed over absolutely nothing.

I love my friend, Mary, and will celebrate her hundredth birthday with her a few years down the road.

ALIGNMENT

A car needs to be in alignment to drive true and function optimally. We also need to be in alignment to drive true and function optimally.

Alignment, in this book, means "to be aligned with," to be centered between the energy of the Earth Mother below and Divinity above. When aligned, these supportive energies flow freely through our physical body and energy fields unimpeded. We are nurtured and empowered. Anything we do while in alignment is enhanced for the force is with us.

Aligning yourself is easy to do, requires no special knowledge, nor requests or suggests that you alter your current spiritual or religious beliefs or practices. It is an enhancement to whatever you are doing.

Here's how to do it. Stand or sit peacefully in presence and close your eyes. Inhale and exhale a few deep slow breaths, and visualize floating over a volcano. Look down through the volcano to the red-hot molten healing earth-core energy at the center of our planet. Inhale and draw that mother-earth energy up to your feet.

Focusing upward, expand your energy toward divinity, merging with the loving healing energies of God, Angels, Saints, Blessed Masters, and past loved ones. Take a few slow deep breaths, visualizing these energies flowing with your breath up and down through you. If appropriate, focus on areas in your body that are injured or traumatized. Visualize these areas returning to their natural healthy state. That's it.

Do this several times each day. It may be done informally, perhaps while washing your hands or anytime you have a few free minutes. It works instantaneously. You will notice immediate improvement in your disposition, painful body parts, and overall demeanor. It will brighten your day and you will be of greater service to yourself and others because you are in alignment. The force is now with you.

A MOUNTAIN IS, A MOUNTAIN IS NOT, A MOUNTAIN IS

The full title reads, "Before I do my work, the mountain is a mountain. While I'm doing my work, the mountain is not a mountain. And after I've completed my work, the mountain is a mountain." The mountain is a metaphor for someone or something in one's life. I'll explain using my father as my mountain.

As a child and until some years into sobriety, my father was my father. He was Mr. God to me and I looked up to him. He was my masculine role model. I simply denied his abusive behaviors toward me. My father was my father.

As I embraced sobriety and began doing my inner-work, I started seeing my father as a wounded man. He never showed emotions and hid his feelings behind a strong rigid facade. I began to see Dad as the angry man he was. I relived his abusive behaviors toward me and hated him for the things he did to me. My father was not my father.

As my work around my father continued, I realized the gifts he brought me and saw the wounds he suffered as a boy. He could not parent any better than he did. I forgave him for his brutality and he became my father again. Now I was free to love him and be with him without being emotionally triggered or drawn into our old story. My father was once again my father.

The only way to heal a relationship with an abusive parent is to embrace the pain and walk through the fire.

IT COULD NOT POSSIBLY HAPPEN - BUT IT DID

It was one of those slip-of-the-finger things that can't possibly happen, yet it did. A response to a Craigslist ad arrived via e-mail and somehow on my magic smart phone I deleted it to the trash folder. Then, trying to undelete it from the trash folder, I deleted it from the trash folder. A help search said that "deleting from the trash folder is a permanent deletion." Then, within a few seconds, the e-mail sync system through my WIFI deleted it from all my other devices as well. That was the end of it. It was gone, and I went from *Yippee!* to *What the heck just happened?*

I felt my energy drop and my world contract. I was very disturbed by this inadvertent act and it bothered me a lot. Being human with an emotional field, I get triggered sometimes and contract into "it's all about ME, ME. ME. ME. ME, and I, I, I, I." *How did this happen? What did I just do? That e-mail was important to ME and now it is permanently deleted!*

I calmed down in a few minutes and took two steps backwards to move away from the event and get a greater perspective. When all I can see is the problem directly in front of me, moving just a few feet aft, broadens my view and softens the event. I noticed how contracted I felt and how small my world was at that moment. I could see nothing except my deleted e-mail and projected this into an "end-of-the-world" scenario.

I set my present activities aside, sat peacefully, followed my breath, and noted that I wanted to tell someone about my misfortune. *Will that help you, Johnny?* I asked myself. *Not at all, but my friend might give me a little sympathy. Does sympathy help? Never!*

I thought of the difference between worry and concern. They are easy to tell apart and very different. Worry is an energy depleting activity, and is sourced from the ego's victim mode. I become a rat running endlessly around a wheel, expending energy, and accomplishing nothing.

Concern is empowering and is the choice of a Spiritual Warrior. Concern has merit and invites me to take responsibility for the situation, consider realistic options, and move forward toward a solution.

I was in victim mode. Victims love sympathy. Don't give it to them.

With a few conscious breaths, reminding myself that "all things pass" and that this event is a deleted e-mail, not a heart attack or life prison sentence, I regained some balance.

It's easy and quite natural to slip into victim mode when unpleasant life events occur. But that serves nothing and no one. That is the path the ostrich takes when it sticks its head in the sand to avoid seeing reality.

When unpleasant events occur, I try to acknowledge the event and allow a few minutes for frustration and emotional release. Then, I apply what I just shared and remind myself that these unpleasant feelings and sensations will shortly dissolve and pass. In effect, I shift to witness mode and observe. Shortly, I'm able to focus on the solution rather than the problem and move forward.

THE PERSONALITY/EGO AND THE SOUL

Journal Entry - Mallorca, Spain - November 2019

Teacher shared in session this morning, "Johnny, you have a kind heart and a huge desire to help. However, yesterday when I fried my electrical power plug adaptor, your offer to fix it came from your personality (ego) not your soul.

"Please note the difference. When offering to help, it is very important to ask yourself, 'where is this desire to help coming from?' Is it from the personality or the soul? As you offer to help, check the source, and ensure that there is no desire for a specific outcome and no desire that your efforts be acknowledged, i.e., that you are not seeking recognition. If it is coming from the personality, you will be attached to the outcome. You will feel disappointment if your efforts are unsuccessful, or if your efforts are not acknowledged with a thank you or more. It's an 'I'll scratch your back if you'll scratch mine' situation as I'll fix it, then you tell me how much you appreciate my efforts and how well I fixed it. This scenario is always energy depleting and leads to disappointment.

"You are good at fixing things and have a genuine desire to help. But you also have a desire to be recognized and rewarded for your efforts. This is the ego expressing itself and the personality wanting to feel important. Your personality desires recognition about how good Johnny MedicineBear fixes things. But this positive recognition of Johnny MedicineBear the pilot, the engineer, the fix-it-guy, the this-and-the-that guy is always fleeting, shallow, and non-sustainable. It rapidly fades.

"The less your mind identifies with your personality and the more your mind identifies with your soul, the less Johnny MedicineBear desires recognition. As one sustains this practice of identifying oneself with the soul, one expands more into the ever-present now.

"With this experience, you have gained some awareness and progressed. Your source point has shifted a bit from the personality toward the soul.

"You've a desire that I be pleasant to you and recognize your efforts and talents. Yesterday, you repaired my electrical power plug adaptor, and I simply took the adaptor from you and walked away. You were deeply disturbed that I didn't even say 'thank you.' Can you see how having desire for a positive response from me creates in you a let-down when I don't provide that positive response? Can you see how not having any desire of a positive response from me is freeing? Can you see that you and you alone are the source of your disappointment and anger, not me? Because I didn't respond how you wanted me to respond, you were disturbed.

"This is the normal scenario when helping from the personality through the egoic mind and most spend their lives here hoping that the world will respond positively to their heart-felt efforts. They feel disappointment when a thank-you is not received. Most stay on this merry-go-round their entire lives out of ignorance, blaming others for their own self-generated misery. They are unaware that they, not the other party, is responsible for their suffering. And their merry-go-round continues round and round.

"When an offer to help is sourced from the soul through an open mind, it is sincere and free of attachments. It is clean and pure. You simply desire to help without any ego stroking, and when complete, you are complete. No matter what the other party does or doesn't do, no matter if they thank you or don't thank you, you remain unaffected. The soul does not seek approval or recognition."

I thanked Teacher for her insights and clarity and settled into a quiet space to allow this awareness to integrate. I'm now aware how I've helped mostly from the personality through my egoic mind and expecting recognition for my efforts for a very long time. Helping from the soul is being of true service. Helping from the personality is engaging in an ego game.

When you next help someone, or volunteer your services, observe where your offers are arising from and consciously begin shifting your source point from the personality toward the soul. Tell yourself that you are doing this deed or performing this service solely for the act itself, not for any recognition. Do this from witness mode and remain detached. Progress in this area is progress in all areas. There is no wasted effort on the spiritual journey.

Resistance to this practice is the ego once again exerting itself and fighting for its life, for the ego sees loss of control as loss of its own life.

WHO AM I

Who am I? Am I Johnny MedicineBear? Am I only this bag of bones? Or am I more? When I take my last breath, what will happen to me?

The physical body is animated by non-physical consciousness. When I take my last breath, my consciousness will detach from my physical body and Johnny MedicineBear will cease to exist as an aspect of "me." Johnny MedicineBear will be no more, and this bag of bones known as Johnny MedicineBear will return to the earth.

My consciousness, including my soul, however, will continue its never-ending journey. This happens to everybody. You cannot taste, touch, smell, hear, or see this higher consciousness through the physical senses, but it is there. It is the everlasting more fundamental expression of who I am.

I've caught a few glimpses here and there over time of my past lives and know that this life is only one of many. Others also have had glimpses of non-physical reality. Cherish these experiences as precious gifts.

So, if asked, 'Who are you, Johnny,' then 'I don't know,' is an honest answer, for I cannot see a lot of who I am while in physical form.

I've obtained a sense of freedom traveling the rocky road of the spiritual pilgrim and relate comfortably to cosmic laws. I believe everyone can relate directly to reality if they open their minds and not resist. Communication may be visual, verbal, dreams, or visions.

Spirit wants everyone to have the most productive and meaningful life possible. We are always supported on our earthwalk by our spiritual friends.

When you catch a little glimpse of reality, you'll know, and you'll smile from ear to ear. You will feel the freedom.

SUFFERING ON THE PILGRIMAGE

Journal Entry - Ireland - 1 November 2019

I'm at my wits end; the end of my rope. I've never felt so alone, dejected, rejected, depressed, lost, afraid, and desperate in my life. There is no place to run, hide, escape, or go for relief.

I finally went to bed in my hotel room last night at 1 am, cried till 2 am, got up and tried to write, couldn't, returned to bed, cried till 4 am, then fell into a restless sleep for a few hours. This morning, I showered, walked about the little Irish village, and cried during the walk. I felt childish and foolish, but I could not stop crying. Several times, I changed direction, or looked away from people to avoid them seeing me in such a miserable state. That's all I do it seems is cry. I am overwhelmed with deep feelings of grief, inadequacy, sadness, fear, and anger. I want to isolate and run away to some place where no one knows me. Visions and thoughts of my Vietnam experiences, low-self-worth, *I don't fit in anywhere, I'm not lovable, I'm a murderer*, are like raw festering sores eating away at my heart.

I had a dream last night during my fitful sleep. I was being nailed to a cross, like The Christ-crucified and left to die. In this dream, my father, my first wife Dee, and ME are nailing ME to a cross. Yes, ME nailing ME to my cross. I try to escape, but cannot. There I hang, screaming as the cross is pushed upright and firmly planted into the ground. ME nailing ME to my cross. This visual is now burned into my mind. Dreams contain powerful messages and gifts. Yet there I hang, miserable, suffering, alone, naked, and completely vulnerable for all to see, and I did it to myself.

I'm realizing that I, and I alone, am responsible for my pain and suffering. But change is possible and, hopefully, this is the way out. When I move beyond the suffering of my doing, I move beyond nailing myself to my cross. Perhaps, someday I'll show up in a future dream delivering flowers to myself.

Mentor Ronnie said some years ago that, "No one has ever done anything to you, Johnny, worse than what you've done to yourself." That was vividly shown to me in this disturbing dream.

Teacher either ignores me or finds fault with most things I do or say. I'm learning that I don't have to respond to everything she says or does, whether I agree with it or not. I'm learning to just sit and allow. If she says something that I disagree with, or know is inaccurate, I do not have to respond. I'm learning that "non-response" is an option in daily events. I'm learning that I don't have to be the expert about everything, even when I know that what she is saying is incorrect or inaccurate. I simply ask myself, *will it really matter or make a difference if I just let it go*? I'm learning to just sit and observe. I'm learning to keep my mouth shut and focus inward. I'm finding that acknowledging with a little bow and saying, "Thank you," is a polite and sufficient response to most encounters. I'm learning to not take life so personally. I'm practicing non-engagement by not responding when appropriate and side-stepping (getting out of the way) of some events.

The oil light in our rental car illuminated while Teacher was driving yesterday. I sat quietly next to her in the passenger seat and observed. Totally ignoring me, she pulled into a service station, got out, and asked the attendant about the oil light.

He poked around under the hood and said, "The oil level is low. Put some in and your oil light will go out." I know that oil lights in cars are about pressure not quantity, unless of course the oil quantity is so low that there is none to pump, hence, no pressure. While Teacher was talking with the mechanic, I checked the car manual which said that *if the oil light illuminates, oil pressure is insufficient for safe engine operation. Shut down the engine, investigate and repair before restarting the engine.*

She never asked my thoughts or wanted to know what the manual said. The service man put oil into our rental and without a word she slid behind the wheel and we drove away. I silently returned the manual to the glove box. The oil light remained illuminated, she ignored it, and we keep driving. I sat in the passenger seat and did not say one word during the entire event.

The oil light experience was incredibly painful for me. To know and to not say one word is what it takes to soften the ego. And my ego was screaming to tell her that, "I'm a guy and I've been under car hoods for about sixty years and I know all about cars and oil lights and I'm going to tell you all about cars and oil lights because I know all about cars and oil lights and you obviously know nothing about cars and oil lights and I'm right and you're wrong, so there, blah, blah, blah." Those were my thoughts and what "Engineer Johnny" wanted to say. On the 3-D physical plane, there is truth here and I am right and she is wrong.

But I am on a spiritual pilgrimage attempting to engage reality from a soul perspective NO MATTER WHAT. Keeping my mouth shut was agonizing. My ego was screaming for me to show her the manual, tell her what needed to be done, and if she resisted, politely tell her to sit down and shut up or get out of the car and walk home. I wanted to choke her. To not say one word was beyond agony. But I did it, and somehow the rental car kept running with the oil light illuminated for several more days till we returned it and simply mentioned that the oil light was on. What a powerful lesson Teacher presented for me.

Later, I did some writing on the anger and rage I was feeling toward Teacher as I continue to feel like I want to die and end my misery. I cannot seem to get out of this miserable place.

But I'm feeling that my ego is losing its grip. I know that all my current pain and suffering is the acting-out of my personality making me miserable and beckoning me to find immediate short-term relief by returning to my old ways, control ways, my-way-or-the-highway ways, totally 3-D ways. That's what this pain and suffering is really about.

But if I give in to my ego, I'll return to my contracted 3-D world with all my fears, anger, and control issues. And perhaps at some future time, I'll begin again to walk through this same fire that I'm in right now. I realized also that this work is essential for me to authentically write *From Savage to Shaman*. Giving in to my ego meant also giving up this project. That was not even an option. So, I suffered onward.

The next morning, I met Teacher at 11 am at the car. "How was your night, Johnny?"

"I cried all night." We drove off in silence, and I cried again for several hours until we arrived at our new hotel in another little village in Ireland at 3 pm. I hate feeling this way. The desire to scream, "THE HELL WITH IT ALL," is overwhelming, yet I persevere and stay in the pain.

"You do not have to identify with Little Johnny anymore if you surrender," Teacher said. "Just let that story of you as Little Johnny go. You will remember all about Little Johnny, but you won't be triggered by the thoughts and feelings of inadequacy and fear. Just surrender; stop resisting; let go." Easy to say, challenging to accomplish.

We drove off, and I felt the tears welling up in me and begin crying softly once more. Soon, I was having a full-blown meltdown. I visualized Dutch's kitchen, the cutlery drawer, opening the drawer, reaching in, grabbing the big knife, and plunging it into my stomach, and twisting it around to ensure that my guts were destroyed. I felt my stomach contract and doubled over in pain. I died, again. After some time, my sobbing subsided. I extracted the knife, saw the wound heal and relaxed. Exhausted, I slumped in the passenger seat.

It is 10:30 pm and I can't sleep. I read about prana and pranayama from a yoga book and deluded myself into believing that I would begin a breathing practice in the morning.

This suffering I am experiencing is necessary. Aside from our meditations and group sessions, Teacher has assumed my father's personality. It's her way or the highway. She is authoritative, arrogant, disrespectful, and disregards my voice, suggestions, or contributions. We don't dialog or discuss things. It is incredibly frustrating to be with her just like it was with Dad.

But underlying these behaviors, she is providing a support system for me to experience this pain and suffering within her safety net. She is protecting me from falling into the bottomless pit of remorse, despair, and suicidal depression. Without her presence, this healing would not occur. Please remember that doing this level of work alone is dangerous and potentially suicidal.

Note from June 2021: In November 2019, when I wrote this journal entry, I did not and could not appreciate what I now know of Teacher's role in my growth and transformation. But today, I do. Teacher supported me, guided me, and allowed for these deep dark energy patterns to play out and clear. The mantra of not giving in to the ego continues.

I shout, "I will not live like this. I will not give into fear, false thoughts, old patterns, and ego. DAD HAS PASSED AND FORMER WIFE DEE IS NOT IN MY LIFE, and I will not carry them with me anymore. They are history. Refocus, stay the course, and remember that I am a "divine being of light, in service to all beings." Stay in presence, Johnny, with no regrets of the past and no fear of the future.

THE CLOAKROOM

Journal Entry - November 2019

A few days after the oil light experience, I had the following dream. I saw myself wearing five different suits of clothes representing five different personas or personalities from different times in my life. These five suits of clothes were hanging on hooks in my familiar grade school cloakroom.

The first was "Little Johnny" wearing casual school clothes. He was my kindergarten-through-high-school persona. The second was "Young Adult John" wearing casual college clothes (including my fraternity letters emblazoned on my Rutgers's University sweater). He was my late-teens-and-early-twenties-college-John persona. The third was "Fighter Pilot JC" wearing his Air Force flight suit (complete with fighter pilot sunglasses and flight cap tilted just the right way to look cool). He was my live-fast-drink-hard-fighter-pilot-in-the-Air-Force persona. The fourth was "American Airlines Captain JC" wearing my American Airlines captain's uniform. He was the sober-AA-captain-full-of-gratitude persona. And the fifth was "Johnny MedicineBear" wearing casual clothes and sporting large, bear-claw and turquoise Native American jewelry. He was the retired-laid-back-open-to-life-adventures persona. My personality assumes one of these five personas as I go about my daily business.

Over time, I've tossed a lot of pieces of me into a big black bag that I've dragged along with me. We all do this. Unresolved fears, angers, resentments, disappointments, and uncertainties are in that bag. Also, there are many gifts that I've also tossed in there as well. My creativity, artistic talents, writing abilities, sense of self, and others. My bag grew quite full and dragging it around required much effort. Poet and author Robert Bly offered this visual of the "shadow bag we drag behind us" in his excellent composition *A Little Book About the Human Shadow*. My work on this spiritual pilgrimage is to clean out my bag, processing the undesirable and embracing the gifts.

Mom told me as a boy that, "Some men process their feelings, Johnny, and some men stuff their feelings. Your father is a stuffer." I took to heart my mother's words and assumed that I was a stuffer as well. Dad was my boyhood hero, and he seemed OK to me. I therefore felt fortunate that I was also born a stuffer and felt no need to alter that.

And that was the end of it until I was in my early fifties. As I grew older, my bag became larger and fuller and the weight increased. I simply smiled more and exerted a bit more effort, dragging my bag with me. I didn't even know that I was dragging a bag behind me.

To survive and "enjoy life," I created a superficial world filled with addictions and sensory pleasures to keep my attention away from my big black shadow bag. Alcohol, parties, fast airplanes, sports cars, and rock 'n roll provided one thrill after another, followed always by a hangover or a letdown. The never-ending roller coaster went up and down, round and round, endlessly. Feeling unworthy, I also refused to explore my creative gifts as well. Most of me, it seemed, was in that bag.

This morning, during our meditation, something marvelous and significant occurred. I experienced some separation between my soul and my personality. I saw my five personas hanging on hooks as suits of clothes in my grade-school cloakroom. I also saw my soul as shimmering blue-white light, also in the cloakroom, visually observing the five suits of clothes hanging on hooks. I observed it all from detached witness mode.

Merging with the shimmering light, I stepped out of the cloakroom without putting on one of the suits. My soul has no personality. There they were, all five suits hanging in the cloakroom, and ME, shimmering blue-white light. No personality desired, and no personality required. I was free, engaging life from the no personality soul.

Later, in the kitchen, I poured some tea and habitually reached for the honey to sweeten my drink. I stopped in mid-stride and asked, *where is this desire for honey coming from?* Immediately, the old habit pattern of using honey to sweeten my tea surfaced, and I just observed my desire for sweetness and allowed it to fade. This is a habitual old-habit pattern I thought, as I always put honey in tea. But today, I prepared my tea without honey. There was no argument, no sense of disappointment, or feelings of *I must have honey in my tea or it won't taste good*. There was no attachment to the honey, and perhaps I'll experience a new taste sensation.

Perhaps this sounds trivial, but it is huge and it metaphorically illustrates engaging life from the ever present now or soul. No past behaviors and preferences were present to interfere with this "now" moment.

My five suits are still hanging in the closet and I may wear any of them whenever I desire. I simply slip on a suit and engage the world from that persona. It is only when I wear a suit without acknowledging the underlying soul, that I identify the persona as "ME." I know through experience that there are deeper and more fundamental components of "ME" than my five suits of clothes. I can now put on my Little Johnny suit, and go out and play feeling alive with child-like wonder, love, and joy without being triggered into anger and/or fear. Presence is very pleasant and freeing.

It's now 8 pm and Teacher and I went for food about 3:30ish to a little café, then drove on to visit a sacred spiritual site. On the way, I tried unsuccessfully to book a hotel on my smart-phone as the car was moving about. I asked her to pull over so I could more easily use the phone keypad. She said, "Give it another try, you can do it, Johnny." I felt no resistance to her suggestion and simply tried again, and it worked. My response to this event differed from my response to the oil light experience of yesterday. Perhaps I've surrendered a bit more. Perhaps I've released a bit more of the shadow baggage. Anything done in presence is easy for it's done without resistance, and without ego. Much more may be accomplished when one surrenders to presence.

On our way home, Teacher drove twisty hilly Irish back country two-lane roads in dark, rainy weather on the unfamiliar left side of the road using only two speeds, way-too-fast and stop. Also, she drove the entire way on low beams, so forward illumination was significantly reduced. It was dangerous, yet somehow, I felt no anxiety. I did not utter one word. I simply sat there and observed and we arrived back at our hotel unscathed.

RESISTING

Why do I resist something that is a bit uncomfortable to do when I know that it is in my best interest to do it? I resist change, I suppose, because change brings in unknowns and I'm never as comfortable in the unknown as I am in the known.

When I acquire something, I tend to keep it for a long time. I wear clothes till they are in rags, it seems. Worn clothes are familiar and comfortable. So, it was with motorcycle Harley. I purchased him new in September 2005, and rode him 180,000 miles in seventeen years. During that time, I had no car. It's unusual to ride that many years and do it on the same bike. I also take care of my belongings as they are family to me. Family and familiar share the same Latin root word "familia."

But sometimes, change is necessary. Occasionally, I resist change with a lame excuse like, "My current experience is just fine," or "It doesn't get any better than this." But I don't really know if the new is better, or the old is better till I try them both. Sometimes, I'm lazy and just settle for the status quo.

From experience, I've learned that I must get uncomfortable to grow. With every breath, I have choice to live from my personality (ego) or from my soul. The personality desires and guides me toward short-term pleasures while the soul is focused on long-term growth and spiritual expansion. If my personality had its way, and I had an unlimited budget, I'd live 24/7 in luxury and excess. My home would be a pleasure palace with every desire and fantasy fulfilled. But I've lit the flame of growth and have a strong desire to "wake-up" to a more meaningful life. I want to live more consciously, perhaps a bit closer to the bone.

I've remained totally 100% vegetarian and mostly vegan since June 2019, with little resistance from my personality. I know the taste of T-bones and lobsters in butter. But I passed through some invisible barrier and thoughts of consuming these foods have faded significantly. Today, the desire for these foods is minimal.

It would be a huge compromise to consume animal meat. Like abstinence from alcohol, non-consumption of animals is important to me. I don't think about it much anymore, I just do it.

I live this way so I don't participate in the senseless destruction of my earthling brothers and sisters. Secondary are the obvious health benefits of a totally plant-based diet. Validation and support of this are widespread on the internet.

From years past, the concept of "if one is good, two is twice as good, and four is twice as good as that," stops by and says hello occasionally. I know that this is false information, however. I sometimes finish a meal and immediately reach for a "few extra bites." I'm familiar with this behavior and have done it since childhood. Yet, I still resist changing this obviously detrimental behavior.

I remember doing the same with cigarettes while I was smoking in my early twenties. I'd awake on a Sunday morning, coughing up a storm from Saturday night's party, light up and take a few deep drags to "get my lungs going again." Then I'd laugh and joke about it. I did the same with alcohol and recall being totally blitzed and reaching for another drink. I'd then brush aside this obvious insanity with a smile and a laugh. I recognize this same pattern today with food.

The ego resists positive change with lies, tricks, and deceptions of all sorts. This resistance invites me to muster greater effort to change. The more effort I exert, the more my ego resists, for the ego believes it is fighting for its life. It takes a lot of energy and effort to loosen the ego sufficiently for it to give-in, give-up, and dissolve. If change was easy, everyone would do it and we'd have an addiction-free, loving, nurturing, compassionate world community. I'm not holding my breath for that.

With every extra bite I eat after I push away from the table, I experience a little hangover and within a few minutes will say, "I wish I hadn't done that." There must be pain for there to be gain.

"Johnny, you don't have to put up with even a little bit of discomfort," whispers my ego. "Have a little snack to ease this little bit of discomfort. You can start tomorrow on your program of this or that." Start tomorrow! I know what that's all about, Mr. Ego! Tomorrow never gets here, so starting never gets here, either.

I always feel better, more alive, more awake, and more authentic when I make choices in alignment with my soul than choices in alignment with my personality. Just little things are all it takes.

Perhaps I want a little snack to ease the growl in my gut at 3 pm. A few bites of apple or a glass of water would suffice, but my ego says, 'Put some peanut butter on the apple, Johnny, you'll enjoy it more.' And, many times, I mindlessly cave in and say, "OK what the hell, it won't matter too much, it's just a little peanut butter on the apple slice." Ten minutes later, I've consumed the entire apple and two or three tablespoons of peanut butter and there I am licking the spoon and feeling compromised. *What the hell did I do that for? You know better than that, Johnny!* Now I've opened the door for self-degradation, self-judgement, and other negative emotions and feelings to flood in. Just one little event is all it takes. A few tablespoons of peanut butter invites a flood of self-judgement and negative self-criticism.

Teacher often said, "When choosing what to do, Johnny, ask yourself, is this choice in my best interest? Is this choice coming from my personality or my soul?"

Am I running toward life or running away from it? I'm doing one or the other as it's impossible to straddle the fence for very long.

When I move toward life, I move toward my soul. I engage life with responsibility, compassion, authenticity, and love. These are attributes of the soul. I cannot realize these attributes while engaged in addictive activities. Am I in for the ego "me" or in for the soul's "I am." Moving toward the soul and making choices from the soul raises my vibration. I become more, and I experience soul-wisdom. I move up a few steps in the Building-of-Life.

This work, it seems, is not just mine or yours, but everyone's. When the dust settles on my earthwalk and I take my final breath, it will not matter how much money I've made, how many toys I've acquired, how many parties I've gone to, how much booze I've drunk, or how many diplomas I have hanging on the wall. It only matters where my soul is.

If one spends their life lying and cheating, it may not be pleasant when they awaken in the next chapter of their never-ending story. The quality of one's next experience depends on how one has lived this experience. Most religions seem to foster that concept. Raising one's vibration through acts of kindness and compassion is everything. Nothing else really matters.

I cut myself slack sometimes and consciously enjoy whatever I want to enjoy. I honor my humanness and occasionally indulge in sensory pleasures.

How did I feel physically, emotionally, and spiritually thirty, twenty, ten, five, or two years ago? I look for gradual, yet significant, positive changes and keep walking the path of the spiritual pilgrim.

It is also extremely important to not degrade or diminish myself. Resistance is a measure of my unwillingness to change, take a risk, upset the status quo, or live in presence. Dissolve the ego and resistance also dissolves. This clears the path toward freedom and joy.

THE MASTER - TEACHER'S ROLE

I read this book and it helped me understand the Master-Teacher's role in relationship with a student. Perhaps you will find it helpful also.
On the Road to Freedom, A Pilgrimage in India, Vol 2, by Swami Paramatmananda.

As we sat around Amma (an enlightened master) later that evening, as if intuiting what were my thoughts of the day's activities and her strange ways, she said, Surrender isn't something that can be forced by the Master. Surrender happens naturally within the disciple. There is a change in his attitude, in his understanding, and in the way he does things. A change takes place in the inner world; the whole focus of life changes. A true Master, however, will never force the disciple to surrender. To force in any way would be harmful, like the injury done to a flower bud, if you were to forcefully open its petals. Such force would destroy the flower. Opening up is something that happens spontaneously, provided the conducive circumstances are created.

The Master creates the necessary situations for this opening up to happen. In reality, a true Master is not a person; he is not the body, for he has no ego. His body is just an instrument that he carries around, so that he can be in this world for the benefit of the people.

Two persons can force ideas on each other, because they are identified with their egos. But a Satguru (Master), who is an embodiment of the Supreme

Consciousness, cannot force anything on anyone, because he is beyond body-consciousness and the mind. The Master is like open space or the boundless sky. He simply exists.

If someone tries to force their rules or ideas on you, you should know that he is a false teacher, even if he claims to be a self-realized Master. A true Master makes no claims about anything. He is simply there. He doesn't care whether you surrender to him or not. If you surrender, you will benefit; if you don't surrender, you will remain the same. In either case, the Master is untouched.

He doesn't worry about anything. In the mere presence of a Master, opening up just happens naturally. The Master does nothing in particular for this to happen. He is the only one who can train you without teaching you directly. His very presence automatically creates a constant wave of situations, wherein you can experience the Supreme Reality in all its fullness. But there is no force involved, nor does he make any claims.

Surrender will develop within you from the tremendous inspiration you receive through the Master's physical presence, for the Master is the embodiment of all divine qualities. In the Master, you observe true surrender and acceptance, and thus you are given a real example that you can relate to.

This should answer all questions that might have sprung up in the reader's mind. Why does a real Guru sometimes act in an unreasonable, contradictory, or even crazy way? It is only to give the disciples the chance to surrender their minds and receive Divine Knowledge. As long as the individual mind exists, the disciple cannot attain wisdom. The disciple who wants to maintain his or her individuality cannot, at the same time merge into the Universal Mind. Surrender and obedience are necessary.

Meditation, study, and other spiritual disciplines are easy when compared to the practice of surrendering to the Guru. Please remember that this is not one person surrendering to another. Any Guru who truly deserves the title has attained unity with the Transcendent Reality. He has merged his individuality in the Universal Existence and has become an instrument of that. Surrendering to him amounts to surrendering to God, merging in God, and becoming one with Him. Amma's strange actions and words must be seen in this light. The Master, taught sometimes with strange and indirect ways and sometimes right in my face ways. In either case, the responsibility for growth is always mine.

. . .

Author's Note: This book helped me to understand why Teacher was sometimes abrupt, disrespectful, impatient, and "in my face." She repeatedly said, "This is not me, Johnny, it is Spirit working through me." It took quite a while to realize this but it helped me to get out of my ego and not resist her.

THE WOUNDED MASCULINE

"What is destroying our planet, Johnny," Teacher asked? There are many answers to this question I thought, and at some level, I suppose, many are true. It is a very broad question. However, she was guiding me to look at what energy, what aspect of consciousness is primarily responsible for human's obvious disregard for the health of our planet. "It is the wounded-masculine, Johnny, that is alive and active in many mature men and woman today that is destroying our home."

The wounded-masculine aspect of consciousness forms within the personality of the wounded child. A baby is born a radiant bundle of love and divinity. But from conscious and unconscious words and actions of parents and others, the child absorbs wounds and the wounded-masculine aspect of consciousness forms.

Masculine consciousness is about protection, and provision. It has a sense of primitiveness and is fundamental to the survival of the family unit. Feminine consciousness is about love and compassion and nurtures the family unit. When formed, the wounded-masculine aspect of consciousness distorts the energies of protection and provision and projects them outward as destructive thoughts, words, and actions.

Both male and female beings embrace both masculine and feminine aspects of consciousness. They are not gender specific.

Most humans on our planet today are wounded, many severely. A wounded being receives its guidance from the ego-personality, while the unwounded or divine-being receives its guidance from the soul.

As a young child matures and absorbs wounds from parents, teachers, and others in authority, the connection to their soul weakens. They become lost, fearful, and uncertain. They begin to shift their source connection away from the soul and seek guidance and gratification from the personality. As they shift their focus away from the soul, the ego strengthens. They seek short term sensory pleasures and engage in shallow personality-gratifying activities. Denial systems support these actions. They believe that they are living in truth and integrity, and see themselves in that light. Their reality becomes distorted and they become delusional.

The wounded being sees themself as separate and apart from other humans and all of nature. Their reality becomes self-centered, uncaring, narcissistic, and contracted. They slide into a protective mode and begin to build walls between themselves and the outer world. The degree of this separation is proportional to the severity of their wounds. They live this way to survive and retain a sense of self. They believe they are in control of their life.

These beings are oblivious to the detrimental effects their negative words and actions have on others. This delusional perspective is supported by ever strengthening denial systems. Inappropriate and destructive behaviors continue and increase. It matters not that others are hurt or injured. They rationalize away their dishonest, manipulative, and injurious actions with thoughts like, *they had it coming to them*, or *they got what they deserved*, or *you should see what they did to me*.

Believing that others are wrong and that the world is out to get them, the severely wounded-masculine pushes against everyone that disagrees with them and treats them as enemies. They believe that they are always right and that others are always wrong. There is no discussion nor compromise with this person.

They believe that animals and plants have no rights and see all of nature as lesser than themselves and a commodity to be exploited. They believe that there are no consequences for their words and deeds. Their perspective is short-term and self-serving, and their strong denial systems render them unaccountable.

Irrefutable proof contrary to their thinking, beliefs, and actions has no effect on the severely wounded-masculine being. Those that try to reason with them are part of a ploy to take them down. They are never wrong. This person is unconscious.

Such a person has lost their soul connection, lost their source of love, and lost their way. Having no compassion, they use and abuse animals and plants, pollute the environment, and are inappropriate, disrespectful, and degrading to their human brothers and sisters. They are unpredictable, unreliable, and dishonest. They will join the military and fight for causes that they know little or nothing about. Feigning friendship and affection, they live shallowly and nervously, expecting the other shoe to fall shortly. Such a person is not disturbed by humans' wanton destruction of forests or the extinction of animal species.

To an awake being however, such destructive events are unconscionable. To an awake being, everything is alive, everything has consciousness, and everything is a sacred thread woven into the tapestry of reality. An awake being is strongly connected to their soul and embraces the aspects of the divine-masculine.

How does one change? How does one become conscious? How does one replace destructive behaviors with loving caring behaviors? This is a whole life's work. If you feel uncomfortable reading this chapter, it is probably resonating with your wounded-masculine. If you embrace some of these suggestions and don't put this book down and run away, you've begun your journey out of the destructive darkness and into the light. Awareness is the genesis of the journey.

As you shift your energy and actions toward compassion, caring, and love, you source more from your soul and less from your personality. You engage life at a deeper, more fundamental level. You are discovering who you really are.

Take ownership of yourself one small piece at a time. Refuse to participate in destructive and dishonest activities. Walk your path slowly and consciously. Note deeply what activities attract you and what you cherish as sacred. Be firm and assertive, without aggression or arrogance, and question everything especially what you already believe as true. Listen more to the soft gentle voice of your inner-self and less to the voices of the outer world. Above all, be gentle with yourself as you journey inward.

It takes great courage to break through the steel armor plating encasing a severely wounded-masculine being but it is possible. Twelve-step programs all speak of letting go of the personality and allowing divinity to shine through.

As you heal yourself and your destructive behaviors drop away, you will become more loving and compassionate toward friends and family that are close to you. This breaks the chain and you will not pass on to your children the destructive behaviors that were passed on to you. You are now contributing to the health and well-being of all. You're now part of the solution, not part of the problem.

WHY WE FIGHT WARS AND THE WAY OUT

Humans have engaged in horrific wars for a very long time and continue to do so. Why haven't we learned from these horrors and stopped this insanity? There is an answer, for there is reason and rationale for everything that occurs, including wars. And, everyone may contribute to the cessation of war by refusing to participate. Become the embodiment of peace.

Trying to understand and stop war with a mind trapped on the physical planes is impossible, as that mind is of the same consciousness as the mind that supports war. One's awareness must rise above "war consciousness" to appreciate why humans create and fight wars. Once that occurs, one may focus on creating peace.

On the lower/physical planes of consciousness, the personality rules and fights for survival and control. Conflict is the norm in our chaotic world today with examples everywhere. It's this person versus that person, this group versus that group, or this country versus that country.

Wars are fought by men and woman willing to follow, obey, and die for causes, countries, and tyrants. They are recruited with baseless promises of self-righteous glory. And if that doesn't draw them in, then threats follow with unpleasant consequences for non-participation.

Rewards of rank, participation medals, and privileges are given for obedience and compliance.

People deeply conditioned, cannot see outside their box or make decisions guided by their inner consciousness. They live in duality, an "us or them" reality. These individuals are easily recruited by slick people promoting lies, half-truths, and shallow promises. They trust, are obedient to, and give their personal power to causes and tyrants they know little or nothing about. They love to belong to groups with a cause, for it gives them purpose and they feel important. They surround themselves with like-minded people and do not have to think on their own. Eventually, they become unable to decide for themselves and believe with all their heart that they have no choice other than to follow a cause, country, or tyrant. They are absolutely convinced that they are doing the right thing. These people lack self-worth and mindlessly follow the masses.

Tyrants are everywhere in our world today. Egos are fighting egos on the individual level, community level, corporate level, and national level. But a tyrant only has as much power as their followers give them. With no followers, there is no supporting power, and the tyrant dissolves.

A tyrant is a recalcitrant child, who's super-inflated ego will do anything to increase his or her power base. Tyrants are savages and have no conscience.

Some disempowered people see tyrants as heroes and believe them without question. These people do not recognize who the tyrant is and establish denial systems that prevent them from seeing reality and truth. These people support tyrants for their own behavior patterns are similar to the tyrants. They live in a delusional world. Common sense, logic, and the obvious, will not deter them from following their "heroes." To see the tyrant for who the tyrant truly is, requires one to see oneself for who one truly is. These people are trapped.

So how do we end wars? We refuse to participate. We refuse to follow tyrants and shallow causes. We think for ourselves and make decisions using logic, common sense, the obvious, and our own sense of discernment. But this requires insight, strength, courage, and a willingness to do one's inner work. Denial systems supporting a delusional reality must be released. The Building-of-Life metaphor, found elsewhere in this book, points to the escape route. Simply put, one must raise their consciousness to a level higher than the level of consciousness that supports war.

How does one rise? They do their inner work. One must find the stairway and climb, for one's salvation and freedom lies at higher levels of consciousness. Refuse to blindly follow. Just because everyone else in your family or community is following, doesn't mean you must follow as well. Use your intuition, check in with your soul, and follow your inner guidance. Don't be enticed by slick salesmen with promises wrapped in glitter and gold just because "everyone else is doing it." It's always easier to follow the crowd than to stand alone. Most cave in and fall into this trap. By walking your own path, you will meet disapproval, anger, resentment, and perhaps even violence from your community. But you will be following your heart, not your ego. This is true self-love.

Tyrants do not want individuals to question, think for themselves, or act from their own intuition. They want people to blindly follow them without question. Become the spiritual warrior and rise above the masses. Become a seeker of truth. Transform yourself, elevate your consciousness, and your actions and behaviors will follow. Your higher consciousness, like a beacon, will be the guiding light for others to follow. The only way out is up.

Wars will cease when there is no longer a need for war.

PUSHING MY BUTTON

While traveling with Teacher in her van yesterday, I asked her to stop at a convenience store so that I could purchase a few small items. She curtly refused, and I sat stunned, frozen in silent anger.

I was deeply disturbed by her refusal and later, after checking into our hotel, I went for a long walk. Returning, I slipped into bed disturbed and could not sleep. Every hour I was up, pacing around, disturbed by her actions. I could not understand why Teacher would not honor my simple request to stop at the convenience store. It made no sense to me. "I'm getting a no on this, I'm getting a no on that," were her simplistic and final responses to my repeated requests.

Anger has its roots in the personality, not the soul. When my request was not granted, I got angry. I didn't pound the table or become explosive, I just experienced anger as tightening of muscles, seething, and wanting to smack her for being so inconsiderate. I internalize anger rather than releasing it outwardly. And, I cannot simply turn this anger response off. To get past it, I must own it, diffuse it, and rise above it.

About 4:00 am, having not slept a wink, I had my little speech all ready to let her have it in the morning about how inconsiderate she was and why couldn't she just honor this simple request? Why couldn't she just be reasonable? I was going to straighten her out when the light bulb came on. She was pushing my button to provoke my anger response. She was my father, my ex-wife Dee, and "Monster Boy" pushing my button. I realized that there will always be someone pushing, or attempting to push, my button.

The solution is to disconnect or remove the button. I sat quietly with these thoughts and realized that if I don't "knee jerk" react when someone jams a finger on my button, but accept whatever comes my way with an open mind and loving heart, my life will be easier and much more pleasant. I will be in alignment with my higher self and I won't be triggered emotionally and experience pain and suffering. Johnny MedicineBear, the personality wants life to unfold his way, while the soul only knows acceptance and love. It is my choice to engage life from the personality or the soul. Experiencing the pain of yesterday and continuing through my sleepless night loosened Johnny a bit and allowed some ego to release. I now have other choices available.

My pain and suffering are of my own making and come from a bruised ego. I went right to sleep after this. This was a powerful lesson.

THE MAN IN THE MIRROR

My perception of how the world is treating me is the direct result of how I am treating myself.

When I feel that the world is out to get me and everything is going wrong, I become hostile. Denial of truth creates in my mind a hostile outer world and I direct my anger, rage, or worse, at the world that is hostile toward me. However, the outer world that I experience IS my inner world projected outward.

Denial and ignorance prevent me from seeing truth. What I experience "out there" is a projection of my inner condition. The more disturbed I am, the harder I push, and the harder I push, the more disturbed I become. I create a vicious downward spiral.

But no matter how hard I pushed outward, Teacher stood fast and held a mirror in front of me so that I could see the true source of my chaos, pain, and suffering.

I saw my face in the mirror, and rather than pushing the mirror away and hating the man in the mirror (me) I learned to embrace the man in the mirror. By doing the work, I'm wiping my mirror clean and seeing the truth of reality and the truth of who I am. Loving the man in the mirror is my path toward freedom.

THE MAN IN THE MIRROR

The man in the mirror is frightening to me,
Stares back with eyes full of hatred and fear.
I hold my gaze on this stranger I see,
Yet I've known him for many a year.

Am compelled to stay gazing at sunken eyes,
Feeling much turmoil within.
He stares right through me, sees through my lies,
Confused, my mind starts to spin.

I try to leave with feet glued to the floor,
Can't lift them, they weigh a ton.
Heart starts to race I want to run out the door,
The man in the mirror's not fun.

Feeling strange movements deep down inside,
Hatred and rage slowly soften.
Behind his dark gaze is love ossified,
His face reflects sadness most often.

"It's not me that's cloudy," says mirror-man,
"The mirror is what needs cleaning.
I'm reflecting truth back to you,
Now polish your mirror to shining."

Ego creates dirt to disguise truth,
Reality is hidden from view.
Clean the mirror, have faith, beyond logical proof,
Is work I'm committed to do.

Ego dissolving as I wipe away dirt,
Reality begins to reveal.
With no place to hide, the ego soon dies,
Revealing the "me" that is real.

Deceptions, lies, fears and untruths,
My mirror is wiped clean of debris.
Love, compassion, integrity, truth,
Shines the man in the mirror as me.

jmb

Here is an exercise for cleaning your mirror.

Sit in front of a mirror and look deeply at yourself. Sit silently without expectation and without judgement. Be loving, not critical, and accept yourself as you see yourself in the mirror. Say your name three times and note how you present yourself to the world. This is how others see you.

Begin now to look through your physical body at your deeper more fundamental self (your soul). See the true expression of who you are. Look deeply into your eyes until you find your center of compassion and love. Notice how you feel when you honor your deeper self. Repeat the following mantra three times: "I am (name), a beautiful being of light and love. I am an extension of divinity and am of service to myself and all beings." Do this for ten minutes every day for three consecutive days.

After one month, repeat the exercise again for three consecutive days, noting the differences from the previous experience. This exercise will clean your mirror, strengthen your ties with divinity, and help merge your personality with your soul.

QUICK TO DEFEND

Teacher pointed out that I am quick to defend some of my behaviors and she is right. Yesterday at a restaurant, I was gazing deeply at her while she was engaged with her meal. She glanced up and saw me staring at her and asked, "Why are you staring at me?"

"I'm not staring at you," I said, but I was. I felt like a child caught with my hand in a cookie jar. I lied to protect myself. I lied to Teacher just like I lied to Dad as a child to protect myself from him. I learned to lie as a child for self-preservation whenever I felt threatened. Teacher is not my father, but I projected my fear of Dad on her and lied.

It takes effort and commitment to break old habit patterns that no longer serve. This pattern that I'm still carrying with me today at age seventy-five had its genesis in me at age five. Now that I'm aware of my response, I can do some work around it and release it.

When my attack dogs want to jump out and protect me, I'll pause, tell them to go back home, and simply answer honestly. "I don't know," is a valid and truthful response to many questions.

SOLLER, MALLORCA, SPAIN

Our spiritual pilgrimage began three-and-a-half months ago in Ashland, Oregon and deposited us today in the town of Soller, on the isle of Mallorca, in the Mediterranean Sea off the coast of Spain. This culture is vertical, with traditions and roots extending back further than I can see. There is community everywhere. Family is deeply rooted here with parents, grandparents, and grandchildren interacting and playing together everywhere. I miss never experiencing safety with a nurturing and loving family. My childhood experiences seem shallow as I stand outside our 150-year-old hotel across the town square from the 700-year-old cathedral in the center of Soller.

Vertical means the culture is steeped in tradition and wisdom, honors and respects their elders, and considers the effects of their current actions and behaviors on future generations. It is also where families live in the same house for hundreds of years and are not threatened by corporate interests. Farms are sustained within a family also for hundreds of years and the dinner table is blessed every meal with locally grown food.

It is where several generations of families live harmoniously in the same home. It is where everyone interacts with everyone else and the children learn experientially from their grandparents who take their last breath in their own beds surrounded by family. Many trace their roots seven or more generations back in the same village, perhaps even in the same house. They are rooted, like an old rock-solid oak tree.

Adjacent to the massive bronze front doors of Soller's cathedral, the little plaque reads, "The old part of this church was constructed in the 1300s with the new additions completed in the 1800s." The 1300s! That's more than a hundred years before Columbus and his crew arrived in the Bahamas. Nothing like this exists anywhere in the United States. Homes and buildings on Mallorca are constructed with quality materials to last for a very long time. "Vertical awareness" is an integral part of everything here. It differs greatly from the horizontal society that we've created and support in the USA, where fast-food prevails and long-term planning and the effects of current endeavors on future generations appears non-existent.

This morning in Soller, my camera invited me for a walk with intention of being a creative photographer, not a tourist taking pictures. I saw beauty in everything.

The village trolley runs through the center of the town square and has been in continuous service for about 120 years. Silently, it glided into the square, discharged and retrieved a few passengers, and silently moved on. Life flows effortlessly in this place. I imagine it unthinkable to even suggest replacing the trolley with a slightly more efficient bus system that would reduce costs. The street trolley IS Soller, and that's all there is to it. Rather than replacing the existing with something cheaper and more efficient, this culture seems content to continue using and improving the established.

There is character and consciousness everywhere here. If it's working, use it, enjoy it, and leave it alone. I love the warm feeling of being in a vertical society.

The locals tend to respect elders, traditions, established ways, and each other. No one appears threatened, and I saw not one homeless person on any street anywhere on Mallorca for the month that I was there.

I am more sensitive to the energies of divinity here and feel grounded and safe. I feel at home.

THE WATER-FAST

On the Isle of Mallorca, I was away from my comfortable and familiar Dutch and Harley surroundings. Being in this space with Teacher, there was no place to run and no place to hide. We each had our own bedrooms and mine included an adjoining bathroom. The old house provided a quiet space for writing and inner work.

Returning from a restaurant on a Friday evening a week after we arrived, I went to my room and retired for the evening. On Saturday morning, I felt guided to stay alone in my room over the weekend, behind closed doors, and not leave for any reason. I consumed no food and drank only the hi-quality tap water from the bathroom sink. I felt no resistance, so on Saturday morning, I texted Teacher and shared my intentions. She returned a supportive reply.

I had my iPhone, iPad, internet connection, and a portable keyboard. Guided to use this time to meditate, stay in silence, and continue writing this book, I fasted through the weekend consuming only water. It was easier than expected.

On Monday morning, I received spiritual guidance to extend the water-fast through Wednesday morning. Texting Teacher my intention to remain in my bedroom for two additional days, she responded again with a supportive reply.

Wednesday morning, Spirit encouraged me to stretch further and remain on this water-fast through Saturday morning. I thought of those that have survived horrific conditions without food and minimal water for several weeks. This wasn't even close to that. I knew that I could do this and that the pain and suffering, albeit minimal, would be beneficial. I texted Teacher my intentions and continued my fast through days five, six, and seven. On Saturday morning, after seven days and eight nights, I left my bedroom and joined Teacher for "break-fast" in the kitchen. I was supported, encouraged, and protected through the entire experience by Teacher. The following are my journal entries from the water-fast week.

Journal Entries - 8 - 16 November 2019

I awoke this morning on day one, Saturday, with no fear, no dread, no pain, and a lot of enthusiasm for this experience that is happening right now. I feel light-hearted, and eager. There is none of the "I can't wait till this is over" feelings that has darkened similar experiences in the past, like seven-day juice-cleanses which I've done several times before. I'm not counting down the days till it's over and I can eat again. I'm not fantasizing about food. I've historically looked forward to ending similar experiences, so that I can celebrate with sensory pleasures once again. But this is not just about cleansing the body, but about spiritual transformation. I hope to sustain whatever I take from this experience. My intention is to not simply hang an accomplishment plaque on the wall to enhance the personality of Johnny MedicineBear so he may enjoy his sensory pleasures a little bit more.

My soul is joyful and alive this morning, participating in this spiritual endeavor. I'm becoming very clear of the difference between the soul, (higher-self, transcendent-self), and the physical, (Johnny MedicineBear the personality, transient-self, ego-self). The soul is the everlasting component and the personality is the transient physical component.

I have no fear or anxiety and am not wishing I was doing something else. I know I'm moving forward by participating in this experience. I am alive. My gut gurgles a bit, but I don't feel massively hungry and I remain in witness mode. I am observing how I feel and observing the emotions that arise. I'm centered in my soul and observing this experience.

It's 11:45 am on day two, Sunday, of my water-fast. I've been in solitude since 8:00 pm Friday evening and have not left this room. I've consumed no food, and I mean nothing, no snacks, cough drops, supplements, or additives to the water such as tea-bags, or lemon drops. Nothing means nothing. I am challenging Johnny MedicineBear. I'm hungry this morning, but it's manageable.

From witness mode, I note that it is Johnny MedicineBear, the personality, not the soul that is hungry and the more detached I remain, the less I notice my hunger. It really helps to remove the personality from the equation. The hunger seems distant.

Last night, a beautiful woman came to me in a dream and enveloped me with her arms and held her body tightly to me. We merged into one and I felt her warm, sweet body and loving energy. I was filled with joy. It was very real.

Awakening, I calmed my heart and sensed that the dream was a bit more than a visual fantasy. Perhaps my Goddess energy, the energy of love and compassion, is shifting. Perhaps that piece of me, the Divine Feminine is working its way back home. Perhaps it is becoming safer for me to be around me. And perhaps it is becoming safer for others to be around me as well.

At 7:30 pm, I watched a webinar about conscious healing then sat and gently cried for several hours. It was not unpleasant and no specific reason surfaced. I just cried. Drained, I went to bed.

It's 10 am on day three, Monday, and I am not hungry this morning. Guidance last night before sleep said to "swim in the quiet and focus on meditations." Resistance to sitting still has been prevalent and the norm most of my life. Time for stillness, peace, and solitude, for that is where my gold lies hidden, waiting to be discovered.

It's 12:15 pm and I am experiencing deepening commitment to this water-fast. I meditated this morning for an hour and a half, and it went by very quickly. Sitting for that long is unusual for me and I was pleased.

I read about a man that did a forty-five-day water-fast. Apparently, he does these extended water-fasts rather frequently, and he claims that it is totally safe and healthy. He's forty-seven and during the water-fasts takes no supplements, salts, or anything. I am confident that I can do this seven-day experience. I have no headaches, muscular discomfort, and haven't any health or safety concerns.

Obsessions with time as in how long I've been on this fast, or how many hours till it ends, or exactly when is it half over, are not present. Doing stretches this morning, the question arose, *why did I wait so long to seriously embark on this spiritual pilgrimage?* Immediately, I heard a voice say, "Johnny was having way too much fun and still had too many parties to attend. He wasn't quite ready for this level of work. He simply could not access the energies required to sustain this pilgrimage." Johnny's resistance was way too high.

5:15 pm: I sat in meditation this afternoon for about an hour. I've never felt desire to meditate before, and am enjoying this new feeling. During this meditation, my head did not bob and drop as it usually does, as I tend to nod off.

It's 12:30 pm on day four, Tuesday, and I'm feeling very low and empty. I'm having trouble focusing on anything. I'm easily distracted today. The house water was shut off this morning for several hours but is working now and guidance this morning said stay for three more days and complete one week of water-fast.

Upon awakening, I didn't want to get up and am having trouble just functioning. I feel lousy and want to end it all. I think about crawling down the rabbit hole and dying. Distractions seem rampant and my mind is everywhere. It is challenging to hold space and remain present at all. I forced myself to sit, and the meditation dragged on forever, it seemed. Perhaps this discomfort is a bit of my ego/personality letting go. I hope so.

It's 5:00 pm and I cried uncontrollably for a while. Perhaps I released some trauma or deep sadness. A darkness covers me now and I want to run away and call it quits.

It's 12:45 pm on day five, Wednesday, and I cried all night in bed last night. I tried over and over to just crawl into the rabbit hole and stay there. And every time I started down the hole, I paused, tried to regain presence and open to the light and gifts that abound in my life. It was a challenging night.

I never in a million years thought I'd go for seven-days with no nourishment, but that's what I'm doing and where I'm going. Today,

I'm more solid in self and more focused than yesterday. Perhaps something released. I'm feeling, at least a bit, more appreciative and alive today. My body is doing fine with no pains or headaches. I'm low on energy.

I'm spending hours every day writing the "Darkness" and "Shadow" sections of this book and I'm most grateful for this opportunity. I feel like I'm being of service.

It's now 8:00 pm of day six, Thursday and I spent most of the day writing on my iPad parts of the "Shadow" section of this book. Trying to save my work, it somehow disappeared and I cannot find it anywhere on my iPad. I'm a Windows guy going all the way back to the DOS computers of the late 1980s, complete with two floppy disks and a giant twenty-megabyte hard drive. But Apple and MS-Word? They are not my favorite platforms to use or write with and it hurts a lot when a day's work is lost. Writing with MS-Word on my iPad is far different than writing with WordPerfect on my Windows-ten desktop.

I looked for months for the "save" button on my iPad version of MS-Word and could not find it anywhere. That button ought to be obvious, and perhaps to some it is, but not to me. It's just not there. After my work was lost, I fiddled with MS-Word and when I turned off the auto-save function, a big "save" button popped up. Voila! So, my left analytical brain is now running full force and I'm reminded that having an engineer's brain is extremely frustrating sometimes because not everyone thinks logically like an engineer.

It only took about twenty-years for me to realize that not everyone can think logically. But, as with flying a jet plane, the logical engineer that resides in me is occasionally very helpful.

Johnny, you are on day six of a seven-day water-fast and perhaps, just perhaps, you're running a bit low on energy and patience. Let it all go, and perhaps you'll find today's lost files tomorrow. Bitching is not in alignment with the divine plan. But I feel like I'm bitching in presence. Bitching in presence, now that's a topic for a PhD in Spiritual Maturity.

You are safe, you are beautiful and you are on your way to the next great adventure of your life, Johnny MedicineBear, so let today go into the history book and go to bed with a grateful heart. And shortly I did.

I'm also experiencing how it feels to be hungry, and it's not pleasant. Many people regularly have very little food available every day and routinely experience what I'm experiencing this week. I can now relate to what starvation feels like.

As I laid on my pillow, a voice whispered, "Perhaps you will find your lost work tomorrow, Johnny, it's not really gone. Stay focused on a positive outcome."

It is the evening of day seven, Friday, and it was challenging to sustain today. I stayed busy looking for yesterday's lost work and rewriting a bit of what is gone. The day passed rather quickly. I was very careful today about regularly saving my work and even e-mailed myself the working files several times to ensure that I'd have my work tomorrow. But the nice big "save" button on my iPad version of MS-Word did not disappear.

It feels like much released this week and I suffered no ill effects from one week of only water. There were no huge lightning flashes of insight or burning bush experiences, but I know that my personality, the ego, has loosened its grip a bit and my soul, my authentic self, has expanded. I cannot explain this any better, for it is simply a deep feeling coming from my core. It feels like "truth of the soul." I am a bit more solid because of this experience.

"It is not so important what I learn from an experience, it is much more important what I become by it."

I slept well Friday night, awoke, showered, and joined Teacher for a small breakfast on Saturday morning. The water-fast experience would not have happened without Teacher's support.

THE SPIRITUAL PILGRIMAGE – MALLORCA, SPAIN

Here are some journal entries from mid-November, 2019 while Teacher and I were staying in a rental home on the island of Mallorca, off the coast of Spain in the Mediterranean Sea. Our little home, in a small community, was very private and allowed for creative writing and the inward journey.

Although Mallorca, Spain is a vacation paradise, we were on a spiritual pilgrimage and did not engage in sight-seeing or other tourist activities. I took only a few photos for historical record and remained focused on my purpose. Here is my journal from several days of that experience.

Journal Entry - Mallorca, Spain - 19 November 2019

Five months ago today, Teacher arrived in Ashland, Oregon and our spiritual pilgrimage began. Sometimes, five months feels like five days, and sometimes it feels like five years.

I went to bed last night at 9 pm, read for a bit, and fell into a restless sleep. About 10 pm, I was agitated. Teacher, with words and behaviors, reminds me of Dad. My agitation was triggered by her words and actions toward me. She doesn't listen to me, or I don't seem to matter to her, and she's not polite to me. It was all stuff like that. It was rather trivial, but tonight, in bed, her words and actions became very loud. I was disturbed and felt a strange energy flowing through me and I shook uncontrollably. I have experienced nothing like this before. My eyes would not stay closed and I was in and out of bed several times.

At 2 am, I got up, dressed, and walked silently downstairs to be alone outside on our small patio. I stood under the brilliant, starry, moonless night sky when I sensed I was no longer alone. Turning, I saw Teacher waiting for me inside the slightly open front door.

Stepping inside, I shared with her my experience of the previous four hours. A strange sensation began in my body and I heard a buzzing sound in my ears and felt light-headed. I sat down in a lounge chair and within minutes, my legs started trembling and I felt my head expanding and opening.

The crown chakra expansion at the top of my head was very strong, and I felt my head getting larger and opening. Something strange and unusual was happening. I saw in a vision, the top of my head crack open and energy flow in or out. Slumping forward, I sensed that my entire body was opening and energy was flowing in and out in all directions. Tears flowed from appreciation and gratitude that something wonderful was happening.

Teacher sat with me, held the space, and reassured me that all was well. "This, Johnny, is the death of your ego," she said, "this is not *your* death." This sensation lasted perhaps thirty minutes, then slowly subsided as the energy surrounding my head and body diminished. The top of my head remained warm.

We sat together and Teacher shared about initiations, transitions, expansions, and awakenings. At 4 am, I returned to bed.

"Johnny, the initiation you experienced a few days ago elevated your vibration to a higher level." She saw this and cautioned that, "Old habit patterns might pull you back down to lower levels. Waking up means engaging life more responsibly. You may have to discard some old habits," Teacher concluded.

Journal Entry - Mallorca, Spain - 20 November 2019

I'm agitated again tonight and can't sleep. My mind is full of random thoughts and will not calm down. No sleep, no rest, I was up and down a lot.

About 2 am, something shifted, and I felt my consciousness separate from my physical body. I watched myself get up, walk around my room, and return to bed. I did this perhaps six times. Every action or thought that arose, I saw myself sitting on the sidelines, judging my actions. *I shouldn't say that, I shouldn't feel that, I ought to try more, that's a bad thing to say, that's a good thing to say, try this, try that, etc.* Every thought or action that occurred, my ego had some judgemental comment about. That went on most of the night.

At 6 am, I got up for a bit then returned and slept for several hours. At 9 am, I awoke and observed my thoughts and actions without feeling and without judgement. Whatever arose, I observed and allowed it to play out without judgement or comment. My consciousness and my physical body were separate. A sense of peace and freedom prevailed.

At 10 am, I showered, dressed, and went downstairs. About an hour later, I left for a walk and shortly noticed a young couple some distance away, looking with interest at an old building. I observed them without comment or judgement. He reached and took her hand, which she willingly gave and he lovingly held. I was an observer in this beautiful space. There was no sense of wanting what he had, or feeling lonely for not having a companion to share this vacation paradise with. None of that occurred. I was simply present. I sensed his actions were from love, not desire. I witnessed true affection and love. I watched this couple for a while, then moved further along on my walk.

Upon returning home, Teacher and I did an interview video for her website. However, my Canon 5D-Mk-III camera stopped video recording after about 30 minutes. It was strange for there was plenty of space on the 32-gig memory card, and the battery still had 60% charge remaining. I felt that the camera ought to record video till either the storage card is full, or the battery is depleted. Teacher mentioned that we ought to take it to a camera shop and talk to a technician to get guidance and find out why the camera stopped recording.

I said, "Let me check it out first before we talk to a camera tech." Her insistence on taking it to a camera shop tech was more about me opening to help than to finding out why the camera stopped recording. We were revisiting a habit pattern of mine from childhood and I was uncomfortable. The "I can do it myself and not ask for help" behavior goes back to childhood and Dad. We talked about this for a while before I let it go and realized that it was OK to ask for help.

Recognizing my resistance to outside help was the lesson here. As soon as I said, "OK, we'll take it to a camera shop tomorrow," Teacher let the issue go.

Journal Entry - Mallorca, Spain - 21 November 2019

Drifting off to bed at 10 pm last night, I had a strong sense that the camera issue was in the setup menu or a design limitation. An internet search showed that the 5D-Mk-III has a 4-gig video file size limitation. When reached, the camera seamlessly stops and restarts automatically.

Additionally, there is a video time limitation of 30-minutes hard wired into the camera. When that time is reached, video recording shuts off. That's why the camera stopped during our interview. There is no way to avoid this time limitation. This answered all the questions about yesterday's camera shutdown.

Sleep was unsuccessful and at 1 am, I suddenly felt numb or dead. I had no sensations of anger, rage, hatred, fear, love, compassion, or anything else. I lay all night in this strange space and stared at the ceiling for hours. I saw myself in slacks and shirt, lying on the ground outside on a street somewhere, not moving. Nothing else in that vision was moving, either. The entire world appeared lifeless. It was very unsettling. I finally drifted into an uneasy sleep.

I tried to nap this afternoon, could not, came downstairs, and felt rage arise deep inside. I grabbed a pen and paper and wrote hatred, anger, and rage on a pile of papers. It was mostly illegible scribbles; however, the feelings were there and perhaps released through writing.

Teacher said that this anger was from before I could write. It was at a time somewhere from birth to perhaps two years old. Out it came. I've felt totally empty all day. Everything I've done today has been a challenge. I feel like a part of me is dying and perhaps it is. But I'm grateful to have the experience, for I know that this discomfort is on my path of healing. To get past it, I must experience it.

At 7 pm, I walked alone to a restaurant in town for dinner. I realized that no matter what Teacher says or how she behaves, I must stay detached and rooted in truth and integrity. When I am solid, I am not triggered by her. If I am triggered, it is from unresolved trauma remaining in my basement. It's never the other's behavior that is the problem. It is always my unresolved traumas surfacing when given an opportunity. With work, I can heal myself.

Journal Entry - Mallorca, Spain - 22 November 2019

It's 2 am and, again, my mind is going in circles reliving past events, giving away my energy and power, feeling sorry for myself, and wishing life was different. I'm projecting my anger and resentment on Teacher. I continually feel fragile and vulnerable. I wish I was with a desirable woman in this paradise to enjoy the pleasures of her company and the surrounding isle of Mallorca, Spain. But I'm with Teacher, a solid, uncompromising master that is being guided to help me wake up so that I may authentically write *From Savage to Shaman*. I have choice right here in this moment to either cave in to past behaviors and patterns, or stop feeling sorry for myself, and focus on my work. I have an opportunity of a lifetime unfolding right here and all I need do is show up one hundred percent present and not resist, to benefit.

With a few breaths and a bit of refocusing, I shook off the desire to quit and now feel grateful that Teacher is here, dedicating her time and energies to waking me up. My resistance has faded. Hopefully, sleep and peace are forthcoming.

This morning in session, Teacher told me I still hold unreleased anger and rage from my first few years of life. I shared that when Dad came home from WWII (he left just a few days after my birth), I was a one-year-old and cried when he held me. Mom said I resisted Dad for several months. No one could figure out what was wrong with Johnny. Why didn't he like his father and let him hold him? Perhaps I knew what I was in for later in life. After consciousness at about three, I do not remember Dad ever hugging me or being affectionate with me. He was a man's man.

We discussed in session this morning, about the camera and I see how my ego was identifying with the "fix-it guru." There is a difference between having skills and using them, and "being the expert" and using them. Identifying with a persona like the "fix-it-guru" is identifying with the ego and it is a trap.

Johnny MedicineBear, the pilot, the fix-it-guru, the-this expert, the-that expert, are all false identities that are not my true identity. I'm understanding this more. After reading yesterday's journal entries about the camera, I see that I was identifying with *I'm the fix-it-guru here and you better let me have a crack at it first.* I never quite said that but that's what I was feeling. Ego is the trap.

Teacher said, "Imagine if we took your camera to a shop, and the tech told us that there is a 30-minute video recording limitation with this camera and that limitation is addressed in the manual. What a shot that would be to the fix-it guru's ego. But if one is beyond ego, one doesn't experience an emotional response. There is no 'I should have checked the manual first,' or 'I should have known better,' or 'I'm so stupid, blah, blah, blah.' Living beyond ego, one stays in presence and simply says, 'Thank you,' and leaves."

I'm reminded that pilots are all about ego. I land smoother than you, and I fly faster airplanes than you, and I'm Captain Sam Smooth, etc.

A master shared on YouTube how the ego loves big, far away, hard to do, maximum effort, and challenges like going to the moon. The soul, or divine consciousness, loves stillness, presence, and being of genuine service. The soul desires to authentically support others.

All these behaviors, patterns, feelings, sensations, desires, thoughts, and actions of no sleep, restlessness, shortness with Teacher, projection of anger, shallow breathing, and sensitive ego triggers, are all deep traumas releasing. When I'm free of trauma, when my basement is clean, then no matter what anyone says or does, I'll not get triggered.

KILLING MY PARENTS - OVER THE CLIFF THEY GO

P lease remember that I am not killing my parents, but rather killing those aspects of me I acquired from my parents. It is a metaphorical experience, not a literal experience.

I massaged this chapter very little, for I wanted it to retain its original flavor. Perhaps you will find a stepping stone in here for you and your work in this area as you move forward on your spiritual journey.

Journal Entry - 24 November 2019

I walked this morning to the big stone church at the top of the village. There were many steps to climb, metaphorical perhaps for climbing the steps toward higher consciousness. The several-hundred-year-old stone church was beautiful and full of character. There was no one there, and I sat alone in silence for an hour in a little garden adjacent to the church at the highest point in this little mountain village.

Upon leaving the church and descending back down toward the village center, I was drawn to an old window in a stone wall, with wooden shutters partially covering the dirty glass. I sensed an old man locked away in a small prison behind the glass, staring out at me. It reminded me of me in my self-made prison. A knot began forming in my gut and as it increased in intensity, I returned to the meditation garden by the old stone church to sit for a while longer and allow these sensations to pass.

Anger arose and my gut continued to tighten. I knew that this anger was from my very early childhood, i.e., before consciousness. I saw myself as an infant, perhaps one or two years old, very angry, and very frightened.

This angry infant child vision continued as I saw my father approaching. He came to me and tried to hold me. But I resisted his efforts and kicked, screamed, and fought to keep him away.

Many years ago, Mom told me that when Dad returned from WW-II in 1945, when I was just one-year-old, I cried, kicked, and screamed when he tried to hold me. Perhaps I knew what I was in for at that early age and resisted.

My vision continued, and I rapidly grew into "Mature Man Johnny," perhaps thirty years old and very fit. Dad approached, and I physically stood up and began moving. I acted out the remaining portion of this vision. Walking toward Dad, we met face-to-face at the edge of the garden.

For the first time in my life, I faced my father and felt no fear. As we locked eyes and stared at each other, I felt my muscles tighten. Then he stepped toward me with the familiar "I'm going to teach you a lesson" look in his eyes. As he reached for me, I threw a punch at him. "Wham" I smashed him in his face. First one, then another and soon I was pounding him and landing punches on his face, chest, and stomach. I shadow boxed and ducked every punch he threw at me. Dad went down, but I pulled him back up and the thrashing continued. I was really into it, and with a racing heart and clenched fists, I danced with the punches, ducking, faking, and jabbing him with all the strength I had. I heard and felt my punches landing on his face and body. Rage toward my father was pouring out and I beat the living tar out of him.

Then Mom appeared and screamed at me to stop beating up Dad. I told her to step aside, for Dad's got this coming. Over and over, I hit Dad, smashing him in the face and chest. When he'd go down, I'd pull him back up. He staggered around a bit in a daze and as soon as he turned toward me, I'd smash him again. I punched Dad till he was out cold and down for the count.

I reached down, picked him up over my head, and tossed him over the side of the hill. Over the edge he went, unconscious, with Mom screaming at me to not do it. Then I turned, grabbed Mom, picked her up over my head, and, with her screaming and thrashing, threw her over the side of the hill to join Dad at the bottom of the drop.

I felt GREAT! My heart was racing, I was breathing fast, and my fists were clenched as I began to slowly allow my body to unwind and relax. I shook the tightness out of my shoulders, checked my body for damage, and found that all was well. I was standing near the edge and shouted over the cliff, "You are never to return as my angry raging father or my passive enabling mother." I walked away and began the slow trek home.

Along the path, I checked in with "Infant Johnny" as a toddler and saw a happy, giggling, smiling baby. Gazing at the sea a half mile distant, I noticed two little light beings or orbs gently hovering and knew that they were my parents. They had no personality, just their essence, and I felt love from them. I continued down the streets toward home. Tears flowed as I shared this loving space with my parents this day in Mallorca, Spain.

This was a very powerful and significant event. I emphasize that this was not about actually harming my parents, but killing and releasing the aspects of them I still carried. Tossing them over the cliff to their destruction was wiping them clean from my emotional fields. I was clearing out my basement of fear and anger from my parents. It was a wonderful experience.

After this event, I began relating to my parents in a more positive and peaceful light. I saw their humanness, their vulnerabilities, their gifts that they gave me, and their struggles growing up and as adults. They are now blessed beings on an earthwalk. And they did the very best that they could with the conditions and circumstances that they had. I don't resist my parents anymore. My mother comes to me occasionally in a dream and vision as a supportive loving mother and whenever I reach for a tool to build or repair something, Dad joins me for the fun.

DEEP WORK IS HARD WORK

Journal Entry – Mallorca, Spain - 25 November 2019

This Chapter is from my written journal of November 2019, while Teacher and I were sharing a house on the Isle of Mallorca, in the Mediterranean Sea off the coast of Spain. We were not tourists enjoying this vacation paradise, but rather seekers on a spiritual pilgrimage.

Last evening, I had an overwhelming urge and watched insane battlefield combat videos about the Roman Army on YouTube. These are battles where 100,000 soldiers engage in close-up combat with spears and swords and at day's end 50,000 soldiers and 10,000 horses lay dead or dying. I was glued to this bloody insanity until I couldn't watch it any longer. Disturbed, I noticed my hard breathing, and turned it off. What was that all about I wondered? *What's going on, Johnny*, I asked myself? No answers came forward.

Watching this graphic violence seemed as insane as the actual battles must have been. I realized that these battles from several hundred years BC also occur occasionally in my mind. Sometimes my in-house terrorist group pays me a visit. Watching these disturbing, violent videos touched me deeply.

This morning in session, I shared the video piece with Teacher. She tied this piece to my latent desire for revenge on my mother and father. "It's there, Johnny, but don't go after it," she said, "or judge it, or wish it was different. You are not to manipulate or divert that energy. Just observe from witness mode and allow it to surface, diffuse, and release on its own.

"Knowing that your rage is there, Johnny, and that you could act as a Roman Soldier and consciously thrust a sword through someone brings this shadow piece out of the basement and into consciousness. Once aware of your rage, you will not act out, for that's not who you are.

"It's much safer knowing that you could perform a violent act than retaining it in your unconscious shadow. Repressed, unresolved shadow, will likely act out on its own at a time of its choosing. This is powerful and important stuff," she continued. "This IS the deep work that is fraught with dangers and therefore must only be done with the guidance and protection of a trusted Teacher."

In Vietnam, I was distant from the "action" and saw very little of it because I flew mostly at night in darkness. I heard very little of it because I was far from the bomb explosions. And I felt very little of it because I was snugly sealed in my Phantom jet-fighter. I anesthetized myself daily with alcohol and flying my Phantom jet-fighter at night was, to me, a very realistic video game. Killing didn't feel like killing. Like the YouTube videos of the Roman Army, a bombing mission into North Vietnam was a video game and I was simply an actor on a stage playing a part. It was not real to me.

Again, tonight I watched about 45 minutes of the same insane battlefield action. Recognizing that I have this killing potential in me is both frightening and freeing. I have hit no one in my life out of anger, for I have a deep fear of retaliation. Standing up for myself and fighting was whipped out of me by my father many years ago. I'm not a hands-on fighter. However, Teacher suggested that I might have avoided fights for my deeper self knew of this unresolved rage, and if released, I might have killed my opponent. It's frightening to imagine my pent-up rage released.

Teacher said that she was aware of and felt my latent rage for a while now, yet stayed the course to work with me. She knew of the danger to herself should this rage emerge. She also knew that my latent rage had to be resolved for me to authentically write this book. She is courageous to stay the course with me.

At seventy-five years old, I realized and acknowledged for the first time that I have this potentially dangerous raging aspect. But once diffused and brought into consciousness, it resolves into a non-issue.

I shared also that I feel a big dead dark weight, like a bowling ball, in my gut. I wake up most mornings feeling half dead and full of dread. This dark shadow, the silent revengeful piece, is that bowling ball. The basement door is now open and I can witness what is in the basement and work with what surfaces. Teacher stressed, "Do not try to fix or manipulate anything, Johnny, and do not wish it was different."

After this morning's session, I felt lighter. I journaled a bit then walked around town paying attention to feelings and thoughts without judgement or manipulation. I also felt closer to Teacher. I accepted her suggestions and didn't resist. We travel to India soon.

Teacher shared that living in the mind is living from the past. It is living from the past memory of everything. Choices are based on this. If it feels good, do it again. If it doesn't feel good, don't do it again. That applies to all our sensory and emotional sensations. Where I go, who I choose to be with, and how I function is all from memory. It is all from the past. This morning, listening to a Guru on YouTube, he was asked, 'What is the difference between an enlightened being and a non-enlightened being?' He said the same thing that Teacher did, that enlightened people live in presence and non-enlightened people live from memory, for it's all they have.

It is uncomfortable living outside the box, and living in presence is living outside the box. Living in presence is living in the unknown. It's taking risks. However, every time I've experienced significant change, I've been outside the box and uncomfortable. Discarding cigarettes and alcohol, was extremely uncomfortable at first. But new awareness came through and unexpected, not from memory experiences began to appear in my life. I'm at the same juncture today with awakening. If I cling to memory and live from memory, I will live from the past, and I'll continue to get the same results.

Teacher suggested meditation at 4 am. I immediately felt resistance and appreciate that my resistance is much more than just doing meditation at 4 am. Getting up that early for meditation is outside the box and outside my comfort zone. Rather than resist and reject it, I agreed to it without reservation. Going on this spiritual pilgrimage is way outside my comfort zone. But significant changes have already occurred because I got out of my comfort zone and am doing the required work.

If I live from memory, I stifle expansion. "Go into the unknown, Johnny, and release the past, ALL OF IT. Don't just let go of the convenient past, let go of all of it. This is essential and once released, there is room for true creativity," she said. This morning was validation of this work.

I awoke in presence and gratitude this morning with no big black bowling ball in my gut. I showered, walked, meditated by the church at the top of the village, enjoyed an orange juice at a local café and came home. I asked for a sign from Spirit of validation and my eyes were drawn to a small car parked in a drive. On the rear panel in chrome letters was the model of this car. It was an "UP." I never heard of an UP. But the way to divinity is always UP. I smiled.

I shared in session that I "was feeling gratitude."

"When you feel it, Johnny, it's the mind taking over the experience. If there is an emotion that comes with any experience, then it's the mind that's speaking to you. You might say I feel like I learned something which differs from I learned something. Don't judge or try to get out of the mind or beyond the mind. It's impossible to do that by trying. Just recognize what's going on and stay in presence. Always come back to the breath."

I went for a drive in our rental car, enjoyed dinner and stopped at a small sea-port for a while. This was the first time I've driven any car since I drove Teacher's car in Asheville, North Carolina several months ago. I've also eaten several meals in restaurants and feel olive oil logged. Everything here is cooked in olive oil. I've never been this sensitive to food before. Whenever I'm "feeling" about anything, it's from the mind. Perhaps if I keep moving, the space beyond the mind, the space of true creativity and freedom will emerge.

I slept fitfully last night and this morning, I feel like I am going to explode. I've had enough. I cannot sleep and there is an active terrorist group in my head. I went out yesterday in our rental car for a few hours and still feel myself shaking from just being outside and breathing new fresh air, driving around this lovely island and taking a few photos of the local scenery. I'm a total wreck and I'm in "Max Overload Mode." I want to run away, yet there is nowhere to run. I feel horrible inside and out and yet don't want to be the wimp and complain or quit.

I'm shaking right now and can't control it. Visions of the roman soldiers and savages killing each other play over and over in my mind. I feel like I'm having a serious major meltdown, or worse. I don't like myself. No! I hate myself. I hate how I feel, what I'm doing, and what I'm not doing. I HATE EVERYTHING.

"Whenever you are feeling some relief, it's always because your ego has found an escape, Johnny, or you're in your head," says Teacher over and over. I'm frigging sick of hearing that. I don't care if it's true or not. I'M GOING TO SCREAM. I've been working intensely for about five months, 24/7, non-stop, and I'm at the end of my rope. I'm in explode mode and I obviously don't get it.

The Beatles and Donovan went to India in the 1960s and stayed with a Master in his Ashram. They were joyful and laughed, played guitars, sang, wrote songs, and meditated. Waking up and becoming aware ought to be somewhat pleasant, at least sometimes.

It's not happening for me. I'm going to quit, but quit what? Where do I go? When I think of my old life of ten, twenty or more years ago, I'm as frightened or worse than sitting in the pain I'm in now. I just want to get it over with. I haven't danced, sung, played any music, or done anything other than work, write, sit, work, write, sit, work, write, and sit some more.

Teacher says, "You're in your head, you're in your head," and I'm ready to explode. I've had enough! Enough of what? How much more can Johnny take till I either wake up from this nightmare, go back to my old nightmares, or kill myself to escape either fate. I don't know, but it's time for our morning session.

Teacher immediately sensed my low vibe and knew that it was triggered by me "escaping" in the car for several hours yesterday. She guided, I resisted, she guided, I resisted, she guided, I resisted less, she guided, I resisted even less, she guided, I broke down in a flood of tears, crying and wailing uncontrollably. Deep sadness flew across my mind's movie screen. Deep, deep, sadness. She's always right, not in a right wrong sense, but as one that sees and knows, and is detached from this experience. She is here to guide me into waking-up so that I may be of divine service. This is necessary for me to be authentic writing *From Savage to Shaman*. This release went on for a few hours.

Teacher received some personal items from a friend in England yesterday and at noon came into the kitchen wearing a beautiful dress. A Divine Goddess ascended into our kitchen. She was all beauty, and I told her so.

Coming out into the living room, she told me that she tried to use her electronic plug adaptor. "I plugged it into the wall, Johnny, and it smoked and apparently is fried. I'll get another next trip downtown."

I asked to see this one and told her I'd look at it and see if I could fix it.

"It's fried Johnny! Might as well toss it."

"Well, maybe it is but I want to look at it anyway to verify that it's dead and then you can get another one."

She resisted giving me this adaptor and we got into it. Our discussion rapidly escalated into a shouting session with her screaming at me that I was being aggressive toward her and she felt my energy grabbing for her. I got in her face and shouted that, **"I bought the God-damn plug adaptor and that the God-damn plug adaptor is mine not yours, and before I lay out another God-damn ten-dollars for a new God-damn plug adaptor, I want to make God-damn sure this one is God-damn dead! Now give me the God-damn plug adaptor!"**

She couldn't hear that. I'm speechless and standing there with my mouth open. She asked me to help and I tried to help gently at first and since she didn't seem to hear that very well, I'm now trying a bit more assertively to help. She's lovely in her dress and I've genuinely complimented her on how beautiful she looks. And she's screaming at me about my aggressive grabbing energy. She's frigging crazy and I'm getting out of here.

So once again Teacher retreats into her room to get away from me. I'm pissed-off and do not understand how she can be so unreasonable. I'm hurt, confused, and want to run away. Under my breath, I'm cussing her out for being so frigging rude to me. *I don't get it*, goes around and around in my head over and over.

Half an hour later, Teacher came out and shared. "Johnny, your help comes from your ego that wants to help as in you scratch my back and I'll scratch yours. There is a payoff you want from me. You want me to be nice to you, thank you for being such a nice man and helping, and all of that. This is understandable, as this is how you and everyone else you've ever known has lived their entire lives.

"Your help does not come from your soul of selfless love and selfless help. The higher space is to simply look at the adapter and do something with it. But you want to look at the adapter and do something with it from, 'I'll help you and you'll like me because I'm the fix-it guru' space. Compliments are unnecessary from the higher space." She explained well and soon I understood.

While she was in her room, I opened the plug adapter, removed the blown fuse, installed the enclosed spare, closed the case, and left it on the kitchen table with a sticky pad note: "fixed." I never heard another word about it.

I realized that I have engaged in all my relationships at this lower "scratching each other's back" level. There has always been this underlying dance of the egos going on that inevitably ends in frustration, anger, disappointment, and separation. Many times, I have wanted Teacher to be nice to me. But we're not here to simply be nice to each other and not hurt the other's feelings for that is the ego-dance. "This is awakening time, not be nice time," she stressed.

I understood and saw the "I want Teacher to like me" piece of my ego. As this pattern revealed itself, and I saw that I've played my part in this game forever, I had another major meltdown. I wailed, cried, and sobbed till the release was complete. Teacher then guided me into a dimension of the void or free space. I witnessed space and emptiness. There was no Johnny MedicineBear, just space or a void, silent and peaceful. Johnny was not there. I witnessed myself from a distance, yet could function as I am now writing this piece. "This space is impersonal, Johnny, and you cannot access this space from the ego."

The things that Teacher has spoken of that were beyond me, I may experience and relate to from this space.

"Total bliss has not yet arrived, Johnny, but this space is on the path. There is room for original thought and creativity in this space."

"I want to help you so you'll compliment me and stroke my ego," and "I want to help you because I just want to help you," are energetically different. They appear superficially identical to the shallow and the blind, but they are very different. You can now see the difference and another block is removed along your path toward spiritual maturity.

HOW TO FIND AUTHENTIC SPIRITUAL TEACHERS (AND KNOW THAT THEY ARE AUTHENTIC)

How do you, *Dear Reader*, find an authentic teacher, spiritual community, or institution to assist you on your spiritual journey? For simplicity, I'll reference only the teacher, but the same applies to a community or institution.

One must use caution when selecting a teacher for there are many charlatans and much false information available. How do you know that your teacher is truly authentic and that they are guiding you in a proper manner?

There are certain qualities and traits that authentic teachers embrace. An authentic teacher will never promise you a reward for doing what they suggest, nor threaten you with a punishment for not doing what they suggest. Also, an authentic teacher will never try to persuade you into believing or accepting something they tell you as a truth. They present and you decide.

Authentic teachers will encourage you to question everything and will never request you to accept answers based on trust or faith alone. All truths will always stand-up to the tests of logic, common sense, and the obvious. If your teacher's doctrine fails any of these tests, leave and look somewhere else.

Authentic teachers demonstrate the path of self-discovery and will always encourage you to validate and verify what you learn from your own experience. Authentic teachers are guides and point the way, where you learn from self-participation. They also provide a safety net for you when the going gets rough. Spiritual work is hard work fraught with dangers and an authentic teacher will protect you from outside interference and self-destruction along your journey.

Observe your teacher's behaviors, actions, and demeanor, especially under trying conditions. If they practice equanimity and express compassion for all, then retain them. If they do not exhibit these qualities, then look elsewhere for someone that does.

Here's an example of an authentic teacher and an authentic experience: suppose you have never felt, tasted, or in any way experienced water. Desiring to learn about water, you visit an authentic teacher that knows all about water and ask the teacher to please tell you about water.

Suppose you are the teacher. Can you tell me about water? Can you express in words what water feels like, or what it tastes like? You may need to think about this a while, but eventually you will agree that it is impossible to express in words what water feels or tastes like. But it is not impossible to have a direct experience with water. The teacher instructs you to open the spigot, fill the bucket, have a drink, then place your hand in the bucket of water. Once done, you now know about water from direct experience. This is what a true teacher does. Anything other than direct experience falls short.

Direct experience is the only way to *knowing* and the water metaphor applies to everything. You cannot become an experienced sailor by reading an instructional book while sitting on the deck of a sailboat moored to the dock. To become a sailor, you must go to open water and encounter a few storms. Experience is your teacher.

The water and sailing examples are metaphors for spiritual growth also. No one can tell you about divinity. You must open your heart and experience it directly. A trusted authentic teacher is essential for the spiritual pilgrim, the seeker of truth, the spiritual warrior and you, *Dear Reader*, on your spiritual journey.

INDIA - ARRIVAL

The morning sun was well below the horizon as we left our rental home on the isle of Mallorca in the Mediterranean Sea off the coast of Spain, in darkness on Thursday, the fifth of December, 2019. The following afternoon we arrived at the SWAN Meditation and Yoga Retreat Center (https://swan-yoga-goa.com/) in the state of Goa near the Arabian Sea in southwest India. We made it in four hops, sleeping a few hours on airport benches, and eating very little. I was grateful that my seventy-five-year-old body traveled comfortably.

While sitting peacefully at an airport waiting for our flight, I was overwhelmed by a sensation of incredible peace. Words cannot describe the sense of freedom and awe that arose and sustained for a while. Something unusual occurred on that airport bench. During that time, nothing outside of myself mattered much. I was totally content to just experience that peaceful state regardless of the events going on around me. Slowly, this euphoric space dissipated. I was very grateful to have experienced this gift.

In the late 1940s, the population of India was about 350 million. Roughly 70 years later, while at the SWAN Center in late 2019, the population of India was about 1.4 billion all living in an area roughly one-third the size of the USA. The population had quadrupled in 70 years There are a lot of people everywhere in India.

I didn't drive a car while in India and thought the drivers insane and the traffic conditions total chaos. Yet somehow, with all those cars, trucks, busses, motorcycles, scooters, mopeds, bicycles, people, and animals everywhere going every which way, I saw few accidents. There seemed to be an unspoken flow of movement like I've witnessed with swarms of fish and birds that move in unison this way than that way in one fluid motion.

In the US, it seems the most important component of a car is not its engine, brakes, or tires, but its video screens and sound systems. In India, it is the horn. Several taxi drivers blew the horn every time they shifted gears, whether in dense city traffic or totally alone on a country road. It didn't seem to matter. Habit, I guess.

Spiritual practice is an integral part of Indian culture with Ashrams, Temples, and Shrines everywhere. Most appeared open and available 24/7/365. Meditation is practiced openly, with many sitting here and there peacefully in silence. Spiritual practice is integral to the Indian culture.

I never felt threatened or in danger while walking around cities, towns, or marketplaces and I could feel the roots of this society going back thousands of years. I was comfortable in India.

INDIA - THE SWAN

The weather during December and January while at the SWAN Retreat and Yoga Center was balmy and pleasant. The little Ashram was a rustic jungle paradise. But I was on my spiritual pilgrimage, not a vacation so I rarely ventured off the grounds and stayed engaged in meditation practice, mantra chanting, yoga, and writing this book. I benefitted by being there.

Upon our arrival at the SWAN, Teacher reframed our relationship and left me on my own. She did her work, and I did mine. Although she supported me energetically and was my spiritual safety net, our interactions on the physical plane were minimal. Daily group-sessions, shared meals, and time together became rare.

Fears I harbor of someone or something outside of myself are projections of fears I harbor within. I saw that all fears and anger I experience from external conditions have their genesis within. I learned this as my relationship with Teacher shifted, and I was now on my own 12,000 miles away from the comforts and security of my home. I wanted to run and play, explore the area and culture, and take a zillion photos. But I knew that holding the line was critical if I were to move beyond my current emotional and spiritual state. Teacher's presence supported me as I felt again a tidal wave of sensory pleasures moving toward me full force. I had inner work to do, and this was the place to do it.

Our initial program at the SWAN was an intensive meditation and yoga practice. At 6 am, our group of five gathered in the rustic meditation hall for guided and silent meditation. Just being in the presence of the meditation instructor and our group, benefitted me. My hardest challenge was to still my mind. Over and over, I brought myself "back to my breath" and followed the simple mantra, "I breathe in, I breathe out." This released thoughts and returned me to center. Initially, meditation is practiced to quiet the mind of its endless chatter. Sitting peacefully following my breath seems so easy conceptually, yet in practice it is a huge challenge. But any effort at stilling the mind is never wasted.

Yoga, as practiced in India, is much more than the asanas (body positions) as practiced here in the west. Yoga is a comprehensive discipline of healing the body, mind and spirit and has been practiced for at least 2,500 years. It was inspiring to lie on my yoga mat and do some of the simple asanas with the instructor. And when the challenges were too great, I was encouraged to lie on the mat or sit peacefully and follow as best I could.

One morning about 3:30 am I received this insight. With no secrets, I have nothing to hide. With nothing to hide, my ego has nothing to protect and therefore it softens. I become an open book. Hence, I may remain undisturbed even if surrounded by external chaos for there is nothing within me that matches the vibration of the external chaos. This idea was not new, however, it was now more than an intellectual concept. It shifted from belief to knowing. I learned that whenever I wish the world to be different than it is, my ego is exerting my will, my desires, and my control. When someone doesn't do what they have told me they will do, I can either justify my anger toward them and get nowhere, or I can breathe through the event, release it, and move on.

A story of the Buddha spoke of agitators that came to his ashram to heckle him during a dharma talk. Buddha calmly ignored them. They continued to heckle him and create a disturbance. He continued to ignore them until they become frustrated and realized that he was not responding to their antics and left.

Later, a monk asked the Buddha how he could be so calm with the hecklers in his face. He replied, "If someone shows up at your door with a package that you didn't order and your name is not on the package, you simply tell him that it's not yours. You don't accept and open the package. The hecklers and bullies will find someone else who will respond to their heckling."

This is a powerful message. The ego must be sufficiently softened to not want to smash the hecklers in the face. The hecklers want confrontation. By not engaging, the hecklers and bullies will leave, for they only stay when someone responds to their aggressive behaviors.

INDIA - THE PUNDIT MASTER ASTROLOGER

In many places, astrology (the study and interpretation of the influence of celestial bodies on humans) is regarded as a non-logical, non-proven curiosity. Many do not take it seriously. I was one of them. However, I learned that astrology is a science and a tool that provides insight and wisdom into one's life.

The master astrologer arrived at the SWAN center and stayed several days to provide readings for interested guests. This master, in his 60s, was a third-generation astrologer. His father and grandfather, both master astrologers, were his teachers. Astrology was their life profession, and they were recognized in India as pundit masters of astrology.

I filled out a small information sheet including the date, time, and location of my birth the day prior to my reading and submitted it. The following day, I sat in session with the master and he shared that he saw my abusive childhood and that I had no protection from my tyrant father. He shared that I had fought in a military war and that about half way through my life I decided to continue my life toward peace and spiritual growth as opposed to war and destruction.

He shared that I had done much inner work, and that there was more work to do. He shared that I was very involved in a project (this book) and that I would complete the book. He spoke of karma, my soul's journey, and other things that reinforced and validated that I was moving forward on my earthwalk positively. I thanked the master and left with his written reading.

I've included this small section about the master astrologer because for many years I too dismissed astrology as child's-play and referred to astrologers as quacks. Today, I support this discipline and recognize the value of this science. You be your own judge and decide for yourself.

INDIA - DEE - WIFE REVISITED

Teacher suggested that forty years ago while married to Dee, neither of us could have been there for the other, for neither of us had done our work. Both of us carried a ton of childhood trauma. I could barely sustain myself let alone support her. And the same was true for her.

I thought about our time together some forty years distant and recalled that I always felt that I was right and Dee was wrong about most everything we disagreed with. "She" could not see clear logic, and "She" could not do this or that and "She" was not there for me when I needed her. This was correct, but I could not understand that it was impossible for her to relate to my logical brain and that it was also impossible for me to relate to her "less logical" and perhaps more creative ways of seeing things. I was rooted in logic and she was not.

Our happy times were centered on drinking and partying, not on good parenting, communication, understanding, and love. I began to see that I was not there for her and, like me, she also needed understanding and support. We were two lost souls trying desperately to escape life on different spaceships. Now, forty years later, I can see this.

Teacher suggested that I phone Dee and share with her that when we were partners, I could not emotionally support her. I intended to tell her that I understand now what I could not understand forty years ago. And if I could have done it any differently forty years ago, I would have. Today I recognize how limited my awareness was forty years ago and wished to clear that piece with her.

One evening, I phoned Dee from the SWAN Ashram in India, and we had our chat. She listened intently and remarked that she was very surprised and pleased. We cleared away some of the wreckage of our past and closed our conversation positively. It was wonderful to heal this piece with Dee.

INDIA - THE AYURVEDIC DOCTOR

Panchakarma is an Ayurvedic detox procedure that discharges stored toxins and reestablishes the body's natural healing ability. The program at the SWAN called for four weeks of special diet, special massage therapies, and other activities designed to realign the body with its auric systems. It cannot get any more authentic than what I experienced at the SWAN. I embraced the Panchakarma with excitement and commitment.

About one week into the program, I contracted an ear infection. The Ayurvedic Doctor, whose office was a little open tiki hut on the Ashram campus, held my right wrist like he was taking my pulse. He deduced that I had a slight fever, that my blood pressure and pulse were normal, and that I had an infection in my right ear that would require antibiotics to clear. He did all this just by holding my wrist. I was amazed. The whole time, he stayed 100% engaged with me neither writing anything down, nor using a computer. He released my wrist, phoned a doctor friend of his, and scheduled me for a visit to a local hospital to see that doctor the following day.

The following morning, I visited the hospital doctor, and he performed a forty-five-minute comprehensive examination 100% engaged in the exam. There were no computers, no interrupting phone calls, and he took only a few notes. He told me what was out of balance and handed me a script for a round of Z-pak antibiotic and some cough syrup to help with a persistent ongoing cough. He was pleasant and thorough. I thanked him and was directed to the front desk for payment.

At the current exchange of seventy Indian rupees for one US dollar, my doctor visit cost $4.25. My prescriptions were another $4.25 for both the Z-pak antibiotic and the cough syrup. Including the taxi fares to and from the hospital, I spent about $12 on the entire affair. The antibiotic was effective, and my ear cleared within a few days. The Panchakarma detox helped, and I slept more soundly, and felt "cleaner" than I did prior to this cleanse.

Gyanmitra, our respected senior meditation instructor, stopped to chat with me one morning in the garden. He is a kind, gentle man with a quick wit and a loving smile. I felt close to him. Like everyone on staff at the SWAN, he was very engaged with his guests.

"Good morning, Johnny, you are an inspiration to all of us here at the SWAN!"

"How's that, Gyanmitra," I asked?

"Look around," he said, "do you see anyone here either as guest or on staff that is much over fifty-years-old?" I hadn't noticed, but he was right. Everyone was younger than me and many by a large margin.

"Johnny, when people get older and retire, many, perhaps even most, fill their lives with mindless activities like watching endless TV and other similar distractions. Rather than embracing and preparing for the upcoming inevitable transition that awaits everyone. Most run from life pretending that they will live forever. You, however, are here at the SWAN engaged in meaningful and life enhancing activities. You are preparing yourself for your upcoming transition. Few go on a spiritual pilgrimage at seventy-five years of age. You are an inspiration to all of us with a message that 'it is never too late to do one's work.' I commend you, my friend."

I was quite taken by Gyanmitra's sincere comments. Being here at the SWAN in India on a spiritual pilgrimage just seemed like the right thing to do and I was grateful for being in this wonderful place.

INDIA - RELEASING KARMA

Feeling strong and in high spirits, I sang softly as I slowly walked the path toward my little hooch at the beautiful SWAN center carrying my meal tray. All was well when whoops...without warning, my right foot caught the hem of my left leg's baggy Indian bell-bottom pants, and I was on the dirt face down surrounded by my randomly strewn lunch.

Immediately, SWAN staff music director Kacie and others were there to help. And within a few minutes, I was up, uninjured, and smiling. Kacie requested a new lunch be sent to my hooch. And after dusting off, I carefully walked bowlegged back home and resolved to get less-baggy pants or wear shorts. Shivendra, the respected SWAN philosopher said, "Johnny, you just released some Karma."

There are many ways to describe or relate to Karma, but I offer this simplistic explanation to understand what Shivendra meant.

Karma is the energy created by thoughts and actions that we do. There is no escape from this, and no way to alter or manipulate Karma. It just is whether one believes it or not.

The energies of our thoughts and actions invite similar energies to move toward us. In effect, we create our own future by our current actions. This means that whatever we do or think today invites similar experiences to manifest in our future. The experiences that we encounter in our future, however, may appear quite different than what we did to invite them. As example, I may selflessly help someone with a monetary gift. Then a week later, when my car breaks down somewhere, a mechanic in a repair truck miraculously appears, rapidly gets me on my way, and refuses payment saying that, "This just feels like the proper thing to do." That's the universal energetic law of Karma in action.

Somewhere in my past, and it's not important to know what, where, or when, I created some karma that was resolved today by this unpleasant and potentially injurious event. That's what Shivendra meant.

The universal law of Karma transcends the physical and applies to everyone, regardless of race, sex, religion, geographic location, age, etc., and it is irrelevant whether one believes it or not. Karma is! It means that I am responsible for the quality of my life, and am inviting the events heading toward me by the Karma of my current and past actions. Karma must resolve.

Creating a pleasant future existence is done by living a life of compassion, love, and service directed from the heart. It is nice to know that I have a hand in how my life plays out. It puts me in the driver's seat and makes me responsible for the quality of my life. If one lives with deception, dishonesty, manipulation, and other similar activities, their future is guaranteed to attract similar events toward them. The future may be the next few minutes or the next few lifetimes, but it must eventually happen for it is cosmic law.

INDIA - RETURN HOME

After hugging my SWAN brothers and sisters in loving farewell, I walked with the driver to the entry gate and climbed into the rear seat of the taxi. I heard the chanting first, then turned to see several of the SWAN staff with heads bowed and praying hands sending me off with prayers for a safe journey home. Tears welled in my eyes as their love flowed into my heart. Smiling, I waved farewell and the taxi slowly headed for the Goa, India airport. It was late January, 2020.

Five flights and forty-eight hours later, having crossed eleven time zones, I arrived home in Florida and stepped into my beloved Dutch. "What an adventure," I reflected.

During the next few months, I noticed changes in myself and I liked what I was becoming. What had I learned? How had I grown? What can I write in this book that may be of value to my brothers and sisters? How may I be of service to humanity by sharing my life-adventures? Thoughts continued to spill out as I wrote my heart into *From Savage to Shaman*.

OTHER THOUGHTS

This morning I had a vision about addiction. It matters not what the addiction is, for all addictions at core level are escape routes. Addiction is desire at the extreme or simply, "it's never enough." Addictions can never be satisfied.

My stomach growls and I feel hunger, yet I've had a bite to eat this morning and my hunger ought to be satisfied. It is in my best interest to not eat. Yet, I am pulled to remove this discomfort of a little hunger knowing that eating food will only temporarily satisfy the craving for the source of my discomfort is not lack of food. I feel my awareness contract a little as my tummy growls and I consider consuming something.

It doesn't matter what I'm running from specifically, for if I'm "running from," I'm always running from myself. Food and fantasies that move through my body and mind pull me from presence. I feel it on subtle levels.

When I focus on food, I fantasize about ice cream or other goodies and it's the same with any other fantasies. But it's always a fantasy and all fantasies pull me off center. It's that simple.

Being gentle with myself means being gentle with Little Johnny, my active six-and-one-half-year-old aspect of consciousness that lives somewhere inside. He is my spontaneous, playful, creative energy and window to divinity.

I am sitting in Dutch at a motorhome repair shop with a clear mind. I'm not thinking about anything. I notice the shop smells of oil and old tires and observe the men that are here working. I notice a man with a turned-down mouth in a perpetual frown. He appears unhappy. But I simply notice him and not judge him or "try to figure him out" with my projections. He is who he is, and that's the end of it.

I prepare breakfast. I'll enjoy a bit of food, like half a cup of leftover Steve's Stew. Not all of it, and not, *oh well, might as well finish it up, there's only a half a cup left!* But a half a cup and that's it. And I prepare this meal in presence. I enjoy the smells, the feel of the cup, the beauty of the stew, the loving energies of the food and the chef. Presence is the answer.

A few years ago, several campers gathered for dinner at a picnic table in our campground. The conversations were light and pleasant. Paul, sitting across from me began sharing about his flying experiences. He was obviously excited and proud of his flying accomplishments. He had recently received his private pilot's certificate and had flown a small twin-engine six-passenger plane. I smiled and paid attention to him and his story, for his excitement and exuberance were infectious. He loved flying and was rightfully proud of his endeavors. Finally, noticing my interest, he looked directly at me and asked, "You fly airplanes, Johnny?"

"A little bit," I said and that was the end of it.

A few years prior, I would have overrun Paul with my exploits of flying fighter-jets in the USAF including a Vietnam combat tour and as Captain with American Airlines. I loved being the center of attention, telling the best jokes, sharing the biggest stories, and bragging about my exploits. Those needs have diminished appreciably. This is a payoff for doing one's work. I believe that the more solid one is internally, i.e., having a healthy, realistic sense of self and self-worth, the less need one has for external recognition of accomplishments, power, and control over others. The desire to make sure everyone knows that I'm a great pilot is no longer there. Stated a bit differently, the ones that claw their way to the top, stand on a soapbox, and profess to know, are trying to fill their internal void with external recognition.

ENDING

Hopefully, you have found yourself in this book and are applying what I experienced to your life. Keep your life-toolbox open and use your new life-tools as you travel your life-journey.

It's now late summer of 2023 and I'm writing this final chapter from Dutch parked in a rustic campground along the western shores of Lake Superior in Minnesota. I recently celebrated my seventy-ninth birthday and am grateful for my blessings. I feel that I'm an integral part of this web of life, not an outsider merely observing. I sleep quite well and am not haunted by memories of an abusive childhood, failed relationships, traumatizing life-events, or the screams of the dead from a long-ago war.

Past traumas no longer trigger painful emotions. I lovingly remember my parents and my childhood, send blessings to my former wives, and calmly reflect on the war in Vietnam. Do the work and the painful past dissolves.

If you remember only a few things from this book, let this be one of them. "The path to your freedom is through doing your deep inner work. One must embrace their darkest secrets and diffuse their childhood traumas. There is no way to get around this."

In this book, I've offered encouragement and support for you to do your work. This path is not for the faint-of-heart. But without doing your inner work, you will live a mediocre life contaminated by the ghosts that reside in your basement.

Only a few will rise to the challenge and passionately embrace the healing path. But whether you dedicate your life full-time or just part-time to waking-up, you are still doing your work. Please remember that every effort, no matter how large or small, on the path toward spiritual maturity is never wasted. With every act of kindness, generosity, and service, you pour a gallon of water into your reservoir of awareness. Your little boat with you in it floats a little higher, whether you know it or not. If you keep at it, eventually you will spill over the dam and be on your way to freedom down the river of life.

There is nothing in your world more important than you becoming conscious. Think for yourself, don't follow the masses, and make your choices from your heart. Live your life as deeply as you can with all the passion and love you can muster. As your inevitable passing approaches, release your body with love and grace.

And please remember that Johnny MedicineBear walks every step with you. You are never alone.

EPILOGUE

During the writing of this book, I asked myself, *am I qualified to write a book about divinity, Spirit, war, love, and a host of other sensitive personal subjects?* I believe that I can authentically bring this work forward for what I have shared in *From Savage to Shaman* was acquired from my life experiences. It is direct knowledge. I'm not simply passing on what was conditioned into me during my early formative years or what I read somewhere and now believe to be true.

I can speak of the closed, rigid, inflexible mind that invites and participates in violence, war, dishonesty, and other atrocities, for I lived in that mind before waking up to reality. I no longer choose the destructive path. Once beyond the closed rigid mind, I saw myself in others that had not moved beyond and related to them without judging them. I believe that most people are who they are from childhood conditioning, unresolved early-life traumas, and/or ignorance.

Anyone can advance toward peace, compassion, and truth.

I'm not an authority on anything, and never took a psychology or human behavior class. However, I've participated full-time in the "Earthwalk-School-of-Life" lab course since 1985 and plan on staying enrolled till my last breath.

I was in Vietnam flying bombing missions in my Phantom jet in

1972 and 1973. Sobriety came in 1985. By 1995, I realized that I would never be truly free and would lead a mediocre life if I could not come to peace with my participation in Vietnam. I was firmly planted on the trap door that covered my basement holding the ghosts of the dead from the bombs I dropped. I could not move off that door for fear that these ghosts would arise, haunt me, and perhaps even kill me. I learned from my non-physical Vietnamese friend, Mr. Song, that I was directly responsible for sending 1,019 people to their next life. There were many ghosts in my basement.

From Savage to Shaman is my atonement for my participation in war. Understanding and owning my actions, not running from my feelings, and living a life of compassion and selfless service freed me. I no longer hold the basement door closed.

I don't know if everyone can get to this place of peace and freedom, but I am certain that everyone can try. Take the first few steps right now if you've not already done so.

I have bared my heart and soul in this project hoping that some will relate to my story in meaningful ways. Hopefully, some will be motivated to walk their path of awakening a bit further from inspiration gained from this book. If I've shown the way for just one person to move forward just one step, then this project has been double worth it.

For I have been greatly challenged with this project and have prospered from this work. This project has been a great gift to me.

If you take your time and energy to drop me a note at FromSavageToShaman@gmail.com, I will make every effort to answer your note personally.

Thank you from my heart.
Johnny MedicineBear

ACKNOWLEDGMENTS

Gratitude to my spiritual guides and friends for their inspiration, guidance, and encouragement to write and publish *From Savage to Shaman*.

Gratitude to Teacher for her selfless service in guiding me out of my darkness, through my shadow, and into my light.

Gratitude to daughters Sarah and Jennifer, and their men, for their love and support.

Gratitude to my close personal friends, especially Karishma - Goddess of Georgia Football; Brother-Friend Joe - Guru of the Civil War; Marie/Mare - Goddess of Horses; Pamela - Goddess of Green Gardens; Johanna - Goddess of Pauma Valley; Gail-Laughing Water - Goddess of Aviation; Kristen - Goddess of Children's Books; Nancy Kweela Bear - Goddess of the Blue Ridge; Brother-Friend John - Guru of Two-Harbors; Christine - Goddess of Knife River; Gail - Goddess of the Woods; Becky - Goddess of TMP, and numerous others. They listened patiently and provided valuable suggestions.

Gratitude to Gyanmitra, Shivendra, Bodhi, Anamika, Swarnim, Abin, Kacie, Simba, the little "boot-thief," and all my brothers and sisters at the SWAN Meditation and Yoga Retreat Center, Goa, India, for holding me in sacred space and providing ongoing inspiration for this book-project.

Gratitude to proof readers Roger, Sid, Wynn, and English Professor Sarah, for their time, energy and heart-felt suggestions.

Gratitude to Steve, Patti, and Cycuse for paving the way by completing *I am Cycuse* a few months ago.

Gratitude to Skinny Leopard Media publisher and friend Cindy, for putting this whole thing together and making it comfortable and easy for me.

And finally, gratitude to those pieces of me that ran away, returned home, and are now part of the whole.

ABOUT THE AUTHOR

A friend told me that she reads the inside back cover bio and has a genuine interest in the particulars of the author. I never do but she's wiser than me so here goes.

I am Johnny MedicineBear and I am the author of *From Savage to Shaman*. I hold a BS degree in Industrial Engineering from Rutgers's University, and an MS degree in Information Systems from Golden Gate University. After graduation from Rutgers in 1967, I worked only one year in industry then shifted my focus to aviation.

I joined the United States Air Force in 1969 and retired after 20 years as an officer and fighter-pilot. Subsequently, I hired on with American Airlines and left in 2004 as a Super-80 Captain based at Chicago O'Hare International Airport.

I've lived in my forty-foot "Newmar Dutch-Star" motorhome since 2004, parking in Florida during the winter months, and traveling the northern states during summers. For seventeen years, from 2005 to 2022, I did not own a car and my only transportation, other than my bicycle and my legs, was my chromed-to-the-hilt Harley-Davidson motorcycle which traveled behind Dutch in an enclosed trailer.

I've been on a spiritual pilgrimage since sobriety arrived in 1985. I've participated in workshops with an eclectic group of facilitators including psychologists, shamans, Reiki masters, and others. And I practiced meditation and yoga in an Ashram in Goa, India for several months in 2019.

I've also facilitated a variety of workshops on various metaphysical subjects over the years and employ the Native American Flute in many ceremonial activities.

I have two loving daughters and two former wives and I'm on good terms with all of them.

I'm committed to spiritual growth and to being of service for all my brothers and sisters.

And I invite you to visit the website *FromSavageToShaman.com* and leave a note in the guest book or send me a note from the "Contact Johnny" page. Also, you may write to me directly at FromSavageToShaman@gmail.com

That wasn't so painful or hard, and I hope it passes muster with my friend.

Thank you,
Johnny MedicineBear